Seafood

Seafood

How to buy, prepare, and cook the best sustainable
fish and seafood from around the world

Editor-in-Chief **C.J. Jackson**

LONDON, NEW YORK, MUNICH,
MELBOURNE, and DELHI

Photographers
Stuart West, Ian O'Leary, Myles New

Project Editor Andrew Roff

US Editor Rebecca Warren

US Consultant Kate Ramos

Senior Art Editor Sara Robin

Editor Lucy Bannell

Managing Editor Dawn Henderson

Managing Art Editor Marianne Markham

Senior Jackets Creative Nicola Powling

Senior Presentations Creative Caroline de Souza

Senior Production Editor Jennifer Murray

Senior Production Controller Man Fai Lau

Creative Technical Support Sonia Charbonnier

DK INDIA
Senior Editor Chitra Subramanyam

Senior Art Editor Neha Ahuja

Managing Editor Glenda Fernandes

Managing Art Editor Navidita Thapa

DTP Manager Sunil Sharma

Senior DTP Designer Pushpak Tyagi

First American Edition, 2011

Published in the United States by
DK Publishing
375 Hudson Street
New York, New York 10014

11 12 13 10 9 8 7 6 5 4 3 2 1

001–176400–May/2011

Published in Great Britain by Dorling Kindersley Limited.

A catalog record for this book is available from the
Library of Congress.

ISBN 978 0 7566 7554 7

DK books are available at special discounts when
purchased in bulk for sales promotions, premiums,
fund-raising, or educational use. For details, contact:
DK Publishing Special Markets, 375 Hudson Street,
New York, New York 10014 or SpecialSales@dk.com.

Printed and bound in L Rex, China

Discover more at
www.dk.com

Contents

Foreword

I have always been completely fascinated by fish and water. A vivid memory as a child is watching the Saturday matinée of the Ernest Hemingway classic *The Old Man and the Sea* and the battle of an old man trying to land a huge marlin: it remains a favorite movie of mine today.

My family lived an almost self-sufficient lifestyle in Kent, England, and I remember preparing seasonal fruit and vegetables in the kitchen with my Mum, as well as cooking meat and fish. Cooked crab was a particular favorite of mine, which my parents—who enjoyed all things fishy—often served us for dinner. Winkles were a weekend treat and enticing the snail out of the shell and dipping it in vinegar is another treasured early memory.

Childhood holidays were spent on the banks of the River Findhorn on the Moray Firth in Scotland, fishing for salmon and trout. I remember the 30lb salmon we sent for smoking and helping with the cleaning and cooking of other catches. My own first catch was a feisty emerald green eel that kicked up a big fuss and nearly had me in the water! I was less enthused by this (lovely looking, I hasten to add) creature—its strong earthy smell stays with me today.

A career based around food was a natural calling. I trained at the London Le Cordon Bleu school and taught on their courses. French cuisine includes many seafood classics and it was there that I really learnt how to appreciate and cook fish. I always wanted to travel and I spent much time in the 1980s and 1990s globetrotting, which opened my eyes to different cuisines and the seafood they use. But it was at Leith's School of Food and Wine in London that I became so focused on all types of seafood.

Today, as Director of Billingsgate Seafood Training School at Billingsgate Market, the UK's largest inland fish market situated in east London, I learn more about fish every day—and it's all here, in this book.

My passion for fish is based on respect. I find it inspirational and humbling that creatures that live in an environment so different from our own offer us fantastic food. With the vast expanse of the ocean, fish really are the best "free-range" meat. But we must never forget our place. Above all else, we must look out for the well-being of the ocean and its fish.

So many people tell me they would love to cook fresh fish but are not sure where to start. I'm convinced this uncertainty stems from the diversity of seafood: if all fish looked like salmon, for example, we'd all be experts at preparing it. Round fish, flat fish, shrimp, squid, clams, crab: they all have particular preparation techniques. But they're worth mastering. Nothing is quite so rewarding as sitting down to a fish so fresh you had to scale and gut it yourself, or producing your first perfectly skinned Dover sole.

Many countries have feasted on the fish in their oceans for hundreds of years, so it's no wonder that seafood recipes are true classics, all made with fantastic ingredients. I've included all my favorites: simple treats, like fisherman's pies and fishcakes, suitable for anything you might find at the fish market; sushi, so exquisite and delicate but demanding of the freshest fish; the incomparable fish soups for which so many countries are renowned; and old-fashioned hits like traditional poached salmon and the very best shrimp cocktail you'll ever eat. There's a recipe for most fish families and all recipes list alternative fish that work just as well. One important note: it is essential to try to choose responsibly sourced fish where possible—we can all make a difference to the long-term survival of our oceans. If you want to identify something obscure, find the best way

to cook a particular fish, or discover sustainable alternatives for over-fished, but well-loved, varieties, turn to the Fish gallery for the perfect "dip-into" resource. It starts with round fish and flat fish before listing the world's seafood.

The fish world is changing and we now face more issues of sustainability and the responsible sourcing of what we eat. But this just offers us new challenges and opportunities: this is the perfect time to discover a new species and also to support your local fishery—if you are lucky enough to live near a harbor.

I hope that this book inspires you to seek out sustainable seafood and eat more of it. The fish in our oceans are a resource we must treasure and we have a responsibility to make sure they are still swimming—in all their variety—for future generations to enjoy.

C.J. Jackson

Sustainable fish—what's the story?

Mention the words "fish" and "sustainability" and many people think of worrying press headlines about dwindling fish stocks. Such articles often correctly highlight the negative issues but rarely praise the positive work that is being done, resulting in an incomplete and sometimes misleading picture.

What went wrong?

World sustainability of all our food sources is a complex and emotive subject, and this is certainly true when it comes to seafood. There are many different views within and without the seafood industry but all agree that some species of fish are under threat, and some near collapse and extinction. Overfishing is often highlighted as a key culprit, but there are other forces at work here.

Overfishing occurs when a particular species is removed from the water at such a rate that the stock left behind does not have time to replenish itself. Understanding how quickly each species of fish grows and matures is key to the success of fishing. Orange roughy is a popular species caught around the New Zealand coast. It was extensively fished some decades ago, but only when stocks began to dwindle did it become apparent that the fish took many years to mature. This species is now protected and monitored carefully to allow stocks to replenish. It can be difficult for customers to know which fish they should be avoiding to aid this replenishment—the situation is always changing, and moreover it may be the case that stocks of a fish are relatively healthy in one sea area yet worryingly low in another. What is certain though, is that the current situation, whereby there is only serious demand for a few well-known species, is damaging, and matters would be improved if a greater number of species were to be targeted. Different methods of fishing also have a direct effect on the ecosystem. With high-impact methods such as trawling (whereby large nets are dragged through the water behind a

Legislation determines what fishing gear can be used, which varieties of fish can be caught, and the size of the catch.

boat), the fisherman will produce a large bycatch of sealife that he does not want. By the time these creatures are returned to the water, they are often dead or dying. Beam trawling is an even more destructive method whereby the nets are attached to metal beams that drag along the seabed, ploughing up large quantities of flora and fauna and causing enormous damage to the ocean environment. Line-fishing is rightly considered a more responsible way to fish, but it should be noted that this somewhat generic term covers a number of methods, some of which also produce a considerable bycatch. Longlining, for example—a technique whereby hundreds of baited hooks hang from a single main line via a series of branch lines—is known to claim the lives of significant numbers of turtles and sea birds, and is less useful than some nets for allowing immature fish to escape.

What is being done?

Now that these problems are well known, there is more legislation in place. Strict fishing quotas have been introduced by many governments to ensure that their coastal waters are

Trawling for shrimp scoops up other sealife—choose organically farmed specimens.

"Quotas ensure that coastal waters are fished responsibly"

fished responsibly. These "catch quotas", which detail exactly how many specimens of a particular species can be caught over a fixed period of time, are advised upon by government scientists who have researched the subject in detail.

A minimum landing size helps to control the stock levels of many species: if a fish that measures less than the designated size is caught, it cannot be sold as part of the catch. (Traditionally, it would be returned to the water, but with the odds of survival being negligible, several countries have now banned this practice of "discarding", in order that the bycatch figures can be more closely monitored. Action can then be taken—for example, sea areas can be closed for fishing—if the bycatch levels become excessive.) A minimum landing size can change annually, but the idea is that a fish isn't caught until it has reached sexual maturity and produced the next generation. To avoid catching undersize fish, many countries have strict controls to determine the size of mesh that can be used, the intention being that only mature fish will be held in the nets, while younger fish will be able to escape.

There are various bodies committed to supporting such practices. The Marine Stewardship Council (MSC) is an independent international organization that certifies sustainable fisheries. Anyone believing that they are sourcing fish sustainably can apply to the MSC for certification. Currently, there are over 5,000 MSC-labeled products on sale.

The Monterey Bay Aquarium's Seafood Watch program is working to promote sustainability in the US. The program works with consumers and businesses to promote sustainable seafood choices with the aim of ensuring healthy oceans.

The rapidly growing fish farming industry is, by definition, a sustainable way to bring fish to market and about 45 percent of the fish that we now consume is farmed. Commercial fish

Large-meshed nets prevent immature fish from being trapped, allowing those fish to reproduce and replenish the stock.

"The current situation, whereby there is only serious demand for a few well-known species, is damaging"

Alaskan pollock (sometimes sold as imitation crab) is one to try—its taste rivals that of cod and it is considerably more abundant worldwide.

Farmed mussels feed on naturally occurring plankton, so are very sustainable.

Responsible farms are monitored closely to ensure their fish are in good health and their cages are clean and secure.

"Fish farming is seen as one of the best ways to take pressure off wild fish stocks in the long term"

farming is only a few decades old, but in this relatively short space of time, a number of serious issues have had to be confronted. Chemicals that were used to keep fish healthy were affecting other life forms and damaging the environment, while pollution issues arose from both fish feces and wastage of excess food. Much of this has been corrected and tighter laws and legislation are now in place.

While it seems that sustainability might almost be taken for granted in a farming operation, issues have arisen further down the food chain. The fish meal pellets that are used as food for farmed fish are made from smaller wild fish, and if these are not sourced sustainably, there could end up being insufficient levels in rivers and oceans to sustain the larger fish that would naturally feed on them in the wild. Finding solutions to this has proved difficult in some cases, but there

are an increasing number of "responsible" farms where they use fish meal that comes labeled as sustainable, or sometimes even farm the food on the same site as the fish. Efforts will continue to be made to improve fish farming practices, because it is seen as one of the best ways to take pressure off wild fish stocks in the long term.

What should I buy?

You, the customer, can have your say by choosing fish that are caught in a responsible way. Fishing methods that are selective, including hand-lined fishing with large-meshed nets that allow small fish to escape, or, in the case of shellfish, hand-gathered, diver-caught, or any method that catches the seafood alive so that they can be returned easily to the sea if they are too small, are best. Additionally, these methods of fishing generally do little damage to the environment.

There are a number of ways to find out this information. Looking at packaging is one—those large retailers that do source their fish sustainably will often make a feature of it. Meanwhile, any product certified as sustainable by the MSC will feature the organization's logo: a blue oval with a white check mark. Although not all sustainable fisheries subscribe to MSC certification, this is a good place to start.

A number of comparable labeling systems exist in different parts of the world. In the US, the Monterey Bay Aquarium has a sustainability guide called Seafood Watch, which is available online as a downloadable guide that shows what is a sustainable choice and what isn't. Recommendations may come with caveats about where the fish is from or how it was caught. Unfortunately, this key information about a product is not always listed on product labels for the consumer to review.

The same information ought also to be available if you are buying your fish from a fishmonger or fish market where the produce does not come pre-packaged. The seller should be able to help you make the best choice (see below). When weighing up the impact your choice of fish will have on the environment, you might also consider the carbon footprint. Unless you live near the coast, it may not be possible to buy local, and you should consider the merits of buying frozen rather than fresh. In many cases, frozen fish will have been transported over land and sea and will have a smaller carbon footprint than fresh fish that may have traveled considerable distances by air. For the best flavor, look out for fish that is labeled as "frozen at sea", which will have been frozen within a few hours of being landed.

Look for farmed fish that have been responsibly farmed, using sustainable fish meal. In addition, there are some particularly good farmed species of fish to look out for, such as tilapia, which can be sustained partly by a vegetarian diet. When it comes to shellfish, rope-grown mussels are also an excellent choice (see page 352).

Tilapia feeds partly on vegetation, making it an environmentally friendly choice for farming.

"Frozen fish may have a smaller carbon footprint, as it is more likely to have traveled by boat and not air-freighted"

Your decisions in the supermarket can make a difference to the varieties of fish that are caught and sold, and what fishing methods are used to land them. If retailers are convinced that people want responsibly sourced fish, and will buy different varieties rather than just the same old few, then that is what they will offer. Enough people voting with their feet and their wallets is the surest way of hastening a future in which all fish is sourced sustainably.

Questions to ask

Talk to your fish seller. Knowing what questions to ask is imperative for supporting sustainable fishing.
- How and where was the fish caught?
- Is the fish carrying roe (see page 180)?
- Is the fish farmed? If so, where is the farm and what are their policies? Do they use sustainable fish meal, for instance?
- Is the fish certified by any organizations, such as the MSC?

A good fish seller will know where his fish have come from, and will be able to help you choose responsibly sourced species.

RECIPES

Salmon recipes

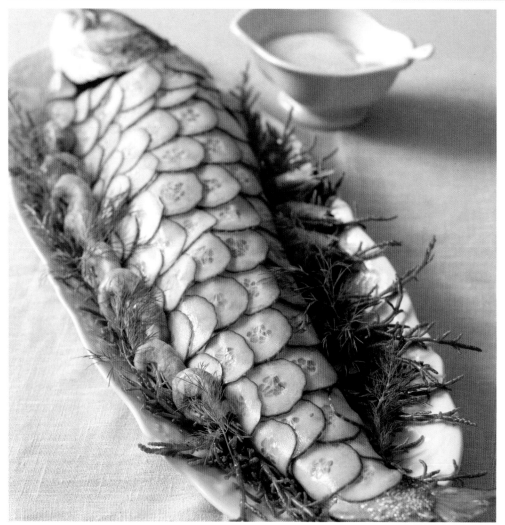

Whole poached and dressed salmon (see page 224)

Salmon jungle curry (see page 154)

Salmon fishcakes (see page 56)

Salmon with mushrooms and bok choy
(see page 196)

**Roasted salmon with Swiss chard
and herb butter** (see page 196)

Salmon en papillote (see page 197)

Asian cucumber salad with smoked salmon (see page 74)

Rich smoked salmon croustades (see page 34)

Salmon rillettes (see page 37)

Further recipes

- **Marinated salmon** (see page 62)

- **Salmon salad with mint yogurt dressing** (see page 75)

- **Salmon chowder with whiskey** (see page 87)

- **Salmon and shrimp fish pie** (see page 117)

- **Salmon in puff pastry** (see page 119)

- **Salmon, horseradish, and kale bake** (see page 126)

- **Crisp salmon with cilantro pesto** (see page 167)

- **Saltimbocca of salmon** (see page 167)

- **Baked salmon with salsa verde and cucumber** (see page 194)

- **Poached salmon with dill butter** (see page 224)

- **Jerk salmon** (see page 246)

- **Smoked salmon and pancetta crostini** (see page 30)

- **Smoked salmon with mustard and dill dressing** (see page 62)

Salmon coulibiac (see page 119)

Trout recipes

Smoked trout mousse (see page 37)

Smoked trout, fennel, and mascarpone crostini (see page 31)

Smoked trout with beet, apple, and dill relish (see page 63)

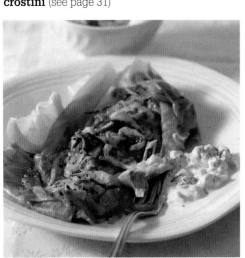

Steamed trout in lettuce (see page 229)

Trout with orange-mustard glaze (see page 236)

Further recipes

- **Smoked trout with pickled cucumber and minted yogurt** (see page 63)

- **Smoked trout and pancetta salad** (see page 75)

- **Creamy smoked trout soup** (see page 87)

- **Pan-fried trout with almonds** (see page 172)

- **Sautéed trout with hazelnuts** (see page 174)

- **Truite au bleu** (see page 220)

Tuna recipes

Tuna and eggplant yakitori skewers with soy dipping sauce (see page 28)

Grilled tuna steaks with salsa (see page 246)

Marinated sweet and hot tuna steaks (see page 242)

Seared tuna with a black sesame seed crust (see page 170)

Further recipes

- **Tuna carpaccio** (see page 60)
- **Salade Niçoise** (see page 73)
- **Tuna and bean salad** (see page 78)
- **Risotto al tonno** (see page 103)
- **Penne with tuna and roasted onion** (see page 111)
- **Tuna and pasta bake** (see page 127)
- **Seared tuna with cucumber and fennel** (see page 170)

Prawn and shrimp recipes

Keralan prawn soup (see page 93)

Shrimp and zucchini balls with caper cream (see page 69)

Spaghetti mare e monti (see page 112)

Tom yum goong (see page 94)

Pan-fried shrimp in garlic butter
(see page 183)

Grilled prawn satay (see page 240)

Shrimp gumbo (see page 137)

Sesame prawn toasts (see page 35)

Further recipes

- **Dublin Bay prawns with lemon and garlic mayo** (see page 28)

- **Classic shrimp cocktail** (see page 55)

- **Shrimp spring rolls** (see page 56)

- **Thai fishcakes** (see page 58)

- **Salt and pepper prawns** (see page 69)

- **Prawn, grapefruit, and avocado salad** (see page 77)

- **Vietnamese salad of shrimp with papaya** (see page 77)

- **Shrimp risotto** (see page 104)

- **Salmon and shrimp fish pie** (see page 117)

- **Pad Thai** (see page 144)

- **Sweet and sour shrimp** (see page 144)

- **Soba noodles with shrimp and avocado** (see page 145)

- **Shrimp diabolo** (see page 146)

- **Green curry of shrimp with eggplant and basil** (see page 161)

- **Prawn dhansak** (see page 161)

- **Green shrimp curry with fresh dill** (see page 162)

- **Prawn balti** (see page 163)

- **Pan-fried shrimp, olives, and tomatoes** (see page 178)

- **Spicy shrimp with garlic** (see page 178)

- **Breaded fried prawns** (see page 187)

- **Egg fu yung** (see page 187)

- **Sesame grilled prawns** (see page 240)

- **Griddled shrimp with hot pepper sauce** (see page 242)

Chile shrimp with cilantro and lime (see page 67)

Scallop recipes

Pan-fried scallops with chile, ginger, and an anchovy dressing (see page 179)

Scallops with bacon (see page 65)

Scallop and pesto crostini (see page 31)

Coquilles St. Jacques (see page 124)

Steamed scallop curry (see page 160)

Broiled scallops with prosciutto and lime (see page 45)

Scallops with sweet chili sauce (see page 66)

Linguine with scallops (see page 112)

Scallops skewered with Parma ham
(see page 45)

Further recipes

- **Scallop and tobiko sashimi** (see page 52)

- **Creamy scallop bisque** (see page 92)

Crab recipes

Crab and mango salad (see page 76)

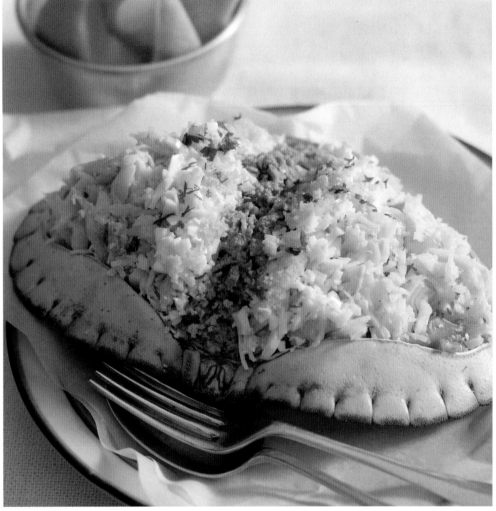

Dressed crab (see page 70)

Crab balls (see page 57)

Pasta with crab and lemon (see page 111)

Crab salad with grapefruit and cilantro (see page 76)

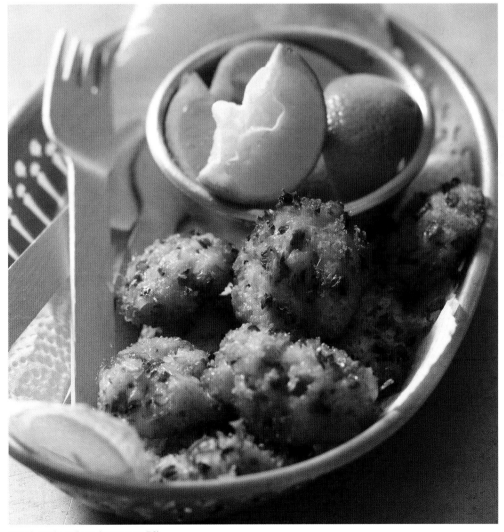

Thai crab cakes (see page 58)

Crab croustades (see page 34)

Further recipes

- **Nori maki** (see page 48)

- **Crab stir-fried with curry powder** (see page 146)

- **Stir-fried yellow curried crabs** (see page 147)

- **Chile crab** (see page 162)

- **Crab and mango curry** (see page 163)

Mussel recipes

Fish soup with fennel (see page 92)

Cod and mussel chowder (see page 86)

Moules marinières (see page 40)

Spaghetti frutti di mare (see page 108)

Laksa lemak (see page 157)

Mussels in ginger and chile broth (see page 132)

Pineapple curry of mussels (see page 150)

Further recipes

- **Mouclade** (see page 90)

- **Waterzooi** (see page 98)

- **Mussels in fennel broth** (see page 132)

- **Bourride** (see page 223)

Starters and Light Bites

Dublin Bay prawns with lemon and garlic mayo

Excellent summer casual entertaining bites. You'll need 6 wooden skewers.

The fish

Dublin Bay prawns, or shrimp, scallops, or monkfish

- **PREP** 30 mins - **COOK** none
- **MAKES** 6 skewers

Ingredients

12 cooked Dublin Bay prawns

2 large mangos, peeled and diced

For the mayonnaise

2/3 cup mayonnaise

5 tbsp crème fraîche or sour cream

1 garlic clove, crushed

grated zest of 1 lemon and juice of 1/2

1 tbsp finely chopped flat-leaf parsley, and sprigs of parsley, to garnish

salt and freshly ground black pepper

lemon or lime wedges, to garnish

1 Peel and devein the prawns (see page 285) and thread on to the skewers with cubes of mango. Arrange on a large platter.

2 Mix together all the ingredients for the mayonnaise and season well to taste. Spoon into a dipping bowl and arrange in the center of the skewers. Garnish with parsley and arrange the lemon wedges around the outside.

Prepare ahead

Mix everything together for the mayonnaise except the parsley. Cover, and chill for up to 1 day. The garlic flavor will become stronger. Mix in the parsley just before serving.

Variations

Grilled monkfish with melon
Cut 1 medium ripe melon into cubes and thread on to skewers with 12oz (350g) grilled, cubed monkfish.

Lobster and papaya
Replace the Dublin Bay prawns with 12oz (350g) lobster meat, and the mango with cubed papaya.

Griddled scallop and avocado
Griddle 24 scallops (see page 306) and thread on to skewers with 3 large avocados, peeled, pitted, and cubed.

Tuna and eggplant yakitori skewers with soy dipping sauce

Bamboo skewers of fish make an excellent canapé or an informal start to any meal. You'll need 12 wooden skewers, soaked in water for 30 minutes to prevent burning.

The fish

Tuna, or swordfish, mahi mahi, or monkfish

- **PREP** 40 mins, plus marinating
- **COOK** 2 mins - **MAKES** 12 skewers

Ingredients

1 large eggplant, cut into 1/2in (1cm) chunks

12oz (350g) tuna steak, cut into 1in (2.5cm) chunks

1 tbsp vegetable oil

shiso leaves, or sprigs of cilantro, to garnish

For the marinade

3 tbsp soy sauce

1 tsp sesame oil

1 tbsp sugar

1 tsp lemon juice

2 tsp mirin

1 tbsp sake (optional)

salt and freshly ground black pepper

1 Put the eggplant into simmering water. Boil for 2 minutes, drain, and cool.

2 Put the eggplant and tuna into a shallow dish. Mix the marinade ingredients and pour over. Stir, cover, and marinate for 30 minutes.

3 Thread 2 pieces of eggplant on to a skewer, a piece of tuna, and 2 more pieces of eggplant. Bring the marinade to a boil in a saucepan.

4 Preheat a griddle pan until smoking. Brush with the oil and put in the skewers. Cook for 2 minutes, turning once, and basting with the marinade. They will be golden brown and shiny. Put the remaining marinade in a small bowl.

5 Arrange on a platter with the dipping sauce and shiso or cilantro and wash down with Japanese beer or sake.

Variation

Scallop and shiitake yakitori skewers
Use 14oz (400g) shiitake mushrooms instead of eggplant and skip step 1. Use 12 large scallops instead of tuna.

TUNA FLAVOR PAIRINGS: A great fish with the Japanese flavors of shoyu, sesame, teriyaki, shiso leaf, rice wine vinegar, and wasabi. It's also good with robust Mediterranean ingredients, such as garlic, tomatoes, and olives.

Smoked salmon and pancetta crostini

The crème fraîche here is light and refreshing against the deep-flavored fish.

The fish

Cold-smoked salmon, or cold-smoked trout

• **PREP** 10 mins • **COOK** 10 mins • **MAKES** 12

Ingredients

12 small slices of bread, cut from a baguette or ficelle

5 tbsp olive oil

6 slices of pancetta

7oz (200g) smoked salmon

7fl oz (200ml) crème fraîche

2 tbsp whole-grain mustard

3 tbsp capers, rinsed, drained, and finely chopped

1 tsp grated lemon zest

1 tsp lemon juice

freshly ground black pepper

12 whole chives, snipped into 1in (2.5cm) lengths, to garnish

1 Preheat the oven to 400°F (200°C). Brush each side of the bread with olive oil, place on a baking tray, and bake for 10 minutes, or until crisp. Leave to cool.

2 Preheat the broiler on its highest setting. Broil the pancetta until crisp on both sides. Drain on paper towels.

3 Cut the smoked salmon into strips about ¾in (2cm) wide.

4 Mix the crème fraîche with the mustard, capers, lemon zest, and lemon juice. Season to taste with pepper.

5 Place the bread slices on a serving plate, divide the crème fraîche mixture between them, and top with smoked salmon, pieces of pancetta, and chives to garnish.

Prepare ahead

The bread slices can be baked up to 2 hours ahead. The crème fraîche mixture can be made 24 hours in advance, covered, and refrigerated. Assemble just before serving.

Anchovy and olive bruschetta

These salty canapés are ideal with pre-dinner drinks.

The fish

Anchovies, or smoked mackerel

• **PREP** 10 mins • **COOK** 5 mins • **MAKES** 12

Ingredients

12 slices Italian bread, such as ciabatta, about ¾in (2cm) thick

½ garlic clove

extra virgin olive oil

3–4 tbsp bottled tomato sauce, or purée

salt and freshly ground black pepper

4oz (115g) mozzarella cheese, drained, and cut into 12 thin slices

1 tsp dried mixed herbs

6 black olives, pitted and sliced

2oz (60g) jar or can anchovies in olive oil, drained, and cut in half lengthwise

1 Preheat the broiler on its highest setting and position the rack 4in (10cm) from the heat. Toast the bread until golden on both sides. Rub 1 side with the cut side of the garlic. Brush the same side of each slice with oil.

2 Spread each bruschetta with 2 tsp tomato sauce and season with salt and pepper. Put a slice of mozzarella on each, sprinkle with herbs and top with olive slices and 2 pieces of anchovy in a crisscross pattern.

3 Broil the bruschetta for 2–3 minutes, or until the mozzarella has melted and is bubbling. Serve hot with chilled prosecco or cold beer.

Prepare ahead

The bruschetta bases can be made 2 hours in advance. Assemble and broil before serving.

Scallop and pesto crostini

These canapés also make a stylish first course.

The fish

Scallops, or shrimp, monkfish, or cockles

- **PREP** 10 mins ▪ **COOK** 7 mins ▪ **MAKES** 12

Ingredients

12 slices Italian bread, such as ciabatta, about ¾in (2cm) thick

½ garlic clove

3 tbsp olive oil

6 scallops, roe removed

1 tbsp lemon juice

salt and freshly ground black pepper

2 tbsp bottled pesto

2 tbsp tomato purée

12 basil leaves, to garnish

1 Preheat the broiler to high. Toast the bread until golden on both sides. Rub 1 side with the cut side of the garlic. Lightly brush the same side of each slice with oil. Set aside.

2 Heat the remaining oil in a large frying pan over medium heat. Add the scallops, sprinkle with lemon juice, and season. Fry for 2 minutes each side, until cooked but tender; keep warm.

3 Spread one half of each crostini with pesto and the other half with tomato purée.

4 Halve each scallop horizontally and put 1 half on each crostini. Grind pepper over and garnish each with a basil leaf. Serve at once.

Prepare ahead

The crostini bases can be made 2 hours ahead.

Smoked trout, fennel, and mascarpone crostini

The fennel lifts the taste of the trout into a truly special mouthful.

The fish

Hot-smoked trout, or smoked mackerel or hot-smoked salmon

- **PREP** 25 mins ▪ **COOK** 15 mins ▪ **SERVES** 4

Ingredients

1oz (30g) slivered almonds

2 tbsp olive oil

4 thick slices crusty sourdough bread

salt and freshly ground black pepper

1 garlic clove

2 hot-smoked trout, about 10oz (300g) each

5½oz (150g) fennel bulb, trimmed, halved, and thinly sliced

4fl oz (120ml) mascarpone cheese

juice of ½ lemon

sprigs of chervil, to garnish

1 lemon, cut into wedges, to serve

1 Preheat the oven to 400°F (200°C). To toast the almonds, spread out over the bottom of a small dry, frying pan. Toast over medium heat for a few minutes, until golden, stirring frequently to prevent them scorching.

2 Pour the olive oil on to a baking tray, then gently press the bread into the oil on both sides. Season with salt and pepper. Bake in the oven for 12–15 minutes until golden brown. Remove, and lightly rub each slice with the garlic. Set aside on a wire rack to keep crisp.

3 Meanwhile, remove the skin and bones from the trout, and gently remove the flesh in big flakes. Put the trout, fennel, mascarpone, almonds, and lemon juice in a bowl. Season with pepper, and gently mix.

4 Arrange the trout mixture over the crostini, season with more pepper, and garnish with the chervil. Serve immediately, with lemon wedges.

Prepare ahead

Make the crostini bases and toast the almonds 2 hours in advance. Assemble the crostini just before serving.

Fried whitebait

Whitebait are very immature members of the herring and sardine family, so should not be eaten regularly. For a similar, but more sustainable recipe, try the Herbed Fish Goujons on page 68.

The fish

Whitebait, smelt, or any mixed, very small fish

- **PREP** 15 mins ▪ **COOK** 20 mins ▪ **SERVES** 4

Ingredients

sunflower oil, for deep-frying

6 tbsp all-purpose flour

1 tsp cayenne pepper

1 tsp salt

1lb (450g) whitebait

1 lemon, cut into wedges, to serve

1 Heat the oil to 350°F (180°C) in a large pan or deep-fat fryer (see page 308).

2 Meanwhile, put the flour, cayenne, and salt in a large bowl and mix together.

3 Toss the whitebait in the seasoned flour, making sure they are evenly coated. Put them into a sieve to shake off the excess flour.

4 Fry the whitebait in batches for 2–3 minutes each, or until they turn lightly golden. (Frying in small batches prevents them clumping together or turning soggy.) Use a slotted spoon to remove them from the oil and drain on paper towels. Serve immediately, with lemon wedges and brown bread and butter.

Marinated anchovies

This is a traditional Spanish recipe, usually served as a chilled tapas.

The fish

Anchovies, or sardines

- **PREP** 35 mins, plus marinating
- **COOK** none ▪ **SERVES** 4

Ingredients

9oz (250g) fresh anchovies

2 tbsp coarse sea salt

1¼ cups sherry vinegar

4 tbsp extra virgin olive oil

grated zest of 1–2 lemons, to taste

sprigs of marjoram or thyme

freshly ground black pepper

1 Rub the scales from the anchovies with your fingers, then gut and bone the fish. Wash and pat dry. Lay them in a single layer in a shallow dish, sprinkle with salt, then pour over the vinegar. Cover and refrigerate for 12–18 hours.

2 Drain away the salt and vinegar cure, and pat the fish dry. Arrange on a clean serving dish and sprinkle with the olive oil, lemon zest (add a squeeze of lemon juice, too, if you like), and marjoram. Season with pepper, and serve with crusty bread, providing toothpicks for your guests to use to spear the anchovies.

Prepare ahead

The anchovies must be cured at least 12 hours ahead, so you will only need to drain away the vinegar, and add the dressing to serve.

ANCHOVY FLAVOR PAIRINGS: The definite, exquisite taste of anchovies is great with sherry or white wine vinegars, shallots, oregano, sage, thyme, parsley, or fruity olive oil.

Rich smoked salmon croustades

Horseradish gives these bite.

The fish

Smoked salmon, or smoked trout

- **PREP** 10 mins, plus chilling ▪ **COOK** 12–14 mins
- **MAKES** 12

Ingredients

4fl oz (120ml) crème fraîche

1 tbsp creamed horseradish

freshly ground black pepper

12 croustade baskets (see Crab croustades, left)

2oz (60g) smoked salmon, sliced

scant 1oz (25g) orange lumpfish caviar

scant 1oz (25g) black lumpfish caviar

1 Mix the crème fraîche and horseradish. Season with pepper, and chill for 30 minutes.

2 Fill each croustade with 1 tsp crème fraîche and horseradish, some smoked salmon, and a little of each type of caviar. Serve within 1 hour.

Prepare ahead

The croustade baskets will keep, in an airtight container, for up to 1 month.

Variation

Salmon and tarragon cream croustades
Mix 4fl oz (120ml) crème fraîche, 5½oz (150g) chopped smoked salmon, 2 tbsp chopped tarragon, 1 tbsp lemon zest, and pepper. Chill for 30 minutes, then spoon into croustades.

Crab croustades

Lightly spiced crabmeat with a crispy case. You'll need a 2 inch (5cm) pastry cutter and a 12-hole mini-muffin pan.

The fish

White crabmeat, or lobster or Dublin Bay prawns

- **PREP** 10 mins ▪ **COOK** 12–14 mins
- **MAKES** 12

Ingredients

4 large slices white or whole wheat bread

1 tbsp melted butter or olive oil

For the filling

7oz (200g) white crabmeat

½in (1cm) fresh ginger, grated

grated zest and juice of 1 lime

3 tbsp mayonnaise

1 tbsp chopped cilantro leaves

2 scallions, finely chopped

salt and freshly ground black pepper

1 red chile, seeded and finely chopped, to garnish

1 Preheat the oven to 350°F (180°C). Remove the crusts from the bread, flatten the slices with a rolling pin, and brush with the butter or oil.

2 Using the pastry cutter, stamp out 3 pieces from each slice of bread. Push the bread, butter-side down, firmly into the muffin pan and bake for 12–14 minutes, or until golden and crisp. Remove from the pan and leave to cool.

3 In a bowl, mix together the crabmeat, ginger, lime zest and juice, mayonnaise, cilantro, and scallions, and season with salt and pepper.

4 Divide the mixture between the croustade baskets and sprinkle each with the red chile. Serve within 1 hour.

Prepare ahead

The croustade baskets will keep, in an airtight container, for up to 1 month. The filling can be made several hours in advance and kept, chilled, until needed. Assemble just before serving.

Anchovy, olive, and basil tarts

Piquant fishy bites, gooey with mozzarella. You'll need a 6-hole muffin pan.

The fish
Anchovy fillets in olive oil

- **PREP** 15 mins, plus chilling
- **COOK** 25–30 mins ▪ **MAKES** 6

Ingredients
oil, for the pan

all-purpose flour, to dust

1 sheet ready-rolled puff pastry (preferably all-butter)

2 eggs

¾ cup heavy cream

2 tbsp freshly grated Parmesan cheese

salt and freshly ground black pepper

6 anchovy fillets in olive oil, drained

6 balls bocconcini (baby mozzarella) cheese, torn

12 kalamata olives, pitted

12 cherry tomatoes, halved

6 fresh basil leaves or small sprigs, plus more to serve

1 Preheat the oven to 400°F (200°C). Lightly brush a 6-hole muffin pan with oil.

2 On a lightly floured work surface, cut the pastry into 6 squares. Use to line the holes in the muffin pan, pushing the pastry gently into the corners. Refrigerate for 1 hour.

3 Combine the eggs, cream, and Parmesan in a bowl, and season. Mix well.

4 Place an anchovy in each of the pastry cases, along with a bocconcini, 2 olives, and 4 cherry tomato halves. Spoon the egg mixture into the cases, and top each with a basil leaf or sprig. Grind over a little pepper.

5 Bake the tarts for 25–30 minutes until golden. Serve warm, garnished with a fresh basil leaf or sprig.

Sesame prawn toasts

A combination of flavors that work surprisingly well together.

The fish
Tiger prawns

▪ **PREP** 25 mins ▪ **COOK** 5 mins ▪ **MAKES** 12

Ingredients
9oz (250g) raw tiger prawns, peeled and roughly chopped (see page 285)

2 scallions, roughly chopped

½in (1cm) fresh ginger, grated

1 tsp light soy sauce

½ tsp sugar

½ tsp sesame oil

1 egg white, lightly beaten

freshly ground black pepper

3 large slices white bread, crusts removed

2 tbsp sesame seeds

vegetable oil, for deep-frying

cilantro leaves, to garnish

1 Put the prawns and scallions in a food processor, and process for a few seconds to make a paste. Transfer to a bowl and stir in the ginger, soy sauce, sugar, sesame oil, and enough egg white to bind. Season with pepper.

2 Cut each slice of bread into 4 triangles and spread thickly with the prawn paste. Sprinkle the sesame seeds evenly over the top.

3 Heat the oil to 350°F (180°C) in a large pan or deep-fat fryer (see page 308). Fry the toasts, in batches, prawn-side down, for 2 minutes. Carefully turn over and fry for another 2 minutes, or until golden brown and crisp.

4 Lift the toasts from the pan with a slotted spoon and drain on paper towels. Serve warm, garnished with cilantro leaves.

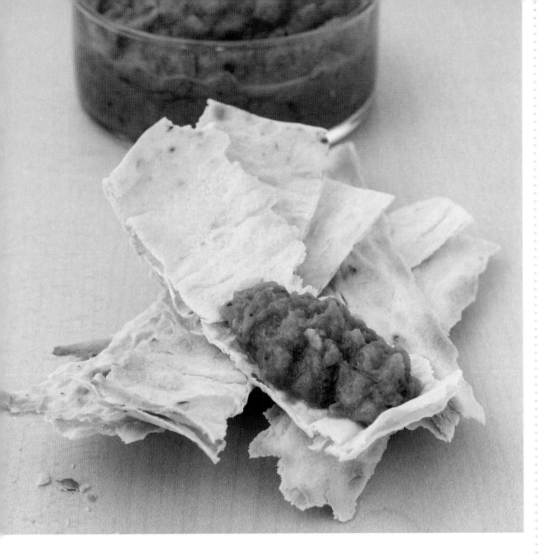

Smoked mackerel pâté

This always disappears quickly.

The fish

Smoked mackerel, or hot-smoked trout

- **PREP** 5 mins ▪ **COOK** none ▪ **SERVES** 4

Ingredients

3–4 smoked mackerel fillets, skinned

10oz (300g) cream cheese

juice of 1–2 lemons

freshly ground black pepper

1–2 tbsp Greek-style yogurt

4 thin slices brown bread, toasted

1 lemon, cut into wedges

1 Break the mackerel into chunks, and add to a food processor. Pulse until broken up.

2 Spoon in the cream cheese, and blend again until smooth. Add the lemon juice, a little at a time, to taste. Season with plenty of black pepper, and blend again.

3 Add the yogurt, and blend again until smooth. Spoon into a serving dish or 4 ramekins. Serve with toasted brown bread and lemon wedges.

Prepare ahead

Make a day ahead, and keep covered in the refrigerator until ready to serve.

Variations

Spicy smoked mackerel pâté
Add a pinch of cayenne pepper.

Light smoked mackerel pâté
Leave out the yogurt to dilute the richness a little, though the pâté will be less creamy.

Salt cod and red pepper dip

An unusual, delicious, and piquant appetizer.

The fish

Salt cod, or salt pollock

- **PREP** 25 mins, plus soaking ▪ **COOK** 1 hr
- **SERVES** 12

Ingredients

2 red peppers

2 garlic cloves

1 small red onion, finely chopped

4 tbsp olive oil

salt and freshly ground black pepper

2 tbsp finely chopped yellow onion

14oz (400g) can chopped plum tomatoes

1lb 2oz (500g) salt cod, soaked overnight

2 tbsp finely chopped marjoram

2 tbsp finely chopped dill

handful of basil leaves, finely chopped

handful of flat-leaf parsley, finely chopped

juice of 1 lemon

1 Preheat the oven to 400°F (200°C). Slice the tops from the peppers, and remove the seeds and membrane. Put a garlic clove and half the chopped red onion in the cavity of each, and lay them on an oven tray lined with parchment paper. Drizzle with 1 tbsp of the oil, and season. Roast for 1 hour. Set aside.

2 Heat the remaining oil in a heavy frying pan over low heat. Add the yellow onion, and sweat for about 5 minutes until soft. Add in the tomatoes, and cook for 10 minutes. Season.

3 Skin the salt cod, and flake the flesh into chunks. Add to the tomato sauce, and cook gently for a further 10 minutes. Set aside to cool.

4 Put the peppers in a food processor with the tomato mixture. Purée until smooth. Transfer to a serving bowl, and season. Stir in the herbs and lemon juice. Serve with crostini.

Prepare ahead

The salt cod dip can be made—without the herbs—up to 2 days in advance, covered, and refrigerated. The flavors will deepen. Stir in the herbs just before serving.

Salmon rillettes

This pâté from France should have a fairly rough texture.

The fish

Hot-smoked salmon, or hot-smoked trout

- **PREP** 15 mins ▪ **COOK** none ▪ **SERVES** 4

Ingredients

2oz (60g) butter, softened

9oz (250g) hot-smoked salmon fillets, skinned

4 tbsp Greek-style yogurt

finely grated zest and juice of ½ lemon

2 tbsp snipped chives

1¾oz (50g) jar keta caviar

handful of watercress, to garnish

lemon wedges, to garnish

1 Put the butter in a bowl and beat with a wooden spoon until smooth. Break up the salmon into small pieces, add to the bowl, and mash with a fork.

2 Add the yogurt, lemon zest and juice, and chives, and stir until evenly combined.

3 Spoon on to serving plates—or small rounds of pumpernickel for canapés—and top with caviar. Garnish with watercress sprigs and lemon wedges.

Prepare ahead

The rillettes can be prepared up to 24 hours in advance, covered, and refrigerated, or frozen for up to 1 month.

Smoked trout mousse

This dish is lifted with pungent horseradish and fragrant dill, and lightened with yogurt. You will need a terrine mold or loaf pan.

The fish

Hot-smoked trout, or smoked mackerel or hot-smoked salmon

- **PREP** 20–25 mins, plus chilling
- **COOK** none ▪ **SERVES** 8–10

Ingredients

2 hot-smoked trout, in total about 1lb 10oz (750g)

1 tbsp powdered gelatin

vegetable oil, for the mold

2 eggs, hard-boiled and chopped

leaves from a small bunch of dill, chopped

3 small scallions, finely sliced

4fl oz (120ml) mayonnaise

4fl oz (120ml) plain yogurt

2oz (60g) grated fresh horseradish, or to taste

juice of 1 lemon

salt and freshly ground black pepper

6fl oz (175ml) heavy cream

bunch of watercress

1 Peel the skin from the trout, then lift the flesh from the bones and gently flake.

2 Sprinkle the gelatin evenly over 4 tbsp cold water in a small bowl and let it stand for 5 minutes, until spongy. Brush a 1.2 quart terrine mold with oil, or line a loaf pan with plastic wrap.

3 Put everything except the cream, watercress, and gelatin in a bowl and stir. Taste; it should be well seasoned.

4 Whip the cream until soft peaks form. Melt the gelatin in a small saucepan over low heat. Add it to the trout mixture and mix thoroughly. At once, fold in the cream. Spoon into the mold and smooth the top. Cover with a lid, or with plasic wrap, and chill for 3–4 hours, until set.

5 Run a knife around the edges of the mold. Dip the base in warm water for a few seconds, then set a plate on top and invert to unmold the mousse. Serve with sprigs of watercress.

Prepare ahead

The mousse can be made up to 3 days ahead, covered, and stored in the refrigerator. Return to room temperature before serving.

Brandade de morue

This dish of creamed salt cod is especially popular in the South of France.

The fish

Salt cod, or salt pollock

- **PREP** 15–20 mins, plus soaking
- **COOK** 15–20 mins ▪ **SERVES** 4

Ingredients

1lb (450g) salt cod

2 garlic cloves, crushed

1 cup olive oil

½ cup hot milk

2 tbsp chopped flat-leaf parsley

freshly ground black pepper

extra virgin olive oil, to drizzle

triangles of white bread, fried in olive oil, to serve

Mediterranean black olives, to serve

1 Soak the fish in a bowl of cold water for 24 hours, changing the water 3 or 4 times.

2 Drain the cod and place in a large, shallow pan, then cover it with fresh cold water and bring to a gentle simmer. Cook for 10 minutes, then remove the pan from the heat and leave the cod to sit in the water for a further 10 minutes before draining.

3 Remove the skin and bones from the fish, then flake the flesh into a bowl and pound to a paste with the garlic.

4 Put the fish paste in a pan over gentle heat. Beat in sufficient olive oil and milk, a little at a time, to make a creamy white mixture that holds its shape. Serve hot, sprinkled with parsley, pepper, and extra virgin olive oil, with the bread triangles and olives.

Prepare ahead

The salt cod and garlic paste can be made up to the end of step 3, then covered, and chilled, for up to 1 day before serving. The flavor of the garlic will deepen. Bring the paste back to room temperature before continuing.

Tapenade

A full-flavored olive and anchovy spread, popular all around the Mediterranean.

The fish

Anchovy fillets in olive oil

- **PREP** 15 mins ▪ **COOK** none ▪ **SERVES** 4–6

Ingredients

2 large garlic cloves

9oz (250g) Mediterranean black olives, pitted

1½ tbsp capers, drained and rinsed

4 anchovy fillets in olive oil, drained

1 tsp thyme leaves

1 tsp chopped rosemary

2 tbsp lemon juice

2 tbsp extra virgin olive oil

1 tsp Dijon mustard

freshly ground black pepper

12 slices baguette, toasted, to serve

1 Place the garlic, olives, capers, anchovies, thyme, and rosemary in a food processor or blender, and process until smooth.

2 Add the lemon juice, extra virgin olive oil, mustard, and black pepper to taste, and blend until a thick paste forms. Transfer to a bowl, cover, and chill until ready to use.

3 Bring to room temperature, and serve with slices of toasted baguette. This is also good to eat with crudités and other Mediterranean appetizers, such as stuffed grape leaves.

Prepare ahead

The tapenade can be made, covered, and chilled for up to 2 days before using. The flavors will deepen. Bring back to room temperature before serving.

SALT COD FLAVOR PAIRINGS: The strong flavors of this preserved fish stand up well to olive oil, garlic, orange, capers, onion, parsley, or even coconut, as they prepare it in the Caribbean.

Taramasalata

"Tarama" is Turkish for the salted fish roe that is traditionally used in this recipe.

The fish

Smoked cod's roe, or salted gray mullet roe

- **PREP** 15 mins, plus chilling • **COOK** none
- **SERVES** 4–6

Ingredients

9oz (250g) piece smoked cod's roe

juice of 1 lemon

2oz (60g) fresh white breadcrumbs, soaked in 3 tbsp cold water

¼ cup extra virgin olive oil

1 small onion, grated, patted dry with paper towels

paprika, for sprinkling

1 Split the roe down the center using a sharp knife and carefully peel away the skin. Place in a blender with the lemon juice and soaked breadcrumbs. Blend well.

2 With the motor running, very slowly add the oil in a thin steady stream until the mixture resembles mayonnaise.

3 Stir in the onion and spoon into a small serving dish. Cover and chill for 30 minutes, then serve sprinkled with paprika.

Prepare ahead

The taramasalata can be prepared up to the end of step 2, covered, and chilled up to 2 days in advance.

Moules marinières

This classic French recipe—mussels in wine, garlic, and herbs—translates as "in the fisherman's style."

The fish

Mussels, or clams

- **PREP** 15–20 mins • **COOK** 15 mins
- **SERVES** 4

Ingredients

4 tbsp butter

2 onions, finely chopped

8lb (3.6kg) mussels, prepared (see page 278)

2 garlic cloves, crushed

2 cups dry white wine

4 bay leaves

2 sprigs of thyme

salt and freshly ground black pepper

2–4 tbsp chopped flat-leaf parsley

1 Melt the butter in a large, heavy saucepan, add the onions, and fry gently until lightly browned. Add the mussels, garlic, wine, bay leaves, and thyme. Season to taste. Cover, bring to a boil, and cook for 5–6 minutes, or until the mussels have opened, shaking frequently.

2 Remove the mussels with a slotted spoon, discarding any that remain closed. Transfer them to warmed bowls, cover, and keep warm.

3 Strain the liquor into a pan and bring to a boil. Season to taste, add the parsley, pour over the mussels, and serve at once.

SMOKED COD'S ROE FLAVOR PAIRINGS:

The taste of this exquisite roe should be enjoyed fairly plain; flatter it with plentiful good-quality olive oil, garlic, and lemon juice.

Oysters Rockefeller

A traditional lunch dish from New Orleans that also makes an excellent first course.

The fish

Oysters

- **PREP** 20 mins
- **COOK** 35 mins
- **SERVES** 4

Ingredients

3½oz (100g) baby leaf spinach
24 oysters, in their shells
2½oz (75g) shallots, finely chopped
1 garlic clove, chopped
4 tbsp chopped flat-leaf parsley
8 tbsp butter
6 tbsp all-purpose flour
2 anchovy fillets in oil, drained and finely chopped
pinch of cayenne pepper
salt and freshly ground black pepper
rock salt
3 tbsp Pernod

1 Wilt the spinach in a pan over medium heat for 5 minutes. Drain well, squeeze to remove excess liquid, and set aside.

2 Discard any open oysters. Shuck the oysters (see page 278), reserve their liquid, then return the oysters to their shells. Separately cover and chill both the oysters and their liquid.

3 Chop the spinach finely and mix with the shallots, garlic, and parsley. Set aside.

4 Melt the butter in a small saucepan over medium heat. Add the flour, and stir for 2 minutes. Slowly stir in the oyster liquid, until smooth. Stir in the spinach, anchovies, cayenne, and salt and pepper. Cover and simmer for 15 minutes.

5 Preheat the oven to 400°F (200°C). Arrange a thick layer of rock salt in 4 serving dishes, then put them in the oven to warm.

6 Uncover the pan and stir in the Pernod. Taste, and adjust the seasoning. Remove the dishes from the oven, and arrange 6 oysters in their shells on each. Spoon the sauce over and bake for 5–10 minutes, or until the sauce looks set. Serve immediately.

Oysters with shallot and vinegar dressing

European tradition, dating back to the Romans, serves oysters raw on the half shell. Both Pacific and native oysters can be used.

The fish

Oysters, or hard-shell clams or whelks

- **PREP** 10 mins
- **COOK** none
- **SERVES** 4

Ingredients

24 oysters, in their shells
crushed ice
4 tbsp red wine vinegar
1 large or 2 small shallots, very finely chopped

1 Shuck the oysters (see page 278), taking care not to pour out any of the juices. Arrange the oysters on a traditional oyster plate with ice, or pack 4 serving dishes with lots of crushed ice and place the oysters on top.

2 Mix the vinegar and shallot together and put into a small dish. Place in the center of the oysters—or the middle of the table—and serve.

Variation

Oysters with lemon and Tabasco
Shuck the oysters as directed and serve on crushed ice, with lemon wedges and Tabasco sauce on the side. Allow your guests to choose their dressing, or to eat the oysters unadorned.

OYSTER FLAVOR PAIRINGS: Briny and mineral-tasting raw oysters work best with punchy red wine vinegar, Tabasco, and lemon juice. When they are cooked, oysters make great partners with anchovy paste, butter, and wilted, drained spinach.

Clams in white wine

Versions of this dish can be found throughout the Mediterranean.

The fish
Clams, or mussels

- **PREP** 10 mins, plus soaking ▪ **COOK** 15 mins
- **SERVES** 4–6

Ingredients
2¼lb (1kg) clams, thoroughly washed

2 tbsp olive oil

1 onion, finely diced

2 garlic cloves, finely chopped

2 bay leaves

1 tsp fresh thyme or a pinch of dried thyme

½ cup dry white wine

1 tbsp chopped flat-leaf parsley

1 Soak the clams for 1 hour to clean them. Discard any that are already open, or that have broken shells. Heat the oil in a large, heavy-bottomed pot. Add the onion and garlic and fry, stirring, for 4–5 minutes, or until translucent.

2 Add the clams with the bay leaves and thyme. Stir thoroughly, cover, and allow to steam for 3–4 minutes, or until the clams have opened. Discard any that remain shut.

3 Add the wine and cook for a further 3–4 minutes, shaking the pot a few times to allow the sauce to thicken slightly.

4 Sprinkle with parsley and serve straight from the pot with crusty bread, to soak up the juices.

Abalone with oyster sauce

Abalone is expensive, but may be found canned. It is particularly popular in China.

The fish
Abalone

- **PREP** 15 mins ▪ **COOK** 10 mins ▪ **SERVES** 4

Ingredients
1 wild or 2 farmed abalone

2 tbsp sunflower or vegetable oil

1 bunch of scallions, finely sliced

1 tsp finely grated fresh ginger

2 tbsp oyster sauce

1 tbsp dark soy sauce

pinch of salt

2 tsp cornstarch

1 Shell the abalone, reserving any juices. To clean, hold the main body and let the viscera hang down. Cut off and discard these. Scrub off the black film along the side of the abalone. Cut off and discard the curled edges and the tough, pointed end. Using a mallet, beat the abalone well to flatten and tenderize. Slice thinly.

2 Heat the oil in a large frying pan, add in the scallions and ginger, and stir over low heat for 3–4 minutes. Add the abalone and toss together to heat through.

3 Mix together the oyster sauce, soy sauce, salt, and 5 tbsp water. Stir in the cornstarch and the reserved abalone juices. Add the sauce to the abalone, and stir over medium heat until it just comes to a boil and the sauce has thickened. Add more water if you would prefer a thinner sauce, and serve.

Prepare ahead
This dish is very quick to make once the abalone has been cleaned, and beaten flat. It can then be covered and refrigerated for up to 1 day. Bring the abalone to room temperature before completing the recipe.

Variation
Canned abalone with oyster sauce
Drain a 12oz (340g) can abalone, reserving the liquid. Slice the abalone thinly. Proceed as above, adding the reserved abalone liquid at the same time as the cornstarch.

Broiled scallops with prosciutto and lime

A delicious, elegant dish.

The fish
Sea scallops, or monkfish or shrimp

- **PREP** 10 mins • **COOK** 5 mins • **SERVES** 6

Ingredients
18 sea scallops

2 tbsp butter, melted

2 garlic cloves, chopped

juice of 1 lime, plus lime wedges to serve

handful of chopped herbs, such as basil, parsley, chives, and cilantro, plus extra to serve

salt and freshly ground black pepper

3 thin slices prosciutto, cut into strips

1 Trim off and discard the small white muscle from each scallop and divide them between scallop shells, or place in an ovenproof dish. Preheat the broiler on its highest setting.

2 Combine the butter, garlic, lime juice, and herbs, and spoon the mixture over the scallops.

3 Season with salt and pepper, and scatter with the prosciutto. Place under the broiler and cook for 5 minutes. Serve immediately with wedges of lime and a scattering of fresh herbs, and warm crusty bread to soak up the delicious flavored butter.

Scallops skewered with Parma ham

Both dainty and meaty, a starter for parties.

The fish
Scallops, or monkfish or shrimp

- **PREP** 10 mins • **COOK** 5–8 mins • **SERVES** 8

Ingredients
8 scallops, halved

1 tbsp olive oil

juice of 1 lemon

salt and freshly ground black pepper

8 slices Parma ham or proscuitto, halved

1 Preheat the oven to 375°F (190°C). Mix the scallops with the oil and lemon, and season.

2 Wrap each scallop half in Parma ham, then thread on to 8 soaked short wooden skewers.

3 Lay the skewers on a baking sheet, and roast in the oven for 5–8 minutes until the ham starts to crisp. Serve hot with a wild arugula salad.

Variation

Marinated skewered scallops
Omit the ham. Marinate the scallops in the lemon mix for 30 minutes. Cook for 5 minutes.

SUSTAINABILITY CHOICE

Be informed

When choosing fish, one of the key things to be aware of is how they were harvested from the ocean. More often than not, this is by net. Fixed nets are considered the most sustainable because, unlike other types of net, they barely touch the seabed and so cause minimal damage to the fishes' environment. Weights anchor the net and floats provide buoyancy to create a structure similar to a tennis net. A trammel net, a type of fixed net (shown here), has three layers of netting. The mesh size is adapted to target certain species, which minimizes the amount of bycatch.

Cured mackerel nigiri

Keep a bowl of vinegared water on hand to prevent the rice from sticking, but avoid using it too much.

The fish
Mackerel

- **PREP** 20 mins • **COOK** none
- **MAKES** 20 nigiri

Ingredients
⅙ recipe sushi rice (see page 293)

a little wasabi paste

1 mackerel fillet, cured and pinboned (see page 294)

1 Take a small amount of rice in dampened hands, gently molding it into a rounded lozenge. Spread a little wasabi over the top.

2 Cut the mackerel into strips and lay across the wasabi, gently pressing together.

Prepare ahead
Cure the fish up to 3 hours in advance, cover, and refrigerate. Return to room temperature before assembling the nigiri sushi.

Variations

Salmon nigiri
Cut 6oz (175g) salmon fillet into strips. Shape the rice as above and top with a little wasabi and then the salmon. Cut a thin strip of nori seaweed and use this to wrap around the middle of the salmon. Makes 20.

Shrimp nigiri
Shape half of the rice and top with wasabi as above. Butterfly 8 large shrimp split open from the base (see page 295) and drape neatly across the top of the rice. Makes 8.

Squid nigiri
Shape the rice and top with wasabi as above. Open 10 squid tubes out flat and carefully score, then cut each in half (see page 282). Drape each lozenge with half a squid tube. Makes 20.

Kingfish nigiri
Shape the rice and top with wasabi as above, using 6oz (175g) kingfish fillet (as prepared for mackerel). Makes 20.

KINGFISH FLAVOR PAIRINGS: The sweet, rich flesh of kingfish is great with wasabi, or in curries with other Asian spices such as hot chile, ginger, and sour tamarind.

Nori maki

You will need a bamboo mat to make these California-style rolls.

The fish
White crabmeat, or surimi (ocean sticks)

- **PREP** 5 mins • **COOK** none
- **MAKES** 16 nori maki

Ingredients
splash of rice vinegar

4 sheets nori seaweed, halved

⅙ recipe sushi rice (see page 293)

a little wasabi paste

½ avocado, thinly sliced

4oz (115g) white crabmeat, or 4 pieces of surimi (ocean sticks), halved

1 Lay a bamboo mat on a board. Have on hand a bowl of tepid water mixed with the vinegar.

2 Lay a half piece of nori seaweed on the bamboo mat, shiny side down. Using wet hands, take a small handful of rice and spread it on the nori, pressing gently, and leaving a 1in (2.5cm) border at one end. Don't use too much water or the nori will become wet and tough.

3 If using a single ingredient (such as the smoked salmon variation below), use a little more rice to fill the rolls. Make an indentation down the center of the rice, spread on a little wasabi paste, the avocado, and crab or surimi.

4 Roll up the sushi, pressing on the bamboo mat to help keep the roll even.

5 To cut the roll, use a very sharp, wet knife and do not saw, but pull the knife toward you. Cut the roll in half, then in half again and stand each upright. Wipe the knife between cuts.

6 Arrange the cut sushi on a large tray to serve. Serve with soy sauce, pickled sushi ginger, pickled daikon, and wasabi paste.

Variations

Smoked salmon nori maki
Substitute 4oz (115g) smoked salmon for the crab, and use only half the nori sheets.

Tobiko and cucumber nori maki
Use only half the nori sheets, fill with strips of cucumber, skin and seeds removed, and top with tobiko (flying fish roe), or salmon keta caviar.

Tuna nori maki
Use only half the nori sheets, and fill with thinly sliced, fresh, sashimi-grade tuna.

Tamaki sushi

An excellent, if slightly cheating, way to serve sushi: get your guests to roll their own!

The fish

Tuna, salmon, snapper, lemon sole, surimi (ocean sticks), tobiko (flying fish roe), or salmon keta caviar

- **PREP** 15–20 mins · **COOK** 5 mins
- **MAKES** 12–14 rolls

Ingredients

For the Japanese omelet (optional)

3 eggs

2 egg yolks

1 rounded tsp cornstarch, mixed with 2 tsp water

splash of vegetable oil

For the rest of the dish

½ recipe sushi rice (see page 293)

2 sheets of nori seaweed per person, cut in two

a choice of fillings, such as 1 fillet per person of sashimi-grade tuna, salmon, snapper, or lemon sole, 2–3 surimi (ocean sticks) per person, 1 jar tobiko (flying fish roe), or salmon keta caviar

a selection of vegetables cut into sticks, such as cucumber, avocado, or green beans and asparagus (both trimmed and blanched for 2–3 minutes in boiling water)

1 Whisk together the eggs, yolks, and cornstarch. Brush a large frying pan with the oil and heat for 1 minute. Pour in enough egg to cover the bottom and cook for a few seconds, or until set. Flip and cook the second side, then slide on to a plate. Cook the remaining mixture. Cut into slices and arrange on a plate.

2 Pile the prepared rice into a bowl and arrange the other ingredients on a large platter.

3 Serve your guests; each person should have a dipping bowl of hand-hot vinegared water. You may need to demonstrate how to assemble the first cornet: hold a piece of nori seaweed in one hand and arrange a little rice across the middle. Make an indentation in the rice and add fillings of your choice. Wrap the ends of the nori seaweed around to form a cornet. It doesn't matter if fillings stick out of the top—this is part of the roll's beauty.

4 Serve with wasabi and Japanese soy sauce for dipping.

Chirashi sushi

This type of sushi requires no rolling and is very easy to make. Serve in individual bowls or on a large platter.

The fish

Tuna, salmon, kingfish, shrimp, mackerel, or squid

- **PREP** 15 mins · **COOK** none · **SERVES** 4

Ingredients

½ recipe sushi rice (see page 293)

Any selection of the following:

shredded daikon

thinly sliced cucumber

1 fillet sashimi-grade tuna, thinly and evenly sliced

1 fillet sashimi-grade salmon, thinly and evenly sliced

1 fillet sashimi-grade kingfish, thinly and evenly sliced

8–12 prepared and cooked shrimp (see page 295)

1 cured mackerel fillet, thinly sliced (see page 294)

1 thin squid tube, scored and cut into pieces (see page 282)

1 Pile the sushi rice into a large, shallow serving dish, or four individual bowls.

2 Arrange the vegetables and fish on top and serve with wasabi and Japanese soy sauce.

Prepare ahead

Prepare and cook the shrimp up to 3 hours in advance, cover, and refrigerate. Return to room temperature before continuing.

SALMON KETA CAVIAR FLAVOR PAIRINGS: The quite exceptional, rich taste of this bright orange roe is great with sushi rice, or melba toast, chopped hard-boiled egg white, and chopped onion.

Scallop and tobiko sashimi

The essence of sashimi is its simplicity, the beauty of the presentation, and for this recipe, the intense freshness of the scallops.

The fish

Scallops, or monkfish, tuna, or salmon, and tobiko (flying fish roe)

■ **PREP** 15 mins ■ **COOK** none ■ **SERVES** 4

Ingredients

16 scallops, roe removed if necessary
2 tbsp tobiko (flying fish roe), green or golden
shiso leaves (perilla), to garnish
Japanese soy sauce, to serve
pickled sushi ginger, to serve
wasabi paste, to serve

1 Cut the scallop meat horizontally into very even ¼in (0.5cm) slices. Arrange, overlapping, on a platter (preferably laquered). Spoon the tobiko around the edge.

2 Decorate with the shiso leaves and add small bowls containing soy sauce, ginger, and wasabi to serve in the center.

Variation

Monkfish, tuna, or salmon, and tobiko sashimi
Slice 1lb (450g) sashimi-grade monkfish, tuna, or salmon and use in place of the scallops.

Cured mackerel sashimi with salad

In spring and summer, mackerel has quite a soft texture; curing it firms the flesh.

The fish

Mackerel, or tuna or bonito

■ **PREP** 30 mins, plus curing ■ **COOK** none ■ **SERVES** 4

Ingredients

2 very fresh mackerel (preferably still with rigor mortis), filleted, cured, and pinboned (see page 294)
2oz (60g) arugula, washed
2 Baby Gem lettuces, washed and torn into strips
large handful of cress, washed
handful of cherry tomatoes, halved
½ small cucumber, peeled and thinly sliced
1 ripe avocado, diced
2 tbsp chopped pickled sushi ginger
Japanese soy sauce, to serve
wasabi paste, to serve

For the dressing

1 tsp honey
1 tbsp mirin
1 tbsp rice wine vinegar
1 tsp sesame oil
2 tbsp sunflower oil

1 Slice the mackerel very thinly, and set aside.

2 Put the salad ingredients into a big bowl and toss together. Put the dressing ingredients into a bowl, whisk to blend, then add to the salad, and toss together.

3 Pile the salad on to a large platter and arrange the sliced mackerel on top. Serve with the soy sauce and wasabi in small dishes on the side.

Prepare ahead

Cure the fish up to 3 hours in advance, cover, and refrigerate. Return to room temperature before assembling the salad.

TOBIKO FLAVOR PAIRINGS: This
fine-grained, crunchy roe can be dyed black with cuttlefish ink, or green with wasabi, and is great with sashimi, or buckwheat blinis, and sour cream.

Escabeche

A Spanish classic traditionally made with mackerel, bonito, tuna, or sardines, escabeche works well with firm white fish, too.

The fish

Any white fish, such as pollock, tilapia, meagre, snapper, and sea bass

- **PREP** 15–20 mins, plus marinating
- **COOK** 15–20 mins ■ **SERVES** 4

Ingredients

1lb (450g) white fish fillets, pinboned and skinned

1 tbsp flour

sea salt and freshly ground black pepper

4 tbsp olive oil

1 tsp paprika

2 garlic cloves, sliced

1 bay leaf

2 strips of orange zest

½ tsp dried thyme

½ tsp dried oregano

6 peppercorns

⅔ cup white wine vinegar

¾ cup medium white wine

handful of arugula leaves, to serve

3 tomatoes, thickly sliced, to serve

1 red onion, finely sliced, to serve

12 black olives, pitted, to serve

1 Cut the fish into 2–2½in (5–6cm) pieces. Put the flour on a plate and season well. Roll the fish in the seasoned flour and shake off excess.

2 Heat half the oil in a frying pan, add the fish in batches and cook for 2–3 minutes each side, or until golden brown. Lift into a deep dish.

3 Put the remaining oil into the pan, add the paprika and garlic and fry for 1 minute. Add the remaining ingredients with ⅔ cup water; take care, as the pan will sizzle when the liquid hits. Bring to a boil and simmer for 3–4 minutes. Remove from the heat and cool.

4 Pour the escabeche over the fish and refrigerate for 12 hours, preferably overnight.

5 Lift from the marinade and put on a platter, with arugula, tomatoes, onion, and olives.

Prepare ahead

The escabeche must be made at least 12 hours, preferably 1 day, before you need it.

Classic shrimp cocktail

A 1960s shrimp cocktail was served with shredded soft lettuce, but the Iceberg leaves used here don't turn limp so quickly.

The fish

Shrimp, or lobster tails, or cockles

- **PREP** 15 mins ■ **COOK** none
- **SERVES** 4 generously

Ingredients

1lb (450g) cooked shrimp

½ cup mayonnaise (or mixed crème fraîche and mayonnaise)

4 tbsp ketchup

1 tsp tomato purée

2–3 tsp Worcestershire sauce

2–3 tsp creamed horseradish

1 tsp brandy

salt and freshly ground black pepper

splash of Tabasco

lemon juice, to taste

½ small Iceberg lettuce, very finely shredded

½ tsp paprika

thinly sliced brown bread, lightly buttered, to serve

1 Peel and devein all but 8 of the shrimp, and discard the shells (see page 285). Set aside.

2 Mix the mayonnaise, ketchup, tomato purée, Worcestershire sauce, horseradish, and brandy together. Season and add the Tabasco and lemon juice to taste.

3 Divide the lettuce evenly between 4 large wine glasses, or glass bowls.

4 Mix the shrimp into the mayonnaise and pile on top of the lettuce. Dust lightly with paprika. Arrange 2 unpeeled shrimp on top of each glass and serve with brown bread and butter.

Variation

Shrimp cocktail, Mexican-style

Omit the mayonnaise flavorings above and instead use 1 tbsp sun-dried tomato purée, 1 tbsp chopped cilantro, 1 small diced avocado, 2 tbsp corn kernels, the juice of 1 lime, and Tabasco sauce. Stir in the shrimp and serve as above, topped with sprigs of cilantro.

POLLOCK FLAVOR PAIRINGS: The firm, meaty, yet subtly flavored flesh of pollock works well with tomatoes, chile, bacon, pancetta, or basil.

Shrimp spring rolls

"Spring" rolls are named because they were eaten to celebrate Chinese New Year, or the first day of spring.

The fish

Shrimp, or white crabmeat

▪ **PREP** 25 mins ▪ **COOK** 15 mins ▪ **SERVES** 12

Ingredients

8oz (225g) raw shrimp, peeled, deveined, and chopped (see page 285)

½ red pepper, seeded and finely chopped

4oz (115g) mushrooms, chopped

4 scallions, thinly sliced

4oz (115g) beansprouts

¾in (2cm) fresh ginger, grated

1 tbsp rice wine vinegar

1 tbsp dark soy sauce

vegetable oil, for shallow frying

8oz (225g) cooked chicken, chopped

1 tbsp cornstarch

12 spring roll wrappers

6 Chinese cabbage leaves, halved

sweet chili sauce, to serve

1 In a bowl, mix together the shrimp, red pepper, mushrooms, scallions, beansprouts, ginger, vinegar, and soy sauce.

2 Heat 2 tbsp oil in a frying pan, add the shrimp mixture, and stir-fry for 3 minutes. Set aside to cool, then stir in the chicken.

3 In another small bowl, mix the cornstarch with 4 tbsp cold water.

4 Lay a spring roll wrapper on a work surface and top with half a cabbage leaf and 1 tbsp of the shrimp mixture. Brush the edges of the wrapper with the cornstarch mix and roll up, tucking in the sides and pressing the brushed edges together to seal. Repeat with the remaining wrappers and filling.

5 Shallow-fry the rolls in hot oil until golden brown. Drain on paper towels and serve with sweet chili sauce.

Prepare ahead

Make the shrimp filling up to 3 hours in advance (only add the chicken when it is completely cold), cover, and refrigerate. Assemble the rolls just before frying.

Salmon fishcakes

The classic fishcake. Use leftover cooked salmon instead, if you have it.

The fish

Salmon, or trout or haddock

▪ **PREP** 15 mins ▪ **COOK** 30 mins ▪ **SERVES** 4

Ingredients

2lb (900g) potatoes, peeled and cut into chunks

knob of butter

2lb (900g) salmon fillets, skinned

handful of curly parsley, finely chopped

salt and freshly ground black pepper

all-purpose flour, for dusting

vegetable oil, for shallow frying

tartar sauce, to serve

lemon wedges, to serve

1 Boil the potatoes in salted water for about 15 minutes or until soft, drain well, and mash with the butter until smooth. Set aside.

2 Put the salmon in a large frying pan, and cover with water. Poach for 5–8 minutes. Remove. Using your fingers, flake into pieces.

3 Gently mix the fish with the potato. Add the parsley, and season well. Take a small handful of the mixture at a time, roll into balls, then flatten into cakes. Dust each with flour.

4 Heat a little oil in a frying pan over medium heat. Fry the fishcakes for 5 minutes each side. Serve with tartar sauce and lemon wedges.

Prepare ahead

Make these up to 1 day ahead, cover, and chill. Return to room temperature before frying.

Variation

Maryland crab cakes

Mix the juice from 1 lemon with 2¼lb (1kg) crab, 4½oz (125g) breadcrumbs, chopped parsley and dill, 4 tbsp mayonnaise, 2 beaten eggs, and salt and pepper. Form into 16 cakes. Fry for just 3–4 minutes, and serve with a corn relish and lemon wedges. Serves 8.

Smoked haddock and herb fishcakes

Crisp fishcakes make a great starter, and the smoky flavors here work well with mustard.

The fish

Smoked haddock, or smoked cod

- **PREP** 10 mins, plus cooling ▪ **COOK** 30 mins
- **SERVES** 6

Ingredients

10oz (300g) smoked haddock fillet, pinboned and skinned

5oz (140g) potatoes, peeled and cut into chunks

salt and freshly ground black pepper

knob of butter

½ tsp Dijon mustard

3 scallions, finely chopped

grated zest and juice of ½ lemon

1oz (30g) chopped flat-leaf parsley

1½oz (45g) all-purpose flour

1 egg, beaten

3oz (85g) dried breadcrumbs

sunflower oil, for shallow frying

1 Preheat the oven to 375°F (190°C). Place the haddock in an ovenproof dish with 2–3 tbsp water, cover with foil and bake for 15 minutes. Leave to cool, then flake into pieces.

2 Boil the potatoes in salted water for about 15 minutes until soft. Drain well, and mash with the butter until smooth.

3 Place the mashed potato, mustard, scallions, lemon zest and juice, and parsley in a large bowl, add the smoked haddock and mix well. Season to taste.

4 Divide the mixture into 12 equal portions and shape each portion into rounds. Place the flour in a small dish, the egg in another dish, and the breadcrumbs in a third. Roll each fishcake in the flour, then dip into the egg, and finally coat with breadcrumbs.

5 Shallow fry the fishcakes in a little oil, in batches, for 5–7 minutes, turning once, or until crisp and golden all over. Drain on kitchen paper, and serve hot with a simple salad of arugula and watercress, and tartar sauce or mayonnaise for dipping.

Prepare ahead

You can prepare these up to the end of step 3 several hours in advance. Chill until required.

Crab balls

These Thai-style bites are a great alternative to Thai fishcakes (see page 58).

The fish

White crabmeat

- **PREP** 10 mins ▪ **COOK** 15 mins ▪ **SERVES** 4

Ingredients

12oz (350g) fresh white crabmeat, or canned white crabmeat, drained

1 red chile, seeded and roughly chopped

2 garlic cloves, roughly chopped

handful of fresh cilantro

grated zest and juice of 1 lemon

1 tsp Thai fish sauce

2 eggs, beaten

salt and freshly ground black pepper

4½oz (125g) fresh breadcrumbs

3 tbsp vegetable oil, for shallow frying

dark soy sauce, to serve

sweet chili sauce, to serve

1 Put the crab, chile, garlic, cilantro, lemon zest and juice, and fish sauce in a food processor. Blend until a rough paste forms, then add the egg and plenty of salt and pepper. Blend again.

2 Scoop the mixture up and roll into 1in (2.5cm) balls. Put the breadcrumbs on to a plate, and roll the crab balls in them until well covered.

3 Heat a little of the oil in a frying pan over medium heat. Add a few of the balls at a time to the pan, to cook in batches. Shallow fry for about 5 minutes until golden all over, moving the balls around the pan so that they brown evenly, topping up with more oil as needed. Drain on paper towels.

4 Serve hot with soy sauce and sweet chili sauce for dipping.

Prepare ahead

The spiced crab paste can be blended up to 4 hours in advance, covered, and refrigerated. Add the egg when ready to continue.

Thai fishcakes

Universally popular, these make a piquant, sophisticated first course.

The fish

Shrimp, or cod or monkfish

- **PREP** 15 mins ▪ **COOK** 15 mins ▪ **SERVES** 4

Ingredients

10oz (300g) cooked shrimp, peeled and deveined (see page 285)

3 garlic cloves

small handful of fresh cilantro

2 hot jalapeños, seeded

splash of Thai fish sauce

splash of dark soy sauce

small handful of basil leaves (preferably Thai basil)

juice of 2 limes

1 egg

salt and freshly ground black pepper

3–4 tbsp vegetable or sunflower oil

sweet chili sauce, to serve

arugula leaves, to serve

1 Put the first 8 ingredients in a food processor, and whizz into a rough paste. Add the egg and plenty of salt and pepper, and whizz again.

2 Heat a little of the oil in a frying pan over medium-high heat. Scoop out a tablespoon of the mixture, then carefully slide it into the pan and flatten to about ¾in (2cm) thick. Repeat until the pan is full, and shallow-fry for 1–2 minutes each side until golden. You will need to cook in batches, adding more oil as needed. Drain the fishcakes on a plate lined with paper towels.

3 Serve hot with a drizzle of sweet chili sauce and some arugula leaves.

Prepare ahead

The fishcake mixture can be blended, covered, and chilled up to 1 day ahead. The flavors will deepen. Return the mix to room temperature before continuing.

Thai crab cakes

These make a delicious starter, or transform into a main course with rice noodles.

The fish

White crabmeat, or salmon

- **PREP** 20 mins, plus chilling
- **COOK** 5–10 mins ▪ **MAKES** 20

Ingredients

1lb 2oz (500g) white crabmeat

4oz (115g) green beans, trimmed and finely chopped

1 green or red chile, seeded and very finely chopped

1 tsp lemongrass, very finely chopped

finely grated zest of 1 lime

1 tbsp Thai fish sauce

1 tbsp finely chopped Chinese chives or garlic chives

1 egg white, lightly beaten

flour, to dust

vegetable oil, for deep-frying

lime wedges, to serve

1 Flake the crabmeat into a bowl, picking it over carefully to remove any small, sharp pieces of shell. Mix in the green beans, chile, lemongrass, lime zest, fish sauce, and chives.

2 Add the egg white, stirring to bind the mixture together. Dust your hands with flour and shape the mixture into 20 small balls. Flatten them slightly into round cakes, place on a plate or board, spaced slightly apart so they don't stick together, and chill for 1 hour, or until firm.

3 Heat the oil to 325°F (160°C) in a large pan of deep-fat fryer (see page 308). Dust the crab cakes with flour and deep-fry them in batches for 3 minutes, or until golden. Drain on a plate lined with paper towels and serve warm with lime wedges.

Prepare ahead

The crab cakes can be assembled, covered, and chilled up to 1 day ahead. The flavors will deepen. Return them to room temperature before continuing.

COD FLAVOR PAIRINGS: Sweet and succulent cod teams well with the sharp flavors of dill, parsley, lemon, capers, and garlic, as well as with gentler bay leaf and butter.

Tuna carpaccio

The fish must be of the very best quality for this recipe, because it will be eaten raw.

The fish

Tuna, or salmon

- **PREP** 10–15 mins • **COOK** 20 mins
- **SERVES** 4

Ingredients

1 sprig of thyme, leaves chopped

2 tsp finely grated lemon zest

5 tbsp extra virgin olive oil

5 Fingerling potatoes, unpeeled

salt and freshly ground black pepper

4 tbsp mayonnaise

1 heaped tbsp small capers, rinsed

2 tbsp olive oil, for frying

14oz (400g) sashimi-grade tuna loin, cut into 8 equal pieces

1 Mix together the thyme, lemon zest, and extra virgin olive oil.

2 Boil the potatoes for 15 minutes, or until tender. Drain, and peel once cool enough to handle. Cut into thick slices and place in a bowl. Season to taste with salt, add a little of the flavored olive oil, and mix with the mayonnaise; set aside.

3 Pat the capers dry with a paper towel. Fry them in the olive oil for 2 minutes, or until crisp, then drain off the oil.

4 Pound each piece of tuna between 2 pieces of plastic wrap until uniformly very thin, then peel off the wrap. Scatter with fried capers, season to taste, and drizzle over the remaining flavored olive oil. Serve with the potatoes.

Seafood ceviche

A brief, light pickling of raw fish conserves its freshness and brings out the true flavor.

The fish

Any firm-fleshed fish, such as halibut, turbot, salmon, or monkfish

- **PREP** 20 mins, plus freezing and marinating
- **COOK** none • **SERVES** 4

Ingredients

1lb (450g) very fresh, firm-fleshed fish fillets, pinboned and skinned

1 red onion, finely sliced

juice of 2 lemons or limes

1 tbsp olive oil

1/2 tsp hot paprika

1 chile, finely chopped

salt and freshly ground black pepper

2 tbsp finely chopped flat-leaf parsley

1 Wrap the fish in plastic wrap or foil, and put it in the freezer for 1 hour to firm up the flesh. This will make it easier to slice. With a sharp knife, slice the fish into very thin slivers.

2 Spread the onion evenly in the bottom of a shallow, non-metallic dish. Pour over the lemon juice and olive oil, then sprinkle with the paprika and chile.

3 Place the fish on the onion, gently turning to coat with the marinade. Cover and marinate in the refrigerator for at least 20 minutes, preferably more than 1 hour. Season, sprinkle with parsley, and serve with crusty bread.

Prepare ahead

The ceviche can be assembled, covered, and chilled up to 2 hours in advance. Return it to room temperature before serving.

HALIBUT FLAVOR PAIRINGS: Fresh halibut can be served almost raw; it needs a gentle soaking in citrus first to tenderize the flesh. It's excellent with butter, nutmeg, pickles, capers, and lemon juice.

Marinated salmon

A Scandinavian favorite, and a refreshing change from smoked salmon.

The fish

Salmon, or trout or sea bass

- **PREP** 20 mins, plus marinating ▪ **COOK** none
- **SERVES** 6–8

Ingredients

2 salmon fillets, about 5oz (140g) each, skin on

3 tbsp coarse sea salt

3 tbsp sugar

1 tbsp coarsely crushed black peppercorns

3 tbsp aquavit or vodka

4 tbsp chopped dill, plus extra sprigs to serve

1 lemon, cut into wedges, to garnish

For the mustard sauce

4 tbsp Dijon mustard

4 tbsp sunflower or vegetable oil

3 tbsp sugar

2 tbsp white wine vinegar

1 tsp sour cream

pinch of salt

1 Score the salmon skin, making cuts ⅛in (3mm) deep. Mix the salt, sugar, and pepper, and sprinkle a quarter onto a nonmetallic dish. Place 1 fillet in the dish, skin-side down, and sprinkle with half the aquavit, another quarter of the salt mixture, and half the dill.

2 Sprinkle the flesh of the second fillet with another quarter of the salt mixture and place it, skin-side up, on top. Rub in the remaining salt and sprinkle with the remaining aquavit. Cover with plastic wrap, then place a large flat plate on top, and weigh it down with food cans. Refrigerate for 24 hours, draining off any liquid after 5–6 hours, then again after a further 5–6 hours. Turn the salmon and chill for another 24 hours, turning twice.

3 Place the sauce ingredients into a blender and process. Chill for 1 hour, covered. Before serving, add 2 tbsp chopped dill.

4 To serve, scrape the seasonings from the salmon. Place skin-side down on a board. Slice thinly on the slant, away from the skin. Serve with the sauce, lemon wedges, and dill.

Prepare ahead

The fish must be prepared 48 hours in advance.

Smoked salmon with mustard and dill dressing

Prepared in a flash while chatting to friends.

The fish

Smoked salmon, or very fresh raw salmon or cold-smoked trout

- **PREP** 5 mins ▪ **COOK** none ▪ **SERVES** 4

Ingredients

12oz (350g) good-quality smoked salmon

juice of 1 lemon

½ cucumber, finely chopped

For the dressing

⅓ cup extra virgin olive oil

3 tbsp white wine vinegar

1 tsp whole-grain mustard

1 tsp honey

salt and freshly ground black pepper

handful of fresh dill, finely chopped

1 Divide the salmon among 4 serving plates, and squeeze over the lemon juice.

2 Put the olive oil, vinegar, mustard, and honey in a small bowl. Whisk until well combined, then season. Sprinkle in half the dill, and whisk again. Taste, and adjust the seasoning.

3 Toss the cucumber with the remaining dill, then spoon it on to the plates. Drizzle over the dressing, and serve with brown bread.

Prepare ahead

The dressing can be prepared 1–2 hours ahead and kept, covered, in the refrigerator.

Smoked trout with beet, apple, and dill relish

A simple assembly job, but with eye-popping colors and great earthy and smoky flavors.

The fish
Hot-smoked trout, or smoked mackerel

■ **PREP** 15 mins ■ **COOK** none ■ **SERVES** 4

Ingredients
3–4 tsp creamed horseradish

½ red onion, finely diced

1–2 heads Belgian endive, leaves separated and rinsed

2 large hot-smoked trout fillets, about 8oz (225g) each, flaked

drizzle of olive oil

juice of ½ lemon

salt and freshly ground black pepper

2–3 apples

2 whole cooked beets, diced

handful of fresh dill, finely chopped

1 In a small bowl, mix together the horseradish and half the onion. Set aside.

2 Arrange the endive and trout on a serving plate, and drizzle with oil and lemon juice. Sprinkle over a pinch of salt and some pepper.

3 Peel, core, and chop the apple into bite-sized pieces. Put in a separate bowl with the beet and dill, and mix together.

4 To serve, spoon the beet relish over the leaves and fish. Sprinkle over the remaining onion, and serve with the horseradish on the side.

Smoked trout with pickled cucumber and minted yogurt

A refreshing mix of avocado, yogurt, and fish.

The fish
Hot-smoked trout, or hot-smoked salmon or smoked mackerel

■ **PREP** 15 mins ■ **COOK** none ■ **SERVES** 4

Ingredients
1 avocado, halved, pitted, and peeled

juice of 1 lemon

2 tbsp white wine vinegar

2 tsp superfine sugar

1 fresh red chile, seeded and finely chopped

½ large cucumber, peeled and halved lengthwise, seeded, and sliced

4 tbsp Greek-style yogurt

handful of mint leaves, chopped

2 large handfuls of mixed salad leaves

12 green olives, pitted

2 hot-smoked trout fillets, about 7oz (200g) each, flaked

salt and freshly ground black pepper

1 Cut the avocado into slices lengthwise, then sprinkle with the lemon juice. Set aside.

2 To make the pickled cucumber, whisk the vinegar, sugar, and chile in a small bowl until combined. Add the cucumber, and toss. In a separate small bowl, stir the yogurt and mint until well mixed.

3 Arrange the salad leaves and olives in a large salad bowl or on 4 individual plates. Top with the flaked trout and avocado. Season with a pinch of salt and some pepper. Spoon over some of the pickled cucumber, and serve the rest on the side with the minted yogurt.

Scallops with bacon

Bacon, chorizo, and pancetta are all excellent to serve with pan-fried scallops.

The fish

Scallops, or shrimp, or monkfish cheeks

- **PREP** 5–10 mins ▪ **COOK** 15 mins
- **SERVES** 4

Ingredients

4 bacon strips, diced

12 scallops

1 tbsp chopped flat-leaf parsley

squeeze of lemon juice

salt and freshly ground black pepper

handful of arugula, to serve

1 Heat a frying pan and add the bacon. Cook over medium heat until the bacon is brown and frazzled. Lift on to a plate.

2 Remove the roe from the scallops, if present. Fry the scallops in the bacon fat for 1–2 minutes on each side or until golden brown. Do not put too many in the pan at once, because they will not brown. Lift on to a plate.

3 Reduce the heat in the pan and fry the roes, if using; these are likely to pop in the hot fat. They are cooked when they are firm.

4 Return the scallop muscles and bacon to the pan, add the parsley, and the lemon juice. Season, and serve with arugula leaves.

Fried calamari

A tempting Mediterranean dish, served as a tasty appetizer.

The fish

Squid, or cuttlefish

- **PREP** 15 mins ▪ **COOK** 10–15 mins
- **SERVES** 4

Ingredients

2 eggs

2 tbsp chilled soda water

6 tbsp all-purpose flour

1 tsp red pepper flakes

1 tsp salt

1lb 2oz (500g) small squid, gutted, cleaned, and cut into $\frac{1}{2}$in (1cm) rings (see page 282)

9fl oz (250ml) vegetable or sunflower oil

lemon wedges, to serve

1 Break the eggs into a bowl, add the soda water, and whisk well. Put the flour, pepper flakes, and salt on a plate and mix well. Dip each piece of squid into the egg mixture and then the flour, ensuring they are evenly coated.

2 Heat the oil to 350°F (180°C) in a large pan or deep-fat fryer (see page 308), then carefully add the squid, a piece at a time. Do not overfill the pan. Cook in batches for 2–3 minutes, or until golden brown. Carefully remove with a slotted spoon and place on paper towels to soak up excess oil. Keep warm while you fry the rest, then serve with lemon wedges.

SCALLOP FLAVOR PAIRINGS: Despite their sweetness, scallops can take on the strong flavors of bacon, chorizo, red bell peppers, red onions, and olive oil, or the Asian tastes of sesame oil, black beans, scallions, ginger, and chile.

Scallops with sweet chili sauce

It's so easy to make sweet chili sauce; almost as quick as opening a jar.

The fish

Sea scallops, or monkfish or shrimp

- **PREP** 10 mins, plus marinating
- **COOK** 5 mins ▪ **SERVES** 4

Ingredients

4 garlic cloves, grated

3 red chiles, seeded and finely chopped

3 tbsp dry sherry

1 tsp sugar

2 tbsp olive oil, plus extra for frying

12 sea scallops, roe removed

1 Put the garlic, chiles, sherry, and sugar in a bowl and mix until the sugar dissolves. Add the oil and scallops, toss together, then leave to marinate for at least 30 minutes.

2 Transfer the scallops to a plate, using a slotted spoon. Reserve the marinade. Heat a little olive oil in a non-stick frying pan and cook the scallops over high heat for 1 minute on each side. Remove from the pan and pour in the marinade. Cook over high heat for 3 minutes, then pour it back over the scallops. Serve with a crisp green salad.

Squid in olive oil and paprika

Use sweet or smoked paprika if you prefer.

The fish

Squid, or cuttlefish, baby octopus, whelks, or periwinkles

- **PREP** 5 mins ▪ **COOK** 5 mins ▪ **SERVES** 4

Ingredients

1lb (450g) squid, gutted and cleaned (see page 282)

2 tbsp olive oil

2 garlic cloves, finely chopped

salt

2 tsp hot paprika

1 tbsp fresh juice

lemon wedges, to serve

1 Slice the squid tubes into rings, and cut each tentacle in half.

2 Heat the oil in a frying pan over medium heat, add the garlic and fry for 1 minute, stirring, then increase the heat and add the squid. Fry for 3 minutes on high heat, stirring frequently.

3 Season to taste with salt, then add the paprika and lemon juice.

4 Transfer to small serving plates and serve immediately, with lemon wedges. This is particularly good as part of a spread of other tapas, such as chorizo and olives.

Gefilte fish

Traditionally in this Jewish recipe, the mixture would have been stuffed into the skin of the deboned carp.

The fish

Carp, or pike or cod

- **PREP** 25 mins **COOK** 6–10 mins
- **SERVES** 4

Ingredients

2lb (1kg) carp fillets, pinboned and skinned

1 tbsp oil

1 onion, finely chopped

2 eggs

1 tsp sugar

salt and freshly ground white pepper

2oz (60g) medium matzo meal

2½ cups (600ml) fish stock

beet and horseradish relish, to serve

1 Put the fish and oil into a food processor and pulse until very well chopped. Transfer to a bowl.

2 Put the onion, eggs, sugar, salt, pepper, and matzo meal into the food processor, and pulse until well combined. Add to the fish and work into a paste by hand.

3 Shape the paste into balls the size of a small apple, and chill until required.

4 Bring the stock to a gentle simmer in a large saucepan. Drop in the fish balls, and poach gently for 6–10 minutes, or until firm. Serve with a beet and horseradish relish.

Prepare ahead

The gefilte fish balls can be made up to 1 day ahead, covered, and refrigerated. Return to room temperature before poaching and serving.

Chile shrimp with cilantro and lime

Sparkling citrus and hot chile bring out the sweetness of the shrimp.

The fish

Shrimp, or scallops

- **PREP** 15 mins **COOK** none **SERVES** 4

Ingredients

14oz (400g) can butterbeans, drained and rinsed

16 cooked shrimp, peeled and deveined, tails left on (see page 285)

handful of fresh cilantro, finely chopped

1–2 red chiles, seeded and finely chopped

2 handfuls of arugula

juice of 1 lime

salt and freshly ground black pepper

splash of sweet chili sauce

1 To soften the butterbeans a little, put them in a bowl, and cover with hot water. Leave to stand for 10 minutes, then drain well.

2 Put the shrimp in a large bowl. Add half the cilantro and all the chiles, and mix well. Add in the butterbeans, and toss again.

3 Arrange the arugula in a large serving bowl or on 4 individual plates. Sprinkle over a little of the lime juice, a pinch of salt, and some pepper. Add the remaining lime juice to the shrimp, stir, then taste and adjust the seasoning.

4 Spoon the shrimp mixture over the arugula, then drizzle with sweet chili sauce, and sprinkle over the remaining cilantro. Serve immediately.

Herbed fish goujons

Fish fingers for grown-ups.

The fish

Any white fish, such as haddock, cod, plaice, lemon sole, saithe, or pollock

- **PREP** 20 mins - **COOK** 10–15 mins
- **SERVES** 4–6

Ingredients

4oz (115g) fresh breadcrumbs

handful of flat-leaf parsley, chopped, plus a few sprigs, to garnish

½ tsp smoked paprika

salt and freshly ground black pepper

3oz (85g) all-purpose flour

1 large egg

8oz (225g) white fish fillets, pinboned and skinned

sunflower oil, for frying

lemon wedges, to serve

1 Place the breadcrumbs, chopped parsley, and smoked paprika in a bowl, season to taste with salt and pepper, and mix thoroughly.

2 Place the flour in a bowl, whisk the egg with 1 tbsp water in another bowl, and spread the breadcrumb mixture into a third.

3 Slice the fish into thin strips. Dust the strips with flour, then dip into the egg, then place in the breadcrumbs, turning to coat completely. Place them on a plate and chill until needed.

4 Heat 1in (2.5cm) sunflower oil in a frying pan until it is hot enough to sizzle when the fish is added. Fry the fish for 1 minute each side, or until crisp, then drain on paper towels. Serve with sprigs of parsley and lemon wedges. These are good with a herbed mayonnaise.

Prepare ahead

Prepare the goujons, cover, and refrigerate up to 1 day in advance. Return to room temperature before frying. Or lay the goujons on a baking sheet, cover, and freeze, then put into a plastic freezer bag to store for up to 1 month.

Broiled sardines on toast

The posh version of a classic snack, great for a late supper, and very healthy.

The fish

Sardines, or herrings, sprats, or small mackerel

- **PREP** 10 mins, plus marinating
- **COOK** 6 mins - **SERVES** 4

Ingredients

8 sardines, scaled, gutted, and boned through the stomach (see page 267) or filleted

4 tbsp olive oil

3 garlic cloves, finely sliced

1 fresh green chile, seeded and finely chopped

juice of 1 lemon

1 tsp crushed fennel seeds

2 tbsp finely chopped flat-leaf parsley

salt and freshly ground black pepper

ciabatta, sliced and toasted, to serve

1 Brush the sardines with a little of the oil and cook under a medium broiler for 3 minutes on each side. Remove, and allow to cool.

2 Meanwhile, put all the remaining ingredients except the bread in a mixing bowl and combine well. Add the sardines, then leave to marinate for 20 minutes, if you have time.

3 Serve the marinated sardines on the warm, toasted ciabatta.

Prepare ahead

Make the recipe to the end of step 2, cover, and refrigerate for up to 1 day in advance. Return to room temperature before serving on toast.

Variation

Anchovies on toast

Cut 2 baguettes in half lengthwise and toast on both sides. Rub with 2 halved tomatoes, squeezing out the seeds and flesh on to the bread. Discard the tomato skins. Lay over 1¾oz (50g) drained anchovy fillets in oil. Slice 2 more tomatoes and arrange on top, drizzle with extra virgin olive oil, season, and scatter with finely chopped shallots and parsley. Top with 1¾oz (50g) more anchovies, and serve.

Salt and pepper prawns

You will find that you can't stop eating these!

The fish

Tiger prawns, or squid, or scallops

- **PREP** 10 mins • **COOK** 10 mins • **SERVES** 4

Ingredients

2 tbsp cornstarch

1 tbsp sea salt

1 tbsp cracked black pepper

16 raw tiger prawns, peeled and deveined (see page 285)

4 tbsp vegetable oil

3 fresh hot red chiles, seeded and finely sliced

3 garlic cloves, grated or finely chopped

6 scallions, cut into 2in (5cm) pieces, then halved lengthwise

dark soy sauce, to serve

1 In a bowl, mix together the cornstarch, salt, and pepper. Add the prawns, and toss until well combined. Set aside.

2 Heat 1 tbsp of the oil in a frying pan over medium heat. Add the chiles, garlic, and scallions, and stir-fry for 3–5 minutes. Remove from the heat, and cover with a lid to keep warm.

3 Heat the remaining oil in a separate frying pan over high heat. Add the prawns, and cook for 3–5 minutes, tossing them gently until they are completely pink.

4 Remove the prawns from the pan with a slotted spoon, and divide among 4 serving plates. Top with the chile and scallion mixture, and serve immediately with a splash of soy sauce.

Shrimp and zucchini balls with caper cream

An unusual and incredibly tasty starter.

The fish

Shrimp, or smoked haddock

- **PREP** 30 mins, plus marinating
- **COOK** 20 mins • **SERVES** 6–8

Ingredients

1¼lb (550g) raw shrimp, peeled, deveined, and finely chopped (see page 285)

9oz (250g) zucchini, grated

1 garlic clove, crushed

2 tbsp finely chopped flat-leaf parsley

grated zest and juice of 1 small lemon

2 eggs, beaten

salt and freshly ground black pepper

8fl oz (250ml) sour cream

1 tbsp capers, rinsed and chopped

1 tbsp finely chopped fresh dill

16fl oz (500ml) olive oil, for frying

1 In a bowl, combine the shrimp, zucchini, garlic, parsley, lemon zest and juice, and eggs. Season and mix well by hand. Cover with plastic wrap, and marinate in the refrigerator for 1 hour. Meanwhile, put the sour cream, capers, and dill in a separate bowl, and season with pepper. Stir, cover with plastic wrap, and chill until needed.

2 Pour the oil into a wide, heavy frying pan over medium-high heat. Roll the shrimp mixture into walnut-sized balls.

3 When the oil is hot, gently drop in the balls. Fry for 4–5 minutes, or until golden brown, turning. Do not overcrowd the pan; cook in batches if necessary. Remove from the pan with a slotted spoon, and drain on paper towels.

4 Serve the shrimp and zucchini balls with bowls of caper cream.

Prepare ahead

Make the shrimp balls and the caper cream up to 1 day in advance. Cover both, and refrigerate until ready to cook.

Crawfish sauté with spicy tomatoes

Crawfish are much-loved in the American South, and especially in Louisiana, so in this recipe Creole flavorings are used to add zip to sweet crawfish.

The fish

Freshwater crawfish, or squid, or shrimp

- **PREP** 10 mins ▪ **COOK** 15–20 mins
- **SERVES** 4

Ingredients

3 tbsp butter

1 onion, finely chopped

1 garlic clove, grated or finely chopped

1 carrot, finely diced

1 tbsp creamed horseradish

2 tbsp whole-grain mustard

1 tsp English mustard

½ tsp cayenne pepper

1 tbsp Creole spice mix

14oz (400g) can tomatoes, chopped

salt and freshly ground black pepper

2 tbsp chopped flat-leaf parsley

5 tbsp mayonnaise

1lb (450g) cooked, peeled, and deveined freshwater crawfish tails, patted dry

1 Melt the butter in a large saucepan, add the onion, garlic, and carrot and cook over low heat for 4–5 minutes or until the onion is soft. Add the horseradish, mustards, cayenne, and Creole spices. Stir over the heat for 1 minute, then add the tomatoes, bring to a boil and simmer for 7–8 minutes or until thick and pulpy.

2 Season the mixture to taste and add the parsley and mayonnaise. Stir in the crawfish and heat through until piping hot. Do not overheat, or they will become tough.

3 Pile the crawfish into a bowl. For a more substantial dish, serve some boiled rice on the side.

Prepare ahead

The tomato sauce in step 1 can be made up to 2 days in advance, covered, and refrigerated. The flavors will deepen. Return to a simmer before continuing.

Dressed crab

A quintessential English classic, perfect for a summer's day. For the best results, buy the crab live and cook it yourself (see page 289).

The fish

Crab

- **PREP** 35–40 mins ▪ **COOK** none ▪ **SERVES** 2

Ingredients

1 brown crab, about 3¾–4½lb (1.3–2kg), cooked

splash of oil

2–3 tbsp fresh white breadcrumbs

dried English mustard, to taste

cayenne pepper, to taste

Worcestershire sauce, to taste

freshly ground black pepper, to taste

1 egg, hard-boiled

chopped flat-leaf parsley, to garnish

1 Remove the brown and white meat from the crab and set aside separately. The mouth, stomach sac, and gills must all be discarded (see pages 288–89).

2 Wash the shell well and brush with a little oil. Mix the brown meat with enough breadcrumbs to bind. Add mustard, cayenne, Worcestershire sauce, and pepper, to taste. Flake the white meat into a bowl, taking care to locate and discard any chips of shell.

3 Neatly arrange both white and brown meat back in the cleaned shell and garnish with chopped hard-boiled egg white, sieved hard-boiled egg yolks, and parsley. Serve with bread and wedges of lemon.

Prepare ahead

Pick out the crab meat, put the white and brown meat into separate bowls, cover, and chill for up to 1 day before continuing.

CRAWFISH FLAVOR PAIRINGS: Enhance sweet crawfish with cayenne pepper or paprika, enjoy simply with lemon, garlic, and tarragon, chives, and dill, or even use Asian ingredients such as lemongrass, soy sauce, and chile.

Yam pla fu

This classic Thai recipe is served with a chili dipping sauce and mango or papaya salad.

The fish

Snapper, or meagre or gray mullet

- **PREP** 15 mins **COOK** 20–25 mins
- **SERVES** 4

Ingredients

1 large snapper, scaled, filleted, and pinboned

1 tsp oil, plus more for deep-frying

2 tsp salt

3oz (75g) dry roasted peanuts, to serve

nam prik (hot chili dipping sauce), or sweet chili sauce, to serve

For the mango salad

2 green mangos or papayas, shredded, or riper fruits, diced

1 carrot, peeled and shredded

2 scallions, finely sliced

1/2 cucumber, peeled, seeded, and shredded

2oz (60g) bean sprouts

For the dressing

1 tbsp palm sugar or dark brown sugar

zest and juice of 1 large lime

1 garlic clove, grated or finely chopped

1 tbsp grated fresh ginger

splash of Thai fish sauce, to taste

1–2 bird's eye chiles, finely chopped, to taste

large handful of cilantro, chopped

large handful of mint, chopped

1 Preheat the oven to 400°F (200°C). Rub the fish with the 1 tsp oil and the salt and arrange on a baking sheet. Roast in the oven for 12–15 minutes, until the skin crisps. Cool.

2 Put the fish in a food processor and whizz until finely chopped. Shape into golf balls. Heat the oil for deep-frying to 350°F (180°C) in a large pan or deep-fat fryer; do not allow it to become too hot (see page 308).

3 Drop each fish ball into the hot oil and deep-fry in small batches for about 3 minutes until brown and crispy. Lift on to paper towels to drain, and keep warm.

4 Toss all the salad ingredients together in a shallow bowl until evenly mixed.

5 Whisk the dressing ingredients together and toss into the salad with the peanuts. Serve with the fish balls, lime wedges, and chili sauce.

Salade Niçoise

This well-known French salad is substantial enough to serve as a main course for two.

The fish

Tuna, or swordfish

- **PREP** 15 mins **COOK** 7–8 mins **SERVES** 4

Ingredients

5 1/2 oz (150g) green beans, trimmed

4 tuna steaks, about 5 1/2 oz (150g) each

5fl oz (150ml) extra virgin olive oil, plus extra for brushing

salt and freshly ground black pepper

2 tsp Dijon mustard

1 garlic clove, crushed

3 tbsp white wine vinegar

juice of 1/2 lemon

8 anchovy fillets in olive oil, drained

1 red onion, finely sliced

9oz (250g) plum tomatoes, quartered lengthwise

12 black olives

2 romaine lettuce hearts, trimmed and torn into bite-sized pieces

8–10 basil leaves

4 eggs, hard-boiled and quartered

1 Cook the beans in a saucepan of gently boiling water for 3–4 minutes, or until just tender. Drain the beans and quickly put them into a bowl of iced water.

2 Preheat a ridged griddle pan over medium-high heat. Brush the tuna steaks with 1–2 tbsp olive oil and season to taste. Sear the steaks for 2 minutes on each side; the centers should be slightly pink. Set aside. Drain the beans again.

3 Meanwhile, whisk together the mustard, garlic, vinegar, lemon juice, and remaining olive oil. Season to taste.

4 Place the beans, anchovies, onion, tomatoes, olives, lettuce, and basil in a large bowl. Drizzle with the vinaigrette and gently toss.

5 Divide the salad among 4 plates and top with the eggs. Cut the tuna steaks in half and arrange on top of each plate.

RED SNAPPER FLAVOR PAIRINGS:

Snapper is always great with the Asian tastes of sesame oil, soy sauce, ginger, garlic, cilantro, palm sugar, and Thai or Vietnamese fish sauces.

Asian cucumber salad with smoked salmon

Cucumber slices combine well with the flavor of smoked salmon.

The fish

Smoked salmon, or cold-smoked trout

- **PREP** 10 mins ▪ **COOK** none ▪ **SERVES** 6

Ingredients

2 large cucumbers

salt and freshly ground black pepper

14oz (400g) smoked salmon, cut into long strips

1 lime, cut into wedges, to garnish (optional)

For the dressing

1 garlic clove, grated or finely chopped

1 tbsp fish sauce

2 tbsp peanut oil

¼ cup white wine vinegar

1 tbsp Thai sweet chili dipping sauce

2 tbsp chopped cilantro leaves

1 With a vegetable peeler, slice the cucumbers lengthwise into ribbons, discarding the central core and seeds. Place the pieces in a bowl.

2 Put the dressing ingredients into a large, screw-top jar and shake well. Alternatively, whisk the ingredients together in a bowl. Ten minutes before serving, pour the dressing over the cucumber and season to taste with salt and pepper. To serve, pile the cucumber on to individual plates, and arrange the smoked salmon on top. Sprinkle with pepper and garnish with lime wedges (if using).

Layered marinated herring salad

For convenience, this recipe uses ready-marinated herring fillets from the supermarket or deli.

The fish

Marinated herring, or marinated anchovies

- **PREP** 15 mins, plus soaking and chilling
- **COOK** none ▪ **SERVES** 6–10

Ingredients

1 sweet onion, finely sliced

2 cups sour cream

½ cup plain yogurt

1 tbsp fresh lemon juice

¼ tsp superfine sugar

2 tart dessert apples, peeled, cored, and finely sliced

2 dill pickles, sliced or chopped

salt and freshly ground black pepper

10oz (300g) marinated herring fillets, drained

2 cooked potatoes, diced (optional)

1 cooked beet, sliced (optional)

1 tbsp chopped dill, to garnish

1 Put the onion in a bowl, cover with cold water, and leave to soak for 15 minutes. Drain well, then toss with the sour cream, yogurt, lemon juice, and sugar. Stir in the apple and pickle, and season to taste with salt and pepper.

2 Place half the herring in a serving dish and top with the potatoes and the beets (if using). Cover with half the sour cream sauce. Layer on the remaining herring, potatoes, and beets, then add the remaining sauce.

3 Cover the dish tightly with plastic wrap and refrigerate for at least 5 hours. Sprinkle with dill just before serving. Good with sourdough or pumpernickel bread.

Prepare ahead

The salad benefits from being assembled up to 2 days in advance and chilled.

Smoked trout and pancetta salad

The bitter leaves and radishes combine well with smoky fish in this light lunch or starter.

The fish

Hot-smoked trout, or hot-smoked salmon, or smoked mackerel

▪ **PREP** 10 mins ▪ **COOK** 5 mins ▪ **SERVES** 6

Ingredients

12oz (350g) hot-smoked trout fillets

12 thin slices of pancetta

2 bunches of watercress, washed

2 heads of Belgian endive, leaves divided

5oz (140g) feta cheese, cubed

5 small radishes, finely sliced

2 shallots, finely sliced

For the dressing

1 tbsp red wine vinegar

⅓ cup extra virgin olive oil

1 tsp superfine sugar

juice of ½ lemon

1 tsp Dijon mustard

salt and freshly ground black pepper

1 Skin the trout, if necessary, and carefully remove any bones. Heat a frying pan and fry the pancetta for 5 minutes, or until crisp.

2 Make the dressing by placing all the ingredients in a jar and shaking well. Season. Place the watercress and endive on to a serving plate, scatter over large flakes of trout, then add the pancetta, feta, radishes, and shallots. Drizzle with the dressing and serve.

Prepare ahead

The dressing can be made, covered, and chilled up to 1 week in advance. Whisk before using.

Salmon salad with mint yogurt dressing

So fresh tasting and glamorous, yet one of the easiest dishes to make.

The fish

Salmon, or trout or tuna

▪ **PREP** 15 mins ▪ **COOK** 25 mins ▪ **SERVES** 4

Ingredients

2 tbsp red wine vinegar

2 tbsp finely chopped fresh mint, plus extra mint leaves to serve

4 tbsp Greek-style yogurt

salt and freshly ground black pepper

1¼lb (550g) salmon fillet, pinboned and skinned

handful of chopped fresh dill

1 lemon, sliced

1 Preheat the oven to 400°F (200°C).

2 Put the vinegar, mint, and yogurt in a bowl, season, and whisk. Set aside.

3 Lay the salmon on a large piece of foil. Sprinkle with the dill, and overlap a few slices of lemon on top. Season, and loosely seal the foil to make a parcel. Place on a baking tray, and bake in the hot oven for 20–25 minutes. Allow to cool.

4 Transfer the salmon to a plate, drizzle over the dressing, and scatter with fresh mint leaves. Serve with a cucumber salad.

Crab and mango salad

With fruity mango, this makes a lovely summer lunch. Buy the crab the day you make it.

The fish

Crab, or lobster or Dublin Bay prawns

- **PREP** 15 mins ▪ **COOK** none ▪ **SERVES** 4

Ingredients

a few mint leaves, roughly chopped

handful of cilantro leaves, roughly chopped

handful of mixed salad leaves, such as arugula, spinach, and watercress

1 shallot, finely chopped

12oz (350g) fresh crab, white and brown meat separated

1 ripe avocado, sliced lengthwise

For the dressing

1 ripe mango, roughly chopped

zest and juice of ½ lime

3 tbsp olive oil

1 To make the dressing, put the mango, lime zest and juice, and olive oil in a food processor and blend until smooth. Add a little water if it's too thick.

2 For the salad, mix together the herbs and salad leaves. Add the shallot and toss in a little of the dressing. Divide the salad between 4 plates and arrange a spoonful each of the white and brown crabmeat on top. Serve with the avocado slices and the remaining dressing on the side, and slices of warm brown bread and butter.

Prepare ahead

Make the dressing up to 3 hours in advance, cover, and refrigerate. Whisk well before using.

Crab salad with grapefruit and cilantro

For a professional finish, tightly pack the crab for each serving into a small pastry cutter, then slide out on to the plates.

The fish

White crabmeat, or shrimp, or cockles

- **PREP** 10 mins ▪ **COOK** none ▪ **SERVES** 4

Ingredients

12oz (350g) fresh white crabmeat, or canned white crabmeat, drained

handful of baby salad leaves

handful of cilantro

2 pink grapefruits, peeled, segmented, and pith removed

For the dressing

3 tbsp extra virgin olive oil

1 tbsp white wine vinegar

pinch of sugar

salt and freshly ground black pepper

1 Make the dressing by placing all the ingredients in a jar and shaking vigorously.

2 Mix the crab with a drizzle of the dressing. Divide the salad leaves and half the cilantro leaves among 4 serving plates, and scatter over the grapefruit segments.

3 When ready to serve, drizzle the salad with the remaining dressing. Divide the crab among the plates, spooning it neatly on top of the leaves. Scatter over the remaining cilantro, and serve immediately.

Prepare ahead

Make the dressing up to 1 week in advance, and keep in a jar in the refrigerator. Shake to re-emulsify before use.

Variation

Chile crab with grapefruit and cilantro
Add a pinch of red pepper flakes or a seeded and chopped fresh chile to the dressing.

Prawn, grapefruit, and avocado salad

Simple enough for brunch, but special enough to serve to dinner guests.

The fish

Tiger prawns, or lobster, white crabmeat, squid, or scallops

• **PREP** 15 mins • **COOK** none • **SERVES** 6

Ingredients

30 cooked tiger prawns, peeled and deveined (see page 285)

2 large pink grapefruit, peeled, segmented, and pith removed

handful of mint leaves, torn

3 radishes, finely sliced

3 scallions, finely sliced

2 avocados, peeled and cut into chunks or slices

bunch of watercress

salad leaves

For the dressing

3 tbsp Thai fish sauce

3 tbsp lime juice

2 tbsp sugar

2 tbsp olive oil

1 Make the dressing by placing all the ingredients in a jar and shaking vigorously.

2 Pat the prawns dry with paper towels, then toss them in a little of the dressing.

3 Place the remaining salad ingredients in a large bowl and toss well with a little more dressing. Divide between 6 plates. Arrange the prawns on top of each plate and drizzle with some of the remaining dressing to serve.

Prepare ahead

The dressing can be made several days in advance and kept refrigerated. Shake the jar to re-emulsify before use.

Vietnamese salad of shrimp with papaya

A beautiful mix of fresh, clean flavors.

The fish

Shrimp, or squid or scallops

• **PREP** 15 mins • **COOK** 2–3 mins • **SERVES** 4

Ingredients

12 large raw shrimp, peeled and deveined, heads and tails removed (see page 285)

2 tbsp vegetable oil

1 tsp rice wine vinegar

1 tsp sugar

1 red chile, seeded and very finely chopped

2 garlic cloves, crushed

2 tbsp Vietnamese or Thai fish sauce

1 tbsp lime juice

1 tbsp chopped mint (preferably Vietnamese mint), plus extra sprigs to serve

1 green papaya, seeded, quartered lengthwise, and thinly sliced

½ cucumber, seeded and shredded

1 Preheat the broiler on its highest setting. Spread the shrimp out on a foil-lined broiler pan, brush with the oil, and broil for 2–3 minutes, or until they turn pink.

2 Meanwhile, whisk the vinegar, sugar, chile, garlic, fish sauce, lime juice, and 2½fl oz (75ml) cold water in a bowl until the sugar dissolves. Add the shrimp and stir to coat in the dressing. Leave to cool completely.

3 Add the mint, papaya, and cucumber and toss. Transfer the salad to a serving platter, with the shrimp and mint sprigs on top.

Prepare ahead

Steps 1 and 2 can be completed several hours in advance. Store, covered, in the refrigerator. Return to room temperature before serving.

Tuna and bean salad

This classic recipe calls for canned tuna, although you can sear fresh tuna to serve with these beans, if you prefer.

The fish

Canned tuna, or canned salmon or canned mackerel

- **PREP** 20 mins ▪ **COOK** none ▪ **SERVES** 4

Ingredients

2 x 4oz (110g) cans tuna in spring water, drained

1 x 14oz (400g) can mixed beans, drained

1 red onion, finely chopped

4 tbsp chopped flat-leaf parsley

1 red bell pepper, seeded and finely diced

salt and freshly ground black pepper

1 garlic clove, halved

For the dressing

4 tbsp extra virgin olive oil

1 tbsp lemon juice

pinch of sugar

1 Put the tuna into a bowl and break into large chunks with a fork. Add the beans and mix.

2 Stir in the onion, parsley, and red pepper and season generously with salt and pepper.

3 Make the dressing by whisking the olive oil with the lemon juice and sugar. Season to taste.

4 Rub the cut side of the garlic around a large salad bowl. Add the dressing to the tuna and beans, toss, and pile into the bowl. Serve with garlic bread.

Prepare ahead

The salad can be made up to 1 day ahead, covered, and chilled. The flavors will deepen. Bring to room temperature before eating.

Herring salad with potatoes and beets

Oil-rich and packed with omega 3, herrings have a fairly short shelf life, so preserving them is common.

The fish

Pickled herring, or pickled sprats, marinated anchovies, or smoked mackerel

- **PREP** 15 mins ▪ **COOK** 15 mins ▪ **SERVES** 4

Ingredients

1lb (450g) salad potatoes, scrubbed

4 large beets, cooked, peeled, and diced

4 scallions, finely sliced

1lb (450g) cured or pickled herring, or rollmops, cut into 2in (5cm) pieces (see page 297)

sprigs of dill, to serve

For the dressing

$2/3$ cup mayonnaise

1 tbsp creamed horseradish

lemon juice, to taste

1–2 tsp German or Dijon mustard

salt and freshly ground black pepper

1 Cook the potatoes in boiling water for about 15 minutes, or until tender, drain, and thickly slice. Put into a bowl, and add the beets and scallions.

2 In a separate bowl, mix the mayonnaise, horseradish, lemon juice, and mustard to taste. Season with salt and pepper. Add to the potato and beets and toss until well coated.

3 Divide the potato salad between 4 dishes and top with the herrings and dill to serve.

Prepare ahead

You can make the potato salad in advance, cover, and chill for 1–2 days. Bring to room temperature before continuing.

SPRAT FLAVOR PAIRINGS: These startlingly silver fish are lovely with earthy beets, piquant white or red wine vinegars, or with cilantro and spicy coriander seeds.

Lobster salad with watercress

A very special summer salad, ideal for outdoor dining.

The fish

Lobster, or white crabmeat, Dublin Bay prawns, or shrimp

▪ **PREP** 20 mins ▪ **COOK** none ▪ **SERVES** 4

Ingredients

½ red onion, finely sliced

1 tsp red wine vinegar

4 cooked lobster tails, halved

1 large bunch of watercress, tough stalks removed

½ fennel bulb, very finely sliced

8 sun-dried tomatoes, chopped

fresh herbs, such as chervil, dill, or chives, to garnish

For the dressing

1 egg

1 egg yolk

2 tsp Dijon mustard

zest and juice of 1 lemon

1¾ cups sunflower oil

¼oz (10g) chervil or chives

salt and freshly ground black pepper

1 To make the dressing, place the egg, egg yolk, mustard, and lemon zest and juice into a blender. Blend on a low speed while slowly adding the oil. Add the chervil. Season to taste with salt and pepper. Set aside.

2 Place the red onion in a bowl with the vinegar, and leave to stand for 10 minutes.

3 Remove all the meat from the lobster tails, keeping the pieces of meat as whole as possible.

4 Arrange the watercress on plates, scatter over the fennel, the drained onion slices, and the tomatoes. Place the lobster meat on top, drizzle with the dressing, and garnish with the herbs.

Prepare ahead

The dressing can be made, covered, and chilled up to 1 day in advance, but only stir in the herbs just before using, to prevent discoloration.

Calamari salad with mint and dill

Fresh herbs and grilled squid make a delicious warm salad.

The fish

Squid, or cuttlefish

▪ **PREP** 20 mins, plus marinating
▪ **COOK** 5 mins ▪ **SERVES** 4

Ingredients

2¼lb (1kg) small squid, gutted and cleaned (see page 282)

3oz (85g) lamb's lettuce, or watercress

12 sprigs of mint

1 small red onion, finely sliced

salt and freshly ground black pepper

juice of 1 lime

2 tbsp chopped dill

4 tbsp extra virgin olive oil

For the marinade

2 tbsp chopped flat-leaf parsley

1 tbsp chopped mint

1 garlic clove, crushed

2 tsp ground coriander

1 tsp ground cumin

2 tsp paprika

4 tbsp olive oil

1 Cut off the squid tentacles and remove the beak-like mouth from the center. Cut the body in half lengthwise and score the flesh to form a diamond pattern. Cut the tentacles into bite-sized pieces. Place in a bowl.

2 Combine the marinade ingredients, adding the oil gradually to make a paste. Coat the squid in the mixture. Cover, chill, and marinate for at least 30 minutes.

3 Combine the lamb's lettuce with the mint and onion. Set aside.

4 Preheat the broiler on its highest setting. Arrange the squid on a foil-lined broiler pan and broil for 4–5 minutes, turning once. Season to taste and sprinkle with a little lime juice.

5 Place the remaining lime juice, the dill, and extra virgin olive oil in a pitcher, season, then whisk well. Pour the dressing over the salad and top with the squid. Serve immediately.

Seafood and fennel salad with anchovy dressing

This crisp, sweet, mixed-seafood salad can be assembled in an instant.

The fish
Any mixed seafood, such as shrimp, mussels, or squid rings

- **PREP** 15 mins ▪ **COOK** none ▪ **SERVES** 4

Ingredients
handful of mixed crisp lettuce leaves, such as Romaine

1 fennel bulb, finely sliced

1lb (450g) ready-cooked mixed seafood, rinsed and dried

6 anchovy fillets in olive oil, drained

1 jalapeño chile, seeded and finely chopped

handful of cilantro, roughly chopped

lemon wedges, to serve

rice noodles, to serve

For the dressing
3 tbsp extra virgin olive oil

1 tbsp white wine vinegar

6 anchovy fillets in olive oil, drained and finely chopped

pinch of sugar

handful of flat-leaf parsley, finely chopped

salt and freshly ground black pepper

1 Make the dressing. In a bowl, whisk together the oil and vinegar. Add the anchovies, sugar, and parsley, season well, and whisk again.

2 In a bowl, toss together the salad leaves, fennel, seafood, anchovies, jalapeño, and cilantro. Pour over the dressing, and carefully mix together. Pile up in a shallow serving bowl, and serve with lemon wedges for squeezing over, and some rice noodles.

Prepare ahead
Make the dressing up to 1 day ahead, cover and chill. Add the parsley just before serving.

Marinated squid salad

An economical and dramatic-looking dish.

The fish
Squid, or cuttlefish or baby octopus

- **PREP** 15 mins, plus marinating
- **COOK** 3 mins ▪ **SERVES** 4

Ingredients
10oz (300g) small squid, gutted and cleaned

1 cup olive oil

salt and freshly ground black pepper

2 tbsp white wine vinegar

3 garlic cloves, crushed

1 tsp paprika

handful of flat-leaf parsley, finely chopped

1 Cut the squid into pieces—a mixture of strips and rings—brush with a little oil and season well.

2 Heat 1 tbsp of the oil in a frying pan, add the squid, and cook over medium heat, stirring constantly, for 2–3 minutes, or until the squid is cooked. Remove from the heat and transfer to a serving bowl.

3 Mix the remaining oil with the vinegar, garlic, paprika, and parsley, then season with salt and pepper. Pour over the squid, combine well, and leave to marinate for at least 30 minutes. Serve with fresh crusty bread and a green salad.

Soups

New England clam chowder

Clams must be cooked on the day of purchase, so when you find great clams, make sure you also have all the ingredients in your kitchen for this fabulous soup.

The fish
Clams, or mussels

- **PREP** 25–30 mins ▪ **COOK** 35–40 mins
- **SERVES** 4

Ingredients

1¾ (800g) clams, thoroughly washed

1 tbsp oil

4oz (115g) thick-cut bacon strips, diced

2 floury potatoes, such as Russet Burbank, peeled and cut into chunks

1 onion, finely chopped

2 tbsp all-purpose flour

2 cups whole milk

salt and freshly ground black pepper

½ cup half-and-half

2 tbsp finely chopped flat-leaf parsley, to garnish

1 Discard any open clams, then shell the rest, reserving the juices (see page 279). Add enough water to the juices to make 2 cups. Chop the clams. Heat the oil in a large, heavy saucepan, and fry the bacon over medium heat for 5 minutes, or until crisp. Remove.

2 Add the potatoes and onion and fry gently for 5 minutes. Stir in the flour for 2 minutes, then add the clam juice and milk, and season. Cover, reduce the heat, and simmer for 20 minutes, or until the potatoes are tender.

3 Add the clams and simmer, uncovered, for 5 minutes. Stir in the half-and-half and reheat without boiling. Serve sprinkled with bacon and parsley, and provide saltines or oyster crackers on the side.

Variation

Manhattan cod and mussel chowder
Replace the clams with 2¼lb (1kg) mussels, adding 1 cup of dry white wine to the juices before topping up with water. When adding the potatoes, add 2 x 14oz (400g) cans tomatoes, 4 garlic cloves, finely chopped, and 1–2 tbsp tomato purée. Use only half the flour and replace the milk with fish stock. Add 2¼lb (1kg) cod fillets, cut into chunks, at the start of step 3. Omit the half-and-half. Sprinkle with thyme and serve with whole wheat bread.

Brodetto abruzzese

This very plain and simple fish stew heralds from Tuscany and was made by impoverished fishermen landing their catch in the Adriatic.

The fish
Any mixed fish, such as hake, mullet, John Dory, rascasse, or sea bass, and mussels, or clams

- **PREP** 30–40 mins ▪ **COOK** 1 hr ▪ **SERVES** 4

Ingredients

1½lb (700g) white fish fillets, pinboned and skinned

5 tbsp extra virgin olive oil

2 garlic cloves, chopped

½ tsp red pepper flakes

8 tomatoes, skinned and chopped, juices reserved

2 tsp tomato purée

⅔ cup medium white wine

sea salt and freshly ground black pepper

12oz (340g) mussels, prepared (see page 278)

crusty bread, to serve

For the stock

1 tbsp olive oil

1 garlic clove, chopped

1 onion, thickly sliced

4–5 fish heads, gills removed, well washed

4 tbsp white wine vinegar

1 bay leaf

1 Cut all the fish into roughly even 1–2in (3–5cm) pieces, and refrigerate.

2 Heat the oil for the stock in a large saucepan, add the garlic, and onion, and fry for 3–4 minutes, then add the fish heads and stir well for a further 3–4 minutes. Add the vinegar, bay leaf, and water to cover. Bring to a boil, reduce the heat to very low, and simmer gently for 25 minutes. Strain.

3 Heat the oil for the soup in another large saucepan over medium heat, add the garlic and red pepper flakes and fry for 1 minute, then add the tomatoes, juices, and tomato purée. Cook over medium heat so the tomatoes break down, then add the wine; simmer for 3 minutes. Pour over 4 cups of the stock, bring to a boil, reduce the heat, and simmer for 10 minutes. Season.

4 Spoon a little soup into a large casserole, top with the fish and mussels and pour over the remaining soup. Place over low heat and cook for 12–15 minutes, or until the fish is cooked and the mussels have opened. Serve with crusty bread.

HAKE FLAVOR PAIRINGS: Economical, and meaty, hake is a great favorite in Spain, so try it with Iberian ingredients such as fruity olive oil, garlic, chorizo, cured ham, and smoked paprika.

Brandied lobster chowder

A luxurious treat, the sweet lobster meat is flattered by warming brandy.

The fish
Lobster, or white crabmeat

- **PREP** 20 mins ▪ **COOK** 1 hr ▪ **SERVES** 4

Ingredients
1 small cooked lobster

⅔ cup dry white wine

1 bay leaf

knob of unsalted butter

2 shallots, finely chopped

¼ cup brandy

1 large tomato, peeled and diced (see page 112)

2 tsp anchovy paste

4 large new potatoes, peeled and diced

8 baby corn, cut in short lengths

salt and freshly ground black pepper

2oz (60g) snow peas, cut in short lengths

¼ cup heavy cream

4 thick slices of lemon, to serve

4 sprigs of parsley, to serve

1 Remove the meat from the lobster (see page 291). Roughly chop the shell and put it in a saucepan with the claw shells and legs. Add 3¼ cups water, the wine, and bay leaf. Bring to a boil, reduce the heat, cover, and simmer for 30 minutes. Strain and reserve the stock.

2 Melt the butter in a large saucepan over low heat. Add the shallots and stir for 1 minute. Add the brandy, ignite, and shake the pan until the flames subside. Add the tomato, anchovy paste, potatoes, and corn. Pour in the stock, season, and bring to a boil. Reduce the heat, cover, and simmer gently for 20 minutes.

3 Meanwhile, blanch the snow peas in boiling water for 2 minutes. Drain. Add them to the soup with the cream and lobster meat. Taste and season again. Reheat the soup, but do not boil. Serve with lemon slices and sprigs of parsley, nutty rye bread, and butter.

Prepare ahead
Make the soup base up to the end of step 2, then cool, and chill, covered, for up to 1 day. Bring to room temperature before continuing.

Cod and mussel chowder

A hearty soup laden with chunks of cod, with mussels to add color and flavor. This is a great, warming dish for the colder months, wonderfully tasty and satisfying.

The fish
Cod, or saithe or pollock and mussels, or clams

- **PREP** 45–50 mins ▪ **COOK** 60 mins ▪ **SERVES** 8

Ingredients
3 potatoes, about 1lb 2oz (500g) in total

2¼lb (1kg) cod fillets, pinboned and skinned

4¼ cups fish stock

2 bay leaves

½ cup white wine

6oz (175g) bacon, diced

2 onions, finely chopped

2 celery sticks, finely chopped

1 carrot, finely chopped

2 tsp dried thyme

1 tbsp all-purpose flour

2¼lb (1kg) mussels, prepared

2 cups heavy cream

salt and freshly ground black pepper

leaves from 5–7 sprigs of dill, finely chopped, to serve

1 Peel and dice the potatoes into ½in (1cm) cubes. Cut the cod into 1in (2.5cm) cubes.

2 Put the stock and bay leaves into a large saucepan and pour in the wine. Bring to a boil and simmer for 10 minutes.

3 Put the bacon in another large saucepan and stir over medium heat until crisp. Add the onions, celery, carrot, and thyme. Stir until soft. Sprinkle in the flour and cook for a minute. Add the stock and bring to a boil, stirring until thickened. Add the potatoes and simmer for about 40 minutes, until very tender.

4 Crush some potatoes against the pan and add in the mussels. Simmer for 1–2 minutes, then add the cod for 2–3 minutes more. Pour in the cream, season, and bring just to a boil.

5 Discard any mussels that have not opened. Ladle into warmed bowls and sprinkle with dill.

Creamy smoked trout soup

This comforting soup is made with a roux-based sauce, so use good stock to make it really sing.

The fish
Hot-smoked trout, or hot-smoked salmon or smoked mackerel

- **PREP** 15 mins ▪ **COOK** 10 mins ▪ **SERVES** 6

Ingredients
3 tbsp butter

1 tbsp all-purpose flour

3¼ cups hot vegetable or fish stock

1 cup heavy cream

¼ cup white wine

2–3 tsp Worcestershire sauce

salt and freshly ground black pepper

squeeze of lemon juice

13oz (375g) hot-smoked trout fillets, skinned and flaked

2 tbsp chopped parsley, to serve

1 Over low heat, melt the butter in a pan, stir in the flour, and mix until smooth. Cook for 2–3 minutes, stirring constantly. Gradually whisk in the hot stock, making sure there are no lumps. Bring to a boil, then cook, uncovered, over low heat for about 3 minutes, stirring.

2 Add the cream, wine, Worcestershire sauce, salt and pepper to taste, and lemon juice, then bring back to a boil.

3 Add the fish pieces and heat them through. Sprinkle the soup with parsley and serve.

Prepare ahead
Make the soup base up to the end of step 2, then cool, and chill, covered, for up to 2 days. Bring to room temperature before continuing.

Salmon chowder with whiskey

Salmon makes a rich soup. Blend in 1 tbsp of cornstarch with the whiskey for a thicker soup.

The fish
Salmon, or trout

- ▪ **PREP** 20 mins ▪ **COOK** 40 mins ▪ **SERVES** 4–5

Ingredients
1 onion, chopped

1 leek, sliced

1 tbsp butter

1 large waxy potato, peeled and diced

10oz (300g) salmon, skinned and cut into small chunks

2oz (60g) fresh or frozen corn

2oz (60g) fresh or frozen peas (optional)

2½ cups fish or chicken stock

⅔ cup dry white wine

1 bay leaf

1 large tomato, peeled, seeded, and chopped

salt and freshly ground black pepper

2 tbsp whiskey

¼ cup heavy cream

chopped parsley, to serve

1 Fry the onion and leek gently in the butter, stirring for about 5 minutes until soft, but not brown. Add the remaining ingredients except the whiskey, cream, and parsley. Bring to a boil, reduce the heat, partially cover, and simmer for 30 minutes until the potatoes are tender.

2 Remove the bay leaf. Stir in the whiskey and cream, and simmer for 1 minute. Taste and adjust the seasoning, if necessary. Ladle into warm bowls and sprinkle with parsley.

SUSTAINABILITY CHOICE

Buy local

Buying local supports the local economy and small, independent fishing businesses. Local fleets tend to be responsible fishers because they need to maintain fish stocks to preserve their own livelihoods. Smaller, local boats also produce a high-quality catch—they spend relatively small periods of time at sea (between 2 and 10 hours) and the fish are placed on ice very soon after catching. Also, buying local cuts down on food miles; many fresh fish are air-freighted over large distances. If you buy local it is easy to establish exactly where and how the fish were caught.

Mouclade

An aromatic and wonderfully rich soup from France's Atlantic coast.

The fish

Mussels, or clams

- **PREP** 20 mins ▪ **COOK** 30 mins ▪ **SERVES** 4

Ingredients

3lb 3oz (1.5kg) small mussels, prepared (see page 278)

3 tbsp butter

1 large shallot, chopped

1½ cups dry white wine

several sprigs of flat-leaf parsley

¼ small fennel bulb, roughly chopped

1 bay leaf

sea salt and freshly ground black pepper

pinch of cayenne pepper

1 large egg yolk

5 tbsp sour cream or crème fraîche

1 large garlic clove, crushed

½ tsp mild paprika or 1 tsp mild curry powder

a few strands of saffron or ¼ tsp ground saffron

chunks of fresh warm bread, to serve

1 Put a large sauté pan over moderate heat. Add in the mussels with 1 tbsp of the butter, the shallot, wine, and 1½ cups of water. Add the parsley, fennel, and bay leaf, season, and add the cayenne. Increase the heat and bring to a boil. Cover and cook for 4–5 minutes, or until the mussels open, shaking a few times.

2 Lift out the mussels, discarding any that haven't opened. Strain the liquor through a muslin-lined sieve and set aside. Shell all but 12 mussels, place in a bowl, and moisten with cooking liquid. Keep warm.

3 In a small bowl, mix the egg yolk and cream. In a separate bowl, mash the remaining butter with the garlic, paprika, and saffron.

4 Put a large saucepan over low heat. Add the butter mixture and, when it bubbles, the mussel liquor, and bring to a simmer. Remove 3 tbsp of this and whisk it into the egg mixture, then whisk this back into the pan. Divide all the mussels between 4 warmed bowls. Pour the broth over and serve with the bread.

Prepare ahead

You can prepare this ahead, but reheat the mussels as gently as possible or they will become tough and overcooked.

Lobster bisque

A rich and luxurious shellfish soup.

The fish

Lobster, or shrimp

- **PREP** 35 mins ▪ **COOK** 1 hr 15 mins
- **SERVES** 4

Ingredients

1 lobster, about 2¼lb (1kg) in total, cooked

3 tbsp butter

1 onion, finely chopped

1 carrot, finely chopped

2 celery stalks, finely chopped

1 leek, finely chopped

½ bulb fennel, finely chopped

1 bay leaf

1 sprig of tarragon

2 garlic cloves, crushed

2½oz (75g) tomato purée

4 tomatoes, coarsely chopped

½ cup Cognac or brandy

⅔ cup dry white wine or vermouth

6 cups fish stock

½ cup heavy cream

salt and freshly ground black pepper

pinch of cayenne pepper

juice of ½ lemon

snipped chives, to garnish

1 Split the lobster and remove the meat (see page 291). Crack all the shells with the back of a knife. Chop the shells into coarse pieces and put the meat into the refrigerator.

2 Melt the butter in a large pan over medium heat, add the vegetables, herbs, and garlic, and cook for 10 minutes, or until softened, stirring occasionally. Add the lobster shells. Stir in the tomato purée, tomatoes, Cognac, white wine, and stock. Bring to a boil and simmer for 1 hour.

3 Let cool slightly, then pulse-blend in a food processor until the shell breaks into very small pieces. Push through a coarse sieve, then pass through a fine sieve. Return to the heat.

4 Bring to a boil, add the lobster meat and cream, then season, adding cayenne and lemon. Serve in warmed bowls, with chives.

Prepare ahead

The bisque can be made to the end of step 3 up to 1 day in advance. Cover, and chill. Finish the recipe just before serving.

MUSSEL FLAVOR PAIRINGS: The feisty taste of mussels is equally good with dry white wine, butter, cream, parsley, and garlic, and with pungent ginger, lemongrass, chile, and spices, or even aniseed fennel and Pernod.

Creamy scallop bisque

A rich broth with sweet scallops and spicy chorizo. Serve as a starter at a dinner party.

The fish

Shrimp, cod or pollock, and scallops

- **PREP** 20 mins ▪ **COOK** 40 mins ▪ **SERVES** 4

Ingredients

10fl oz (300ml) dry white wine

1 tbsp butter

1 small onion, finely chopped

1 small shallot, very finely chopped

1 ripe tomato, chopped

7oz (200g) raw shrimp, peeled and deveined (see page 285)

3½oz (100g) cod, pinboned, skinned, and cut into chunks

12 small or 6 large scallops

2 tbsp chopped flat-leaf parsley

2 tsp dill seeds

3 tbsp brandy

sea salt and freshly ground black pepper

3½fl oz (100ml) half-and-half

2½oz (75g) chorizo, diced

1 tbsp finely chopped chives, to garnish

1 Bring 3¼ cups water to a boil with the wine. Meanwhile put the butter in a pan over medium heat. Add the onion and shallot and soften until golden. Add the tomato, shrimp, fish, scallop roes, parsley, and dill seeds; stir for 5 minutes. Add the brandy, and cook for 1 minute. Pour in the boiling wine and season. Reduce the heat, and simmer for 10 minutes. Leave to cool, then roughly mash with the back of a spoon. Gently heat the half-and-half.

2 Purée the soup in a blender, strain back into the pan and stir in the half-and-half. Return to a simmer. Remove from the heat, adjust the seasoning, and keep warm.

3 Put a frying pan over medium heat. Add the chorizo and fry until crisp. Set aside on a plate lined with paper towels and keep warm.

4 Quickly add the scallop muscles to the pan for 2 minutes, turn, and cook for 1 minute. Ladle the soup into bowls and add the scallops. Scatter over the chorizo to serve.

Prepare ahead

Make the soup to the end of step 2, cover, and refrigerate for 1 day. Reheat gently.

Fish soup with fennel

Robustly flavored with brandy and orange.

The fish

Mussels, any firm white fish, such as monkfish, and tiger prawns

- **PREP** 10 mins ▪ **COOK** 1 hr ▪ **SERVES** 4–6

Ingredients

2 tbsp butter

3 tbsp olive oil

1 large fennel bulb, finely chopped

2 garlic cloves, crushed

1 small leek, sliced

4 ripe plum tomatoes, chopped

3 tbsp brandy

¼ tsp saffron threads, infused in a little hot water

grated zest of ½ orange

1 bay leaf

5¼ cups fish stock

10½oz (300g) potatoes, diced and parboiled for 5 minutes

4 tbsp dry white wine

1lb 2oz (500g) mussels, prepared (see page 278)

salt and freshly ground black pepper

1lb 2oz (500g) firm white fish, cubed

6 raw tiger prawns, deveined (see page 285)

parsley, chopped, to garnish

1 Heat the butter with 2 tbsp of the oil in a large, deep pan. Stir in the fennel, garlic, and leek, and stir over moderate heat for 5 minutes, or until softened and lightly browned.

2 Stir in the tomatoes and brandy, and boil for 2 minutes, or until reduced slightly. Stir in the saffron, orange zest, bay leaf, stock, and potatoes. Bring to a boil, reduce the heat and skim any scum from the surface. Cover and simmer for 20 minutes, or until the potatoes are tender. Remove the bay leaf.

3 Meanwhile, bring the remaining oil and the wine to a boil in a deep pan. Add the mussels, cover tightly, and shake well over high heat for 2–3 minutes. Discard any mussels that do not open. Strain, add the liquid to the soup and season. Bring to a boil, add the fish and prawns, reduce the heat, cover, and simmer gently for 5 minutes. Add the mussels and return almost to a boil. Serve sprinkled with parsley.

Prepare ahead

The soup can be made to the end of step 2, covered, and refrigerated up to 3 days in advance. Reheat gently before continuing.

Cotriade

This soup from Brittany was originally a way to use the leftover catch of the day.

The fish

Any mixed fish, such as haddock, pollock, or ling

- **PREP** 20 mins ▪ **COOK** 30 mins ▪ **SERVES** 4

Ingredients

2 large floury potatoes, peeled

2 tbsp mild olive oil

2 tbsp butter

2 yellow onions, coarsely chopped

4¼ cups light fish stock

3 sprigs of thyme

3 bay leaves

3 sprigs of flat-leaf parsley

sea salt and freshly ground black pepper

1¾lb (800g) mixed fish, skinned, cut into large chunks

4 thick slices country bread, to serve

For the dressing

5–6 tbsp mild olive oil

½ tsp Dijon mustard

sea salt and freshly ground black pepper

1 tbsp white wine or cider vinegar

2 tbsp finely chopped flat-leaf parsley

1 Cut the potatoes into chunks. Put the oil and butter in a large, heavy sauté pan. Add the onions and soften over moderate heat until just golden, stirring frequently. Add the stock, then add in the potatoes and herbs. Season lightly, stir, cover and cook for 12–15 minutes or until the potatoes are almost cooked.

2 Place the fish in the pan and season lightly. Gently stir, then cook for 10 minutes, or until the fish just starts to flake when pressed.

3 Meanwhile, in a cup, mix the oil and mustard, and season, then whisk in the vinegar until emulsified. Stir in the parsley.

4 Remove the soup from the heat and adjust the seasoning. Lift out the herbs. Put the bread in 4 warmed bowls and moisten with a little dressing. Ladle over the soup and drizzle on the remaining dressing. Serve hot.

Prepare ahead

Make the dressing up to 6 hours ahead, and cover. Whisk to re-emulsify before use.

Keralan prawn soup

This fragrant soup is from southern India. If you use dried curry leaves, add with the stock.

The fish

Tiger prawns

- **PREP** 20 mins ▪ **COOK** 40 mins
- **SERVES** 4–6

Ingredients

1 tsp black peppercorns

¾ tsp mustard seeds

2 tsp coriander seeds

½ tsp fenugreek seeds

2–3 large red chiles

4 garlic cloves, chopped

2in (5cm) fresh ginger, chopped

2–3 tbsp vegetable oil

small handful of fresh curry leaves

2 onions, finely chopped

3¼ cups fish stock

8fl oz (250ml) coconut milk

9oz (250g) raw tiger prawns, peeled and deveined (see page 285)

1 tbsp coconut cream

2 tbsp chopped cilantro leaves

juice of 1 lime, or to taste

1 Heat a sturdy frying pan over low heat. Roast the peppercorns, mustard, coriander, and fenugreek seeds together for about 30 seconds, until the mustard seeds start to pop. Grind to a powder, and set aside.

2 Roughly chop the chiles (for a mild flavor, use 2 chiles and remove the seeds). Put in a food processor with the garlic and ginger. Pour in 4 tbsp hot water and process to a paste. Set aside.

3 Heat the oil in a wok or saucepan. When hot, toss in the curry leaves and fry for 20 seconds. Be careful; they will spatter. Add the onions, cover, and soften for 10 minutes, stirring occasionally.

4 Stir in the chile paste and fry for 2–3 minutes, until the water evaporates. Add the ground spices and stir for 30 seconds. Pour in the stock and simmer for 20 minutes, or until reduced by one-third. Stir in the coconut milk and reheat, then add the prawns for a further 4–5 minutes. Add the coconut cream and finish with the cilantro leaves and enough lime juice to sharpen.

Prepare ahead

Make this soup up to the point that the fish stock has been reduced, cover, and refrigerate for 1 day. Reheat gently before continuing.

Potage poissonière

This classic cream of whiting soup seems plain, but if using very fresh fish is utterly delicious.

The fish
Whiting, or haddock, cod, or ling

- **PREP** 20 mins ▪ **COOK** 45 mins ▪ **SERVES** 4

Ingredients
2¼lb (1kg) whiting, filleted, with head and bones
1 small carrot, sliced
1 celery stalk, sliced
1 onion, finely diced
handful of parsley sprigs
sprig of thyme
1 small bay leaf
large pinch of salt
2 cups milk
4 tbsp butter
3 tbsp all-purpose flour
1–2 tbsp creamed horseradish, to taste
grated nutmeg, to taste
freshly ground black pepper
2 tbsp chopped flat-leaf parsley
5 tbsp half-and-half
croutons, to serve

1 Pinbone and carefully skin the whiting fillets (see page 271). Set aside.

2 To make the stock, put all the whiting skin, the bones, and head (remove the gills) in a large saucepan, pour over 2¼ cups of water, and add the carrot, celery, onion, herbs, and salt. Slowly bring to a boil, then cook over very low heat, uncovered, for 25–30 minutes. Strain.

3 Put the whiting into a large saucepan, add the milk and poach over low heat for 5–6 minutes. Strain the liquor and reserve. Put the fish into a food processor and whizz to a paste. Set aside.

4 Melt the butter in the rinsed-out saucepan, blend in the flour, and cook over low heat for 1 minute. Blend in the milk and stock, and bring slowly to a boil. Simmer for 2–3 minutes.

5 Remove from the heat and whisk in the fish and horseradish, adding nutmeg, salt, and pepper. Add the parsley and half-and-half, adjust the seasoning. Serve, with the croutons in a separate bowl.

Prepare ahead
Make the stock 1 day in advance, cover, and chill until needed.

Tom yum goong

Tamarind gives the right piquant note to this key Thai recipe for hot and sour prawn soup.

The fish
Tiger prawns, or scallops

- **PREP** 10–15 mins ▪ **COOK** 15 mins
- **SERVES** 4

Ingredients
1 tbsp sunflower or peanut oil
1 tsp shrimp paste
2 bird's eye chiles, finely chopped, and seeded (if preferred)
2 garlic cloves, finely chopped
2 tsp palm sugar
2 scallions, finely sliced
2oz (60g) shiitake mushrooms, trimmed and sliced
2 tbsp tamarind paste, to taste
1 quart well-flavored fish stock
1 stalk lemongrass, halved
2in (5cm) piece galangal or fresh ginger, peeled and finely sliced
a few kaffir lime leaves
1–2 tbsp Thai fish sauce, to taste
1 tsp sesame oil
1lb (450g) raw tiger prawns, peeled but tail intact, deveined and butterflied (see page 285)
squeeze of lime juice, to taste
handful of roughly chopped cilantro leaves

1 Heat the oil in a large pan, add the shrimp paste, and cook over low heat for 1–2 minutes until aromatic. Add the chiles, garlic, palm sugar, scallions, and mushrooms; stir for 2 minutes.

2 Add the tamarind, stock, lemongrass, galangal, and lime leaves. Bring to a boil and simmer for 2–3 minutes. Season with fish sauce and add the sesame oil and prawns. Poach over low heat for 3–4 minutes or until the prawns are cooked.

3 Add lime juice, or more tamarind, or fish sauce to taste. Stir in the cilantro and serve.

Variation
Tom yum talay
Begin as above, adding 3 chiles, 1 tbsp palm sugar, 3 scallions, and 1 diced red bell pepper. Omit the mushrooms. Add a 14oz (400g) can of coconut milk. Bring to a boil, simmer for 3 minutes. Add 2 cups of stock, the lemongrass, galangal and lime leaves; omit the tamarind and sesame oil. Simmer for a few minutes. Add 2–3 tbsp Thai fish sauce and 1lb (450g) mixed seafood (add squid at the last minute), lime, and cilantro leaves.

WHITING FLAVOR PAIRINGS: Enjoy the delicate flavor of whiting with sweet butter, milk, and parsley, as in potage poissonière, or the equally subtle tastes of olive oil, or delicate, aniseed chervil.

Büsumer fish soup

From the German region of Schleswig-Holstein on the North Sea coast.

The fish
Any mixed, firm white fish, such as pollock or haddock, and tiger prawns

- **PREP** 15 mins • **COOK** 20 mins • **SERVES** 6–8

Ingredients

2 large carrots, chopped

1 large potato (Russet Burbank or Yukon Gold), peeled and diced

1 large onion, diced

4¼ cups hot vegetable stock

1 bay leaf

salt and freshly ground black pepper

juice of 1 lemon

1lb 2oz (500g) white fish fillets, pinboned, skinned, and cut into bite-sized pieces

7oz (200g) button or cremini mushrooms, sliced

3½oz (100g) raw tiger prawns, peeled (see page 285)

½ cup heavy cream

½ bunch of dill, chopped, to garnish

1 Put the carrots, potato, and onion into a saucepan, add the hot stock and bay leaf, and bring to a boil. Reduce the heat and simmer for 10 minutes.

2 Sprinkle a little salt and pepper, and half the lemon juice, over the fish, then add it to the stock with the mushrooms. Simmer for another 5 minutes over low heat.

3 Add the prawns and the remaining lemon juice, and cook for 3 minutes, or until the prawns turn pink. Remove the bay leaf and season to taste. Stir in the cream and half the dill and serve immediately, using the remaining dill to garnish.

Prepare ahead
Make the soup base up to the end of step 1, then cool, and chill, covered, for up to 3 days. Reheat over moderate heat to a simmer before continuing.

Potato and clam soup

This is a delicious autumn soup for all the family to enjoy.

The fish
Clams, or mussels

- **PREP** 25 mins • **COOK** 1 hr 15 mins
- **SERVES** 4–6

Ingredients

2¼lb (1kg) clams, thoroughly washed

½ cup dry white wine

2–3 tbsp olive oil

2 celery stalks, finely diced

1 red onion, finely chopped

1 carrot, finely chopped

4 tomatoes, peeled, seeded, and chopped

2 potatoes, peeled and diced

1 sprig of rosemary

1 tbsp finely chopped flat-leaf parsley or chervil

salt and freshly ground black pepper

4–6 slices country bread

1 Throw away any clams with broken shells and any that are open and won't close when gently tapped. Put them in a large frying pan with the wine, cover, and place on high heat for 5 minutes or until the shells open. Discard any that remain shut. Drain, reserving the liquid. Remove the clams from their shells, place in a bowl, cover, and refrigerate. Strain the cooking liquid through a fine sieve.

2 Heat the oil in a large, heavy-bottomed pan, add the celery, onion, and carrot, and cook on low heat for 10 minutes or until lightly browned. Add the tomatoes, potatoes, reserved cooking liquid, and 4¼ cups water, and bring to a boil. Add the rosemary, then reduce the heat, cover, and simmer for 1 hour.

3 Stir in the clams and parsley or chervil, then season. Remove the rosemary, put a slice of bread in each bowl, and ladle over the soup.

Cullen skink

Named after Cullen, in north-east Scotland, where "skink" is the name for a soup or stew.

The fish
Finnan haddock, or smoked trout or smoked cod

- **PREP** 20 mins ▪ **COOK** 25 mins ▪ **SERVES** 4

Ingredients
8oz (225g) potatoes, peeled and diced

salt and freshly ground black pepper

2 tbsp butter

2 whole Finnan haddock (or 4 small smoked haddock fillets)

1 onion, finely chopped

1¼ cup milk

1 Simmer the potatoes in salted water for 15 minutes, or until tender. Drain, then mash with the butter. Set aside.

2 Put the fish into a sauté pan. Pour in 1¼ cup water and add the onion. Poach for 8–10 minutes. Lift the fish on to a plate and pull away the flesh in large flakes. Set aside.

3 Return the fish skin and bones to the water and cook for a further 15 minutes. Strain this stock into a large pitcher, then add as many of the chopped onions as possible. Stir in the milk.

4 Put the milk, stock, and onion back into the saucepan, place over medium heat and whisk in enough of the mashed potato to form a thick, creamy consistency. Season to taste and add the flaked fish. Serve immediately.

Mango and snapper broth

A complete meal in a bowl. Green mangos add bite to a citrussy, fiery soup.

The fish
Red snapper, or sea bream or sea bass

- **PREP** 15 mins, plus marinating
- **COOK** 10 mins ▪ **SERVES** 4

Ingredients
1 tbsp light soy sauce

2 tbsp Thai fish sauce

1 tbsp toasted sesame oil

1 tbsp mirin

1 tsp sugar

juice of 2 limes, or to taste

1lb 2oz (500g) red snapper fillets, pinboned, skinned, and cut into 1in (2.5cm) cubes

2 stalks lemongrass, finely chopped

2 tbsp vegetable oil

4 red bird's eye chiles, finely sliced

4 scallions, finely sliced

2in (5cm) fresh ginger, finely shredded

4 garlic cloves, roughly chopped

4 small green (under-ripe) mongos, peeled and finely chopped

2 tsp palm sugar or dark brown sugar

2 tbsp rice wine vinegar

4¼ cups fish stock

8 lime leaves, torn

3½oz (100g) egg noodles

3½oz (100g) green beans, halved

salt

2 tbsp chopped cilantro leaves

1 tbsp shredded mint leaves

1 Combine the soy sauce, half the fish sauce, sesame oil, mirin, sugar, and juice of 1 lime, and spoon over the fish. Refrigerate for 20 minutes. Pound the lemongrass to a paste with a dash of water, using a mortar and pestle. Set aside.

2 Heat the oil in a wok or large pan and fry the chiles, scallions, ginger, and garlic for 30 seconds over high heat. Add the mongos and fry for 1 minute. Stir in the sugar until it begins to caramelize. Add the vinegar, lemongrass, stock, lime leaves, and remaining fish sauce. Bring to a boil.

3 Stir in the noodles, beans, and fish pieces (not the marinating liquid). Simmer for 3–5 minutes, until the noodles are cooked and the fish flakes easily. Season with salt, sharpen with lime juice, and add the herbs.

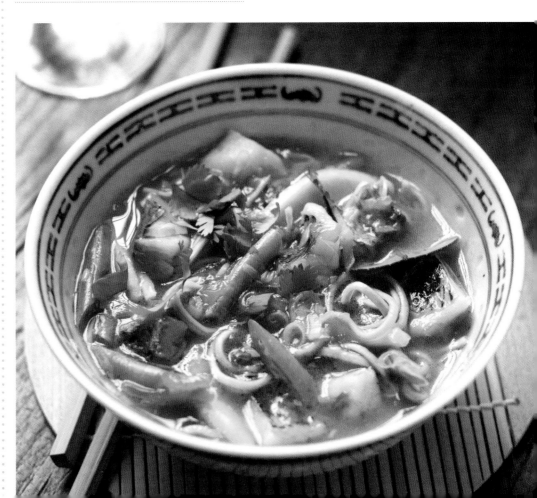

Waterzooi

A delicious Flemish soup in which aniseedy tarragon really lifts the flavors. Perfect on a cold spring day, when asparagus is in season.

The fish

Mussels, or clams, and monkfish, or any firm white fish, and lemon sole, or any flat fish

- **PREP** 20 mins • **COOK** 30 mins • **SERVES** 4

Ingredients

2 cups light chicken or fish stock

½ cup dry white wine

3 large scallions, finely chopped

1 large waxy potato, peeled and cut into batons

1 large carrot, cut into batons

1 medium-large zucchini, sliced on the diagonal

14oz (400g) asparagus, chopped into 2in (5cm) lengths

1lb 2oz (500g) mussels, prepared (see page 278)

½ cup whipping cream

salt and freshly ground black pepper

10oz (300g) monkfish, cut into chunks

1 lemon sole, filleted and skinned, fillets halved

1 tbsp finely chopped tarragon, to serve

1 Put the stock, wine, and most of the scallions in a casserole. Bring to a boil over moderate heat. Add the potato, reduce the heat to a simmer, and cook for 5 minutes, then add the carrot for 5 minutes. Add the zucchini and asparagus for 1–2 minutes, or until all is *al dente*. Lift out the vegetables and set aside.

2 Bring the stock to a boil and reduce by a third. Reduce the heat to a simmer, add in the mussels, cover and cook for 3–4 minutes. Strain through a muslin-lined sieve into a bowl, cool briefly, then discard any that haven't opened. Shell the rest and set aside. Return the stock to a simmer over moderate heat, then stir in the cream and season. Add the monkfish, cook for 2–3 minutes, add the sole and cook for 1 minute, then return the vegetables and mussels for 2 minutes.

3 Using a slotted spoon, lift the vegetables into 4 warmed bowls. Place the fish on top, ladle over the broth, and scatter with mussels, tarragon, and the reserved scallions.

Soupe de poissons

Complement this flavorful soup with garlic croûtes spread with rouille, and topped with Gruyère cheese.

The fish

Any white fish, such as pollock or saithe, and seafood

- **PREP** 20 mins • **COOK** 1 hr • **SERVES** 6

Ingredients

5 tbsp olive oil

4 onions, chopped

2 leeks, chopped

3lb 3oz–4½lb (1.5–2kg) mixed white fish and seafood

½ tsp of fennel seeds

4 ripe tomatoes, quartered

9 garlic cloves, crushed

5 sprigs of flat-leaf parsley

3 bay leaves

large strip of dried orange peel

1 tbsp tomato purée

salt and freshly ground black pepper

pinch of saffron threads

6 croûtes, to serve

1 Put the oil in a large, heavy saucepan. Add the onions and leeks, and soften over moderate heat until just golden.

2 Scale and gut the fish. Rinse all the fish and seafood. Stir into the pan, then add the fennel, tomatoes, garlic, parsley, bay leaves, orange peel, and tomato purée. Cook for 8–10 minutes until the fish is just beginning to flake. Pour in 2 quarts hot water and season. Reduce the heat and simmer for 20 minutes.

3 Remove from the heat. Leave to cool a little, stirring and mashing down the fish with the back of a large wooden spoon. Remove the orange peel and bay leaves. Whizz the soup to a rough purée in a blender, then push it through a fine sieve into a clean saucepan. Return to a simmer over moderate heat.

4 Soften the saffron in a ladleful of the soup, then stir into the rest of the soup in the pan. Taste, and adjust the seasoning. Ladle into bowls, and serve hot, with the croûtes.

Prepare ahead

This soup can be made 1–2 days in advance and kept, covered, in the refrigerator. Reheat gently to serve.

SAITHE FLAVOR PAIRINGS: This meaty fish is excellent cooked with beer, or try it with a very creamy white sauce flavored with leeks, a little parsley, and fennel.

Paella, Pasta, and Risotto

Paella

This Spanish rice dish has many regional variations. This marinera version contains a delicious mix of seafood.

The fish

Tiger prawns, squid, Dublin Bay prawns, mussels, or any mixed seafood

▪ **PREP** 10 mins ▪ **COOK** 30 mins ▪ **SERVES** 4

Ingredients

1 quart hot fish stock

large pinch of saffron threads

2 tbsp olive oil

1 onion, finely chopped

2 garlic cloves, crushed

2 large tomatoes, skinned and diced

12 raw tiger prawns, peeled and deveined (see page 285)

8oz (225g) squid, gutted, cleaned, and sliced into rings (see page 282)

14oz (400g) paella rice

3oz (85g) peas

4 raw Dublin Bay prawns, or very large shrimp, head-on

12–16 mussels, prepared (see page 278)

1 tbsp chopped flat-leaf parsley, to garnish

1 Pour a little of the hot stock into a bowl, add the saffron, and set aside. Heat the oil in a large frying or paella pan, and fry the onion and garlic until softened. Add the tomatoes, cook for 2 minutes, then add the peeled tiger prawns and squid for 1–2 minutes.

2 Stir in the rice, saffron liquid, peas, and 2¼ cups of stock. Simmer, uncovered, without stirring, over low heat for 12–14 minutes, or until the stock has evaporated and the rice is just tender, adding extra stock if necessary.

3 Meanwhile, cook the Dublin Bay prawns in ⅔ cup of simmering stock for 3–4 minutes, or until cooked through. Transfer to a warm plate with a slotted spoon. Tap the mussels and discard any that do not close. Add the mussels to the stock, cover, and cook over high heat for 2–3 minutes. Remove with a slotted spoon, discarding any that have not opened.

4 Reserve 8 mussels for garnish. Remove the rest from their shells and stir into the paella. Arrange the reserved mussels and Dublin Bay prawns on top, and garnish with parsley.

Risotto al tonno

This creamy fish risotto uses canned tuna, so it's a great pantry recipe.

The fish

Canned tuna

▪ **PREP** 15 mins ▪ **COOK** 40 mins ▪ **SERVES** 4

Ingredients

2 tbsp butter

4 tbsp extra virgin olive oil

1 large onion, finely chopped

1 garlic clove, chopped

9oz (250g) risotto rice

½ cup medium white wine

4¼ cups hot fish stock

1 tbsp tomato purée

6oz (200g) can tuna in spring water, drained and flaked

12 cherry tomatoes, halved

2 tbsp chopped flat-leaf parsley

salt and freshly ground black pepper

1 Heat the butter and half the oil in a large saucepan. Add half the onion and cook over low heat for 8–10 minutes until soft. Add the garlic and cook for a minute. Add in the rice and cook for 2 minutes, until it turns translucent. Add half the wine and simmer for a couple of minutes. Stir in the stock a ladleful at a time, stirring frequently, and only adding more when the previous amount has been absorbed, for 20–25 minutes.

2 Meanwhile, in a separate pan, heat the remaining oil and add the remaining onion, cook for 8–10 minutes until soft. Add the tomato purée and stir for 2 minutes. Pour in the remaining wine, bring to a boil, and simmer for 5 minutes. Add the tuna and stir for 2–3 minutes. Add the tomatoes and parsley.

3 When the risotto rice is *al dente* and the stock all absorbed, stir in the tuna mixture, season to taste and serve.

Variation

Risotto nero

This recipe can be turned into risotto nero with the addition of 1 sachet of squid or cuttlefish ink (about 1oz/25g), to the rice, just before the stock.

DUBLIN BAY PRAWN FLAVOR PAIRINGS:

When cooked very simply, Dublin Bay prawns benefit from the gentle flavors of lemon juice or mayonnaise, but can also stand up to bolder garlic, paprika, sage, and chile.

Shrimp risotto

Perfect for a cold night, serve this as soon as it is ready.

The fish
Shrimp, or scallops

- **PREP** 15–20 mins - **COOK** 25–30 mins
- **SERVES** 6

Ingredients
⅓ cup olive oil

1lb 2oz (500g) shrimp, peeled and deveined (see page 285)

2 garlic cloves, grated or finely chopped

leaves from 1 small bunch of flat-leaf parsley, chopped

salt and freshly ground black pepper

4 tbsp dry white wine

4 cups fish or chicken stock

1 onion, finely chopped

15oz (420g) risotto rice

1 Heat a third of the oil in a saucepan, and add the shrimp, garlic, parsley, and salt and pepper.

2 Cook, stirring, until the shrimp turn pink. Pour in the wine and stir thoroughly. Transfer the shrimp to a bowl; set aside. Simmer the liquid in the pan for 2–3 minutes, until reduced by three-quarters. Add the stock and 1¼ cups water, and heat to boiling. Keep the mixture simmering.

3 Heat half the remaining oil in a large saucepan. Add the onion and cook for 2–3 minutes, until soft but not brown. Add the rice, and stir until coated with oil. Add the stock, a ladleful at a time, stirring until it is absorbed before adding more. Continue until the rice is cooked but still has a bit of bite; it should take about 20 minutes.

4 Stir in the shrimp and remaining olive oil, and season. Spoon into warmed bowls, and serve immediately.

Haddock, green bean, and artichoke paella

Use paella rice if you can find it for this recipe, instead of the basmati.

The fish
Haddock, or cod or any other white fish

- **PREP** 15 mins - **COOK** 30 mins - **SERVES** 4–6

Ingredients
1 tbsp olive oil, plus extra if needed

1 onion, finely chopped

salt and freshly ground black pepper

pinch of turmeric

2 garlic cloves, grated or finely chopped

7oz (200g) green beans, trimmed

9½oz (280g) jar artichoke hearts, drained and rinsed

4 tomatoes, skinned, seeded, and chopped

pinch of hot or regular paprika

14oz (400g) basmati rice

5 cups hot vegetable stock

1½lb (675g) haddock fillets, pinboned, skinned, and cut into chunky pieces

handful of dill or flat-leaf parsley, finely chopped

juice of 1 lemon

1 Heat the oil in a large, heavy frying pan over medium heat. Add the onion and a pinch of salt, and sauté for about 5 minutes until soft and translucent. Stir in the turmeric, then add the garlic, beans, and artichokes. Cook gently for about 5 minutes until the beans begin to wilt, adding a little more oil if needed.

2 Now add the tomatoes and paprika, and cook for 5 minutes. Add in the rice, and stir. Pour in half the hot stock. Bring to a boil, then reduce the heat and simmer for about 15 minutes. Add the remaining stock and the fish, cover, and cook over low heat for 10 minutes, or until the rice and fish are cooked.

3 Keep the lid on the pan until ready to serve, then stir in the fresh herbs and lemon juice. Taste, adjust the seasoning, and serve.

Prepare ahead
Cook the vegetables up to the point of adding the rice (do not add the rice), cool, cover, and refrigerate up to 6 hours in advance. Reheat gently before continuing.

Smoked fish kedgeree

This classic Anglo-Indian recipe became a popular breakfast dish in Victorian times.

The fish

Smoked haddock, or kippers or smoked mackerel

- **PREP** 15 mins **COOK** 25–30 mins
- **SERVES** 4

Ingredients

6oz (175g) long-grain rice

4½oz (125g) frozen peas

8oz (225g) smoked haddock fillet

4 eggs

2 tbsp butter

½ tsp ground cumin

freshly grated nutmeg, to taste

salt and freshly ground black pepper

2 tbsp chopped flat-leaf parsley

2–4 tbsp half-and-half, to taste

1 Boil the rice according to the package instructions. Drain well, then spread out in a wide dish, and fork through the grains to fluff up. Leave until cold. Boil the frozen peas according to the package instructions, drain, and set aside.

2 Meanwhile, place the haddock in a sauté pan and half-cover with water. Bring slowly to a boil, and simmer gently for 6–7 minutes. Drain well. When cool enough to handle, break the fish into large flakes, discarding any skin and pinbones.

3 Bring a saucepan of water to a boil, and drop in the eggs. Boil for 7–8 minutes. They will be hard-boiled, but the yolks will remain moist. Drain, and shell. When cold, cut into quarters.

4 Melt the butter in a sauté pan over medium heat. Add the rice, and stir to coat the grains. Gently mix in the fish and peas. Add the cumin, nutmeg, salt and pepper, and half the parsley. Stir in the half-and-half, and cook, stirring occasionally, until piping hot.

5 Top with the hard-boiled egg quarters, sprinkle over the remaining parsley, and serve.

Prepare ahead

Cook the rice, peas, haddock, and eggs up to 1 day ahead. Cover, and refrigerate separately. Return to room temperature before continuing with the recipe.

Seafood risotto

Replace the scallops and shrimp with squid for a more economical dish.

The fish

Shrimp and scallops, or squid, and any mixed white fish, such as haddock and pollock

- **PREP** 20 mins **COOK** 30 mins **SERVES** 8

Ingredients

2–3 tbsp olive oil

1lb (450g) raw shrimp, peeled and deveined (see page 285)

salt and freshly ground black pepper

1lb (450g) mixed white fish, cubed

16 scallops, roe removed

2 knobs of butter

2 onions, finely chopped

4 garlic cloves, grated or finely chopped

8 cups hot vegetable or fish stock

1½lb (675g) risotto rice

1 cup medium white wine

6 tomatoes, skinned, seeded, and finely chopped

large handful of flat-leaf parsley, finely chopped

handful of dill, finely chopped

lemon wedges, to serve

1 Heat half the oil in a frying pan, add the shrimp and seasoning, and cook for a couple of minutes. Remove and set aside. Add the fish, and more oil, if needed, and cook for a couple of minutes, or until cooked. Remove and set aside.

2 Season the scallops, add to the pan with more oil, if needed, and cook for 2 minutes each side. Remove and set aside. Add a knob of butter to the pan, then the onions, and cook over low heat for 5–8 minutes, until soft. Stir in the garlic. Put the stock in a large pan and keep on a low simmer.

3 Stir the rice into the onions. Season, then pour in the wine and increase the heat. Allow to boil for a few seconds while the alcohol evaporates. Add the stock, a ladleful at a time, stirring until it is absorbed before adding more. Continue until the rice is cooked but still has a bit of bite; it should take about 20 minutes.

4 Stir in the tomatoes, seafood, and fish, then the herbs and remaining butter. Taste and season, then serve with lemon wedges.

Fideua

This Spanish pasta dish, with a tasty mixture of seafood, is hearty and filling.

The fish

Shrimp, scallops, clams, or any shellfish, and any firm white fish, such as cod or monkfish

- **PREP** 15 mins · **COOK** 25 mins · **SERVES** 4

Ingredients

pinch of saffron threads

2½ cups hot fish stock

2–3 tbsp olive oil

1 onion, fincly chopped

2 garlic cloves, crushed

3 ripe tomatoes, skinned, seeded, and chopped

1 tsp sweet or smoked paprika

10oz (300g) spaghetti or linguine, broken into 2in (5cm) lengths

8oz (225g) raw shrimp, peeled, but tails left intact, and deveined (see page 285)

8 small scallops, cut in half

10oz (300g) clams, thoroughly washed

8oz (225g) firm white fish, cut into ¾in (2cm) pieces

5oz (140g) peas

salt and freshly ground black pepper

2 tbsp chopped flat-leaf parsley

1 Put the saffron in a small bowl and add 2 tbsp of the hot stock. Set aside.

2 Heat the oil in a large frying or paella pan over medium heat. Add the onion and garlic and fry for 5–8 minutes, or until soft, stirring frequently. Add the tomatoes and paprika and cook for a further 5 minutes. Add the saffron with its liquid and half the remaining stock, increase the heat, and bring to a boil.

3 Add the pasta, reduce the heat, and simmer, uncovered, stirring occasionally, for 5 minutes. Add the shrimp, scallops, clams, white fish, and peas, and cook for a further 5 minutes, or until the pasta and fish are cooked. If the mixture begins to dry out, add a little more stock. Season to taste, sprinkle with parsley, and serve hot, straight from the pan. It's good with aïoli and crusty bread.

Prepare ahead

The base of the fideua can be made in advance up to the end of step 2. Pour into a bowl, cool, cover, and refrigerate for up to 2 days. Reheat gently, then return to a boil before continuing.

Linguine alle vongole

Versions of this popular classic are cooked all along the Italian Mediterranean and Adriatic coasts.

The fish

Clams, or mussels

- **PREP** 5 mins · **COOK** 20 mins · **SERVES** 4

Ingredients

2 tbsp olive oil

1 onion, finely chopped

2 garlic cloves, grated or finely chopped

14oz (400g) can chopped tomatoes

2 tbsp sun-dried tomato purée

½ cup dry white wine

1lb 5oz (600g) clams, shelled, juices reserved (see page 279)

salt and freshly ground black pepper

12oz (350g) linguine

4 tbsp finely chopped flat-leaf parsley, plus extra to garnish

1 Heat the oil in a large saucepan over medium heat. Add the onion and garlic and fry, stirring frequently, for 5 minutes. Add the tomatoes, tomato purée, wine, and clam juices, and season. Bring to a boil, stirring. Reduce the heat to low, partially cover, and leave to simmer for 10–15 minutes.

2 Meanwhile, bring a large pot of salted water to a boil. Add the linguine, and boil according to the package instructions, until tender to the bite. Drain and shake to remove excess water.

3 Add the clams and parsley to the sauce and simmer for 1–2 minutes. Season to taste.

4 Add the linguine to the sauce and toss to coat. Sprinkle with extra parsley and serve at once with crusty Italian bread and green salad.

Prepare ahead

The tomato sauce in step 1 can be made a day in advance, covered, and refrigerated. Reheat gently before continuing.

Variation

Canned clam linguine

This dish can also be made using canned clams. For this, use 2 x 5oz (140g) jars clams in natural juice, strained, with the juice reserved. Because they won't be quite as flavorsome, the sauce will benefit from a large pinch of red pepper flakes, for added zing.

CLAM FLAVOR PAIRINGS: Partner this shellfish with a sauce either of cream, onions, herbs, and white wine, or tomatoes, garlic, parsley, bacon, and a touch of chile.

SQUID FLAVOR PAIRINGS: When cooked alone, try squid perked up with a sprinkling of chile, or breadcrumbed and served with garlic mayonnaise, or simply with olive oil and lemon.

Spaghetti puttanesca

A spicy pasta dish popular with everyone.

The fish
Anchovy fillets in olive oil

- **PREP** 15 mins - **COOK** 25 mins - **SERVES** 4

Ingredients
4 tbsp extra virgin olive oil

2 garlic cloves, grated or finely chopped

½ red chile, seeded and finely chopped

6 anchovy fillets in olive oil, drained and finely chopped

4oz (115g) black olives, pitted and chopped

1–2 tbsp capers, rinsed and drained

1lb (450g) tomatoes, peeled, seeded, and chopped (see page 112)

1lb (450g) spaghetti

chopped flat-leaf parsley, to serve

Parmesan cheese, to serve

1 Heat the oil in a saucepan, add the garlic and chile, and cook gently for 2 minutes, or until slightly colored. Add the anchovies, olives, capers, and tomatoes, and stir, breaking down the anchovies to a paste.

2 Reduce the heat and simmer, uncovered, for 10–15 minutes, stirring frequently.

3 Meanwhile, cook the spaghetti in lightly salted boiling water according to the package instructions. Drain.

4 Toss the spaghetti with the sauce, and serve sprinkled with parsley and Parmesan, with a spinach salad and crusty bread.

Prepare ahead
The sauce can be made up to 2 days ahead, covered, and refrigerated. The flavors will deepen. Return to a brisk simmer before adding to the pasta.

Spaghetti frutti di mare

A traditional Italian dish with a hint of spice and the freshest seafood.

The fish
Mussels, baby squid, shrimp, or any mixed seafood

- **PREP** 25 mins - **COOK** 20 mins - **SERVES** 4

Ingredients
3 tbsp olive oil

1 small onion, finely chopped

2 garlic cloves, grated or finely chopped

2 cups chunky tomato sauce

¼ tsp red pepper flakes

1lb (450g) mussels, prepared (see page 278)

1lb (450g) baby squid, gutted and cleaned and sliced into rings (see page 282)

4 tbsp dry white wine

½ lemon, sliced

1lb (450g) spaghetti

12 large shrimp, peeled, but tails left intact, and deveined (see page 285)

3 tbsp chopped flat-leaf parsley

salt and freshly ground black pepper

1 Heat the oil in a large saucepan and cook the onion and garlic over low heat, stirring, for 3–4 minutes, or until softened. Add the sauce and red pepper flakes, then simmer for 1 minute.

2 Tap the mussels and discard any that do not close. Place the mussels and squid in a large pan with the wine and lemon, cover, and bring to a boil. Cook for 3–4 minutes, or until the mussel shells have opened, shaking. Strain the liquid through a fine sieve and reserve. Discard the lemon and any unopened shells. Reserve a few mussels in their shells and shuck the rest.

3 Cook the spaghetti in lightly salted boiling water according to the package instructions.

4 Meanwhile, add the mussel liquor to the sauce and simmer, uncovered, for 2–3 minutes, or until slightly reduced. Add the shrimp and simmer for 2 minutes. Add the mussels and squid, and parsley, and season to taste.

5 Drain the pasta, return to the pan, and toss in the sauce. Transfer to a bowl, place the reserved mussels in their shells on top, and serve.

Prepare ahead
The tomato sauce in step 1 can be made up to 3 days in advance, covered, and refrigerated. Return to a simmer before continuing.

Spaghetti with clams

This simple seafood pasta brings out the best in the fresh, briny clams.

The fish

Clams, or mussels, whelks, periwinkles, or cockles

- **PREP** 20 mins - **COOK** 15 mins - **SERVES** 4

Ingredients

2½lb (1.1kg) clams

1 tbsp butter

5 tbsp olive oil

2 garlic cloves, coarsely chopped

4oz (115g) fresh breadcrumbs

salt and freshly ground black pepper

12oz (350g) spaghetti

½ tsp red pepper flakes

¼ cup dry white wine

1 tbsp extra virgin olive oil, to serve

2 tbsp grated Parmesan cheese, to serve

4 tbsp chopped flat-leaf parsley, to serve

1 Scrub the clams well under cold running water. Discard any with cracked shells, or that are open and do not close when firmly tapped.

2 Heat the butter with 2 tbsp of the oil in a large, heavy frying pan and stir in half the garlic. Add the breadcrumbs and fry gently, stirring, for 2 minutes, or until golden. Remove from the heat and season.

3 Cook the spaghetti in a large pan of lightly salted boiling water according to the package instructions, or until it is cooked, but still has a bit of bite to it. Drain, keeping back a tiny amount of the cooking water.

4 Meanwhile, heat the remaining oil in a large, deep pan, add the remaining garlic and the red pepper flakes, and stir over moderate heat for 1 minute. Add the wine, season, bring to a boil, then add the clams. Cover and cook over high heat for 4–5 minutes, shaking often, until all the clams have opened.

5 Remove the clams with a slotted spoon, then boil the juices rapidly, uncovered, until reduced by about half.

6 Return the clams to the pan with the pasta; toss lightly. Serve drizzled with extra virgin olive oil, sprinkled with the garlic breadcrumbs, Parmesan, and parsley.

Spinach linguine with white clam sauce

Immensely satisfying and quick to make, this dish will soon become part of your regular repertoire.

The fish

Clams, or mussels

- **PREP** 20–25 mins - **COOK** 5–10 mins
- **SERVES** 4–6

Ingredients

1¾lb (800g) clams

1 onion, finely chopped

1 cup dry white wine

salt and freshly ground black pepper

10oz (280g) fresh spinach linguine

4 tbsp olive oil

2 garlic cloves, finely chopped

2 tbsp chopped flat-leaf parsley

1 Scrub the clams well under cold running water. Discard any with cracked shells, or that are open and do not close when firmly tapped. Put them in a large pan that has a lid, with the onion and wine. Place over high heat, bring to a boil, cover, and shake once or twice. After 2–3 minutes, the shells will have opened.

2 Strain the clams and reserve their liquor. When cool enough to handle, discard any clams that have not opened, and remove most of them from their shells. Return the cooking liquor to the pan over high heat, and boil to reduce to about 1 cup of liquid.

3 Bring a large pot of salted water to a boil, add the linguine, and cook according to the package instructions. Meanwhile, heat the oil in another pan over medium heat, add the garlic, and sauté until aromatic. Add the clams, parsley, and cooking liquor, and season.

4 Drain the linguine, keeping back a tiny amount of the cooking water, and add the pasta to the clams. Mix everything together until piping hot, then serve on warmed plates.

Penne with tuna and roasted onion

This recipe uses fresh tuna steaks, but you can use a 6oz (170g) can of good-quality tuna in olive oil; add it to the pasta without cooking.

The fish
Tuna, or mackerel or bonito

▪ **PREP** 10 mins ▪ **COOK** 20 mins ▪ **SERVES** 4

Ingredients
3 red onions, cut into wedges

handful of cherry tomatoes

few sprigs of thyme

3 tbsp olive oil

salt and freshly ground black pepper

2 tuna steaks, about 6oz (175g) each

12oz (350g) penne

grated zest of ½ lemon

pinch of red pepper flakes

drizzle of good-quality balsamic vinegar, to serve (optional)

1 Preheat the oven to 400°F (200°C). Place the onions, tomatoes, and thyme in a large roasting pan, drizzle with 2 tbsp olive oil, season with salt, then mix well with your hands. Roast for 15 minutes, or until soft and lightly charred.

2 Meanwhile, heat a pan or griddle until hot. Rub the tuna steaks with the remaining oil and season. Fry for 3–4 minutes on each side (depending on thickness and how you like it), remove, and put to one side to rest.

3 Cook the pasta in a pot of boiling salted water for 10 minutes or until it is cooked, but still has a bit of bite to it. Drain, keeping back a tiny amount of the cooking water. Return the pasta to the pan and toss together with the roasted onions and tomatoes.

4 Slice the tuna into chunks, add to the pan with the lemon zest and red pepper flakes, and toss gently. Season to taste, then drizzle with balsamic vinegar (if using), and serve.

Pasta with crab and lemon

A light, fragrant, and elegant dish for a summer's evening.

The fish
Crab, or lobster or shrimp

▪ **PREP** 5 mins ▪ **COOK** 10 mins ▪ **SERVES** 4

Ingredients
1 tbsp olive oil

1 large onion, finely sliced

salt and freshly ground black pepper

2 garlic cloves, finely sliced

grated zest and juice of 1 lemon

handful of flat-leaf parsley, finely chopped

7oz (200g) fresh white crabmeat, or canned white crabmeat, drained

12oz (350g) linguine or spaghetti

chili oil, to serve (optional)

1 Heat the olive oil in a large frying pan, add the onion and a pinch of salt, and cook over low heat for 5 minutes, or until soft and translucent. Stir in the garlic and lemon zest, and cook for a few seconds more.

2 Stir in the parsley and crab, then season well with salt and lots of pepper. Add lemon juice to taste.

3 Meanwhile, cook the pasta in a large pot of boiling salted water according to the package instructions, or until it is cooked, but still has a bit of bite to it. Drain, keeping back a tiny amount of the cooking water. Return the pasta to the pan and toss with the crab sauce, drizzle with chili oil (if using), and serve.

Variation

Piquant pasta with crab and lemon
Add 1 tsp rinsed capers, or a chopped green bell pepper, to the crab.

Linguine with scallops

A hint of chile and lime make this a perfect pasta dish for supper, or even entertaining.

The fish
Sea scallops, or monkfish or shrimp

- **PREP** 10 mins - **COOK** 8 mins - **SERVES** 4

Ingredients
14oz (400g) linguine

juice of 1 lime

5 tbsp olive oil, plus extra for brushing

1 red chile or jalapeño, finely chopped

2 tbsp chopped cilantro

salt and freshly ground black pepper

12 sea scallops, roe removed

1 Cook the pasta in a large pot of boiling salted water according to the package instructions, or until it is cooked, but still has a bit of bite to it. Drain, keeping back a tiny amount of the cooking water, and keep warm.

2 Meanwhile, whisk the lime juice with the oil. Stir in the chile and half the cilantro. Season to taste. Toss the dressing with the linguine, and keep warm.

3 Heat a large griddle pan or heavy frying pan over high heat. Brush the scallops with oil, place in the pan and sear for 3 minutes, turning once. Do not overcook.

4 Divide the linguine between 4 serving plates and arrange the scallops on top. Serve immediately, with the remaining cilantro sprinkled over, with crusty bread and salad.

Spaghetti mare e monti

The ingredients of this well-known dish come from the sea and the mountains.

The fish
Shrimp

- **PREP** 15 mins, plus soaking - **COOK** 15 mins
- **SERVES** 4

Ingredients
½oz (15g) dried porcini mushrooms, rinsed

6 ripe plum tomatoes

2 tbsp extra virgin olive oil

5½oz (150g) baby button mushrooms

2 garlic cloves, grated or finely chopped

1 bay leaf

⅔ cup medium white wine

8oz (225g) cooked shrimp, peeled and deveined

salt and freshly ground black pepper

14oz (400g) spaghetti

1 Place the porcini in a bowl and pour over ⅔ cup of boiling water. Leave to soak for 30 minutes. Chop the mushrooms, then strain the liquid through a fine sieve and reserve.

2 Meanwhile, put the tomatoes in a heatproof bowl. Make a nick in the skin of each, then cover with boiling water. Leave for 30 seconds, then drain, peel, seed, and roughly chop.

3 Heat the oil in a large frying pan. Add all the mushrooms and fry until golden. Add the garlic for 30 seconds. Pour in the porcini liquid, add the bay leaf, and simmer briskly until reduced to a glaze. Reduce the heat to low.

4 Pour in the wine and tomatoes and simmer for 7–8 minutes, or until the tomatoes break down. Remove the bay leaf, add the shrimp, and cook for 1 minute. Season to taste.

5 Meanwhile, cook the pasta in a large pot of boiling salted water according to the package instructions, or until it is cooked, but still has a bit of bite to it. Drain, keeping back a tiny amount of the cooking water, then return to the pan. Add the sauce, toss, and serve.

Prepare ahead
Make the sauce up to the point when the tomatoes have broken down up to 2 days in advance, cover, and refrigerate. Reheat gently before continuing.

Pasta with seafood and tomatoes

This recipe uses raw seafood, but you can use cooked seafood if it's more convenient.

The fish
Any mixed seafood, such as shrimp, squid, and mussels

- **PREP** 5 mins ▪ **COOK** 20 mins ▪ **SERVES** 4

Ingredients
1 tbsp olive oil

1 onion, finely chopped

salt and freshly ground black pepper

3 garlic cloves, grated or finely chopped

14oz (400g) can chopped tomatoes

12oz (350g) linguine or spaghetti

12oz (350g) mixed raw seafood

handful of flat-leaf parsley, finely chopped

1 Heat the oil in a large frying pan, add the onion and a pinch of salt, and cook over low heat for 5 minutes or until soft and translucent. Stir in the garlic and cook for a few seconds more. Add the tomatoes, bring to a boil, then simmer gently for 10–12 minutes.

2 Meanwhile, cook the pasta in a large pot of boiling salted water according to the package instructions, or until it is cooked, but still has a bit of bite to it. Drain, keeping back a tiny amount of the cooking water. Return to the pot.

3 Stir the seafood into the tomato mixture for the last few minutes of cooking. Season well with salt and pepper, stir in the parsley, then toss with the pasta, and serve.

Pasta with anchovies, chile, and lemon

You should find white anchovies in oil at the deli counter of the supermarket.

The fish
Anchovy fillets in olive oil

- **PREP** 10 mins ▪ **COOK** 10 mins ▪ **SERVES** 4

Ingredients
1 tbsp olive oil

2 red onions, finely chopped

salt

2 garlic cloves, grated or finely chopped

1 red chile or jalapeño, seeded and finely chopped

1 green chile, seeded and finely chopped

grated zest of 1 lemon

12oz (350g) linguine or spaghetti

12 white anchovy fillets in olive oil, drained

handful of finely chopped flat-leaf parsley

juice of 1 lemon, to serve

1 Heat the oil in a large frying pan, add the onions and a pinch of salt, and cook over low heat for 5 minutes, or until soft. Add the garlic, chiles, and lemon zest, and cook for a few minutes more, stirring to make sure the mixture does not brown.

2 Meanwhile, cook the pasta in a large pot of boiling salted water until it is cooked, but still has a bit of bite to it. Drain, keeping back a tiny amount of the cooking water. Return the pasta to the pan.

3 Stir the anchovies into the onion mixture, then toss with the pasta, add the parsley, and toss again. Serve with a squeeze of lemon.

Pies, Tarts, and Bakes

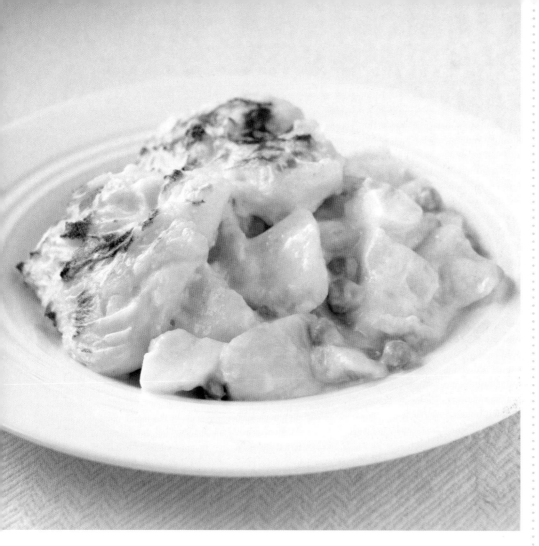

Quick fish pie with peas

Easy to make even after a hard day at work, and universally popular.

The fish

Any firm white fish, such as haddock, ling, cod, or pollock (or even salmon)

- **PREP** 15 mins ▪ **COOK** 25 mins ▪ **SERVES** 4

Ingredients

2lb (900g) floury potatoes, peeled and quartered

3 tbsp milk

salt and freshly ground black pepper

1½lb (675g) white fish, pinboned, skinned, and cut into chunks

⅔ cup milk, plus more if needed

6oz (175g) frozen peas

4 eggs, hard-boiled and coarsely chopped

For the sauce

2 tbsp butter

2 tbsp all-purpose flour

1¼ cups milk

1 tbsp Dijon mustard

1 Preheat the oven to 400°F (200°C), or the broiler to high. Boil the potatoes in salted water for 15 minutes, or until soft. Drain well, add the milk, season, and mash. Set aside.

2 Put the fish in a shallow pan. Season well. Pour over enough milk to cover, and poach over medium heat for 3–4 minutes. Remove the fish with a slotted spoon, and transfer to an ovenproof dish.

3 For the sauce, melt the butter in a pan. Remove from the heat, and stir in the flour with a wooden spoon until smooth. Return to the heat, and stir in the milk, little by little, then cook for 5–10 minutes until thickened. Add more milk if needed. Stir in the mustard, and season. Add the peas and eggs (if using).

4 Spoon the sauce over the fish, top with the mashed potato, and fork to form peaks. Dot with extra butter if you wish, then cook in the oven or under a hot broiler for about 10 minutes until crisp and golden.

Prepare ahead

Assemble 1 day ahead and keep, covered, in the refrigerator, before baking or broiling.

Fish and leek pie

This recipe requires a 9-inch pie dish.

The fish

Any firm white fish, such as haddock or pollock

- **PREP** 15 mins ▪ **COOK** 50 mins ▪ **SERVES** 4

Ingredients

1 tbsp olive oil

1 onion, finely chopped

salt and freshly ground black pepper

4 leeks, finely sliced

1 tsp all-purpose flour

⅔ cup hard cider

handful of flat-leaf parsley, finely chopped

⅔ cup heavy cream

1½lb (675g) white fish, skinned and cut into chunks

10oz (300g) ready-made puff pastry

all-purpose flour, to dust

1 egg, lightly beaten, for egg wash

1 Preheat the oven to 400°F (200°C). Heat the oil, add the onion and a little salt, and sweat gently. Add the leeks, and cook for 10 minutes. Remove from the heat, stir in the flour, and a little cider. Return to the heat, pour in all the cider, and cook for 5–8 minutes. Stir in the parsley and cream, and spoon into the pie dish with the fish.

2 Roll out the pastry on a floured work surface so it is 2in (5cm) larger all around than the dish. Cut a 1in (2.5cm) strip from the edge. Wet the edge of the dish; fit the pastry strip around, and press down. Brush with egg wash, then top with the pastry. Press the edges to seal. Make 2 slits to allow steam to escape. Brush with egg wash, and bake for 20–30 minutes until puffed and golden.

Prepare ahead

Make the filling 1 day ahead, cover, and chill.

Salmon and shrimp fish pie

This luxurious version of everyone's favorite pie is made in a 9-inch ovenproof dish.

The fish

Cold leftover salmon, or cold leftover trout, and shrimp

- **PREP** 15 mins **COOK** 35 mins **SERVES** 2

Ingredients

1½lb (675g) potatoes, peeled and quartered

1¼ cups milk, plus 2 tbsp extra

salt and freshly ground black pepper

12oz (350g) leftover baked salmon, flaked

7oz (200g) cooked shrimp, peeled and deveined

knob of butter, plus extra for topping

1 tbsp all-purpose flour

1 tbsp wholegrain mustard

1 Preheat the oven to 400°F (200°C). Boil the potatoes in salted water for 15 minutes, until soft; drain. Add 2 tbsp milk, season, and mash.

2 Arrange the salmon and shrimp in the ovenproof dish. Season, and set aside.

3 Gently melt the butter in a pan. Remove from the heat, and stir in the flour. Add a little milk and beat until smooth. Return the pan to the heat and continue adding the milk, a little at a time, stirring constantly, until thickened. Whisk to get rid of any lumps, then stir in the mustard.

4 Pour the sauce over the salmon, cover with the potato, and dot with extra butter. Bake in the oven for 15–20 minutes until crisp and golden.

Prepare ahead

Assemble 1 day ahead and keep, covered, in the refrigerator.

Fisherman's pie

There are never any leftovers of this great but simple fish pie; the eggs and shrimp help to make it incredibly moreish. You'll need a 9-in pie dish.

The fish

Any firm white fish, such as haddock, hake, cod, or pollock, and shrimp

- **PREP** 35–45 mins **COOK** 50 mins
- **SERVES** 6

Ingredients

1lb 6oz (625g) potatoes, peeled and quartered

4¼ cups milk, plus ¼ cup

salt and freshly ground black pepper

10 peppercorns

2 bay leaves

1 small onion, quartered

1lb 10oz (750g) white fish fillets, skinned and cut into large chunks

6 tbsp butter, plus more for the dish

¼ cup all-purpose flour

leaves from 5–7 sprigs of parsley, chopped

4½oz (125g) cooked, peeled, and deveined shrimp

3 eggs, hard-boiled and coarsely chopped

1 Preheat the oven to 350°F (180°C). Boil the potatoes until tender; drain. Add ¼ cup milk, salt, and pepper. Mash.

2 Pour the remaining milk into a pan, add the peppercorns, bay leaves, and onion. Bring to a boil, remove from the heat, cover and let stand for 10 minutes. Add the fish, and simmer for 5–10 minutes. Strain off and reserve the liquid.

3 Gently melt the butter. Whisk in the flour, then the reserved liquid. Return to the heat and stir until thickened. Add the parsley.

4 Butter the pie dish. Spoon in the fish, sauce, prawns, and eggs. Spread over the potato, and bake for 20–30 minutes.

Prepare ahead

Assemble 1 day ahead and keep, covered, in the refrigerator.

Variation

Individual fish crumbles
Make the fish and shrimp mixture, but not the potato. Rub 6 tbsp butter into ¾ cup all-purpose flour. Add 1 tbsp chopped parsley, 3 tbsp rolled oats, 1 tbsp grated Parmesan cheese, salt, and pepper. Butter 6 ramekins and fill with the fish, then top with the crumble. Bake for 20–25 minutes.

Salmon coulibiac

A classic Russian speciality. You can vary it, authentically, by using pancakes in place of the rice to layer with the fish filling.

The fish

Salmon, or trout or sturgeon

- **PREP** 40 mins ▪ **COOK** 45 mins
- **SERVES** 4–6

Ingredients

1lb (450g) puff pastry

2 tbsp butter

1 small onion, finely chopped

2oz (60g) button mushrooms, finely chopped

5 tbsp milk

9oz (250g) cooked salmon (poached or canned), skinned, pinboned, and flaked

2 hard-boiled eggs, diced

4oz (115g) cooked long-grain rice, chilled

1 tbsp finely chopped flat-leaf parsley

1 tbsp finely chopped dill

salt and freshly ground black pepper

1 egg, beaten, for glazing

1 Roll one-third of the pastry into a 10 x 6in (25 x 15cm) sheet. Lay it on a baking sheet and pierce all over with a fork. Chill for 10 minutes. Preheat the oven to 400°F (200°C). Roll out the remaining pastry to about one-third larger than the base. Chill.

2 Melt the butter in a saucepan, add the onion and cook over low heat for 4–5 minutes until soft. Increase the heat and add the mushrooms. Fry for 2–3 minutes. Add the milk and simmer until the mushrooms are cooked. Cool.

3 Cook the pastry base in the oven for 5–10 minutes or until crisp; cool on a wire rack.

4 Mix the salmon, hard-boiled eggs, rice, and herbs, season, and add the mushroom mixture.

5 Spoon the salmon mixture over the base. Lay the second sheet of pastry on top, tucking the edges under the cooked pastry to seal.

6 Cut small fishes or leaves from the pastry trimmings. Make a small hole on the coulibiac, brush with beaten egg, and decorate the top. Chill for 15 minutes. Brush again with egg and bake for 25–30 minutes until golden brown.

Prepare ahead

Assemble the coulibiac to the end of step 5, cover, and chill for up to 2 days before baking. Return to room temperature before continuing.

Salmon in puff pastry

Baking salmon en croûte ("in a crust") keeps it moist and succulent.

The fish

Salmon, or trout

- **PREP** 25 mins ▪ **COOK** 30 mins ▪ **SERVES** 4

Ingredients

3oz (85g) watercress, coarse stems removed, very finely chopped

4oz (115g) cream cheese

salt and freshly ground black pepper

14oz (400g) puff pastry

all-purpose flour, for dusting

1lb 5oz (600g) salmon fillet, pinboned, skinned, and halved

oil, for greasing

beaten egg or milk, to glaze

1 Preheat the oven to 400°F (200°C). Place the watercress in a bowl, add the cream cheese, season generously, and mix well.

2 Roll out the pastry on a lightly floured surface to ⅛in (3mm) thick. It should be 3in (7.5cm) longer than the salmon pieces and more than twice as wide. Trim the edges. Transfer to a lightly oiled baking tray.

3 Place 1 piece of salmon in the middle of the pastry. Spread with the watercress cream and place the other piece of salmon on top. Lightly brush the pastry edges with water, then fold the 2 ends over the salmon. Fold in the sides so they overlap slightly and press together. Brush with beaten egg, and make 2 or 3 holes with a skewer to allow steam to escape. Bake for 30 minutes, until well risen and golden.

4 Remove from the oven and allow to stand for a few minutes, then slice and serve.

Prepare ahead

The dish can be assembled up to 12 hours before baking. Cover and chill, then return to room temperature before continuing.

SALMON FLAVOR PAIRINGS: Classically matched to the fragrance of dill, tarragon, sorrel, and lemon, salmon also works well with ginger, or even the Indonesian thick soy sauce kecap manis.

Pissaladière

This is a French version of pizza.

The fish

Anchovy fillets in olive oil

- **PREP** 20 mins, plus rising ■ **COOK** 85 mins
- **SERVES** 4 as main course, 8 as canapés

Ingredients

For the topping

4 tbsp olive oil

2lb (900g) onions, finely sliced

3 garlic cloves

a few sprigs of thyme

1 tsp *herbes de Provence*

1 bay leaf

3½oz (100g) jar or can anchovy fillets in olive oil

12 black Niçoise olives, pitted, or Italian olives

For the crust

2 cups bread flour, plus extra for dusting

salt and freshly ground black pepper

1 tsp brown sugar

1 tsp active dried yeast

1 tbsp olive oil

1 Combine the flour, 1 tsp salt, and pepper in a large bowl. Pour ½ cup tepid water into another bowl, and whisk in the sugar, then the yeast. Set aside for 10 minutes to froth, then pour into the flour with the oil.

2 Mix to a dough, adding more water if it is too dry. Knead on a floured surface for 10 minutes, or until elastic. Shape into a ball, return to the bowl, and cover with a kitchen towel. Leave in a warm place for 1 hour, or until doubled in size.

3 Put the oil in a saucepan over low heat. Add the onions, garlic, and herbs, cover and simmer for 1 hour, or until the onions become a stringy purée. Set aside, discarding the bay leaf.

4 Preheat the oven to 350°F (180°C). Knead the dough briefly on a floured surface. Roll it out to fit a 13 x 9in (32.5 x 23cm) jelly roll pan, and prick all over with a fork.

5 Spread the onions over the crust. Drain the anchovies, reserving 3 tbsp oil, and halve lengthwise. Embed the olives in rows in the dough, and drape the anchovies in a criss-cross pattern on top. Drizzle with the anchovy oil, and sprinkle with pepper. Bake for 25 minutes. Serve warm or cool, cut into rectangles.

Tarte au poissons

Make this cooked fish tart in a tart pan. It's great for leftovers. You will need baking beans for the pastry shell.

The fish

Cooked trout, or cooked salmon, cod, or haddock, cooked smoked fish, or cooked shrimp

- **PREP** 45 mins, plus chilling ■ **COOK** 55 mins
- **SERVES** 4

Ingredients

8oz (225g) pastry dough

all-purpose flour, for dusting

1 onion, finely chopped

3 tbsp butter

4 ripe tomatoes, peeled, seeded, and diced (see page 112)

1 small garlic clove, crushed

2 tsp chopped thyme leaves

large pinch of freshly grated nutmeg

½ cup half-and-half

2 eggs, beaten

salt and freshly ground black pepper

6oz (175g) cooked trout, pinboned, skinned, and flaked into large pieces

1 tbsp grated Gruyère cheese

1 Roll the pastry dough on a floured surface to a 10in (25cm) circle and use it to line a 8in (20cm) tart pan. Chill for 15 minutes. Preheat the oven to 350°F (180°C).

2 Line the pastry shell with parchment paper and baking beans. Bake for 12–15 minutes, or until set. Lift out the paper and beans and return to the oven for another 5 minutes. Allow to cool. Reduce the oven temperature to 300°F (150°C).

3 Cook the onion in the butter for 4–5 minutes, or until translucent. Add the tomatoes and garlic, then cool. Stir in the thyme, nutmeg, half-and-half, and eggs, and season well.

4 Put the fish into the pastry shell and spoon in the tomato mixture. Sprinkle with the Gruyère. Return the tart to the oven and bake for 25–35 minutes, or until set and golden brown. Serve warm or cold.

Prepare ahead

Bake the pastry shell up to 1 day ahead, cool completely, and store in an airtight container at room temperature.

TROUT FLAVOR PAIRINGS: Try white wine vinegar, or lemon, to enhance and sharpen the trout's sweet flesh, or match with rich pastry, almonds, or hazelnuts, and highlight with chives.

Smoked mackerel and scallion tart

This tart transforms the humble smoked mackerel into a sophisticated and luxurious treat. You will need a 7 inch (18cm) round, loose-bottomed, straight-sided tart pan and baking beans.

The fish
Smoked mackerel, or smoked salmon

- **PREP** 15 mins ▪ **COOK** 50 mins ▪ **SERVES** 4

Ingredients
9oz (250g) pastry dough

all-purpose flour, for dusting

2 eggs, plus 1 extra for brushing

1 tbsp olive oil

1 bunch of scallions, finely chopped

salt and freshly ground black pepper

2 smoked mackerel fillets, about 3½oz (100g) each, skinned and flaked

7fl oz (200ml) crème fraîche or sour cream

handful of flat-leaf parsley, finely chopped

1 bunch of chives, finely chopped

1 Preheat the oven to 400°F (200°C). Roll out the pastry on a floured work surface, and use to line the pan. Trim the excess, line with parchment paper, and fill with baking beans. Bake for 15–20 minutes until the edges are golden. Remove the beans and paper, brush with egg wash, and return to the oven for 2–3 minutes to crisp. Reduce the oven temperature to 350°F (180°C).

2 Heat the oil in a frying pan over low heat. Add half the scallions and a pinch of salt, and cook gently for 5 minutes. Spoon over the pastry with the raw scallions. Scatter on the mackerel, and season with pepper.

3 Mix the crème fraîche and the 2 eggs. Add the herbs, season with a little salt, and mix. Carefully pour into the tart shell, then bake for 20–30 minutes until set and golden. Leave to cool for 10 minutes before releasing from the pan. Serve with tomato and cucumber salad.

Prepare ahead
The tart shell can be baked 1 day ahead. Cover, and store at room temperature.

Smoked haddock, leek, and grainy mustard tart

Use dyed smoked haddock for this recipe, so it shows up well. You'll need a 8–10 inch (20–25cm) tart pan and baking beans.

The fish
Smoked haddock, or smoked cod or canned salmon

- **PREP** 15–20 mins, plus chilling
- **COOK** 1 hr 10 mins–1 hr 20 mins ▪ **SERVES** 4

Ingredients
10oz (300g) pastry dough

all-purpose flour, for dusting

12oz (350g) dyed smoked haddock fillet, with skin

1¼ cup milk

sprig of thyme

1 bay leaf

4 tbsp unsalted butter

1 leek (white part only), very finely sliced

1 tbsp all-purpose flour

1 egg, plus 1 egg yolk

salt and freshly ground black pepper

1 tbsp grainy mustard

2 tbsp grated Parmesan cheese

1 Roll out the pastry on a floured surface to line the tart pan, and chill for 30 minutes. Preheat the oven to 375°F (190°C). Line the pastry with parchment paper and fill with baking beans. Bake for 15–18 minutes. Remove the paper and beans and cool. Reduce the oven temperature to 340°F (170°C).

2 Put the fish in a sauté pan. Pour over the milk, thyme, and bay leaf. Bring to a boil, reduce the heat, and simmer for 5–6 minutes. Skin, and break into large flakes. Strain the milk.

3 Melt the butter in a saucepan, add the leek, cover, and cook for 6–8 minutes. Stir in the flour and cook for 1 minute. Remove the pan from the heat and slowly blend in the milk. Return to the heat, bring to a boil, then cool. Stir in the egg, yolk, and seasoning.

4 Spread the mustard on the pastry. Arrange the fish on top and spoon on the sauce. Sprinkle with Parmesan and bake for 30–40 minutes. Cool for a moment before serving.

Prepare ahead
Assemble the tart—ensuring all elements are completely cold before placing into the pastry shell—up to 1 day ahead, cover, and chill.

Smoked haddock with spinach and pancetta

This deliciously satisfying dish is great for a quick supper.

The fish
Smoked haddock, or smoked trout

- **PREP** 10 mins ▪ **COOK** 15–20 mins
- **SERVES** 6

Ingredients
1 tbsp butter, plus extra for greasing

1 tbsp olive oil

1 onion, finely chopped

3½oz (100g) pancetta or bacon, chopped

1lb (450g) spinach

3½oz (100g) crème fraîche or sour cream

salt and freshly ground black pepper

2½oz (75g) Parmesan cheese, grated

1¾lb (800g) smoked haddock fillets, skinned

juice of ½ lemon

1oz (30g) breadcrumbs

1 Preheat the oven to 375°F (190°C) and butter an ovenproof serving dish. Melt the oil and butter together in a frying pan and fry the onion and pancetta for 5 minutes.

2 Add the spinach and stir until wilted, then stir in the crème fraîche, seasoning, and most of the Parmesan. Simmer until slightly thickened.

3 Spoon the spinach mixture into the dish and place the fish on top. Sprinkle with lemon juice. Scatter with breadcrumbs and the remaining Parmesan, and bake for 15–20 minutes, or until the fish is cooked through and flakes easily.

Prepare ahead
Assemble up to 1 day in advance, cover, and refrigerate until ready to bake.

Smoked fish and anchovy gratin

A wonderfully rich and flavorsome recipe for a cold winter evening.

The fish
Smoked mackerel and smoked salmon, or any mix of smoked fish

- **PREP** 10 mins ▪ **COOK** 30 mins ▪ **SERVES** 4

Ingredients
4½oz (125g) smoked mackerel fillet, skinned

4½oz (125g) smoked salmon

8–12 anchovy fillets in olive oil, drained

4 waxy potatoes, peeled, boiled, and sliced

knob of butter, melted

For the sauce
knob of butter

1 onion, finely chopped

1 garlic clove, grated or finely chopped

1 tbsp all-purpose flour

1¼ cup milk

salt and freshly ground black pepper

handful of curly parsley, finely chopped

1 Preheat the oven to 400°F (200°C). To make the sauce, melt the butter in a pan over low heat. Add the onion, and sweat gently for about 5 minutes until soft and translucent, then add the garlic and cook for a few seconds more. Remove from the heat and stir in the flour, then add a little of the milk and beat until smooth.

2 Return the pan to the heat, and slowly add the rest of the milk, stirring until thickened. Season well, and stir in the parsley.

3 Layer the smoked fish and anchovies in an ovenproof dish, then spoon over the sauce and gently combine. Top with a layer of potatoes, brush with melted butter, and bake in the oven for 15–20 minutes until golden, crispy, and heated through. Serve with a crisp green salad.

Prepare ahead
Cool the sauce completely, then assemble the dish, cover, and chill up to 2 days in advance. Return to room temperature before baking.

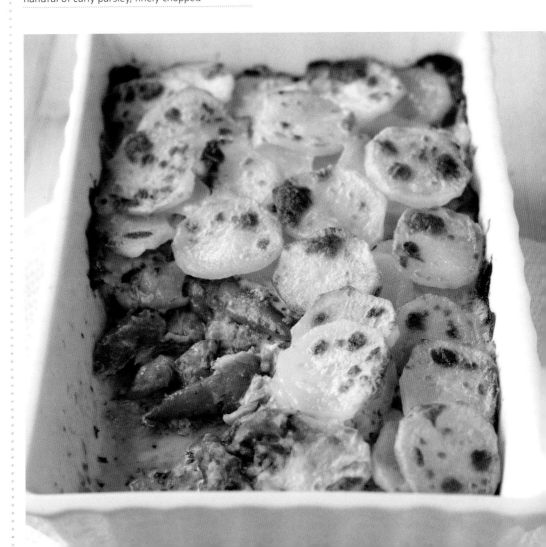

Empanadas

These savory Spanish pastries make very versatile but substantial nibbles. You'll need a 3½ inch (9cm) round pastry cutter.

The fish

Canned tuna, or canned sardines

- **PREP** 45 mins, plus chilling
- **COOK** 40–50 mins ▪ **MAKES** 24

Ingredients

1lb (450g) all-purpose flour, plus extra for dusting

salt and freshly ground black pepper

6 tbsp butter, diced

2 eggs, beaten, plus extra for glazing

1 tbsp olive oil, plus extra for greasing

1 onion, finely chopped

1 cup canned tomatoes, drained

2 tsp tomato purée

5oz (140g) can tuna in spring water, drained

2 tbsp finely chopped flat-leaf parsley

1 To make the pastry, sift the flour into a large mixing bowl with ½ tsp salt. Add the butter and rub in with your fingertips until it resembles fine breadcrumbs. Add the eggs with 4–6 tbsp water and combine to form a dough. Cover with plastic wrap and chill for 30 minutes.

2 Meanwhile, heat the oil in a frying pan, add the onion, and fry over medium heat, stirring, for 5–8 minutes, or until translucent. Add the tomatoes, tomato purée, tuna, and parsley, and season. Reduce the heat and simmer for 10–12 minutes, stirring occasionally.

3 Preheat the oven to 375°F (190°C). Roll out the pastry to ⅛in (3mm) thick. Using the pastry cutter, cut out 24 rounds. Put 1 tsp of the filling on each, brush the edges with water, fold over, and pinch together.

4 Place the empanadas on an oiled baking tray and brush with egg. Bake for 25–30 minutes, or until golden. Serve warm.

Prepare ahead

Cool the tuna filling completely, then assemble the empanadas, cover and chill for up to 2 days. Bring to room temperature before baking.

Variation

Empanaditas

Cut smaller circles of pastry for bite-sized versions, which make ideal canapés. Bake for just 15–20 minutes.

Coquilles St. Jacques

An elegant main course. You'll need 4 scallop shells or ramekins, and a piping bag.

The fish

Sea scallops, or cockles

- **PREP** 20 mins ▪ **COOK** 50 mins ▪ **SERVES** 4

Ingredients

1lb (450g) floury potatoes, peeled and cut into chunks

6 tbsp butter

large pinch of grated nutmeg

salt and freshly ground black pepper

3 egg yolks

8 sea scallops, roe removed

6 tbsp medium white wine

1 bay leaf

3in (7.5cm) piece of celery stalk

4 black peppercorns

small sprig of thyme

8oz (225g) button mushrooms

juice of ½ lemon

1 tbsp all-purpose flour

6 tbsp heavy cream or crème fraîche

1¾oz (50g) Gruyère or Emmental cheese, grated

1 Boil the potatoes and mash with 2 tbsp of the butter, nutmeg, and seasoning; beat until fluffy. Stir in the yolks. Spoon into a piping bag and pipe a border around each shell or ramekin.

2 Preheat the oven to 425°F (220°C). Place the scallops in a medium saucepan, add ⅔ cup of water, the wine, bay leaf, celery, peppercorns, thyme, and a pinch of salt. Bring to a boil, cover, and simmer for 1–2 minutes, or until the scallops whiten. Strain, reserve the liquid, and discard the vegetables.

3 Gently cook the mushrooms with the lemon juice, 2 tbsp water, and salt and pepper in a covered pan for 5–7 minutes. Uncover. If any liquid remains, simmer until it evaporates.

4 Melt the remaining butter in a pan. Stir in the flour, and cook for 1 minute. Gradually stir in the reserved scallop liquid. Slowly bring to a boil, and stir until thickened. Season, and simmer over low heat for 4–5 minutes. Stir in the cream and half the cheese. Cut each scallop in 2, and stir into the sauce with the mushrooms.

5 Spoon the mixture into each shell or ramekin, and sprinkle with the remaining cheese. Bake for 15 minutes, or until golden, and serve.

CANNED TUNA FLAVOR PAIRING:

The bold taste of canned tuna is great against onion, olives, tomatoes, and garlic. Or make it shine against gentle pasta and creamy cheese sauces.

Salmon, horseradish, and kale bake

When paired with healthy kale, horseradish makes the perfect bake for winter.

The fish
Salmon, or smoked haddock

- **PREP** 10 mins • **COOK** 35 mins • **SERVES** 4

Ingredients
4 salmon fillets, about 5½oz (150g) each, pinboned and skinned

2½ cups milk

2 handfuls of kale

2 tbsp butter

1 tbsp flour

½ cup strong Cheddar cheese, grated

1–2 tbsp creamed horseradish

1 Preheat the oven to 400°F (200°C). Put the salmon in a frying pan, and pour in enough milk to cover. Poach gently over low heat for about 10 minutes until opaque and cooked, then transfer the salmon to an ovenproof dish using a slotted spoon. Strain and reserve the milk.

2 Trim the tough stalks from the kale, and roughly chop the leaves. Boil or steam for about 5 minutes until nearly soft, then drain, and add to the salmon. Combine gently.

3 Melt the butter in a saucepan and stir in the flour. Cook for 1 minute, until foaming, then gradually add the poaching milk, whisking constantly to remove lumps. Bring to a boil and cook, stirring, for 4–5 minutes, until thickened. Remove from the heat and add the cheese, stirring, until it melts, then the horseradish.

4 Pour the cheese sauce over the salmon, and bake for about 15 minutes until golden.

Prepare ahead

The whole dish can be assembled, covered, and chilled several hours in advance. Bring to room temperature before baking.

Haddock mornay

With a layer of spinach under the poached haddock, this is a colorful one-pot meal.

The fish
Haddock, or smoked cod or smoked pollock

- **PREP** 10 mins • **COOK** 30 mins • **SERVES** 4

Ingredients
1½lb (675g) haddock fillet, pinboned, skinned, and cut into 4 equal pieces

⅔ cup fish stock or water

1¼ cups milk

3 tbsp butter, plus extra to grease

3 tbsp all-purpose flour

½ cup Cheddar cheese, grated

salt and freshly ground black pepper

9oz (250g) spinach leaves, chopped

pinch of grated nutmeg

½ cup fresh whole wheat breadcrumbs

2 tbsp chopped flat-leaf parsley

½ cup Parmesan cheese, grated

1 Place the fish in a deep frying pan, pour in the stock and milk, and slowly bring to a boil, then cover and simmer for 6–8 minutes, or until the fish is cooked. Lift the fish from the pan and keep warm. Reserve the poaching liquid.

2 Melt the butter in a pan and stir in the flour until smooth. Cook for 1 minute, then gradually whisk in the poaching liquid. Stir over the heat until thickened. Stir in the Cheddar, season, and remove from the heat.

3 Put the spinach in a pan, cover, and cook for 1 minute over a low heat, until wilted. Season with the nutmeg and spread out in a greased, shallow, ovenproof dish. Preheat the broiler.

4 Place the haddock on the spinach and pour over the sauce. Mix the breadcrumbs, parsley, and Parmesan, and sprinkle over. Broil until golden, and serve.

Prepare ahead

The whole dish can be assembled, covered, and chilled several hours in advance. Reheat gently before broiling.

Tuna and pasta bake

This is a quick, one-dish, pantry meal that is ideal at the end of a busy day. You'll need a 2-quart ovenproof serving dish.

The fish

Canned tuna, or canned mackerel

- **PREP** 10 mins ▪ **COOK** 40 mins ▪ **SERVES** 6

Ingredients

salt and freshly ground black pepper
7oz (200g) pasta shells
oil, for the dish
1 can condensed cream of mushroom soup
½ cup milk
7oz (200g) can tuna in spring water, drained
7oz (200g) can corn, drained and rinsed
1 onion, finely chopped
1 red pepper, cored and finely chopped
¼ cup chopped flat-leaf parsley
pinch of chilli powder (optional)
½ cup Cheddar cheese, grated

1 Bring a large saucepan of salted water to a boil over high heat. Add the pasta, stir, and cook for 2 minutes less than the time specified on the package. Drain the pasta and set it aside.

2 Preheat the oven to 425°F (220°C) and oil a 2-quart ovenproof serving dish.

3 Heat the mushroom soup and milk over low heat in the saucepan used for the pasta. Stir in the tuna, corn, onion, pepper, parsley, chilli powder (if using), and half the cheese. Once the soup is heated, stir in the pasta. Season to taste.

4 Pour the mixture into the dish and smooth the top. Sprinkle with the remaining cheese. Bake for 30–35 minutes, or until golden brown. Serve hot, straight from the dish, with hot garlic bread and a green salad.

Prepare ahead

The whole dish can be assembled, covered, and chilled several hours in advance. Bring to room temperature before cooking.

Monkfish Americaine

The firm texture of monkfish makes it an excellent candidate for this dish, which is traditionally made with lobster.

The fish

Monkfish, or shrimp or lobster

- **PREP** 45–50 mins ▪ **COOK** 1 hr
- **SERVES** 4–6

Ingredients

3lb (1.35kg) monkfish, with its bone
2 onions, chopped
½ cup dry white wine, or juice of ½ lemon
1 tsp peppercorns
3–5 sprigs of parsley
30g (1oz) plain flour
salt and freshly ground pepper
2 tbsp olive oil
½ cup butter

For the Americaine sauce

1 carrot, diced
2 garlic cloves, finely chopped
14oz (400g) can chopped plum tomatoes
⅔ cup dry white wine
3 tbsp Cognac
leaves from 3–4 sprigs of tarragon, chopped, stalks reserved
pinch of cayenne pepper (optional)
1 bouquet garni
¼ cup heavy cream
1 tbsp tomato paste
pinch of sugar (optional)

1 Cut the fish into ½in (1cm) slices. Slightly flatten each with the side of a broad knife.

2 Put half the onions in a large saucepan and add the fish bone, wine, peppercorns, parsley, and 2 cups of water. Bring slowly to a boil, then simmer, uncovered, for 20 minutes. Strain and reserve.

3 Put the flour on a plate and season. Lightly coat the fish slices. Heat the oil and a quarter of the butter in a sauté pan, add half the fish and sauté for 2–3 minutes. Transfer to a plate. Sauté the remaining fish.

4 Add the carrot, garlic, and remaining onion to the pan and cook for 3–5 minutes until soft. Add the tomatoes, wine, Cognac, tarragon stalks, salt, pepper, cayenne, and bouquet garni. Pour in the stock. Bring to a boil and simmer for 15–20 minutes.

5 Sieve the sauce into a large saucepan, pressing down with a ladle. Boil for 5–10 minutes, until thickened. Whisk in the cream and tomato paste. Taste, adding sugar if you like.

6 Add the monkfish and simmer for 5–10 minutes. Take from the heat and add the remaining butter in small pieces, shaking. Sprinkle with tarragon and serve.

One Pot

Caldereta asturiana

This iconic stew, from the Asturias region of Spain, traditionally uses the day's catch.

The fish

Any mixed white fish, such as hake, monkfish, or red mullet, and shellfish, such as squid, mussels, shrimp, or clams

- **PREP** 25 mins ▪ **COOK** 40 mins ▪ **SERVES** 6

Ingredients

2¼lb (1kg) white fish fillets, pinboned and skinned

4 small squid, gutted and cleaned (see page 282)

1lb 2oz (500g) each mussels, prepared (see page 278) and clams, thoroughly washed

½ cup dry white wine

3 tbsp extra virgin olive oil

1 large Spanish onion, chopped

3 garlic cloves, grated or finely chopped

large pinch of cayenne pepper

1 heaping tbsp all-purpose flour

1 cup fish stock

large bunch (8–10 tbsp) flat-leaf parsley, chopped

9oz (250g) large raw shrimp, peeled and deveined (see page 285)

2 large red bell peppers, seeded and quartered

salt and freshly ground black pepper

lemon juice, to taste

1 Preheat the oven to 350°F (180°C). Cut the fish fillets into large pieces and the squid into large squares. Chill until needed.

2 Make sure the mussels and clams are shut, or close when tapped sharply. Add the wine to a large saucepan, bring to a boil, add the mussels and clams, and cook over medium heat for 3–4 minutes, or until open. Discard any that remain shut. Strain the liquor and reserve. Remove the shellfish from their shells.

3 Heat the oil in a flameproof casserole, add the onion, and cook until softening. Add the garlic, cayenne pepper, and flour; stir for 1–2 minutes. Add the mussel liquid, fish stock, and parsley.

4 Add the raw seafood and peppers and season. Cover and cook in the oven for 20–25 minutes. Add the mussels and clams, and return to the oven for 5 minutes. Sprinkle with lemon and serve with crusty bread.

Prepare ahead

Make the sauce base in step 3 up to 2 days in advance, cover, and refrigerate. Return to a simmer before continuing.

Ligurian fish stew

An easy, but very impressive stew.

The fish

Red mullet, John Dory, red snapper, cod, or tilapia, and clams, or any mixed seafood

- **PREP** 20 mins ▪ **COOK** 20–25 mins
- **SERVES** 6–8

Ingredients

3 medium red mullet, scaled and filleted

4 small John Dory fillets, skinned

8oz (225g) red snapper or tilapia fillet, skinned

8oz (225g) cod fillet, skinned

½ cup olive oil

1 onion, finely chopped

2 celery ribs, finely sliced

2 small carrots, finely sliced

1 bulb fennel, finely sliced

3 garlic cloves, crushed

1 tsp tomato purée

3 tbsp Pernod

½ cup dry white wine

8 plum tomatoes, seeded and coarsely chopped

2 tsp thyme leaves

2 tsp marjoram leaves, chopped

1 quart fish stock

salt and freshly ground black pepper

8oz (225g) clams, thoroughly washed

1 Pinbone the mullet, Dory, and red snapper or tilapia fillets (see page 271) and halve. Trim the cod fillet and cut into large pieces. Set aside.

2 Heat most of the oil in a flameproof casserole. Add the vegetables and garlic and cook over low heat for 4–5 minutes. Stir in the tomato purée, then the Pernod, wine, tomatoes, and herbs. Bring to a boil and simmer for 5 minutes. Add the stock and simmer for 5 minutes. Season.

3 Add the fish and cook over low heat for 4–5 minutes or until opaque and firm. Add the clams and cook until the shells have opened. Adjust the seasoning and serve with warm ciabatta, drizzled with the remaining oil.

Variation

Seafood and tomato cioppino

Replace the clams with mussels, small scallops, and 2 whole cooked crabs, chopped into pieces. Reduce the total weight of white fish to 1lb 2oz (500g). Omit the celery, carrots, and fennel. Sprinkle with chopped flat-leaf parsley to serve.

JOHN DORY FLAVOR PAIRINGS:

A tomato accompaniment, as in Ligurian fish stew, suits John Dory, although it's also great with creamy sauces, wild mushrooms, sage, capers, lemon, and rich crème fraîche.

Mussels in fennel broth

A great pick-me-up, aromatic and healthy.

The fish

Mussels, or manila or little neck clams

- **PREP** 10 mins ▪ **COOK** 20 mins ▪ **SERVES** 4

Ingredients

1 tbsp olive oil

1 onion, finely chopped

1 fennel bulb, finely chopped

salt and freshly ground black pepper

2 garlic cloves, grated or finely chopped

2 waxy potatoes, peeled and finely diced

1¼ cups hot vegetable stock or fish stock

14oz (400g) can coconut milk

3lb (1.35kg) mussels, prepared (see page 278)

handful of basil leaves, torn

1 Heat the oil in a large pan over low heat. Add the onion, fennel, and a pinch of salt, then sweat for about 5 minutes until softened. Add the garlic and potatoes, and cook for a few more minutes, being careful not to allow anything to brown.

2 Pour in the stock, and bring to a boil. Add the coconut milk, reduce the heat slightly, and simmer gently for about 10 minutes, or until the potatoes are cooked. Return to a boil, add the mussels, and cover. Cook for about 5 minutes, until the mussels are open (discard any that remain shut).

3 Stir in the basil, and adjust the seasoning. Serve immediately.

Prepare ahead

Make the broth up to the point when the potatoes are cooked, cover, and refrigerate for up to 2 days. Reheat gently before continuing.

Mussels in ginger and chile broth

These succulent mussels in a moat of gingery juices are terrific with a mound of fluffy rice.

The fish

Mussels, or palourde or hard-shell clams

- **PREP** 20 mins ▪ **COOK** 25 mins
- **SERVES** 2–4

Ingredients

3lb 3oz (1.5 kg) mussels, prepared (see page 278)

7 tbsp butter

2 onions, finely chopped

2 red bird's eye chiles, finely chopped

2in (5cm) fresh ginger, shredded

5 large garlic cloves, grated or finely chopped

2 stalks lemongrass, split lengthwise and lightly bruised

½ cup ginger wine or sherry

1¾ cups fish stock

⅔ cup coconut milk

3 tbsp coconut cream

salt and freshly ground black pepper

juice of 1–2 limes, to taste

3 tbsp chopped cilantro leaves

1 Tap the mussels and discard any that do not close.

2 Melt the butter in a large pan over low heat, and gently cook the onions, chiles, ginger, garlic, and lemongrass for 10 minutes until soft but not colored.

3 Increase the heat to high and add the wine and stock. Bring to a boil before adding in the mussels. Cover and cook for 5–7 minutes, until they have opened. Discard the lemongrass along with any mussels that remain closed.

4 Pour in the coconut milk and cream, and bring to a boil. Season, sharpen with lime juice, stir in the cilantro leaves, and serve.

Mixed fish stew with croutons

A hearty dish ideal for a large gathering.

The fish
Any mixed fish, such as haddock, monkfish, or plaice, and any shellfish, such as shrimp

- **PREP** 15 mins - **COOK** 30 mins - **SERVES** 8

Ingredients
5lb (2.25kg) mixed fish fillets, scaled and pinboned, and shellfish, shelled

3 tbsp olive oil

4 garlic cloves, grated or finely chopped

2 tbsp tomato purée

1 onion, finely chopped

8 tomatoes, skinned, seeded, and chopped (see page 112)

1 tsp fennel seeds

a few strands of saffron

pinch of paprika

4 cups fish stock

salt and freshly ground black pepper

1 baguette

4½oz (125g) Gruyère cheese, grated

handful of flat-leaf parsley, finely chopped

1 Wash the fish, then cut it into chunky bite-sized pieces and set aside. Put the oil in a large wide pan, add the garlic, tomato purée, and onion, and cook over very low heat for 5–8 minutes, or until the onion begins to soften, but not color.

2 Add the tomatoes, fennel seeds, saffron, and paprika, pour in the stock, and season with salt and pepper. Bring to a boil, then reduce to a simmer, and cook for 10 minutes. Add the fish and shellfish and simmer for 10 minutes more, or until the fish is cooked.

3 Slice the bread on the diagonal and toast. Serve the soup with the croutons, and sprinkle over the cheese, and parsley.

Prepare ahead
Make the soup base up to just before adding the fish, cover, and refrigerate for up to 2 days. Return to a simmer before continuing.

Spicy, saucy monkfish

A satisfying meal for a cold winter's night.

The fish
Monkfish, or gray mullet or red snapper

- **PREP** 30–35 mins - **COOK** 30–35 mins
- **SERVES** 6

Ingredients
4 tbsp vegetable oil

2 onions, finely sliced

2 tbsp paprika

1¼ cups fish stock

2 x 14oz (400g) cans tomatoes

6 garlic cloves, grated or finely chopped

4 bay leaves

2 celery stalks, peeled and finely sliced

2 carrots, finely sliced

salt and freshly ground black pepper

2¼lb (1kg) monkfish fillets, skinned and cut in 1in (2.5cm) cubes

For the spicy sauce
2 tbsp butter

1 onion, finely chopped

1 apple, peeled, cored, and diced

1 tsp ground cumin

1 tsp ground coriander

½ tsp ground ginger

½ tsp ground cloves

¼ tsp cayenne pepper, or ½ tsp red pepper flakes

½ tbsp cornstarch

¾ cup coconut milk

⅔ cup fish stock

1 For the sauce, melt the butter in a saucepan. Add the onion and apple and cook gently for 3–5 minutes, until soft. Add the spices and stir for 2–3 minutes. Blend the cornstarch to a paste with 2–3 tbsp of the coconut milk.

2 Add the remaining coconut milk and stock to the pan and bring to a boil. Stir in the cornstarch paste; the sauce will thicken. Set aside.

3 Heat the oil in a heavy-bottomed pot. Add the onions and cook until soft. Add the paprika, stock, tomatoes, garlic, bay leaves, celery, and carrots. Season and bring to a boil. Reduce the heat and simmer to reduce by one-third.

4 Add the sauce and return to a boil. Add the fish. Cover and simmer for 12–15 minutes. Discard the bay leaves and serve in warm bowls.

Prepare ahead
Make the spicy sauce and the stew base up to 3 days ahead, mix, cover, and refrigerate. Return to a boil before adding the fish.

SUSTAINABILITY CHOICE

Diversify

Try out less popular fish to take pressure off the more extensively fished species. You can also expect more for your money, because there isn't high demand for them. Aim to vary your choices, however, as less popular species may not yet have been monitored for stock levels and they may quickly become overfished themselves. In the US, sole (shown here) is a great example of an underutilized species that should be enjoyed more often. Look out for lesser-known species of fish in responsible supermarkets and restaurants and give them a try.

Shrimp gumbo

A classic from Louisiana, this has a brown roux base and is thickened with okra (gumbo).

The fish

Shrimp, or kingfish or cod, and crabmeat

- **PREP** 30 mins • **COOK** 1 hr • **SERVES** 6–8

Ingredients

6 tbsp butter

2¼lb (1kg) raw shrimp, peeled and deveined (see page 285)

4 tbsp crabmeat

2 tbsp all-purpose flour

½ tsp cayenne pepper

1 large onion, finely chopped

2 garlic cloves, grated or finely chopped

4oz (115g) okra, trimmed

1 large red bell pepper, seeded and diced

2 x 14oz (400g) cans tomatoes, or 1lb 10oz (750g) fresh tomatoes, halved

4¼ cups shellfish stock

1 bay leaf

2 sprigs of thyme

grated zest of 1 lemon

1 tbsp filé powder (optional)

salt and freshly ground black pepper

1 Melt the butter in a large saucepan, add the shrimp in batches and stir-fry over medium heat for 2–3 minutes or until cooked. Lift on to a plate and cool.

2 Add the crab and flour to the butter, cook over low heat for 3–4 minutes or until the flour is golden brown. Add the cayenne, onion, and garlic, and cook for a further 3 minutes.

3 Stir in the okra and bell pepper. Pour over the tomatoes, stock, herbs, and lemon zest. Bring to a boil and simmer for 25–30 minutes until thick.

4 Stir the shrimp into the gumbo to warm through, add filé powder (if using), and season to taste. Serve with rice and Tabasco sauce.

Prepare ahead

The gumbo can be made, cooled, chilled, covered, and refrigerated up to 1 day in advance of serving. Reheat very gently, or the shrimp will toughen.

Bouillabaisse

A delicious soup for a special occasion.

The fish

Any mixed white and oily fish, such as cod, flounder, halibut, and herring, and shellfish, such as shrimp and mussels

- **PREP** 20 mins • **COOK** 45 mins • **SERVES** 4

Ingredients

4 tbsp olive oil

1 onion, finely sliced

2 leeks, finely sliced

1 small fennel bulb, finely sliced

6–7 garlic cloves, grated or finely chopped

4 tomatoes, skinned, seeded, and chopped

2 tbsp tomato purée

1 cup dry white wine

4¼ cups fish or chicken stock

pinch of saffron threads

strip of orange zest

1 bouquet garni

salt and freshly ground black pepper

3lb (1.35kg) mixed white and oily fish fillets, pinboned and cut into chunks, and shellfish

2 tbsp Pernod

4½oz (125g) mayonnaise

1 bird's-eye chile, seeded and roughly chopped

8 thin slices day-old French bread, toasted, to serve

1 Heat the oil in a large saucepan over medium heat. Add the onion, leeks, fennel, and 2–3 of the garlic cloves and fry, stirring, for 5–8 minutes, or until the vegetables are softened. Add the tomatoes, half the tomato purée, and all the wine, and stir until blended.

2 Add the stock, saffron, orange zest, and bouquet garni. Season to taste, and bring to a boil. Reduce the heat, partially cover the pan, and simmer for 30 minutes, or until the soup is reduced slightly, stirring occasionally.

3 Remove the orange zest and bouquet garni from the soup and add the firm fish. Reduce the heat to low and let simmer for 5 minutes, then add the delicate fish and simmer for a further 2–3 minutes. Stir in the Pernod, and season.

4 To make the rouille, place the remaining garlic and tomato purée, mayonnaise, chile, and ½ tsp salt into a food processor and whizz until smooth. Spread each piece of toast with rouille and put 2 slices in the bottom of each bowl. Ladle the soup on top and serve.

CRAB FLAVOR PAIRINGS: Rich, strong, brown crabmeat is great with cayenne pepper or anchovy paste. White crabmeat is best with mild egg or mayonnaise.

Italian seafood stew

A simple fish stew from Tuscany, made by impoverished fishermen making the best of their catch in the Adriatic.

The fish

Gray mullet, sea bass, tilapia, or any mixed white fish, and calamari

- **PREP** 10 mins ▪ **COOK** 20 mins
- **SERVES** 6–8

Ingredients

2 gray mullet, scaled and filleted

4 tilapia, scaled and filleted

1 calamari, prepared (see page 283)

5 tbsp extra virgin olive oil

2 onions, finely sliced

1 red chile, seeded and finely diced

3 garlic cloves, chopped

14oz (400g) can chopped tomatoes

½ cup dry white wine

2 cups fish stock

2 tbsp chopped flat-leaf parsley

salt and freshly ground black pepper

thickly sliced and toasted Italian rustic bread, to serve

1 Pinbone the fish fillets (see page 271). Cut into large pieces. Thinly slice the calamari and set aside.

2 Heat the olive oil and add the onions; cook over low heat for 5–6 minutes or until they are translucent. Add the chile and garlic and cook for a few minutes longer. Stir in the tomatoes, wine, and stock, bring to a boil, and simmer until syrupy. Add the parsley and season to taste.

3 Add the sea bass and tilapia, set the pan over low heat for 6–8 minutes or until the fish is cooked: it will be opaque. Add the calamari and stir into the broth for a minute or so until it has just lost its translucency.

4 Arrange the toasted bread on 6–8 plates and spoon the broth on top.

Prepare ahead

The broth can be prepared up to 1 day ahead, covered, and refrigerated. Reheat gently before continuing with the recipe.

Monkfish in spicy tomato sauce

This classic recipe has fabulously bold and sunshiney flavors.

The fish

Monkfish, or skate, cod, or shrimp

- **PREP** 20 mins ▪ **COOK** 20 mins ▪ **SERVES** 4

Ingredients

2¼lb (1kg) monkfish tail, filleted and trimmed of membrane (see page 270)

2 tbsp extra virgin olive oil, plus a splash for cooking

1 small onion, chopped

2 garlic cloves, chopped

1–2 red chiles, seeded and chopped

10 tomatoes, peeled, seeded, and chopped (see page 112), or 14oz (400g) can chopped tomatoes

½ cup tomato sauce

1 tsp sugar

1 tbsp chopped oregano

12 black olives, pitted and halved

2 tbsp capers, rinsed

salt and freshly ground black pepper

1 Cut the monkfish into 4 even-sized portions; refrigerate until ready to use.

2 Heat the 2 tbsp olive oil in a large sauté pan, add the onion, and cook for 3–4 minutes or until soft. Add the garlic and chile and cook over low to medium heat for another 1–2 minutes.

3 Add the tomatoes, tomato sauce, and sugar, bring to a boil, reduce the heat, and simmer for 5 minutes, or until the tomatoes begin to break down and soften.

4 In a small frying pan, heat the splash of oil and brown the monkfish for 1–2 minutes. Lift into the tomato sauce and cook over low heat for 5–7 minutes or until the monkfish is cooked; it will be firm and opaque in appearance.

5 Stir the oregano, olives, and capers into the sauce and season. Serve with rice or pasta.

Prepare ahead

The tomato sauce can be made ahead, covered, and chilled for up to 2 days. Reheat gently, and add the oregano, olives, and capers just before serving.

GRAY MULLET FLAVOR PAIRINGS

The sometimes earthy taste of this firm fish is enhanced by lemon juice, white wine, and white wine vinegar, or any dish containing tomatoes.

Salt cod braised with vegetables

This Spanish recipe is fragrant with the aromas of garlic, bay, and saffron.

The fish

Salt cod, or salt pollock

- **PREP** 20 mins, plus soaking • **COOK** 40 mins
- **SERVES** 4

Ingredients

1¾lb (800g) thick-cut salt cod, soaked, scaled, and cut into 4 pieces

3 tbsp olive oil

1 onion, finely diced

white parts of 2 leeks, finely sliced

3 garlic cloves, grated or finely chopped

3 tomatoes, peeled, seeded, and chopped (see page 112)

1lb 2oz (500g) potatoes, peeled and diced

salt and freshly ground black pepper

2 bay leaves

large pinch of saffron threads

½ cup dry white wine

2 tbsp chopped flat-leaf parsley

1 Soak the fish for at least 24 hours in enough water to cover, changing the water 2–3 times.

2 Heat the oil in a large, shallow, heatproof casserole. Add the onion and leek, and fry gently, stirring, for 5 minutes, or until soft.

3 Add the garlic and tomatoes, and stir for a further 2 minutes. Add the potatoes, season, and add the bay leaves and saffron.

4 Put the salt cod, skin-side up, on top. Pour in the wine and 1 cup of water, then bring to a simmer and cook for 25–30 minutes. Shake the casserole once or twice every few minutes to help thicken the sauce.

5 Sprinkle over the parsley, and serve straight from the casserole.

Prepare ahead

The vegetable base of the braise—steps 2 and 3—can be cooked up to 2 days ahead, covered, and refrigerated. Return to room temperature before continuing.

Hungarian fish goulash

Paprika flatters the carp in this recipe. Use more of the spice for greater heat.

The fish

Carp

- **PREP** 15–20 mins • **COOK** 25 mins
- **SERVES** 4

Ingredients

2¼lb (1kg) carp fillets, skinned

seasoned flour (see page 55)

3 tbsp sunflower oil, plus more if needed

1 large onion, chopped

1–2 red or green bell peppers, thickly sliced

1–2 tsp paprika, to taste

1 cup medium white wine

1 tbsp chopped dill

1 tbsp chopped flat-leaf parsley

salt and freshly ground black pepper

8fl oz (250ml) sour cream

1 Cut the carp into 1in (2.5cm) chunks. Roll them in seasoned flour.

2 Heat the oil in a large frying pan and cook the carp in batches for 3–4 minutes or until cooked, adding a little more oil between batches if needed. Lift on to a plate and keep warm.

3 Add the onion and peppers to the pan and fry over medium heat for 3–4 minutes or until beginning to soften. Stir in the paprika to taste and cook for a further 2 minutes.

4 Add the wine, bring to a boil, and simmer for 2–3 minutes to reduce by one-third. Return the carp and add the herbs. Season to taste.

5 Swirl in the sour cream and heat through until the goulash just comes to a boil. Adjust the seasoning and serve with rice or noodles.

Prepare ahead

The flavors of the goulash will improve if cooled, covered, and refrigerated for up to 36 hours in advance. Reheat gently before adding the sour cream.

SALT POLLOCK FLAVOR PAIRINGS:

This salted fish is milder than salt cod. Its distinctive flavor works with earthy ingredients, such as potato, onion, and leeks.

OCTOPUS FLAVOR PAIRINGS: The firm, sweet chunks are great with the Asian tastes of a spicy stir-fry, or try it Italian style with red wine, onions, balsamic vinegar, and sage.

Vietnamese caramel monkfish

The caramel here gives the fish an intense sticky sweetness, which is balanced by salty fish sauce.

The fish

Monkfish, or catfish or shrimp

- **PREP** 10 mins ▪ **COOK** 30 mins
- **SERVES** 2–4

Ingredients

1lb 10oz (750g) monkfish tail, filleted and trimmed of membrane (see page 270)

¼ cup granulated sugar

2 tbsp vegetable oil

2 garlic cloves, chopped

4 small shallots, chopped

3–4 tbsp Vietnamese fish sauce

2 scallions, finely sliced

freshly ground black pepper

large handful of cilantro, to garnish

lime wedges, to garnish

1 Cut the monkfish fillets into 1–1½in (3–4cm) cubes. Set aside.

2 Put ½ cup water and the sugar into a heavy saucepan. Cook over low heat, stirring very occasionally, until the sugar has dissolved. Increase the heat and boil steadily until the mixture begins to brown. Cover your hand with a cloth, and swirl the pan so the caramel browns evenly; do not stir. Once the caramel is deep brown and smells nutty, quickly add another ½ cup water. It will splatter, so be careful. Allow the sizzling to subside, then pour into a pitcher.

3 Heat the oil in a large wok, add the garlic and shallots, and stir over medium heat until beginning to color. Add the monkfish and stir-fry over high heat until brown. Stir in the caramel sauce over medium heat until the monkfish is white and firm to the touch. Add the fish sauce and scallions and stir until the onions are slightly soft. Season with pepper.

4 Pile into a serving dish with cilantro and lime wedges. Serve with rice or noodles.

Prepare ahead

Make the caramel a day in advance, cover, and store at room temperature. If it hardens, reheat very gently before continuing.

Spicy stir-fried squid

A traditional Thai recipe, although such recipes are legion in many countries and regions across Asia.

The fish

Squid, or octopus, calamari, or shrimp

- **PREP** 20 mins ▪ **COOK** 5–6 mins
- **SERVES** 2–4

Ingredients

8 small squid, gutted and cleaned (see page 282)

1 tbsp vegetable oil

1 stalk lemongrass, split into 4 lengthwise

2 kaffir lime leaves

1 yellow or orange bell pepper, seeded and diced

handful of basil leaves, preferably Thai, shredded

salt and freshly ground black pepper

For the paste

3 garlic cloves, chopped

2 shallots, coarsely chopped

1 tbsp grated fresh ginger

1–2 red chiles, to taste (seeded for a milder result)

1¾oz (50g) chopped cilantro, preferably both leaves and roots

large splash of vegetable oil

1 tbsp palm sugar or dark brown sugar

1 tbsp Thai fish sauce

1 Score the squid tubes (see page 282) and set aside with the tentacles.

2 To make the paste, put the garlic, shallots, ginger, chile, cilantro, vegetable oil, palm sugar, and fish sauce into a food processor. Process to form a finely chopped green paste.

3 Heat the 1 tbsp vegetable oil in a large wok, add the paste, and cook over low to medium heat for 2–3 minutes or until it smells aromatic. Add the squid, lemongrass, lime leaves, and pepper. Stir-fry, tossing over medium-high heat until the squid is opaque and coated in the other ingredients. (Avoid overcooking the squid, as it will become tough.)

4 Stir in the basil and adjust the seasoning, then remove the lemongrass and lime leaves. Serve with rice or noodles and a green salad.

Prepare ahead

The paste can be made up to 1 day ahead, covered, and chilled. It will become spicier.

Sweet and sour shrimp

Shrimp in a fragrant sauce spiked with chile, garlic, and ginger makes a great main course.

The fish
Shrimp, or squid, scallops, or monkfish

- **PREP** 20 mins ▪ **COOK** 10 mins ▪ **SERVES** 4

Ingredients

3 tbsp rice wine vinegar

2 tbsp honey

1 tbsp granulated sugar

2 tbsp light soy sauce

2 tbsp ketchup

2 tbsp vegetable oil

3 shallots, peeled and sliced

¾in (2cm) fresh ginger, grated

1 red chile, seeded and finely chopped

1 garlic clove, crushed

1 small carrot, cut into matchsticks

1 celery stalk, cut into matchsticks

1 jalapeño, seeded and cut into strips

1lb 2oz (500g) raw shrimp, peeled and deveined (see page 285)

2 scallions, sliced lengthwise, to serve

1 Put the vinegar, honey, sugar, soy sauce, and ketchup in a small saucepan, and heat gently until the honey and sugar melt. Remove from the heat and set aside.

2 Heat the oil in a wok, add the shallots, ginger, chile, garlic, carrot, celery, and jalapeño and stir-fry for 4 minutes.

3 Add the shrimp and stir-fry for a further 2 minutes or until they turn pink. Pour in the vinegar mixture and stir-fry for 1 minute, or until the shrimp and vegetables are coated and everything is heated through.

4 To serve, transfer to a platter and sprinkle with scallions. Serve with boiled rice.

Pad Thai

One of Thailand's national dishes, this is often served rolled up in a thin omelet.

The fish
Shrimp, or squid or monkfish

- **PREP** 20 mins ▪ **COOK** 10 mins ▪ **SERVES** 4

Ingredients

2 tbsp chopped cilantro leaves

1 red bird's eye chile, seeded and finely chopped

4 tbsp vegetable oil

9oz (250g) raw shrimp, peeled and deveined (see page 285)

4 shallots, finely chopped

1 tbsp sugar

4 large eggs, beaten

2 tbsp oyster sauce

1 tbsp Thai fish sauce

juice of 1 lime

12oz (350g) flat rice noodles, cooked according to package instructions

9oz (250g) beansprouts

4 scallions, sliced

4oz (115g) unsalted roasted peanuts, coarsely chopped

1 lime, cut into wedges, to serve

1 Mix together the cilantro, chile, and vegetable oil. Heat half the mixture in a wok, add the shrimp, and stir-fry for 1 minute. Remove and set aside.

2 Add the remaining vegetable oil to the wok and stir-fry the shallots for 1 minute. Add the sugar and eggs, and cook for 1 minute, stirring frequently to scramble the eggs.

3 Stir in the oyster sauce, fish sauce, lime juice, noodles, and beansprouts, and return the shrimp to the wok. Stir-fry for 2 minutes, then add the scallions and half the peanuts. Toss everything together for 1–2 minutes, or until piping hot.

4 Divide between 4 warmed bowls, scatter the remaining nuts on top, and add a lime wedge. This is excellent with a fresh salad of beansprouts and shredded carrot, tossed with lime juice.

Soba noodles with shrimp and avocado

Soba noodles, usually made from buckwheat flour, originate in Japan.

The fish
Shrimp, or scallops

- **PREP** 15 mins, plus standing ▪ **COOK** 15 mins
- **SERVES** 4

Ingredients
9oz (250g) soba noodles

1½oz (45g) dried wakame (seaweed)

2 tbsp vegetable or peanut oil

16 raw shrimp, peeled and deveined, tails left on (see page 285)

6 shiitake mushrooms, sliced

4 cherry tomatoes, halved

2 tbsp pickled ginger, rinsed and finely chopped

4 tbsp mirin

2 tbsp rice vinegar

2 tbsp Japanese soy sauce

1 avocado, sliced

2 tbsp sesame seeds, to serve

2 tbsp roughly chopped cilantro leaves, to serve

1 Cook the noodles in a pot of boiling water according to the package instructions, or until just tender. Drain and rinse under cold water until cool. Drain again, and set aside.

2 Soak the wakame in cold water until soft, then drain, and cut into strips. Set aside.

3 Heat the oil in a wok, add the shrimp and mushrooms, and stir-fry for 1 minute. Add the tomatoes and stir-fry for a further minute. Set aside to cool, then add to the noodles.

4 Make a dressing by mixing the pickled ginger, mirin, vinegar, and soy sauce. Add the dressing, wakame, and avocado to the noodles and vegetables, and toss.

5 Divide among 4 serving plates, and sprinkle with sesame seeds and chopped cilantro.

Prepare ahead
Make the noodles, without the avocado, up to 1 day ahead, cover, and refrigerate. Return to room temperature, add the avocado, and sprinkle with sesame seeds, and cilantro.

Sweet and sour stir-fried fish with ginger

Make sure you buy very firm-fleshed fish for this, so it doesn't fall apart in the wok.

The fish
Any firm white fish, such as haddock

- **PREP** 10 mins ▪ **COOK** 20 mins ▪ **SERVES** 4

Ingredients
1–2 tbsp cornstarch

salt and freshly ground black pepper

1½lb (675g) thick white fish fillets, pinboned, skinned, and cut into strips

1–2 tbsp vegetable or sunflower oil

1 onion, roughly chopped

2 garlic cloves, grated or finely chopped

1in (2.5cm) fresh ginger, finely sliced

large handful snow peas or sugarsnap peas, sliced into strips

For the sweet and sour sauce
1 tbsp white wine vinegar

1 tbsp tomato purée

1 tbsp sugar

1 tsp cornstarch

2 tsp light soy sauce

2 tbsp pineapple juice

1 For the sauce, mix the vinegar, tomato purée, sugar, cornstarch, soy sauce, and pineapple juice in a bowl, and set aside. Put the cornstarch on a plate, season, and toss in the fish.

2 In a wok, heat half the oil until hot, then add the fish. Stir-fry for 5 minutes until golden. Remove with a slotted spoon, and keep warm. Carefully wipe the wok with paper towels, and add a little more oil. When hot, add the onion and stir-fry until it softens, then add the garlic and ginger, and stir-fry for a few minutes more.

3 Pour in the sweet and sour sauce, and let boil for a few minutes, stirring constantly. Reduce the heat to medium, add the snow peas, and stir-fry for 1 minute. Return the fish to the wok, quickly toss together, and serve with rice.

Prepare ahead
Make the sweet and sour sauce up to 2 days ahead and keep, covered, in the refrigerator.

Crab stir-fried with curry powder

This Thai street dish is eaten throughout the country. For eating indoors, you'll need plenty of paper napkins and finger bowls with lemon slices for your diners.

The fish
Crab, or shrimp or scallops

- **PREP** 30 mins ▪ **COOK** 15–20 mins
- **SERVES** 4

Ingredients
1 raw crab, about 2¼lb (1kg) in total

1 egg, lightly beaten

2 large garlic cloves, chopped

1in (2.5cm) fresh ginger, chopped

pinch of salt

2 cups coconut cream

4 tbsp curry powder

4 tsp Thai fish sauce

tiny pinch of white sugar

4 tsp rice vinegar

½ cup coconut milk

1oz (30g) celery stalks (preferably Asian celery), cut into ¾in (2cm) lengths

½ small white onion, sliced

handful of cilantro leaves, chopped

1 Clean the crab (see page 287). If you find any orange roe or mustard-colored tomalley (both are delicacies), set them aside. Segment the crab into about 8 pieces, cracking the claws. Mix any tomalley and roe with the egg.

2 Using a mortar and pestle, pound the garlic, ginger, and salt into a coarse paste. Heat a wok, add 1¾ cups coconut cream and, when sizzling, add the paste. As the paste mixture is beginning to color, add the crab and fry for a few moments over moderate heat. Sprinkle in the curry powder. Continue to fry for a few more moments, stirring. When fragrant, season with the fish sauce, sugar, and vinegar.

3 Add the remaining coconut cream and the coconut milk, stirring well. Cover and simmer until the crab is cooked, tossing regularly.

4 Remove the lid and increase the heat, then stir in the egg mixture until the egg has thickened and begun to separate.

5 Mix in the celery and onion, then sprinkle with cilantro and serve with rice, or stir-fried Chinese broccoli with oyster sauce.

Shrimp diabolo

Quick and easy shrimp in a warming spicy tomato sauce, great to make after a day's work.

The fish
Shrimp, or scallops, monkfish, or squid

- **PREP** 5 mins ▪ **COOK** 20 mins ▪ **SERVES** 4

Ingredients
2 tbsp olive oil

1 onion, chopped

1 red bell pepper, seeded and sliced

3 garlic cloves, crushed

½ cup dry white wine or stock

1 cup passata or tomato purée

1lb (450g) cooked shrimp, peeled and deveined (see page 285)

1–2 tbsp chili sauce

2 tsp Worcestershire sauce

1 Heat the oil in a large saucepan and fry the onion for 5 minutes. Add the red bell pepper and fry for another 5 minutes, or until softened.

2 Add the garlic and fry for a few seconds. Stir in the wine and let it bubble away for 1–2 minutes.

3 Stir in the passata and bring to a boil, stirring, then reduce the heat and simmer for 5 minutes.

4 Stir in the shrimp just until piping hot, then the chili and Worcestershire sauces, and serve immediately with boiled rice.

Prepare ahead
Make the tomato sauce 2–3 days ahead, cover, and chill. Return to a simmer before continuing.

Stir-fried yellow curried crabs

The little-known cuisine of Laos is delicious. Once you've tried this dish, you'll be addicted.

The fish
Crab

- **PREP** 25 mins ▪ **COOK** 20–25 mins
- **SERVES** 4

Ingredients
4 tbsp vegetable oil

5 tbsp Laotian kore (see below)

1 tsp Indian curry powder (optional)

8 small crabs, about 8oz (225g) each, halved or quartered

2 scallions, thinly sliced diagonally

For the Laotian kore
1½ tsp cumin seeds

1 tbsp coriander seeds

1 stalk lemongrass, outer leaves discarded, then chopped

1oz (30g) galangal, chopped

grated zest of 1 kaffir lime

3 large garlic cloves, crushed

1 large shallot, chopped

3 tbsp finely chopped cilantro root

½ tsp turmeric

1in (2.5cm) fresh ginger, chopped

4–6 green or red Thai chiles, seeded

2 tsp Thai shrimp paste

1 tbsp Indian curry powder (optional)

1 To make the Laotian kore, heat a frying pan over medium heat and roast the cumin and coriander seeds until fragrant. Put the lemongrass, galangal, kaffir lime zest, garlic, shallot, cilantro root, turmeric, ginger, chiles, and roasted seeds in a blender. Blend until smooth, adding water to help. Stir in the shrimp paste and curry powder (if using).

2 Heat the oil in a wok over high heat and stir-fry the kore for about 5 minutes or until golden and fragrant. Add the curry powder (if using) and stir to blend well.

3 Reduce the heat to medium and add the crab, tossing. Cover and cook for 5 minutes. Uncover, toss, and cook for 5 minutes more. Transfer to a serving platter and sprinkle with scallions.

Prepare ahead
Make the Laotian kore, cover, and refrigerate up to 2 days ahead. The flavors will deepen.

Fish with tomatoes, potatoes, and onions

Simple, but full of flavor, and hearty.

The fish
Any mixed firm fish, such as red mullet, haddock, bream, sea bass, pollock, or cod

- **PREP** 30 mins ▪ **COOK** 35 mins ▪ **SERVES** 8

Ingredients
3 tbsp olive oil

5 large potatoes, peeled and cut into bite-sized pieces

salt and freshly ground black pepper

4 garlic cloves, grated or finely chopped

handful of flat-leaf parsley, finely chopped

1¼lb (550g) cherry tomatoes, halved

1 cup dry white wine

1½lb (675g) mixed firm-fleshed fish fillets, scaled, pinboned, and cut into bite-sized pieces

16 anchovy fillets in olive oil, drained

1 Heat the oil in a large, shallow, heavy-based pan, add the potatoes, and season well with salt and pepper. Cook over medium heat, stirring frequently, for 10–15 minutes, or until beginning to turn golden brown. Lower the heat, then stir in the garlic and parsley and cook for a few seconds before adding the tomatoes.

2 Cook for 6–8 minutes, or until the tomatoes begin to split, then increase the heat, add the wine, and allow to boil for a couple of minutes while the alcohol evaporates. Reduce the heat to low, add the fish and anchovies, cover, and cook for 10 minutes.

3 Transfer to a shallow serving dish and serve with crisp dressed salad and crusty bread.

Prepare ahead
Make the tomato base until the alcohol has evaporated from the wine. Cover, and refrigerate for up to 3 days. Return to a simmer before continuing.

Curry

Coconut and turmeric curry of red snapper

This curry should be hot, salty, and a little tart.

The fish
Red snapper, or sea bream or sea bass

- **PREP** 20 mins ▪ **COOK** 10–15 mins
- **SERVES** 4

Ingredients

2 cups coconut milk

1 cup light chicken stock or water

2 stalks lemongrass, bruised

pinch of granulated sugar

1 tbsp tamarind paste, or to taste

4 tbsp Thai fish sauce, or to taste

7oz (200g) red snapper fillet or 14oz (400g) whole red snapper, scaled and gutted

handful of torn betel leaves (optional)

½ cup coconut cream

5 kaffir lime leaves, finely shredded

For the curry paste

5–6 dried small red chiles

pinch of salt

2–3 few bird's eye chiles, seeded if preferred

1¾oz (50g) chopped lemongrass

4 tbsp chopped scallions

2½ tbsp chopped garlic

1 rounded tbsp turmeric

1 rounded tbsp Thai shrimp paste

1 Put all the ingredients for the curry paste into a food processor and whizz, adding just enough water to make a smooth paste.

2 Combine the coconut milk with the stock in a saucepan, add the lemongrass and bring to a boil. Season with the sugar, tamarind, and fish sauce, and add 4 tbsp curry paste. Simmer for a minute before adding the fish and betel leaves (if using). Continue to simmer until the fish is cooked.

3 Check the seasoning, adding more fish sauce or tamarind, if you want, then stir in the coconut cream. Sprinkle with the shredded lime leaves and serve with slices of cucumber, sprigs of mint and cilantro, grilled shrimp, and rice.

Prepare ahead
Make the curry paste up to 3 days ahead, cover, and refrigerate. The flavors will deepen.

Pineapple curry of mussels

This Thai curry comes from Phetchburi, a prosperous province in southwest Bangkok.

The fish
Mussels, or clams

- **PREP** 20–25 mins ▪ **COOK** 25 mins
- **SERVES** 4

Ingredients

½ cup coconut cream

2–2½ tbsp palm sugar, to taste

2½ tbsp Thai fish sauce

½ tbsp tamarind paste, or to taste

2 cups coconut milk

10oz (300g) finely chopped pineapple

10oz (300g) mussels, prepared (see page 278)

3 kaffir lime leaves, torn

1 long red or green chile, seeded if preferred, thinly sliced at an angle

For the curry paste

10 dried large red chiles, soaked and chopped

3 heaped tbsp chopped red bird's eye chiles, seeded if preferred

pinch of salt

2½ tbsp chopped galangal

5 tbsp chopped lemongrass

2 tsp finely grated kaffir lime zest

1 tsp chopped cilantro root

5 tbsp chopped garlic

2½ tbsp chopped scallions

1 rounded tbsp Thai shrimp paste

1 Put all the ingredients for the curry paste into a food processor and whizz, adding just enough water to make a smooth paste.

2 Heat the coconut cream over moderate heat, add 4 tbsp of curry paste and fry until fragrant. This can take as long as 10 minutes.

3 Season with the palm sugar and fish sauce (not too much, as the mussels will add salt), then the tamarind. Add the coconut milk, then the pineapple and mussels. Simmer until the shells have opened, stirring regularly. (Discard any mussels that remain closed.)

4 Sprinkle with the lime leaves and chile. Check the seasoning. Serve with steamed rice.

Prepare ahead
Make the curry paste up to 3 days ahead, cover, and refrigerate. The flavors will deepen.

Kenyan fish curry

A fiery, broth-like curry, sharpened with tamarind, and enriched with coconut milk.

The fish

Any white fish, such as haddock, or shrimp or squid

- **PREP** 20 mins **COOK** 35–40 mins
- **SERVES** 4

Ingredients

juice of 1 lime

1 tsp cracked black peppercorns

1lb 5oz (600g) white fish fillet, pinboned, skinned, and cut into chunks

6 tbsp vegetable oil

For the spice mixture

2 dried red chiles

¾ tsp coriander seeds

¾ tsp cumin seeds

1 tsp mustard seeds

¼ tsp turmeric

For the masala

1 red onion, finely chopped

1 red bell pepper, seeded and shredded

1 red chile, finely shredded, seeded if preferred

4 garlic cloves, grated or finely chopped

9oz (250g) plum tomatoes, skinned, seeded, and finely chopped (see page 112)

¾ cup coconut milk

2 tbsp tamarind paste, or to taste

1 To make the spice mixture, roast the chiles and seeds in a frying pan until aromatic, then grind to a powder and add the turmeric.

2 Combine the lime juice and peppercorns and pour over the fish. Heat the oil in a frying pan. Fry the fish for 1 minute each side, until lightly colored. Transfer to a plate, and cover.

3 For the masala, add the red onion to the pan. Cover and cook for 5 minutes. Uncover, add in the red bell pepper, chile, and garlic, and fry until the onions are about to turn color. Stir in the spice mixture and fry briskly for 1 minute. Add the tomatoes, bring to a boil, then pour in ¾ cup of water. Simmer for 15 minutes. Pour in the coconut milk and enough tamarind paste to lend a tang. The curry shouldn't be too thick; aim for a broth-like consistency.

4 Return the fish to the pan and simmer for 5–10 minutes or until cooked through. Serve hot.

Tamarind fish curry

Giant tamarind trees grow everywhere in southern India, offering both shade and their sweet-sour fruits for cooking.

The fish

Any white fish, such as lemon sole, or shrimp or squid

- **PREP** 10 mins **COOK** 35–40 mins
- **SERVES** 6

Ingredients

2 tbsp vegetable oil

1 tsp mustard seeds

10 curry leaves

pinch of fenugreek seeds

2 garlic cloves, chopped

2 onions, chopped

¼ tsp turmeric

½ tsp chili powder

3 tomatoes, chopped

1 tsp tomato purée

sea salt

1 tbsp tamarind paste

1lb 2oz (500g) white fish fillets, skinned

1 Heat the oil in a large saucepan. Add the mustard seeds and, when they begin to pop, the curry leaves, fenugreek seeds, and garlic. Sauté for 1–2 minutes or until the garlic turns brown. Stir in the onions and cook over moderate heat, stirring occasionally, for 10 minutes or until the onions are golden.

2 Add the turmeric and chili powder and mix well, then add the tomatoes, tomato purée, and some salt and cook for a further 2 minutes. Add the tamarind paste and ¾ cup of water. Bring to a boil and simmer for 12 minutes, stirring occasionally, until the sauce thickens. Taste, adding more tamarind paste if you wish.

3 Pinbone the fish, cut it into pieces, and carefully mix into the sauce. Reduce the heat and cook gently for 4–5 minutes or until just cooked through. Serve with plain boiled rice.

Prepare ahead

The curry sauce can be made up to 2 days ahead, covered very well, and refrigerated. The flavors will deepen. Return to a simmer before adding the fish.

Thai green fish curry with snow peas

Thai curries are wonderful because, although they taste hot, the fire dissipates very quickly.

The fish

Any white fish, such as cod or pollock, or shrimp, scallops, squid, cuttlefish, monkfish, snapper, or bream

▪ **PREP** 15 mins ▪ **COOK** 15 mins ▪ **SERVES** 4

Ingredients

2 waxy potatoes, scrubbed, cut into chunks

salt and freshly ground black pepper

4oz (115g) snow peas

14oz (400g) can coconut milk

2 tbsp Thai green curry paste

1¼lb (550g) white fish, pinboned, skinned, and cut into chunks

1–2 thin green chiles, seeded and shredded

a few torn basil or cilantro leaves

1 Boil the potatoes in lightly salted water for about 5 minutes until almost tender. Steam the snow peas in a metal colander or steamer over the potatoes for 3 minutes. Drain the potatoes.

2 Mix the coconut milk with the curry paste in a pan. Add the fish, potatoes, chiles, and a little seasoning. Bring to a boil, reduce the heat, part-cover, and simmer very gently for 10 minutes until the fish and potatoes are tender.

3 Gently stir in the snow peas. Taste and adjust the seasoning, if necessary. Spoon over Thai jasmine rice in warmed bowls. Sprinkle with basil or cilantro leaves.

Variation

With mixed vegetables
This can be cooked with broccoli, green beans, or zucchini instead of the snow peas.

Thai red curry with snapper

Homemade curry paste adds a delicious fragrance and warmth to the curry.

The fish

Snapper, or catfish, rabbit fish, or barracuda

▪ **PREP** 10 mins ▪ **COOK** 20 mins ▪ **SERVES** 4

Ingredients

2 tbsp sunflower oil

2 tsp shrimp paste

1 large onion, finely chopped

2 garlic cloves, crushed

1 tbsp palm sugar, or dark brown sugar

4 tomatoes, seeded and diced

14oz (400g) can coconut milk

1¼ cup fish or shellfish stock

1–2 tbsp Thai fish sauce, to taste

juice of ½–1 lime

4 snapper fillets, about 6oz (175g) each, scaled, pinboned, and halved

3 tbsp roughly chopped cilantro leaves

For the curry paste

4 red chiles, seeded and chopped

1 red bell pepper, broiled, skin removed

1 tbsp ground coriander

2 stalks lemongrass, roughly chopped

2 tbsp grated galangal or fresh ginger

1 tbsp Thai fish sauce

1 tsp shrimp paste

1 tsp palm sugar

1 Place all the ingredients for the curry paste in a food processor and whizz to a paste.

2 Heat the oil in a wok, add the shrimp paste, and stir over low heat for 1–2 minutes. Add the onion and cook for a further 2 minutes; add the garlic, palm sugar, tomatoes, and curry paste. Stir for 2 minutes; add the coconut milk and stock. Bring to a boil and simmer for 4–5 minutes; season with fish sauce and lime juice.

3 Add the snapper, return to a boil, then reduce the heat and simmer for 5–6 minutes or until the fish is just cooked; it will be white and beginning to flake. Sprinkle over the cilantro and serve with steamed rice.

Prepare ahead

The curry paste will keep, covered, in the refrigerator for up to 1 week.

RABBIT FISH FLAVOR PAIRINGS:

This subtle-tasting fish is best with the Thai flavors of the curries here, or try it with Afro-Caribbean tastes of coconut, cilantro, and warming spices.

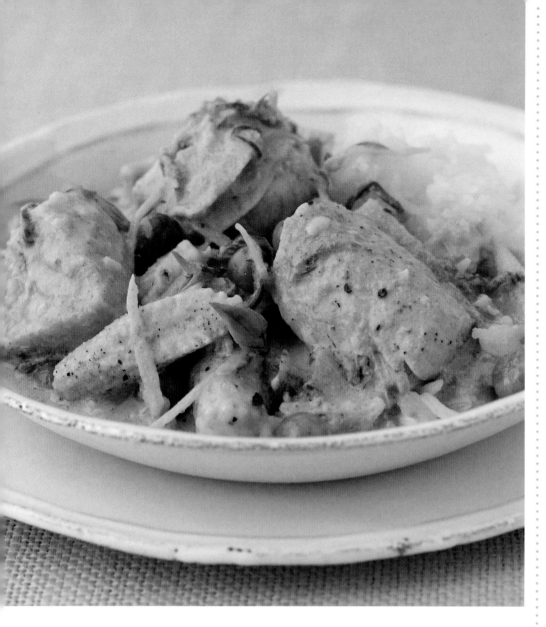

Grilled halibut curry

The addition of freshly grated coconut here gives the curry body and substance.

The fish

Halibut, or turbot or brill

• **PREP** 55 mins • **COOK** 40 mins • **SERVES** 4

Ingredients

1–2 large banana leaves, trimmed

2 cups coconut cream

2½oz (75g) Thai basil leaves

6–10 kaffir lime leaves, finely shredded

4 halibut fillets, about 6oz (175g) each, skinned

For the red curry paste

6–10 dried red chiles, soaked and chopped

a few bird's eye chiles, seeded if preferred

pinch of salt

4 tbsp chopped garlic

5 tbsp chopped shallots

4 tbsp chopped lemongrass

1 rounded tbsp chopped galangal

1 tsp chopped kaffir lime zest

1 tsp chopped cilantro root

1 tsp Thai shrimp paste

pinch of freshly ground white peppercorns

pinch of mace (optional)

For the coconut mixture

1 cup coconut cream

2½ tbsp palm or muscovado sugar

4 tbsp Thai fish sauce, or to taste

3½oz (100g) freshly grated coconut

1 Put the curry paste ingredients into a blender, and whizz, adding water to make a paste. For the coconut mixture, simmer 5 tbsp curry paste in half the coconut cream until fragrant, add the sugar, fish sauce, and grated coconut and simmer, adding the remaining coconut cream.

2 Cut the leaf into 8 pieces, 4 about 6in (14cm) wide and 4 about 8in (20cm) wide. Place each small piece on a large one, shiny sides out.

3 Along half of each inner leaf, smear a little coconut cream, then sprinkle with basil leaves. Spread on a layer of coconut mixture, a little basil, lime leaves, and coconut cream. Place the fish on top, then repeat the layering in reverse.

4 Fold the inner leaf over to cover, then wrap tightly in the outer leaf. Secure with toothpicks. Grill for up to 30 minutes. The outer leaves will char; the inner leaves are for serving.

Salmon jungle curry

Hot, fresh flavors give new life to salmon.

The fish

Salmon, or monkfish

• **PREP** 10 mins • **COOK** 20 mins • **SERVES** 4

Ingredients

2 tbsp vegetable oil

2 tbsp Thai green curry paste

3 garlic cloves, crushed

2in (5cm) fresh ginger, grated

2 hot red chiles, seeded and shredded

14oz (400g) can coconut milk

good splash of Thai fish sauce

7oz (200g) drained bamboo shoots

2 heaped tbsp pea eggplant (if available)

2½oz (75g) baby corn, halved lengthwise

14oz (400g) salmon fillets, pinboned, skinned, and cut into chunks

small handful of basil leaves (preferably Thai basil)

1 In a large frying pan, heat the oil, add the curry paste, and stir. Throw in the garlic, ginger, and chiles. Keep stirring for 2–3 minutes.

2 Now pour in the coconut milk. Bring to a boil, then add the fish sauce, bamboo shoots, pea eggplant (if using), and baby corn. Reduce the heat slightly, and simmer for 5 minutes.

3 Add the salmon and basil, and simmer for another 5–10 minutes until the fish is cooked. Season and serve with sticky Thai jasmine rice.

Prepare ahead

The curry sauce can be made 1 day ahead, covered, and refrigerated. Return to a simmer before adding the fish.

Mahi mahi curry

The rich flavor of mahi mahi works well with this tamarind and coconut milk combination.

The fish
Mahi mahi, or swordfish

- **PREP** 15 mins ▪ **COOK** 25 mins
- **SERVES** 4–6

Ingredients
2 tbsp vegetable oil

½ tsp mustard seeds

10 curry leaves

pinch of fenugreek seeds

1 large onion, chopped

1in (2.5cm) fresh ginger, sliced

½ tsp turmeric

½ tsp chili powder

1 tsp ground coriander

2 tomatoes, chopped

sea salt

1 tbsp tamarind paste

1lb 2oz (500g) mahi mahi fillet, pinboned, skinned, and cut into 1½in (4cm) pieces

¾ cup coconut milk

pinch of crushed black pepper

1 Heat the oil in a large wok. Add the mustard seeds and, when they start to pop, add the curry leaves and fenugreek seeds. Sauté for 1 minute or until the fenugreek turns golden, then add the onion and cook for 5 minutes over moderate heat, stirring occasionally.

2 Add the ginger, turmeric, chili powder, and ground coriander. Mix well, then add the tomatoes and salt to taste. Cook for 5 minutes, stirring constantly. Stir in the tamarind paste and 1¼ cups water and slowly bring to a boil. Reduce the heat, add the fish and simmer for 5–6 minutes until cooked through.

3 Reduce the heat as low as possible and pour in the coconut milk. Add the pepper. Simmer gently for 2 minutes, then remove from the heat. Serve immediately with boiled rice or potatoes.

Prepare ahead
Make the curry sauce up to just before adding the fish, cover, and refrigerate for up to 2 days. Return to a simmer before continuing.

Seafood curry

This quick curry is flavored with chiles, coconut, and lime, and is easy to make for a mid-week supper.

The fish
Any firm white fish, such as cod or haddock, and shrimp

- **PREP** 15 mins ▪ **COOK** 12 mins ▪ **SERVES** 4

Ingredients
1lb 5oz (600g) white fish, pinboned, skinned, and cut into bite-sized pieces, rinsed and patted dry

½ tsp salt and freshly ground black pepper

½ tsp turmeric

½ onion, chopped

½in (1cm) fresh ginger, chopped

1 garlic clove, crushed

2 tbsp sunflower oil

1 tsp black mustard seeds

4 green cardamom pods, crushed

2–4 dried red chiles, crushed

⅓ cup creamed coconut, dissolved in 2 cups boiling water

12 raw shrimp, peeled and deveined (see page 285)

2 tbsp fresh lime juice

cilantro leaves, to serve

lime wedges, to serve

1 Put the fish in a non-metallic bowl, sprinkle over the salt and turmeric, and turn to lightly cover. Set aside.

2 Put the onion, ginger, and garlic in a food processor or blender, and process to a paste. Heat a deep frying pan over high heat until hot. Add the oil and swirl around, then reduce the heat to medium, add the onion paste, and fry, stirring, for 3–5 minutes, or until it just begins to color. Stir in the mustard seeds, cardamom, and chiles and stir for 30 seconds.

3 Stir in the creamed coconut. Leave to bubble for 2 minutes, then reduce the heat to medium-low, add the fish and any juices in the bowl, and spoon the sauce over the fish. Simmer for 2 minutes, spooning the sauce over the fish once or twice as it cooks, taking care not to break up the pieces.

4 Add the shrimp and simmer for 2 minutes, or until they turn pink. Add the lime juice, and serve with cilantro leaves and lime wedges.

Laksa lemak

This Malaysian dish is rich with coconut.

The fish

Mahi mahi, and tiger prawns, mussels, and squid

- **PREP** 20 mins ▪ **COOK** 15 mins ▪ **SERVES** 4

Ingredients

14oz (400g) can coconut milk

1¾ cups shellfish stock

1 stalk lemongrass

4 kaffir lime leaves

1in (2.5cm) piece galangal or fresh ginger, peeled and finely sliced

1lb (450g) mahi mahi fillets, pinboned, skinned, and cut into large chunks

12 raw tiger prawns, peeled, but tails left intact, and deveined (see page 285)

1lb (450g) mussels, prepared (see page 278)

2 squid, gutted, cleaned, and cut into rings (see page 282)

12oz (350g) vermicelli, to serve

lime wedges, to serve

For the curry paste

2 tsp vegetable oil

splash of sesame oil

2 tsp palm sugar

3 garlic cloves, halved

½ bunch of scallions, roughly chopped

1 tsp shrimp paste

2 red chiles, seeded and chopped

1 large bunch of cilantro (with roots, if possible)

1 tsp cumin

1 tsp turmeric

1 tsp salt

1 Put all the ingredients for the curry paste in a food processor and whizz. Blend in half the coconut milk to make a smooth paste.

2 Heat a large wok, add the paste and cook over low heat for 1 minute. Add the remaining coconut milk and the stock, bring to a boil, and add the lemongrass, lime leaves, and galangal; simmer for 5 minutes. Add the fish, prawns, and mussels, cook for 3–4 minutes. Add the squid.

3 Meanwhile, cook the vermicelli according to package instructions. Divide between 4 bowls and ladle laksa on top. Serve with lime wedges.

Prepare ahead

The curry paste can be kept, covered, in the refrigerator for up to 1 week.

Coconut fish curry

This fantastic recipe from southern Kerala is ideal for people who prefer mild curries.

The fish

Any white fish, such as tilapia, or shellfish

- **PREP** 25 mins ▪ **COOK** 20 mins ▪ **SERVES** 6

Ingredients

2 tbsp vegetable oil

7oz (200g) shallots, chopped

10 curry leaves

1lb 2oz (500g) white fish fillets, pinboned and skinned

1 tbsp lemon juice

For the spice paste

3½oz (100g) freshly grated coconut

1 tsp ground coriander

½ tsp chili powder

large pinch of turmeric

1 To make the spice paste, put the coconut, ground coriander, chili powder, and turmeric in a blender. Pour in ¾ cup of water and process to make a smooth paste.

2 Heat the oil in a large frying pan or wok. Add the shallots and curry leaves and cook over medium-low heat for 5 minutes or until the shallots are soft. Stir in the spice paste with 1¼ cups of water and bring to a boil. Cook for about 5 minutes, stirring occasionally, until the sauce has thickened.

3 Cut the fish into 1in (2.5cm) pieces and add to the sauce. Pour in the lemon juice and mix carefully. Cook gently for 4–5 minutes or until cooked through. Remove from the heat and serve with boiled rice or Indian bread.

Prepare ahead

The curry base can be made, covered, and refrigerated for 2–3 days. The flavors will deepen. Reheat gently before continuing with step 3.

TILAPIA FLAVOR PAIRINGS: The sweet, distinctive taste of this fish pairs well with Thai ingredients; try it with bird's eye chiles, kaffir lime, nam pla, shrimp paste, and galangal.

Fish head curry

Fish heads are inexpensive and contain the delicacy of the "pearl" or cheek.

The fish
Salmon, cod, or snapper heads

- **PREP** 15 mins - **COOK** 30 mins - **SERVES** 4

Ingredients
14oz (400g) can coconut milk
2 tbsp vegetable oil
1 onion, finely sliced
10 cardamom pods, split
1in (2.5cm) piece of galangal or fresh ginger, thinly sliced
4 tomatoes, seeded and chopped
1 tbsp tamarind paste
2 cups fish stock
4 large fish heads, gills removed, and washed well
salt and freshly ground black pepper
3 tbsp chopped cilantro

For the paste
1 tbsp chopped macadamia nuts
1 garlic clove, chopped
½ bunch scallions
1 tsp shrimp paste
3 red chiles (more if you like it hot)
1 tsp turmeric
1 tsp ground cumin
2 tsp garam masala
pinch of salt

1 Prepare the paste: put the ingredients into a food processor and finely chop. Add 3 tbsp coconut milk and blend to a smooth paste.

2 Heat the vegetable oil in a large flameproof casserole, add the onion, and cook over medium heat for 8–10 minutes until slightly golden. Add the paste, cardamom, galangal, and tomatoes, and cook for 3–4 minutes. Add the tamarind paste, remaining coconut milk, and stock, bring to a boil, then reduce the heat to a simmer.

3 Add the fish heads, cover, and poach for 12–15 minutes, turning halfway, or until the heads are beginning to break up. Transfer to a serving dish. Bring the cooking liquid to a boil, adjust the seasoning, and stir in the cilantro. Pour over the heads to serve.

Prepare ahead
The paste can be made up to 1 day ahead, covered, and chilled until needed.

Goan curry

Red hot with chile, although this can be tempered to personal taste.

The fish
Snapper, or pomfret or catfish

- **PREP** 10–15 mins - **COOK** 30 mins
- **SERVES** 6

Ingredients
2¼lb (1kg) snapper, scaled and filleted
2 tbsp coriander seeds
1 tsp cumin seeds
6–8 dried red chiles, to taste
3 garlic cloves, chopped
1 tbsp grated fresh ginger
½ tsp turmeric
½ tsp salt
2 x 14oz (400g) cans coconut milk
2 tbsp peanut oil
1 large onion, thinly sliced
2 large tomatoes, seeded and chopped
1–2 green chiles, seeded and chopped
2 tbsp tamarind paste
salt and freshly ground black pepper
lime juice, or a handful of chopped cilantro

1 Pinbone the snapper fillets and cut them into 3, cover, and refrigerate until required.

2 Put the coriander and cumin seeds in a saucepan; stir over medium heat until they begin to pop. Remove and cool. Put the seeds, dried chiles, garlic, ginger, turmeric, and salt into a food processor. Process until well chopped. Add 4–5 tbsp of the coconut milk and pulse to blend.

3 Heat the oil in a large saucepan, add the onion, and cook over low heat for 12–15 minutes, until turning golden brown. Add the tomatoes, green chiles, and spice paste and cook over medium heat for 2–3 minutes until very aromatic. Add the remaining coconut milk, bring to a boil, and simmer for 5–7 minutes. Add the tamarind paste and season.

4 Add the snapper, reduce the heat, and cook for 4–6 minutes or until opaque and firm.

5 Adjust the seasoning and add the lime juice or chopped cilantro. Serve with steamed rice.

Prepare ahead
Prepare the spicy sauce up to the end of step 3, cool, cover, and chill for up to 1 day. The flavors will deepen. Return to a simmer before continuing.

BLACK POMFRET FLAVOR PAIRINGS:
This firm, sweet fish is a natural ingredient in curry, or try it with Middle Eastern tastes such as couscous, orange, plenty of cilantro, or chermoula.

Squid curry

In Sri Lanka, fishermen cook freshly caught squid onboard with spices.

The fish
Squid, or cuttlefish or octopus

- **PREP** 15 mins • **COOK** 30–35 mins
- **SERVES** 4

Ingredients
3 tbsp vegetable oil

½ tsp mustard seeds

2 large onions, sliced

3 green chiles, slit lengthwise

1in (2.5cm) fresh ginger, finely sliced

½ tsp chili powder

½ tsp ground coriander

2 large tomatoes, sliced

14oz (400g) squid, gutted, cleaned, and cut into rings, with tentacles (see page 282)

1 tbsp chopped cilantro leaves, to serve

1 Heat the oil in a large frying pan and add the mustard seeds. When they pop, add the onions and cook for 5 minutes, or until golden.

2 Stir in the green chiles and ginger, then the chili powder and ground coriander. Mix well and add the tomatoes. Cook over moderate heat for 5–10 minutes or until the tomatoes break down to give a thick sauce.

3 Add the squid, and mix thoroughly. Cover and cook over low heat for 15 minutes, stirring occasionally to prevent sticking. If the dish becomes dry, stir in a little water.

4 Serve hot, sprinkled with the cilantro, with paratha or chapatti, or any flavored rice.

Prepare ahead
Make the sauce to the end of step 2, cover, and refrigerate for 2 days. The flavors will deepen. Return to a simmer before adding the squid.

Steamed scallop curry

In Thailand, this is steamed in banana leaves.

The fish
Any white fish, such as turbot, and scallops

- **PREP** 35–40 mins • **COOK** 20–25 mins
- **SERVES** 4

Ingredients
1¾oz (50g) white fish fillets, pinboned and skinned

½ cup coconut cream

1½–3 tbsp Thai fish sauce

pinch of sugar (optional)

1 medium egg

5 kaffir lime leaves, very finely shredded

4 scallops, roe removed, each cut into 3 slices

4 scallop shells, boiled in heavily salted water for several minutes to clean

handful of basil leaves (preferably Thai basil)

1 bai yor leaf, very finely shredded (optional)

few pieces of red chile, shredded, to serve

few cilantro leaves, to serve

For the thickened coconut cream
good pinch of rice flour

5 tbsp coconut cream

pinch of salt (optional)

For the red curry paste
6–8 dried red chiles, soaked and chopped

pinch of salt

2½ tbsp chopped garlic

4 tbsp chopped shallots

4 tbsp chopped lemongrass

1 rounded tbsp chopped galangal

1 tsp chopped kaffir lime zest

1 tsp chopped cilantro root

2 tsp Thai shrimp paste

pinch of freshly ground white peppercorns

1 Put the curry paste ingredients in a blender, and whizz with enough water to make a paste.

2 Purée the fish in a blender, then stir in 4 tbsp curry paste, and the coconut cream. Season with fish sauce and sugar (if using). Add the egg. Stir in most of the lime leaves and the scallops.

3 Generously line the scallop shells with the basil and bai yor (if using). Spoon in the scallop curry mixture. Steam gently for about 15 minutes. When the "mousse" is slightly firm, it is cooked. Do not overcook or it will split.

4 Meanwhile, mix the rice flour with 1 tbsp of the coconut cream. Bring the remaining coconut cream to a boil, then stir in the rice flour mixture. Season with salt, if liked. Spoon the thickened coconut cream over the curry and garnish with the reserved lime leaves, the red chile, and cilantro leaves.

Prepare ahead
The curry paste can be prepared up to 3 days ahead, covered well, and refrigerated. The flavors will deepen.

Prawn dhansak

Increase the number of chiles if you like your curry really spicy. The amount here will give a moderate heat.

The fish
Tiger prawns

- **PREP** 15 mins ▪ **COOK** 30 mins ▪ **SERVES** 8

Ingredients
12oz (350g) red lentils

salt and freshly ground black pepper

2 tbsp vegetable oil, or 1 tbsp ghee

6 cardamom pods, crushed

3 tsp mustard seeds

2 tsp medium chili powder

2 tsp turmeric

2 tsp ground cinnamon

2 onions, finely chopped

4in (10cm) fresh ginger, finely chopped

4 garlic cloves, grated or finely chopped

3–4 green chiles, seeded and finely sliced

1½lb (675g) raw tiger prawns, peeled and deveined (see page 285)

1 pineapple, peeled and cut into bite-sized pieces

8 tomatoes, skinned, seeded, and roughly chopped (see page 112)

handful of fresh cilantro, finely chopped

1 Put the lentils in a large, heavy-based pan, season, then cover with cold water. Bring to a boil, reduce the heat to a simmer, and cook for 20 minutes, or until tender. Drain and set aside.

2 Meanwhile, heat half the oil or ghee in a large, heavy-based frying pan, add the dried spices, and cook, stirring, until the seeds pop. Stir in the onions, ginger, garlic, and chiles, and cook for 5 minutes, or until soft and fragrant.

3 Add the remaining oil or ghee to the pan, then add the prawns. Increase the heat and cook, stirring occasionally, for 6–8 minutes. Stir in the pineapple, lentils, and tomatoes and a little hot water so the mixture is slightly sloppy, and simmer for 5 minutes. Season, stir in the cilantro, and serve.

Prepare ahead
The curry can be prepared to the end of step 2, covered, and refrigerated for up to 3 days. Reheat gently before continuing.

Green curry of shrimp with eggplant and basil

A delicious, thin curry from Thailand.

The fish
Shrimp, or scallops, or any firm white fish

- **PREP** 15 mins ▪ **COOK** 20 mins ▪ **SERVES** 4

Ingredients
5 tbsp coconut cream

1½–3 tbsp Thai fish sauce, to taste

1 cup coconut milk, or chicken or shrimp stock

3 small eggplants, stalk removed, cut into sixths just before cooking

3½oz (100g) pea aubergines, optional

8–12 large, raw shrimp, deveined (see page 285)

3–4 kaffir lime leaves, torn

3 green chiles, seeded and thinly sliced

handful of basil leaves (preferably Thai basil)

1 rounded tbsp shredded fresh ginger

For the curry paste
1 heaped tbsp bird's eye chiles, seeded if preferred

pinch of salt

1 rounded tbsp chopped galangal

2½ tbsp chopped lemongrass

1 tsp grated kaffir lime zest

2 tsp chopped cilantro root

1 tsp turmeric

1 rounded tbsp chopped fresh ginger

2½ tbsp chopped shallots

2½ tbsp chopped garlic

1 tsp Thai shrimp paste

1 tsp white peppercorns

1 tsp roasted cilantro seeds

few blades of mace, roasted (optional)

1 Put the ingredients for the curry paste in a blender and whizz; adding just enough water to make a paste.

2 Heat the coconut cream, add 2½ tbsp of the curry paste, and fry over high heat for about 5 minutes, stirring, until fragrant and oily.

3 Season with fish sauce, then add the coconut milk or stock. Bring to a boil, then add all the eggplant. Simmer for 10–12 minutes, then add the shrimp. Simmer for 3–4 minutes until they are cooked.

4 Add all the remaining ingredients, then allow to rest for a minute or so before serving. The curry should have a dappling of separated coconut cream floating on top.

Prepare ahead
The curry paste can be made 3 days in advance. Cover well, and refrigerate. The flavors will deepen.

Green shrimp curry with fresh dill

Dill mellows the intense flavor of lime leaves.

The fish

Shrimp, or scallops, or sea bass

- **PREP** 30 mins **COOK** 30 mins **SERVES** 4

Ingredients

3 tbsp vegetable oil

5 tbsp Thai green curry paste

1 tbsp shrimp paste

1 tbsp palm or granulated sugar

2 cups coconut milk

2 cups chicken or vegetable stock

4–6 kaffir lime leaves, bruised

Thai fish sauce, to taste

2 large waxy potatoes, peeled, and cut
into 1in (2.5cm) pieces

1½lb (675g) raw shrimp, peeled and deveined
(see page 285)

1 bunch of dill

1 Heat the oil in a pan over medium-high heat
and stir-fry the curry paste for about 2 minutes
or until fragrant. Add the shrimp paste and
sugar, and stir-fry for 1 minute.

2 Reduce the heat and add the coconut milk,
stock, kaffir lime leaves, and fish sauce. Add
the potatoes, cover, and cook for 20 minutes.

3 Add the shrimp and stir well, then cover
again and cook for about 5 minutes, or until
they turn pink. Sprinkle with dill fronds.

4 You can choose to eat this hot, but in Laos
it would be eaten at room temperature with
steamed sticky rice on the side: with your
fingers, pinch and shape a small amount of
rice into a ball and dip into the curry, eating
shrimp along with dill in the same bite.

Prepare ahead

Make the curry base to the end of step 2 up
to 2 days ahead, cover, and refrigerate. Reheat
gently before continuing.

Chile crab

The best way to enjoy this dish is to dress for a
mess: cover yourself with a napkin, roll up your
sleeves, and tuck in. Prepare bowls of warm
water with slices of lemon to rinse fingers.

The fish

Crab, or freshwater crawfish or rock lobster

- **PREP** 10 mins **COOK** 20 mins **SERVES** 4

Ingredients

8 raw, small, blue crabs, or other small crabs,
weighing about 8oz (225g) each

2 tbsp sunflower oil

2 tsp coriander seeds

2 tsp mustard seeds

1 large onion, finely chopped

4 bird's eye chiles, seeded if you like,
and finely chopped

4 garlic cloves, chopped

2 tbsp grated fresh ginger

1 tsp turmeric

2 tbsp palm or dark brown sugar

1 bunch of scallions, finely sliced

3 tbsp tamarind paste

1 tsp cornstarch

⅔ cup shellfish stock

chopped cilantro, to serve

1 Clean the crab if necessary (see page 286).
Cook the crabs in a large pot of boiling water
for 5 minutes (they may need to be cooked in
2 batches). Cut in half and crack the claws.

2 Heat the oil in a large saucepan, add the
coriander and mustard seeds, and cook over
medium heat until they pop. Add the onion
and cook for 3–4 minutes or until translucent.

3 Add the chiles, garlic, ginger, turmeric, and
sugar, and stir for 2–3 minutes or until aromatic.
Add in the scallions and cook for 1 minute.

4 Mix the tamarind paste, cornstarch, and stock
together and blend into the chile and seed
mixture. Bring to a boil, return the crab, and
sprinkle with cilantro to serve.

Prepare ahead

The sauce for this dish can be made 2 days
ahead, covered, and refrigerated. The flavors
will deepen. Gently reheat, and cook and cut
up the crabs when ready to eat.

Crab and mango curry

This delectable curry from the Maldives marries tropical fruit with spices and seafood.

The fish

Crab claws, or shrimp

- **PREP** 15–20 mins **COOK** 25–30 mins
- **SERVES** 4

Ingredients

juice of 1 lime

¼ tsp ground turmeric

¾ tsp cracked black peppercorns

8 raw crab claws

1 firm, slightly under-ripe mango, cut into ¾in (2cm) cubes

1 tbsp palm or dark brown sugar

For the masala

4 tbsp vegetable oil

¾ tsp mustard seeds

2 sprigs of curry leaves (about 2 tbsp leaves)

1½in (4cm) cinnamon stick

1 large onion, sliced

2 red chiles, seeded and chopped

3 garlic cloves, grated or finely chopped

¾in (2cm) piece of fresh ginger, finely chopped

½ tsp ground cumin

½ tsp chili powder

1 tsp fennel seeds, roasted and ground

4 large plum tomatoes, peeled and finely chopped (see page 112)

1 Mix the lime juice, turmeric, and peppercorns. Coat the crab claws in this mixture and set aside.

2 Heat the oil in a wok and add the mustard seeds; they should pop. Toss in the curry leaves and cinnamon. After 30 seconds, add the onion. Reduce the heat, cover, and soften for 5 minutes.

3 Stir in the chiles, garlic, and ginger and cook for 1 minute. Add the cumin, chili powder, and ground fennel. Stir, then add in the tomatoes. Fry until the tomatoes have cooked down.

4 Add the crab claws with the spiced juice, stir, then add the mango and sugar. Fry for 10 minutes over high heat until the crab claws are cooked. You'll need a small hammer or pair of crackers to break the crab shells; it's messy, but great fun. Serve with flatbreads or rice.

Prepare ahead

Make the spiced tomato sauce 2 days in advance. Cover, and refrigerate.

Prawn balti

More common in the UK than in Pakistan, baltis are a hit with curry aficionados.

The fish

Tiger prawns, or sea bass, sea bream, scallops, or monkfish

- **PREP** 20–25 mins **COOK** 15–20 mins
- **SERVES** 4

Ingredients

1lb 2oz (500g) raw tiger prawns, peeled, but tails left intact, and deveined (see page 285)

juice of 1 lime

1½ tsp paprika

For the masala

3 tbsp vegetable oil

1 red onion, diced

1½in (4cm) piece fresh ginger, finely shredded

2 garlic cloves, grated or finely chopped

2 green chiles, shredded

1 red bell pepper, seeded and shredded

half a 14oz (400g) can chopped tomatoes

¼ tsp turmeric

¼–½ tsp chili powder

¼ tsp ground cinnamon

½ tsp garam masala

½ tsp ground coriander

½ tsp sugar

2 tbsp coarsely chopped cilantro leaves

1 Put the prawns in a bowl, squeeze over the lime juice and stir in the paprika. Set aside.

2 Heat the oil in a wok over moderate heat and fry the onion until just beginning to turn golden. Add most of the ginger, the garlic, chiles, and red bell pepper. Fry for 1 minute.

3 Increase the heat and add the tomatoes, turmeric, chili powder, cinnamon, garam masala, ground coriander, and sugar. Cook briskly until the tomatoes have thickened. Pour in ⅔ cup of hot water, stir well and reduce the heat to low. Add the prawns, with any lime juice, and simmer until they turn pink.

4 Sprinkle with chopped cilantro and the remaining shredded ginger before serving.

Prepare ahead

The masala can be made up to 2 days ahead, covered, and refrigerated. The flavors will deepen. Return to a simmer before continuing.

Pan-fried and Deep-fried

Pan-fried mackerel in rolled oats

The lemon wedges and the hot, sinus-clearing mustard make this dish a cold-weather winner.

The fish

Mackerel, or herring or sprats

- **PREP** 15–20 mins - **COOK** 15 mins
- **SERVES** 6

Ingredients

2 eggs

1oz (30g) all-purpose flour

6oz (175g) rolled oats

salt and freshly ground black pepper

6 large mackerel fillets, pinboned and skinned

¼ cup vegetable oil, plus more if needed

lemon wedges, to serve

watercress sprigs, to serve

For the mustard sauce

4 tbsp butter

2 tbsp all-purpose flour

juice of ½ lemon

1 tbsp Dijon mustard, or to taste

1 Beat the eggs in a dish and sift the flour into a bowl. Combine the rolled oats and salt and pepper in another bowl. Turn each fish fillet in the flour, dip in the egg, then coat in oats.

2 For the sauce, melt a third of the butter. Add the flour and whisk until foaming. Whisk in 1 cup of boiling water. Return to the heat and whisk for 1 minute. Remove from the heat, add the remaining butter, and whisk. Add the lemon juice and mustard, and season.

3 Line a baking sheet with paper towels. Heat the oil in a large frying pan. Add half the fish and cook for 2–3 minutes on each side, until crisp and golden. Transfer to the baking sheet and keep warm while you cook the remaining fish. Serve with lemon wedges, watercress, and the sauce.

Shallow-fried masala sardines

These curried fish have a lovely spicy flavor.

The fish

Sardines, or herring or small mackerel

- **PREP** 10–15 mins, plus marinating
- **COOK** 20 mins - **SERVES** 2–4

Ingredients

4 sardines, about 10oz (300g) in total, scaled and gutted

5 tbsp vegetable oil

1 small onion, finely sliced

small handful of chopped cilantro leaves, to serve

lemon wedges, to serve

For the spice paste

1 onion, chopped

2 green chiles, chopped, seeded if liked

½in (1cm) fresh ginger, finely chopped

10 curry leaves

10 black peppercorns

½ tsp chili powder

½ tsp turmeric

2 tbsp wine or cider vinegar

1 tsp lemon juice

salt

1 Place all the ingredients for the spice paste in a blender. Process to make a paste. Set aside.

2 Wash the fish, then pat dry. With a very sharp knife, make slashes about 1in (2.5cm) apart along the fish, on both sides. Place on a baking tray and spread the spice paste all over, and into the cuts. Leave for 15–20 minutes.

3 Heat 2 tbsp of the oil in a large frying pan. Add the onion and cook for 5–6 minutes over very high heat until well browned and crisp. Remove and drain on paper towels.

4 Heat the remaining oil in the same pan over low heat. Place in the fish, cover, and cook for 6 minutes on each side. Lift on to a serving dish. Sprinkle the onions over and serve with cilantro and lemon wedges.

Prepare ahead

Make the spice paste 3 days ahead, cover well, and refrigerate until needed.

Crisp salmon with cilantro pesto

Lightly cooked, fresh, and fragrant, this is a wonderful way to eat salmon.

The fish
Salmon, or sea bass, tuna, swordfish, or skate

- **PREP** 5–10 mins ▪ **COOK** 10–15 mins
- **SERVES** 4

Ingredients
4 salmon fillets, about 6oz (175g) each, with skin, scaled and pinboned

3 tbsp vegetable oil

2 tsp sea salt

lemon wedges, to serve

cilantro leaves, to serve

For the pesto
leaves from 1 large bunch of cilantro

2–3 garlic cloves

2 tbsp pine nuts

$\frac{1}{4}$ cup olive oil

1oz (30g) Parmesan cheese, finely grated

salt and freshly ground black pepper

1 To make the pesto, put the cilantro in a food processor with the garlic, pine nuts, and 2 tbsp olive oil. With the blade turning, slowly pour in the remaining oil in a steady stream. Stir in the Parmesan, season to taste, put into a bowl, and cover.

2 Brush the skin side of each salmon fillet with a little vegetable oil. Heat the remaining oil in a frying pan until hot. Add the salmon, skin side down. Cook over medium heat until the skin is crispy. Increase the heat to high, turn and brown the sides and top of each fillet very quickly. The top should remain slightly soft, showing it is rare.

3 Put the salmon on warmed plates, sprinkle with sea salt and spoon on some pesto. Serve with the lemon wedges and cilantro leaves.

Prepare ahead
The pesto keeps for 2 days in the refrigerator, if the surface is covered with a thin layer of oil to keep it from the air. (If it is not, the cilantro will discolor, and the pesto begin to stale.)

Saltimbocca of salmon

Slices of salmon are marinated, then wrapped around smoked salmon.

The fish
Salmon, monkfish, or tuna, and smoked salmon

- **PREP** 20–25 mins, plus marinating
- **COOK** 1–2 mins ▪ **SERVES** 4–6

Ingredients
$2\frac{1}{4}$lb (1kg) salmon fillet, with skin, pinboned

9oz (250g) smoked salmon slices

leaves from 5–7 sprigs of basil

3 tbsp butter

For the marinade
juice of $\frac{1}{2}$ lemon

$\frac{3}{4}$ cup olive oil

leaves from 3–4 sprigs of thyme

2 bay leaves, crushed

For the tomato-basil garnish
4 tomatoes, skinned, seeded, and chopped (see page 112)

2 tbsp olive oil

leaves from a small bunch of basil, chopped

salt and freshly ground pepper

pinch of sugar

1 With the tail of the salmon fillet facing away from you and working toward it, use a filleting knife to cut 12 diagonal slices, as thin and even as possible. Leave the skin behind.

2 For the marinade, put the lemon juice and oil in a shallow dish with the thyme and bay leaves. Add the salmon slices, cover, and refrigerate for 1 hour.

3 Mix the tomatoes for the garnish with the oil and basil and season, adding sugar to taste. Let stand at room temperature for 30–60 minutes.

4 Lift the salmon from the marinade and pat dry. Cut the smoked salmon slices into pieces the same size as the fresh salmon. Arrange a piece of smoked salmon on top of each fresh salmon slice. Put a basil leaf on top. Roll up as you would a Swiss roll, starting from a long side, and secure with a toothpick.

5 Heat the butter in a frying pan and add the salmon, leaving space around each piece. Cook over high heat, turning, for 1–2 minutes. Remove the toothpicks and serve with the tomato-basil garnish.

Prepare ahead
The marinade and tomato garnish can both be made, covered, and refrigerated 6 hours ahead. Bring to room temperature before continuing.

Vietnamese crispy fish

This classic dish needs plenty of chile for an intense heat that is tempered by palm sugar.

The fish
Snapper, or red mullet

- **PREP** 10–15 mins   **COOK** 15 mins
- **SERVES** 2

Ingredients
2 snapper, about 1lb (450g) each, scaled, gutted, and trimmed, and heads removed

salt

4 tbsp vegetable oil

3 garlic cloves, chopped

6 tomatoes, seeded and roughly chopped

2 red chiles (preferably bird's eye), seeded and finely sliced

1 tbsp palm sugar

2 tbsp nam pla

1 tsp cornstarch

2 scallions, chopped

2 tbsp roughly chopped cilantro

1 Slash the fish on each side and season with salt. Heat half the oil in a large frying pan, add the fish, and fry on each side for 6–8 minutes, or until cooked.

2 Heat the remaining oil in a large pan, add the garlic, tomatoes, and chiles, and cook over high heat until the tomatoes have softened. Add the palm sugar, nam pla, and 6 tbsp water, and cook for a minute or two, or until the mixture is reduced and sticky. Stir in the cornstarch, scallions, and cilantro, and cook for another minute.

3 Lift the fish on to a plate and spoon the sweet, sticky sauce over the top. Serve with rice.

Prepare ahead
The sticky sauce—made in step 2—can be made up to 3 days ahead, covered, and refrigerated. Reheat gently before continuing. It may need a little more water, so adjust the consistency until it is as you prefer.

Shallow-fried red mullet

Pan-frying makes the most of the delicate sweetness of red mullet.

The fish
Red mullet, or gray mullet or sea bream

- **PREP** 5 mins   **COOK** 5 mins   **SERVES** 4

Ingredients
4 red mullet, about 1lb (450g) each, scaled, gutted, and trimmed, and heads removed

sea salt and freshly ground black pepper

cornmeal or polenta, for coating

grapeseed or vegetable oil, for frying

lemon juice, to serve

1 Season the fish, then coat them on both sides with cornmeal or polenta, shaking off any excess. Set a non-stick or cast-iron frying pan over moderately high heat and add enough oil to coat the bottom of the pan.

2 Put the prepared fish into the hot oil, presentation-side (the side that will be uppermost when serving) down. Shallow-fry for 2 minutes, or until the fish is golden brown.

3 Carefully turn the fish using tongs and cook until the other side is golden brown. To test if it is cooked, insert a thin-bladed knife into the center of the fish, then touch the knife tip to your thumb. If it is warm, the fish is ready. Drain briefly on paper towels and sprinkle with lemon juice. Serve with sprigs of watercress.

RED SPOT EMPEROR BREAM FLAVOR PAIRINGS: Try this with tomatoes, garlic, olive oil, marjoram, fennel, and thyme, or with spicier red chile, fish sauce, cumin, and cilantro.

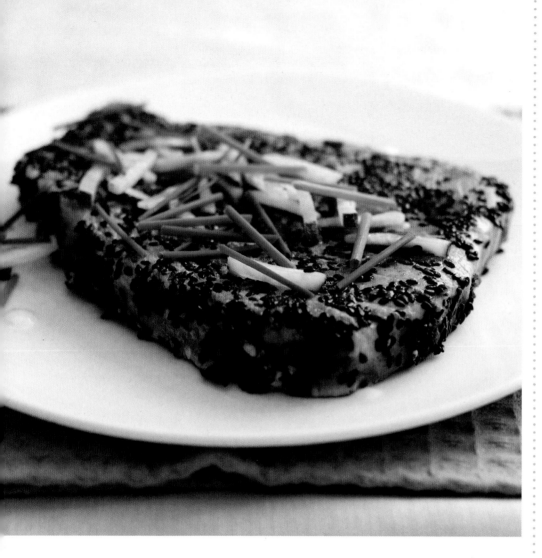

Seared tuna with a black sesame seed crust

A dramatic looking dish, the nutty sesame is a great foil to the juicy tuna.

The fish
Tuna, or swordfish, marlin, or salmon

- **PREP** 10 mins, plus marinating
- **COOK** 1 min **SERVES** 4

Ingredients
¼ cup olive oil, plus extra for searing

1 garlic clove, grated or finely chopped

1 small hot red chile, finely chopped

2 tbsp black sesame seeds, plus extra for sprinkling (optional)

salt

2 tuna steaks, about 10oz (300g) each, halved lengthwise

2 radishes

juice of 1 lemon

½ bunch of chives, chopped into 2in (5cm) lengths

1 Mix the oil, garlic, chile, sesame seeds, and a sprinkling of salt on a large flat dish. Rinse the tuna, and pat dry with paper towels. Carefully press them into the sesame seeds so that they stick. Turn, and coat the other side. Cover, and marinate in the refrigerator for at least 1 hour.

2 Meanwhile, cut the radishes into matchsticks, and put them in a bowl with half the lemon juice, to prevent browning.

3 Heat a little extra oil in a frying pan over high heat. Sear the tuna for 20 seconds on each side. Leave to rest for 5 minutes.

4 Put half a tuna steak on each of 4 serving plates, and drizzle with the remaining lemon juice. Drain the radishes, and scatter over with the chives and extra sesame seeds (if using).

Variation
Black sesame tuna salad
Double the quantities and serve this as a main course with a salad of fresh orange segments, finely sliced cucumber, and sprigs of dill or mint, as well as the radish.

Seared tuna with cucumber and fennel

This tuna is served very rare, so it is essential that it is bought as fresh as possible.

The fish
Tuna, or swordfish or marlin

- **PREP** 15 mins, plus cooling **COOK** 6 mins
- **SERVES** 4

Ingredients
6 tbsp olive oil, plus extra for brushing

4 tuna steaks, about 5½oz (150g) each

salt and freshly ground black pepper

1 fennel bulb, sliced

2 shallots, finely chopped

1 cucumber, seeded, peeled, and finely chopped

2 tbsp mint, basil, and chervil leaves, torn

juice of 1 lemon

8 anchovy fillets in olive oil, drained

lemon wedges, to serve

1 Rub 2 tbsp of oil over the tuna and sprinkle with plenty of pepper. Set aside.

2 Heat 2 tbsp of oil and sauté the fennel for 4–5 minutes until just tender. Season. Put the fennel into a large bowl and set aside to cool a little.

3 Add the shallots, cucumber, and herbs to the fennel. Stir in the lemon juice and remaining oil.

4 Heat a heavy frying pan or grill pan until smoking. Lightly brush the tuna steaks with oil, then pan-fry for 30 seconds. Brush with a little more oil, turn, and cook for a further 30 seconds.

5 Place a tuna steak on each plate, with the fennel salad piled on top, and 2 anchovy fillets draped over. Serve with lemon wedges and warm parsley-buttered new potatoes.

Prepare ahead
Sauté the fennel up to 1 day ahead, cover, and chill. Bring to room temperature before continuing with the recipe.

Fish sticks with chunky tartar sauce

You can bake these for 8 minutes at 400°F (200°C) instead of frying, if you prefer. Children love them, too.

The fish

Any firm white fish, such as haddock, cod, or pollock

- **PREP** 15 mins ▪ **COOK** 7 mins ▪ **SERVES** 4

Ingredients

4oz (115g) fresh breadcrumbs

1½lb (675g) thick white fish fillets (loin works best), pinboned and skinned

1–2 tbsp all-purpose flour

1 egg, lightly beaten

¼ cup Parmesan cheese, finely grated

salt and freshly ground black pepper

1 tbsp vegetable oil

3 tbsp tartar sauce

1 tsp capers, rinsed, drained, and chopped

3 pickles, drained and finely chopped

1 Spread the breadcrumbs on a baking tray, and toast in the oven for about 5 minutes, or until golden. Put them into a food processor, and whizz until fine.

2 Cut the fish fillets into thick, even strips about 1in (2.5cm) wide; you should end up with about 20 "sticks".

3 Put the flour and egg on to separate plates. Mix the breadcrumbs with the Parmesan, and season. Dredge the fish in the flour, then dip in the egg. Finally, press each into the breadcrumb mixture on all sides.

4 Heat the oil in a large frying pan over medium heat. Add the fish sticks, in batches so as not to crowd the pan, and fry for 3–4 minutes. Turn and fry for 2–3 minutes. When cooked, they should flake under the gentle pressure of a finger. Remove, drain on paper towels, and keep warm while you fry the rest.

5 Put the tartar sauce into a bowl, and stir in the capers and pickles. Serve with the hot fish sticks.

Prepare ahead

These can be frozen before frying if the fish has not been previously frozen. Freeze on a baking sheet to keep separate then, when frozen solid, put into a plastic freezer bag to store. Defrost before frying the fish sticks.

Spiced haddock with coconut, chile, and lime

An unusual and delicious midweek supper dish for a cold night.

The fish

Haddock, or salmon, cod, pollock, saithe, or whiting

- **PREP** 10 mins ▪ **COOK** 20 mins ▪ **SERVES** 4

Ingredients

4 haddock fillets, about 1½lb (675g) in total

salt and freshly ground black pepper

14oz (400ml) can coconut milk

1 medium-hot red chile, seeded and finely chopped

juice of 1 lime

splash of Thai fish sauce

pinch of sugar (optional)

5½oz (150g) green beans, trimmed

1 tbsp peanut or sunflower oil

For the spice mixture

1–2 tsp cayenne pepper, to taste

1 tsp paprika

1 tsp ground cinnamon

1 tsp ground coriander

1 tbsp cornstarch

1 To make the spice mixture, mix together the spices and cornstarch in a bowl. Season the haddock fillets, then coat well with the spice mixture. Set aside.

2 Pour the coconut milk into a wide pan, add the chile, and bring to a boil. Reduce the heat to a simmer, then add the lime juice, fish sauce, and sugar (if using). Throw in the green beans, and simmer for about 5 minutes.

3 Meanwhile, heat the oil in a nonstick frying pan over high heat. Add the fish, and fry for about 5 minutes on each side until golden.

4 Either add the fish to the sauce, or serve the sauce on the side.

Pan-fried trout with almonds

This all-time classic is served across Europe. Almonds are typically used, but hazelnuts work equally well.

The fish
Trout, or mackerel

■ **PREP** 10 mins ■ **COOK** 15 mins ■ **SERVES** 2

Ingredients
2 small trout, scaled, gutted, and gilled
2 tbsp seasoned flour (see page 55)
2–3 tbsp vegetable oil
lemon wedges, to serve

For the almond beurre noisette
3 tbsp unsalted butter
1¾oz (50g) blanched almonds, chopped
1 tbsp chopped flat-leaf parsley
juice of 1 lemon

1 Wash the trout and be sure the bloodline has been removed completely (see page 266). The head is traditionally left on, as the eye indicates if the fish is cooked (it turns white) and the cheek or "pearl" is the best morsel.

2 Dry the trout well and roll in the seasoned flour. Heat the oil in a large frying pan, add the trout, and cook over low heat for 4–5 minutes. Turn with tongs or a spatula and cook on the second side for 3–4 minutes or until the fish is cooked. Avoid the temptation to keep turning the fish, as it will begin to break up. Transfer to a warmed serving dish and set aside.

3 Wipe out the frying pan, add the butter, heat until hot and foaming, then add the almonds. Cook, stirring, until toasted and golden brown (too dark and they will taste bitter).

4 As soon as the almonds are the right color, add the parsley and lemon juice. Standing back, as it will splatter, swirl the pan, and, while sizzling, pour over the trout. Serve with lemon wedges.

Balinese spicy mackerel

Typical of the cuisine of Indonesia this recipe uses kecap manis, soy sauce, and molasses.

The fish
Mackerel, or salmon, catfish, or cod

■ **PREP** 10 mins, plus chilling ■ **COOK** 15 mins
■ **SERVES** 4

Ingredients
4 small mackerel, skin on, filleted and pinboned
juice and grated zest of 2 limes
½ tsp ground turmeric or 2 tsp freshly grated turmeric
½ tsp salt
3 tbsp vegetable oil
1 stalk lemongrass, split into 4
3 tbsp kecap manis

For the chile paste
3 red chiles, seeded (optional) and finely chopped
6 shallots, chopped
2 garlic cloves, crushed
5 roasted candlenuts or macadamia nuts
1 tbsp grated fresh ginger
1 tbsp tamarind paste
½ tsp superfine sugar
salt and freshly ground black pepper

1 Cut the mackerel fillets in half lengthwise. Sprinkle with the lime juice, turmeric, and salt, cover, and refrigerate for 15–30 minutes.

2 Put the chiles, shallots, garlic, nuts, ginger, tamarind, and sugar into a small food processor, and process to chop very finely. Season lightly.

3 Pat the mackerel dry with paper towels. Heat the oil in a large frying pan or wok. Cook the mackerel skin side down, a few pieces at a time, until firm, opaque, and brown. Avoid stirring to prevent the fish from breaking up. Remove from the pan.

4 Add the spice paste to the pan and cook over medium heat until fragrant. Add ½ cup of water and the lemongrass, bring to a boil, and simmer for 2–3 minutes. Return the fish and add the kecap manis, stir over low heat until all ingredients are combined and the sauce is reduced and bubbling. Serve with rice and garnish with lime wedges and cilantro.

Prepare ahead
You can make the chile paste up to 1 day ahead, cover, and store in the refrigerator.

MACKEREL FLAVOR PAIRINGS:
Oil-rich mackerel takes well to the Asian tastes of chile, shoyu, sesame seeds, mirin, rice vinegar, daikon, cucumber, and cilantro, or to Mediterranean basil, olive oil, and garlic.

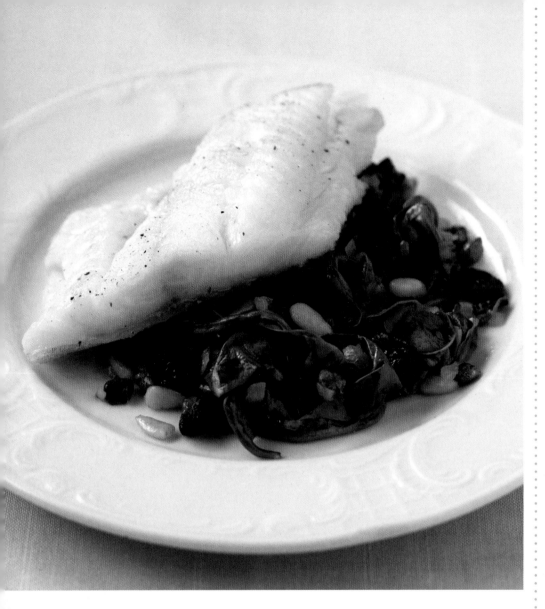

Sautéed trout with hazelnuts

The crunchy topping makes a delicious contrast to the soft-textured fish.

The fish

Trout, or mackerel

- **PREP** 20–25 mins ▪ **COOK** 20 mins
- **SERVES** 4

Ingredients

4 trout, about 10oz (300g) each, scaled and gutted

2oz (60g) hazelnuts

2 lemons

2–3 tbsp all-purpose flour

salt and freshly ground black pepper

8 tbsp butter

2 tbsp chopped flat-leaf parsley

1 Rinse the trout inside and out, and pat dry with paper towels.

2 Preheat the oven to 350°F (180°C). Spread the hazelnuts on a baking sheet and cook for 8–10 minutes, until browned. While hot, rub in a dish towel to remove the skins. Peel the lemons, remove all the pith, and cut into thin rounds. Remove any pips. Set aside.

3 Put the flour on a large plate and season. Press each trout in the flour, turning to coat on all sides. Lift out and gently shake to remove any excess.

4 Heat half the butter in a large frying pan, until foaming. Add 2 trout, and brown over medium heat for 2–3 minutes. Carefully turn and cook for 3–5 minutes more, until the flesh flakes easily under a fork. Keep warm while you cook the remaining fish in the rest of the butter.

5 Add the hazelnuts to the pan, and sauté for 3–4 minutes, until golden brown. Stir in most of the parsley. Serve the fish on warmed plates, spoon over the hazelnuts, and scatter with lemon slices and the remaining parsley.

Prepare ahead

The hazelnuts can be roasted and skinned 1 day ahead. Store in an airtight container at room temperature.

Pollock with spinach and pine nuts

An extremely healthy dish, and very easy to make quickly.

The fish

Any firm white fish, such as turbot, halibut, cod, or pollock

- **PREP** 10 mins ▪ **COOK** 15 mins ▪ **SERVES** 4

Ingredients

4 pollock fillets, about 5½oz (150g) each, scaled and pinboned

salt and freshly ground black pepper

2 tbsp olive oil

1 onion, finely chopped

handful of plump raisins

handful of pine nuts, toasted

1–2 tsp capers, rinsed and gently squeezed dry

2 large handfuls of spinach leaves

1 Season the fish with salt and pepper. Salting the fish—ideally with sea salt—before cooking firms the flesh by removing moisture.

2 Heat half the oil in a large non-stick frying pan over medium heat. Add the fish, skin side down, and cook gently for 5–6 minutes. Turn, and cook on the other side until it just begins to flake when gently pressed; the time this takes will depend on the thickness of the fish, but be careful not to overcook. Remove from the pan, and set aside to keep warm.

3 Carefully wipe out the pan with paper towels, then add the remaining oil. Sauté the onion for about 5 minutes until soft and translucent. Add the raisins, pine nuts, and capers, and cook for a few minutes more, breaking up the capers with the back of a fork.

4 Add the spinach, and cook until just wilted. Taste, and season if needed. Serve the fish on a bed of the wilted spinach mixture.

Omelet Arnold Bennett

This famous dish was specially created for the Victorian novelist at the Savoy Grill, London.

The fish
Smoked haddock, or smoked mackerel

- **PREP** 5 mins ▪ **COOK** 20 mins ▪ **SERVES** 4

Ingredients
8 large eggs, separated

⅔ cup half-and-half

12oz (350g) smoked haddock fillet, poached, skinned, and flaked

4 tbsp grated Parmesan cheese

freshly ground black pepper

4 tbsp butter

1 Beat the egg yolks in a bowl with 2 tbsp of the half-and-half, until smooth and creamy. In a separate, clean bowl, whisk the egg whites until they form soft peaks. Add 1 tbsp of the whites to the egg yolk mixture, to loosen it, then fold in the rest with the haddock, half the cheese, and plenty of pepper.

2 Preheat the broiler on its highest setting. Melt the butter in a large non-stick frying pan and, when foaming, add the egg mixture. Cook until the eggs have set on the bottom, using a spatula to draw the edges into the middle of the pan as they start to set, so the uncooked mixture can run to the sides of the pan.

3 Once set on the bottom, scatter the remaining cheese on top, and pour over the rest of the half-and-half. Put the pan under the broiler until lightly browned and set. Serve at once.

Cod in tomato sauce

Tomatoes add sweetness to this Spanish dish.

The fish
Cod, or haddock, saithe, pollock, or whiting

- **PREP** 10 mins ▪ **COOK** 30 mins ▪ **SERVES** 4

Ingredients
2 tbsp olive oil

2¼lb (1kg) cod fillet, pinboned, skinned, and cut into 4 pieces

1 large onion, finely sliced

1 garlic clove, grated or finely chopped

4 large plum tomatoes, skinned, seeded, and chopped (see page 112)

2 tsp tomato purée

1 tsp sugar

1¼ cup fish stock

½ cup dry white wine

2 tbsp chopped flat-leaf parsley

salt and freshly ground black pepper

1 Preheat the oven to 400°F (200°C). Heat the oil in a flameproof casserole large enough to hold the cod in 1 layer. Fry the fish over medium-high heat for 1 minute, turn and cook for 1 minute more. Remove and set aside.

2 Add the onion and garlic to the casserole and fry over medium heat until softened. Add the tomatoes, tomato purée, sugar, stock, and wine, bring to a simmer, and cook for 10–12 minutes. Top with the fish and bake in the oven for 5 minutes. Lift out the cod, and keep warm.

3 Place the casserole over medium-high heat and simmer the sauce until thickened. Stir in half the parsley and season. Divide the sauce between 4 warmed plates and place the fish on top. Serve sprinkled with the remaining parsley.

Prepare ahead
The tomato sauce can be made up to 2 days ahead, covered, and refrigerated. Return to a simmer before continuing.

Sweet and sour snapper with pineapple

Snapper has a meaty, sweet, and succulent flesh that works well with the classic Chinese sweet and sour flavors.

The fish
Snapper

▪ **PREP** 25 mins ▪ **COOK** 15 mins ▪ **SERVES** 4

Ingredients
1¾lb (800g) snapper fillets, pinboned and scaled

5 tbsp cornstarch

4–5 tbsp sunflower oil, plus extra if needed

1 onion, finely chopped

1 tbsp chopped fresh ginger

1 garlic clove, chopped

1 red and 1 orange bell pepper, seeded and thickly sliced

2 celery stalks, sliced

2 tbsp ketchup

2 tbsp plum sauce

2 tbsp light soy sauce

5 tbsp red wine vinegar

8oz can pineapple chunks in natural juice

1 Cut the snapper into 2in (5cm) pieces, and roll in 4 tbsp of the cornstarch. Heat half the oil in a large wok, and fry the fish pieces, a few at a time, for 3–4 minutes or until cooked; the flesh will be white and firm. You may need to add more oil between batches. Set aside.

2 Heat the remaining oil in the same frying pan. Add the onion, ginger, garlic, peppers, and celery, and stir-fry over high heat, tossing all the time, for 3–4 minutes or until the vegetables soften.

3 Mix the ketchup, plum sauce, soy sauce, vinegar, and drained juice from the pineapple together. Stir in the remaining cornstarch. Add this to the vegetables and cook over gentle heat for 2–3 minutes or until lightly thickened. Return the snapper and add the pineapple chunks. Heat through and serve with rice.

Prepare ahead
The sweet and sour sauce can be made up to 2 days in advance, covered, and refrigerated. Reheat gently. It may need more water, so add a little until the consistency is as you prefer.

Red mullet Dieppoise

A Dieppoise garnish usually contains wine and cream, but vitally mussels from that area.

The fish
Red mullet, or rascasse, pollock fillets, or hake fillets, and mussels, or clams

▪ **PREP** 20 mins ▪ **COOK** 25 mins ▪ **SERVES** 4

Ingredients
1 shallot, finely chopped

⅔ cup dry white wine

1lb 2oz (500g) mussels, prepared (see page 278)

2 tbsp butter

4oz (115g) button mushrooms, thickly sliced

⅔ cup heavy cream

salt and freshly ground black pepper

lemon juice, to taste

2 tbsp olive oil

4–8 small red mullet (depending on size), scaled, gutted, and trimmed (liver left in)

1 tbsp seasoned flour (see page 55)

1 Put the shallot and wine into a small saucepan, bring to a boil, and simmer for 2–3 minutes to reduce by one-third. Add the mussels, cover with a well-fitting lid, and cook over medium heat for 3–4 minutes, or until opened. Try to resist the temptation to lift the lid. Lift on to a plate to cool, and strain the liquid. Discard any muusels that have not opened and lift them from their shells.

2 Heat the butter in a large saucepan, add the mushrooms, and fry over brisk heat for 2–3 minutes or until cooked, then add the mussel liquor and simmer for 2–3 minutes to reduce by half. Add the cream, bring to a boil, and simmer until the sauce is a syrupy consistency. Season, adding lemon juice to taste. Add the mussels and warm through.

3 Meanwhile, heat the oil in a large frying pan, and coat the fish with the seasoned flour. Fry the fish, in 2 batches, in the hot oil for 3 minutes each side. Lift on to a serving dish and spoon the sauce over.

RED MULLET FLAVOR PAIRINGS:
This beautiful fish is great with white wine, cream, mushrooms, tomatoes, garlic, and bell peppers, or with citrus, and herbs such as chervil and tarragon.

Spicy shrimp with garlic

This great recipe is incredibly quick to make—and hard to stop eating!

The fish

Shrimp, or scallops or monkfish

▪ **PREP** 5 mins ▪ **COOK** 10 mins ▪ **SERVES** 4

Ingredients

4 tbsp olive oil

6 garlic cloves, grated or finely chopped

1 tsp red pepper flakes

1 tbsp dry sherry

9oz (250g) raw shrimp, peeled and deveined (see page 285)

salt and freshly ground black pepper

1 Heat the oil in a frying pan over medium heat, add the garlic and red pepper flakes, and cook gently for 2 minutes.

2 Add the sherry and shrimp, increase the heat, and stir for 5 minutes, or until the juices have reduced by half. Season and serve with crusty bread and a crisp salad.

Pan-fried shrimp, olives, and tomatoes

The deep tastes of the Mediterranean in this dish highlight the sweet flavor of the shrimp.

The fish

Shrimp, or monkfish, scallops, or squid

▪ **PREP** 5 mins ▪ **COOK** 15 mins ▪ **SERVES** 4

Ingredients

1 tbsp olive oil

1 onion, finely chopped

2 garlic cloves, grated or finely chopped

12 large raw shrimp, peeled and deveined, tail left intact (see page 285)

splash of dry sherry, or dry white wine

6 tomatoes, skinned, seeded, and chopped (see page 112)

large handful of mixed olives, pitted

salt and freshly ground black pepper

handful of basil and flat-leaf parsley, chopped

1 Heat the oil in a large frying pan over medium heat. Add the onion, and sauté for about 5 minutes until soft and translucent. Add the garlic, and cook for a few seconds, then add in the shrimp and cook over high heat, until they are just turning pink.

2 Add the sherry, and continue cooking for 5 minutes, stirring, until the alcohol has evaporated. Add the tomatoes and olives and cook for a further couple of minutes, stirring occasionally, until the tomatoes start to break down. Season well, and stir in the herbs. Serve immediately with fresh crusty bread.

Pan-fried clams with parsley and garlic

Simple tastes here for a healthy winter feast.

The fish
Clams, or mussels

▪ **PREP** 10 mins ▪ **COOK** 20 mins ▪ **SERVES** 4

Ingredients
1 tbsp olive oil

1 onion, finely chopped

salt

2 garlic cloves, grated or finely chopped

1–2 green bell peppers, seeded and finely chopped

⅔ cup dry white wine

1lb (450g) clams, prepared

handful of flat-leaf parsley, finely chopped

lemon wedges, to serve

1 Heat the oil in a large frying pan over medium heat. Add the onion and a pinch of salt, and sweat for about 5 minutes until soft and translucent. Add the garlic and peppers, and gently sweat until the peppers begin to soften. Increase the heat to high, and add the wine. Cook for a couple of minutes until the alcohol has evaporated.

2 Add the clams, shaking the pan occasionally, and cook for 5–6 minutes until the clams open (discard any that remain shut). Add the parsley, and stir to combine. Serve hot with crusty bread to mop up the juices and some lemon wedges.

Pan-fried scallops with chile, ginger, and an anchovy dressing

An extravagant treat with strong flavors for an adventurous crowd.

The fish
Sea scallops, or squid or monkfish

▪ **PREP** 10 mins ▪ **COOK** 30 mins ▪ **SERVES** 4

Ingredients
2–3 tbsp olive oil

1½lb (675g) waxy potatoes, peeled and thinly sliced

12 sea scallops, roe removed

salt and freshly ground black pepper

1 hot red chile, seeded and finely chopped

1in (2.5cm) fresh ginger, grated

juice of ½ lemon

handful of flat-leaf parsley, finely chopped

For the anchovy dressing
3 tbsp extra virgin olive oil

1 tbsp white wine vinegar

8 anchovy fillets in olive oil, drained and finely chopped

pinch of sugar (optional)

1 Heat 1–2 tbsp of the olive oil in a large non-stick frying pan over medium-high heat. Add the potatoes, and sauté for 15–20 minutes until golden and cooked through. Drain on paper towels, and set aside to keep warm.

2 Meanwhile, make the anchovy dressing. In a bowl, whisk together the extra virgin olive oil, vinegar, and anchovies until well combined. Taste, and add a pinch of sugar if it needs it. Season with pepper.

3 Pat the scallops dry with paper towels, and season with salt and pepper. Put the remaining olive oil in the frying pan over high heat. When hot, add the scallops. Sear for about 1 minute, then turn them over. Add the chile and ginger, and squeeze over the lemon juice, being careful, as it will spit. Remove the pan from the heat, and sprinkle over the parsley.

4 Serve immediately with the sautéed potatoes and a drizzle of the anchovy dressing.

Prepare ahead
Make the anchovy dressing up to 2 days ahead, cover, and refrigerate. Return to room temperature, and whisk before use.

SUSTAINABILITY CHOICE

Buy seafood outside the spawning season

Fish and shellfish spawn at different times of the year, though many spawn in spring and early summer. Avoid buying any fish that are full of roe to give the species the chance to reproduce. Lobster, for example, produces millions of eggs, and only very few will survive, so this slow-growing crustacean needs time to replenish the stock. During the latter stages of roe production and immediately after spawning, fish can also be disappointing to eat, lacking flavor and texture, because their muscles are not exercised as often as at other times of the year.

Pan-fried shrimp in garlic butter

The shrimp can be peeled or not; provide finger bowls and plenty of paper napkins if you leave the shell on.

The fish
Shrimp, or scallops, monkfish, or cod cheeks

- **PREP** 5 mins ▪ **COOK** 10 mins ▪ **SERVES** 4

Ingredients
6 tbsp unsalted butter

juice of 1 lemon, plus more to serve

2 garlic cloves, crushed

2 tbsp finely chopped flat-leaf parsley, plus extra sprigs, to serve

salt and freshly ground black pepper

2 tbsp olive oil

16–20 raw shrimp, peeled, deveined, and butterflied (see page 285)

lemon wedges, to serve

1 Mix the butter, lemon juice, garlic, and parsley together, and season to taste with salt and plenty of pepper.

2 Heat the oil in a large frying pan, add half the shrimp and pan-fry over medium heat for 2 minutes, or until they have lost their translucency and turned pink. Lift on to a large serving platter and keep warm while you cook the remaining shrimp in the same way.

3 Wipe out the frying pan if necessary and add the garlic butter. Heat until hot and foaming and the garlic is soft, but not brown. Add a splash of lemon juice to stop the cooking and immediately pour over the shrimp.

4 Garnish with parsley and lemon wedges, and provide lots of crusty bread to mop up the delicious garlic butter.

Prepare ahead
The garlic butter can be made up to 2 days ahead. Wrap it in parchment paper and store in the refrigerator.

Flounder with smoked bacon

A recipe for a romantic dinner, because it's difficult to pan-fry more than two fish.

The fish
Flounder, or any flat fish such as dab, plaice, or lemon sole

- **PREP** 10 mins ▪ **COOK** 20 mins ▪ **SERVES** 2

Ingredients
2 medium flounder

4oz (115g) thick-cut bacon strips, diced

1 tbsp seasoned flour (see page 55)

lemon wedges, to serve

chopped flat-leaf parsley, to serve

1 Remove the gills, the bloodline, and trim the flounder (see page 272).

2 Heat a large frying pan, add the bacon, and cook until brown and crispy. Lift out on to a plate, but keep the fat in the pan.

3 Dust the fish with the seasoned flour. Pan-fry the flounder one at a time in the bacon fat for 3–4 minutes on each side. Once cooked, lift on to a plate and keep warm.

4 Once both fish are cooked, arrange them on a large plate, and spoon the bacon over the top. Garnish with lemon wedges and parsley. Serve with steamed green beans, or a tomato salad.

PLAICE FLAVOR PAIRINGS: This subtle-flavored, delicate-fleshed fish is best with mild partners; try butter, lemon, parsley, breadcrumbs, sage, mushrooms, or mashed potatoes.

Sole meunière

Pan-frying in clarified butter (*à la meunière*) is a classic French way to cook fish simply.

The fish

Lemon sole, or sand dabs, turbot, or plaice

- **PREP** 5 mins • **COOK** 10 mins • **SERVES** 2

Ingredients

2 lemon sole, skinned, filleted

2 tbsp seasoned flour (see page 55)

6–8 tbsp butter

2 tbsp finely chopped flat-leaf parsley

juice of ½ lemon

1 Roll the sole fillets in the seasoned flour until well coated. Arrange them in a single layer on a plate (do not stack, as they will stick together and the flour will become soggy).

2 To clarify the butter, melt it in a heavy-bottomed saucepan over very low heat. When it stops spitting, carefully pour it into a dish, leaving the white sediment (the milk solids) behind in the bottom of the pan.

3 Heat half of the clarified butter in a large frying pan until it is no longer sizzling. Lower in the fish, and press down gently with a spatula. Pan-fry for 1 minute. Turn the fish over and cook on the second side for another 30 seconds or so; the fish is cooked when it is firm and white. Transfer to a plate and keep warm. (You may need to cook in two batches.)

4 Wipe out the frying pan and add the remaining butter. Allow to cook for a few seconds until it turns golden brown, then add the parsley and a squeeze of lemon juice, and pour, still sizzling, over the fish.

Samak maquli

This is typical Egyptian street food. If you can't find small red mullet, use fillets instead.

The fish

Red mullet, or small gray mullet, sardines, small mackerel, or small pomfret

- **PREP** 15 mins • **COOK** 5–10 mins
- **SERVES** 2

Ingredients

6–8 small red mullet, scaled, gutted, and gills removed

8 garlic cloves, crushed

4 tbsp chopped flat-leaf parsley

grated zest of 1 lemon

salt and freshly ground black pepper

olive oil, for deep-frying

3 tbsp seasoned flour (see page 55)

lemon wedges, to serve

For the sauce

3–4 tbsp tahini paste

4 garlic cloves, crushed

juice of 1–2 lemons, to taste

1 tbsp chopped flat-leaf parsley

1 Rinse the fish to ensure all traces of blood are removed; pat dry on paper towels.

2 Mix the garlic, parsley, and lemon zest and season generously. Use this to rub all over and inside the cavity of the fish.

3 Heat the oil to 350°F (180°C) in a large pan or deep-fat fryer (see page 308).

4 When the oil is hot, dust the fish with seasoned flour and cook 2–3 fish at a time. Once cooked (their flesh will be white and opaque), transfer to a warmed serving dish while you cook the remaining fish.

5 For the sauce, mix the tahini paste, garlic, lemon juice to taste, and parsley. Add water if the mixture is too thick. Serve the fish with the tahini sauce and lemon wedges.

Prepare ahead

Rub the fish with the garlic, parsley, and lemon, and make the tahini sauce, 1 day in advance. Cover both separately, and refrigerate. Bring to room temperature before continuing.

LEMON SOLE FLAVOR PAIRINGS:

Lemon sole is much-prized for its delicate, yet definite sweet flavor and soft flesh. Treat it simply, and pair with seasoned flour or herbed breadcrumbs.

Fish and pumpkin chips

There is nothing quite like fish and chips on a cold night. It's quick, simple, and very tasty.

The fish

Any white fish, such as saithe, pollock, bass, or tilapia

- **PREP** 25 mins ▪ **COOK** 30–40 mins
- **SERVES** 4

Ingredients

1 pumpkin or butternut squash, about 2¾lb (1.25kg)

olive oil, for drizzling

½ cup all-purpose flour, plus more to coat

a pinch of salt

2 tbsp vegetable oil, plus extra for deep-frying

⅔ cup milk

1 large egg white

4 white fish fillets, about 6oz (175g) each, pinboned and skinned

1 Preheat the oven to 475°F (240°C), or its highest setting. Peel the pumpkin and cut into chips. Put them on a baking sheet, drizzle with oil, and cook for 30 minutes, turning halfway, until crisp, but tender inside.

2 Meanwhile, sift the flour into a bowl. Make a well in the middle, add the salt with 2 tbsp oil and the milk, and whisk until smooth. Whisk the egg white until stiff, then fold it in.

3 Heat the oil to 350°F (180°C) in a large pan or deep-fat fryer (see page 308).Coat the fish in a little seasoned flour, then dip it in the batter. Fry the fish, 1 piece at a time, in the oil for 8 minutes until crisp and golden brown. Carefully remove and drain on paper towels. Keep warm while cooking the rest.

4 Serve immediately with the pumpkin chips.

Mixed fried fish

This works best with firm white fish, but you can also use squid, sliced into rings. If using squid, be careful not to overcook, or it will toughen.

The fish

Any mixed fish, such as cod, salmon, and snapper, and tiger prawns, or squid rings

- **PREP** 20 mins ▪ **COOK** 10 mins ▪ **SERVES** 4

Ingredients

4 tbsp all-purpose flour

2 eggs, lightly beaten

3oz (85g) dried white breadcrumbs, or Panko breadcrumbs

3 mixed fish fillets, about 4oz (115g) each, pinboned and skinned

12 raw tiger prawns, peeled and deveined, heads removed (see page 285)

oil, for deep frying

For the sauce

2oz (60g) arugula, plus extra to serve

1 garlic clove, crushed

½ cup mayonnaise

1 tsp lemon juice

salt and freshly ground black pepper

1 Place all the sauce ingredients in a food processor, season, and blend until smooth.

2 Season the flour with salt and pepper. Place the flour, eggs, and breadcrumbs in 3 separate dishes. Cut each fish fillet into 4 pieces. Toss the fish and prawns in the flour, dip in the egg, then coat in breadcrumbs.

3 Heat the oil to 350°F (180°C) in a large pan or deep-fat fryer (see page 308). Fry the fish in batches for 2–3 minutes, or until crisp and golden. Drain on paper towels.

4 Put a few arugula leaves on each plate and top with fish. Serve immediately with the sauce.

Egg fu yung

Light and tasty, these Chinese patties are made with shrimp and stir-fried vegetables.

The fish
Shrimp, or any firm white fish

- **PREP** 15 mins ▪ **COOK** 20 mins ▪ **SERVES** 4

Ingredients
¾ cup vegetable stock

1 tbsp oyster sauce

1 tbsp light soy sauce

1 tbsp Chinese rice wine

vegetable oil, for deep-frying

3 shallots, thinly sliced

2 garlic cloves, crushed

1 green bell pepper, seeded and chopped

1 celery stalk, chopped

3oz (85g) beansprouts

4oz (115g) raw shrimp, peeled and deveined (see page 285)

5 eggs, beaten

2 tsp cornstarch

1 Pour the stock, oyster sauce, soy sauce, and rice wine into a small saucepan. Set aside.

2 Heat 2 tbsp of oil in a wok and stir-fry the shallots, garlic, green bell pepper, and celery for 3 minutes. Add the beansprouts and shrimp. Stir-fry for 2–3 more minutes, until they turn pink. Transfer to a bowl and set aside.

3 When the mixture is cool, stir in the eggs. Wipe the wok with paper towels.

4 Return the wok to the heat and pour in 2in (5cm) oil. When hot, ladle in one-quarter of the mixture and fry for 2 minutes, until browned, spooning over the oil so the top starts to set. Carefully turn and cook the other side. Place on paper towels and keep warm while you cook the rest of the mixture.

5 Mix the cornstarch with a little water until smooth and stir into the stock mixture in the saucepan. Bring to a boil, stirring, and simmer for 1 minute, until thickened. Spoon over the patties and serve with the rice.

Prepare ahead
Make the sauce 1 day ahead, cover, and refrigerate. Reheat gently to serve, adding a little more water if it has become too thick.

Breaded fried prawns

Easy, and far tastier than store-bought.

The fish
Tiger prawns, squid, or scallops

- **PREP** 20 mins, plus chilling ▪ **COOK** 15 mins ▪ **SERVES** 4

Ingredients
12 tbsp dried breadcrumbs

6 tbsp cornmeal

2 tsp dried marjoram or oregano

2 tsp dried thyme

freshly ground black pepper

24 raw tiger prawns, peeled, but tails left intact, and deveined (see page 285)

all-purpose flour, to dust

3–4 eggs, beaten

sunflower or vegetable oil, for deep-frying

1 Mix the breadcrumbs, cornmeal, marjoram, thyme, and pepper, and spread out on a plate.

2 Pat the prawns dry with paper towels and dust with flour, leaving the tails clear. Brush with beaten egg, then press into the breadcrumb mixture to evenly coat. Chill for 30 minutes.

3 Heat the oil to 350°F (180°C) in a large pan or deep-fat fryer (see page 308). Deep-fry the prawns in batches for 2–3 minutes, until the coating is golden and crisp. Drain on paper towels and serve at once, with sweet chili sauce. For a special occasion, add herb-and-chile-flecked thin rice noodles.

Fritto misto di pesce

In coastal Naples and Liguria, *Fritto misto* (little fried morsels) is made with fish; other regions use offal and vegetables instead.

The fish

Any small mixed fish, such as sardines, sprats, anchovies, red mullet, and shellfish, such as squid

- **PREP** 10 mins ▪ **COOK** 10–15 mins
- **SERVES** 4

Ingredients

8 sardines or sprats, scaled and gutted

16 fresh anchovies, if available, or fresh sprats, scaled and gutted

4 small red mullet, scaled and gutted

8 small squid, gutted, cleaned, and prepared (see page 282)

6 tbsp seasoned flour (see page 55)

olive oil, for deep-frying

lemon wedges, to serve

1 Prepare the fish, ensuring they are gutted well, the gills are removed, and any trace of blood is cleaned away. Pat well with paper towels to remove moisture. Dredge all the fish and squid well in seasoned flour.

2 Heat the oil to 350°F (180°C) in a large pan or deep-fat fryer (see page 308).

3 Cook the fish in small batches for 3–4 minutes, depending on species and size (fry batches of same-sized fish together for even cooking), then drain on paper towels.

4 Pile on to a serving dish with lemon wedges for people to help themselves.

Sole colbert

This French Escoffier classic is traditionally served with *pont neuf* (very thin fries).

The fish

Dover sole, or any small flat fish, such as dab, flounder, plaice, or lemon sole

- **PREP** 25 mins ▪ **COOK** 5–7 mins ▪ **SERVES** 2

Ingredients

2 small Dover sole, skinned

vegetable oil, for deep-frying

2 tbsp seasoned flour (see page 55)

1 egg, beaten

6 tbsp dried white breadcrumbs, sieved

For the maître d'hôtel butter

4 tbsp unsalted butter, softened

3 tbsp finely chopped flat-leaf parsley

lemon juice, to taste

salt and freshly ground black pepper

1 Prepare the Dover sole, but do not snip away the backbone (see page 276).

2 Heat the oil to 350°F (180°C) in a large pan or deep-fat fryer (see page 308).

3 Dust the fish evenly with the seasoned flour. Brush thoroughly with the egg and roll in the breadcrumbs. Set aside.

4 Mix all the ingredients for the maître d'hôtel butter, adding lemon juice and seasoning to taste. Roll into a sausage shape, wrap in plastic wrap, and chill.

5 Fry the sole for 5–7 minutes; it will curl slightly and be golden brown. Transfer to paper towels and carefully remove the backbone by snipping at either end and pulling away, so the fillets are separated.

6 Arrange the fish on a serving dish. Slice the butter into ¼in (0.5cm) slices and put 2–3 in the middle of each of the fish. It will melt to create a lovely, if rich, dressing. Serve with fries and a flower salad.

Prepare ahead

The maître d'hôtel butter can be made and refrigerated for 2–3 days before use.

DAB FLAVOR PAIRINGS: Sharpen the subtle taste of this flat fish with white wine vinegar, capers, and lemon juice, or bake with potatoes, sage, and mushrooms.

Deep-fried haddock in beer batter

Skin on or off is down to personal taste, though purists say it should be removed.

The fish
Haddock, or any white fish, such as cod, pollock, saithe, tilapia, or smoked haddock (a revelation)

- **PREP** 10 mins **COOK** 7–10 mins
- **SERVES** 4

Ingredients
oil, for deep-frying

4 haddock fillets, about 6–8oz (175–225g) each, pinboned and skinned

4 tbsp seasoned flour (see page 55)

For the batter
½ cup all-purpose flour

1 tsp baking powder

½ tsp salt

8–10fl oz (250–300ml) pale ale

salt and freshly ground black pepper

1 Sift the all-purpose flour, baking powder, and salt into a bowl. Make a well in the center and add half the ale. Gradually stir in the flour so the batter remains smooth. As it thickens, blend in more ale until the batter is the consistency of half-and-half, and season.

2 Heat the oil to 350°F (180°C) in a large pan or deep-fat fryer (see page 308). Dust the fish with seasoned flour. Using tongs, lower the fish into the batter to coat completely, then lift out and let any excess drip back into the bowl. Swish the fish through the hot oil to allow the batter to start to "set", then let the fish go.

3 Fry for 7–10 minutes or until the batter is golden brown. Lift the fish on to paper towels and sprinkle with salt. Serve with french fries and tartar sauce.

Tempura

Unusually, a good tempura batter should have many small lumps.

The fish
Any white fish, such as snapper, lemon sole, or sea bass, or salmon and a selection of seafood

- **PREP** 25 mins **COOK** 10–15 mins
- **SERVES** 4

Ingredients

For the batter
2 cups cold sparkling water

1 egg, beaten

¼ cup cornstarch

1 cup self-rising flour

For the seafood
oil, for deep-frying

6oz (175g) white fish fillet, pinboned and skinned

4oz (115g) raw tiger prawns, peeled and deveined (see page 285)

8 sea scallops

2 squid, gutted, cleaned, and cut into rings

For the traditional dipping sauce
⅔ cup boiling water infused with 2 tbsp bonito flakes, and strained

⅔ cup Japanese dark soy sauce

1 tbsp granulated sugar

1 tsp grated fresh ginger

For the new-style dipping sauce
2 tbsp syrup from stem ginger (optional)

2 tbsp red wine vinegar

2 tbsp dark soy sauce

1 tbsp honey

2 scallions, finely sliced

1 To make the batter, put the water into a large bowl, add the egg and flours and whisk together to form a batter with lots of fine lumps. Cover and refrigerate for 20–30 minutes.

2 Mix together the ingredients for both the traditional and new-style dipping sauces in two separate bowls.

3 Heat the oil to 350°F (180°C) in a large pan or deep-fat fryer (see page 308). Dip the prepared fish, shellfish, and squid in the batter and fry a few pieces at a time until crisp. The batter should remain quite pale in color. Lift on to paper towels and keep warm while you fry the rest. Serve with both dipping sauces.

HADDOCK FLAVOR PAIRINGS: The briny, wonderfully fresh flavor of haddock is complemented with rich batter and piquant tartar sauce, or even salty dulse seaweed, or Cheddar or mozzarella cheeses.

Baked and Roasted

Baked salmon with salsa verde and cucumber

This is also an excellent way to use up leftover salmon.

The fish

Salmon, or sea bass, sea bream, or gray mullet

- **PREP** 20 mins ▪ **COOK** 10 mins ▪ **SERVES** 4

Ingredients

12oz (350g) salmon fillet, pinboned and skinned

1 tbsp olive oil

1 cucumber

For the salsa verde

handful of basil leaves

handful of mint leaves

handful of flat-leaf parsley

2 tbsp white wine vinegar, plus extra to taste

2 tsp capers, rinsed and finely chopped

2 garlic cloves, grated or finely chopped

8 anchovy fillets in olive oil, drained and finely chopped

2 tsp wholegrain mustard

salt and freshly ground black pepper

6 tbsp extra virgin olive oil, plus extra to taste

1 Preheat the oven to 400°F (200°C). Rub the fish with the olive oil, place on a baking sheet, and bake for 10 minutes, or until opaque, and the flesh begins to flake under the pressure of a finger. Set aside to cool.

2 To make the salsa verde, chop all the herbs finely and put in a bowl. Drizzle with the vinegar and stir. Add the capers, garlic, and anchovies, and stir again. Add the mustard and season well. Slowly stir in the olive oil. Taste, and add more vinegar or oil to taste. Transfer to a bowl.

3 Peel the cucumber, slice in half lengthwise, and scoop out the seeds. Dice the flesh. Put the salmon on a platter. Spoon the salsa verde over the top and place the cucumber on the side.

Prepare ahead

Make the salsa verde 1 day in advance, cover, and refrigerate. The flavors will deepen. Return to room temperature before serving.

Sole with basil and pinenuts

The success of this simple Venetian recipe lies in the quality of the fish, the basil, and Italian olive oil.

The fish

Dover sole, or lemon sole, flounder, or plaice

- **PREP** 10–15 mins, plus marinating ▪ **COOK** 15 mins ▪ **SERVES** 4

Ingredients

4 small Dover sole, about 12oz (350g) each

2 tbsp extra virgin olive oil, plus extra for the baking sheet

juice of ½ lemon

1 tbsp shredded basil leaves

salt and freshly ground black pepper

lemon wedges, to serve

For the sauce

4 tbsp pine nuts

2 tbsp extra virgin olive oil

1–2 tbsp shredded basil, plus extra for garnish

juice of ½ lemon

1 Skin and trim the Dover sole (see page 276) being sure to remove the bloodline. Arrange on a plate and drizzle with the olive oil and lemon juice. Sprinkle with the basil and season lightly. Cover and refrigerate for 30 minutes.

2 Preheat the oven to 415°F (210°C). Arrange the marinated fish on a lightly oiled baking sheet, pouring over the marinade. Roast in the oven for 8–10 minutes or until the flesh of the fish has lost its translucency.

3 Meanwhile, dry roast the pine nuts in a frying pan until just beginning to brown, add the olive oil and basil, and cook together for a few seconds. Add the lemon juice, standing back, as the pan may splatter, and immediately pour over the fish.

4 Return the sole to the oven for another 2–3 minutes then transfer to warmed plates. Serve with the juices from the baking sheet, and lemon wedges.

DOVER SOLE PAIRINGS: The delicate, firm flesh is wonderful with lemon, or try mint and cucumber to lift the tastes. It is also excellent, and indulgent, with truffle oil and wild mushrooms.

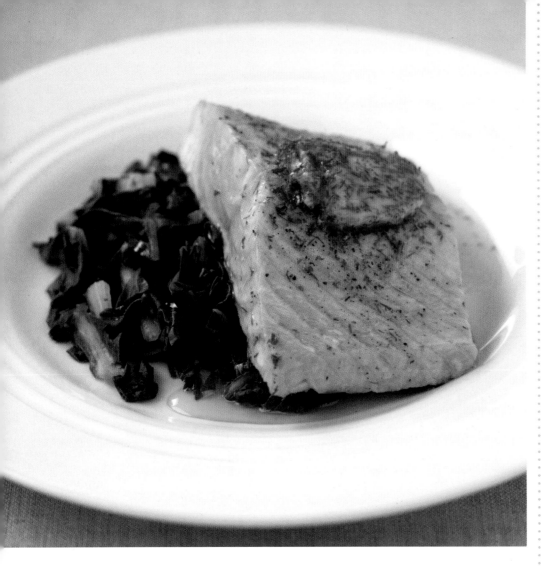

Salmon with mushrooms and bok choy

The piquant flavors of Asian ingredients work beautifully with the salmon in this quick and easy dish—perfect for a weeknight.

The fish

Salmon, or snapper

- **PREP** 15 mins ▪ **COOK** 25 mins ▪ **SERVES** 4

Ingredients

1 tbsp olive oil

1 tbsp dark soy sauce

½ tbsp mirin (Japanese rice wine), or dry sherry

2in (5cm) fresh ginger, peeled and finely chopped

2 garlic cloves, grated or finely chopped

salt and freshly ground black pepper

4 salmon fillets, about 5½oz (150g) each

2 bok choy, quartered lengthwise

7oz (200g) button mushrooms, halved if large

1 Preheat the oven to 400°F (200°C). Put the olive oil, soy sauce, mirin, ginger, and garlic in a bowl, mix well, and season with salt and pepper.

2 Put the salmon, bok choy, and mushrooms in a roasting pan, then drizzle over the oil mixture. Roast in the oven for 20–25 minutes, or until the salmon is cooked through. Serve with rice.

Roasted salmon with Swiss chard and herb butter

This would be equally delicious with curly kale or spinach instead of the chard.

The fish

Salmon, or trout, turbot, or brill

- **PREP** 10 mins ▪ **COOK** 30 mins ▪ **SERVES** 4

Ingredients

4 salmon fillets, about 5½oz (150g) each

1 tbsp olive oil

salt and freshly ground black pepper

2 handfuls of Swiss chard, trimmed and chopped

juice of 1 lemon

pinch of chili flakes

For the herb butter

½ cup butter

handful of curly parsley, finely chopped

handful of dill, finely chopped

1 First, make the herb butter. Put the butter and herbs in a mixing bowl, and beat well. Spoon on to wax paper, then roll into a log. Twist the edges of the paper, and put the roll in the refrigerator.

2 Preheat the oven to 400°F (200°C). Sit the salmon fillets in a nonstick roasting pan, drizzle with the olive oil, and season. Bake for 15–20 minutes until cooked through.

3 Meanwhile, cook the Swiss chard in a large pan of boiling salted water for 5–8 minutes, until it still has a bite to it. Drain well, and transfer to a serving dish. Squeeze over the lemon juice, and stir in the chili flakes. Divide between 4 warmed plates.

4 Place the roasted salmon on top of the Swiss chard, lay a slice of herb butter on each piece, and serve immediately.

Prepare ahead

The herb butter can be made ahead, and stored in the refrigerator for 1–2 days.

Salmon en papillote

Cooking "en papillote"—in a tightly sealed parchment packet—ensures the fish is moist.

The fish

Salmon, or sea bass, bream, red mullet, or snapper

■ **PREP** 25 mins ■ **COOK** 15 mins ■ **SERVES** 4

Ingredients

4 salmon fillets or steaks, about 6oz (175g) each

olive oil, for greasing

4 tomatoes, sliced

2 lemons, sliced

8 sprigs of tarragon

freshly ground black pepper

1 Cut 8 circles of parchment paper large enough for the salmon steaks to fit on half of the circle. Use 2 circles per steak to create a double thickness. Lightly grease the top circle with olive oil. Repeat with the rest.

2 Preheat the oven to 325°F (160°C). Divide the tomatoes among the circles, placing them on one half. Place the salmon on top, then the lemon slices and tarragon. Season with pepper. Fold up the paper to enclose the fish. Crimp the edges to create a tight seal. Place on a baking tray and bake for 15 minutes.

3 Place on warm plates, and serve immediately, with beurre blanc (see page 245).

Prepare ahead

The paper cases can be assembled, and stored in the refrigerator for 2 hours.

Asian halibut en papillote

Because of the paper cases, this dish retains all of its delicious fragrance.

The fish

Halibut, or turbot or brill

■ **PREP** 15–20 mins ■ **COOK** 10–12 mins ■ **SERVES** 4

Ingredients

4½oz (125g) snow peas, trimmed

1oz (30g) black fermented Chinese beans, or 2 tbsp black bean sauce

4 garlic cloves, grated or finely chopped

1in (2.5cm) fresh ginger, peeled and finely chopped

3 tbsp light soy sauce

2 tbsp dry sherry

½ tsp granulated sugar

1 tbsp sesame oil

2 tbsp vegetable oil

1 egg

½ tsp salt

4 halibut fillets or steaks, 6oz (175g) each, skinned

4 scallions, thinly sliced

1 Preheat the oven to 400°F (200°C). Simmer the snow peas in salted water for 1–2 minutes. Drain. If you are using fermented black beans, rinse and coarsely chop.

2 Stir together the garlic, ginger, black beans or black bean sauce, soy sauce, sherry, sugar, and sesame oil. Set aside.

3 Fold a sheet of parchment paper in half and cut out a curve to make a heart shape when unfolded. It should be large enough to leave a 3in (7.5cm) border around a fish fillet. Repeat to make 4. Open each out and brush with oil, leaving a 1in (2.5cm) border. Beat the egg and salt together. Brush on the borders.

4 Arrange the snow peas on one side of each paper heart and set a halibut fillet on top. Spoon over the black bean seasoning and sprinkle with scallions. Fold the paper over and seal the edges.

5 Lay the cases on a baking sheet and bake for 10–12 minutes, until puffed. Allow each diner to open their own aromatic package.

Prepare ahead

The paper cases can be assembled, and stored in the refrigerator for 2 hours.

Sea bream en papillote

A classic method of cooking fish; wrapped in paper with a selection of aromatics.

The fish

Sea bream, or sea bass or snapper

- **PREP** 10 mins ▪ **COOK** 12–15 mins
- **SERVES** 1

Ingredients

1 small sea bream, scaled, filleted, and trimmed

a few slices of scallion or fennel

herbs of your choice (try dill, tarragon, rosemary, or oregano)

1 tablespoon of butter or splash of olive oil

splash of Pernod or white wine

sea salt and freshly ground black pepper

lemon or lime wedges, to serve

1 Pinbone the fish fillets. Preheat the oven to 415°F (210°C). Arrange the fillets, skin-side up, on a large sheet of parchment paper.

2 Arrange the vegetables and herbs around the fish and season lightly. Add the butter or oil, and drizzle with Pernod or wine. Season lightly.

3 Wrap the fish securely, but not too tightly, so that the steam can circulate. Roast in the oven for 12–15 minutes or until cooked through. The flesh will be firm and opaque.

4 Serve directly from the parchment paper. To eat, open the parcel and squeeze the lemon or lime juice over the fish.

Prepare ahead

Assemble the parcel up to 1 day in advance, and refrigerate. Return to room temperature before baking.

Roast hake with remoulade

Remoulade is similar to tartar sauce and both work equally well with deep-fried, pan-fried, or roasted white fish.

The fish

Hake, or Patagonian toothfish, plaice, lemon sole, pollock, or whiting

- **PREP** 5–10 mins ▪ **COOK** 6–8 mins
- **SERVES** 4

Ingredients

4 hake fillets, about 6oz (175g) each, pinboned and skinned

1 tbsp extra virgin olive oil

salt and freshly ground black pepper

4 small sprigs of thyme

sprigs of watercress, to serve

lemon wedges, to serve

For the remoulade

5 tbsp mayonnaise

5 tbsp crème fraîche

1 tsp Dijon mustard

2 tsp chopped capers

2 tsp chopped gherkins

1 tbsp chopped tarragon

1 tbsp chopped chervil, or flat-leaf parsley

$\frac{1}{2}$–1 tsp anchovy paste, to taste

1 Preheat the oven to 400°F (200°C). To make the remoulade, mix all the ingredients in a small bowl and season to taste with anchovy paste and pepper.

2 Brush the hake with the olive oil and season lightly. Arrange on a baking sheet and put the thyme on top. Bake in the oven for 6–8 minutes, or until cooked; it will be opaque and the flesh white and firm. Remove the fish and drain well on paper towels.

3 Transfer the fish on to a warmed serving dish and garnish with the watercress and lemon wedges. Serve the remoulade separately.

Prepare ahead

The remoulade can be made, covered, and chilled up to 1 day ahead. Return to room temperature before serving.

PATAGONIAN TOOTHFISH FLAVOR PAIRINGS:

The dense, sweet flesh of this fish responds well to mayonnaise spiked with capers, or try it with Asian soy sauce, sesame, chile, and cilantro.

Stuffed squid, Naples-style

Squid stuffed with pine nuts and golden raisins, then casseroled in a tomato sauce.

The fish

Squid, or cuttlefish or baby octopus

- **PREP** 35 mins • **COOK** 1 hr 10 mins
- **SERVES** 4

Ingredients

4 large squid with tentacles, gutted

5 tbsp extra virgin olive oil

2 garlic cloves, chopped

1 tbsp chopped marjoram

1 tbsp chopped flat-leaf parsley

2 tbsp golden raisins

2 tbsp pine nuts

12 Italian green olives, chopped

2 anchovy fillets in olive oil, drained and roughly chopped

salt and freshly ground black pepper

5 tbsp fresh white breadcrumbs

For the sauce

2 tbsp extra virgin olive oil

1 small onion, finely chopped

5 tbsp medium white wine

10oz (300g) can tomatoes

pinch of sugar (optional)

1 Prepare the squid, but do not open the tubes out flat (see page 282). Lightly score the tubes and set aside. Chop the tentacles.

2 Heat the olive oil, add the tentacles, garlic, and herbs, toss for 1 minute. Stir in the golden raisins, pine nuts, olives, and anchovies, and season. Add the breadcrumbs, then cool. Preheat the oven to 340°F (170°C).

3 For the sauce, heat half the oil and cook the onion until translucent, add the wine and tomatoes, and simmer for 5 minutes. Season, adding sugar if it tastes acidic.

4 Stuff the squid tubes with the stuffing and seal with toothpicks. Heat the remaining oil in a flameproof casserole and lightly brown the squid. Pour on the sauce, cover, and bake for 1–1½ hours.

5 Lift the squid on to a warmed dish, and remove the toothpicks. Reduce the tomato sauce if necessary, then pour it over, and serve with noodles or rice.

Sea bass with tomato sauce

Make sure you use well-flavored tomatoes, as they make all the difference to the finished dish.

The fish

Sea bass, or sea bream or hake

- **PREP** 10 mins • **COOK** 25 mins • **SERVES** 4

Ingredients

4 small sea bass, about 12oz (340g) in total, scaled, gutted, and trimmed

1 tbsp seasoned flour (see page 55)

5 tbsp Italian extra virgin olive oil

1 onion, finely chopped

2 celery stalks, finely sliced

2 garlic cloves, chopped

8 plum tomatoes, roughly chopped

5 tbsp dry white wine

salt and freshly ground black pepper

pinch of sugar

2 tbsp chopped flat-leaf parsley

1 Preheat the oven to 375°F (190°C). Slash the sea bass 3–4 times on each side. Dust with the seasoned flour and arrange in a baking tray.

2 Heat the olive oil in a frying pan, add the onion, celery, and garlic, and cook over low heat for 2–3 minutes, until softening. Add the tomatoes and wine, and cook for 3–4 minutes, until the juices run. Season and add the sugar.

3 Spoon the tomato sauce over the sea bass and bake in the oven for 15–20 minutes or until cooked. The flesh will be white and opaque.

4 Slide the fish on to a large, warmed serving dish and sprinkle with parsley. Don't forget to take the cheeks from the fish heads; these are particularly delicious.

Prepare ahead

The tomato sauce can be made 2–3 days in advance. Cover, and refrigerate. Bring to room temperature before continuing.

GILT-HEAD BREAM FLAVOR PAIRINGS:

Try this firm, meaty fish with Mediterranean tastes, such as tomatoes, fennel and Pernod, lemon, saffron, parsley, and garlic. It also works well with cilantro.

Baked saithe in wine and herbs

Wholesome and so quick to make.

The fish

Saithe, or any other white fish, such as haddock, pollock, turbot, or cod

- **PREP** 5 mins ▪ **COOK** 20 mins ▪ **SERVES** 4

Ingredients

1½lb (675g) saithe fillets, pinboned, skinned, and cut into 4 pieces

salt

¾ cup white wine

12 cherry tomatoes

handful of flat-leaf parsley, finely chopped

1 Preheat the oven to 375°F (190°C). Sprinkle the fish with salt, then lay it in an ovenproof dish. Pour over the wine, and add the tomatoes and herbs.

2 Cover the dish tightly with foil, then bake in the oven for 15–20 minutes, until the fish is cooked through and the alcohol has evaporated. Serve with salad and fresh crusty bread for a summery dish, or creamy mashed potato in winter.

Swordfish baked with herbs

Rosemary and thyme perfectly complement the strong flavors of this dish.

The fish

Swordfish, or marlin, or tuna

- **PREP** 20 mins ▪ **COOK** 15–20 mins
- **SERVES** 4

Ingredients

4 swordfish steaks, 6oz (175g) each, skinned

freshly ground black pepper

2 tbsp extra virgin olive oil, plus extra for greasing

1 fennel bulb, thinly sliced

4 tomatoes, sliced

1 lemon, sliced

¼ cup chopped flat-leaf parsley

1 tbsp chopped mint

4 sprigs of thyme

2 tsp chopped rosemary leaves

½ cup dry white wine

1 Preheat the oven to 350°F (180°C). Season the swordfish steaks with plenty of pepper. Lightly grease an ovenproof dish with oil and evenly place in the fennel.

2 Lay the fish in the dish in a single layer and top with the tomatoes and lemon. Sprinkle with the herbs, and pour over the wine. Drizzle with the olive oil and cover the dish tightly with foil.

3 Bake for 15–20 minutes, or until just cooked. Serve immediately, spooning the juices in the dish over the fish. New potatoes and broccoli or French beans are good on the side.

Butterflied sardines stuffed with tomatoes and capers

Cheap, healthy, and completely delicious.

The fish

Sardines, or herring or mackerel

- **PREP** 15 mins ▪ **COOK** 10 mins ▪ **SERVES** 4

Ingredients

4–6 tomatoes, peeled and finely chopped

2 tsp capers, drained and rinsed

handful of flat-leaf parsley, finely chopped, plus extra to garnish

2 garlic cloves, grated or finely chopped

salt and freshly ground black pepper

12 fresh sardines, boned through the stomach

a little olive oil

juice of 1 lemon

1 Preheat the oven to 400°F (200°C). Put the tomatoes, capers, parsley, and garlic in a bowl. Season well, and stir.

2 Lay the sardines out on some plates, skin-side down, and spoon on the tomato mixture. Either roll up the sardines or just fold them over, then sit them all in a baking tray. Drizzle with the olive oil and lemon juice.

3 Bake in the oven for 10–15 minutes until cooked through. Garnish with extra parsley, if you wish, and serve with a crisp green salad.

Lemon sole with herbs

The very delicate flavors here perfectly suit this subtle-tasting fish.

The fish

Lemon sole, or plaice, brill, or any other flat fish

- **PREP** 10 mins ▪ **COOK** 20 mins ▪ **SERVES** 4

Ingredients

3 tbsp extra virgin olive oil

1 tbsp white wine vinegar

1 tsp Dijon mustard

small handful of herbs, such as parsley, thyme, and dill, chopped

salt and freshly ground black pepper

4 lemon sole fillets, about 6oz (175g) each

1 Preheat the oven to 400°F (200°C). To make the dressing, whisk together the oil and vinegar in a bowl. Add the mustard and herbs, and mix well. Season well, and mix again.

2 Lay the fish in a roasting pan, then cover with about ¼in (6mm) water. Season well. Bake in the oven for 15–20 minutes, until the fish is cooked through and the water has almost evaporated. To check whether the fish is cooked, poke it to make sure the flesh lifts from the bone easily. It should be white with no traces of pink.

3 Using a spatula, carefully lift the fish on to a warmed serving dish or individual plates. Spoon over some of the dressing. Serve hot with sautéed potatoes and broccoli.

Baked bream

This classic Iberian dish, *besugo al horno*, combines fish and potatoes.

The fish

Sea bream, or snapper or sea bass

- **PREP** 10 mins, plus marinating
- **COOK** 1 hour ▪ **SERVES** 4

Ingredients

2 sea bream, about 1lb 5oz (600g) each, scaled and gutted

1 tbsp tapenade

2 lemon slices, thickly sliced

juice of 1 lemon

3 tbsp olive oil

1½lb (675g) potatoes, finely sliced

1 onion, finely sliced

2 peppers, seeded and sliced into thin rings

4 garlic cloves, chopped

2 tbsp chopped parsley

1 tsp hot paprika

½ cup dry white wine

salt and freshly ground black pepper

1 Make 2 diagonal cuts on each side of the thickest part of both fish. Place in a nonmetallic dish and spread the tapenade over the inside and outside. Tuck a lemon slice into the gills, drizzle with lemon juice, and place in the refrigerator for 1 hour.

2 Preheat the oven to 375°F (190°C). Grease an ovenproof dish with 1 tbsp of the oil. Layer half the potatoes in the dish, then the onion and peppers. Scatter with the garlic and parsley, and sprinkle with the paprika, then layer the remaining potatoes on top. Drizzle over the rest of the oil, and sprinkle with 2–3 tbsp of water. Cover with foil and bake for 40 minutes, or until cooked through and golden.

3 Increase the oven temperature to 425°F (220°C). Place the fish on the potatoes, pour over the wine, season, and return to the oven, uncovered, for 20 minutes, or until cooked. Serve immediately.

Prepare ahead

The fish can be prepared to the end of step 1, covered, and chilled 6 hours in advance. Bring to room temperature before continuing.

Halibut in rosemary and garlic crust

Versatile and quick, this delicious recipe with its couscous crust is popular with children.

The fish

Halibut, or cod, haddock, monkfish, turbot, brill, or salmon

- **PREP** 20 mins ▪ **COOK** 15 mins ▪ **SERVES** 4

Ingredients

2oz (60g) couscous

1 tsp turmeric

1 tbsp chopped rosemary, plus extra small sprigs to garnish

1 large garlic clove, grated or finely chopped

¼ cup pecorino or Parmesan cheese, finely grated

salt and freshly ground black pepper

sunflower or vegetable oil, for greasing

1 egg, beaten

3 tbsp all-purpose flour, seasoned

4 halibut fillets, about 5½oz (150g) each

¾ cup tomato purée

½ tsp honey

1 Preheat the oven to 375°F (190°C). Stir 5 tbsp boiling water into the couscous in a bowl. Cover for 5 minutes, then spread on a plate, and leave to cool. Stir in the turmeric, chopped rosemary, garlic, cheese, and seasoning. Oil a roasting pan and heat it in the oven.

2 Put the egg on one plate, and the flour on another. Dip the fish in the flour, then the egg, then the couscous. Put it in the hot roasting pan. Bake for 15 minutes until golden and cooked through, turning once.

3 Meanwhile, heat the purée and honey together in a pan. Season to taste. Spoon on to 4 warmed plates and top with the halibut. Garnish with sprigs of rosemary and serve with baby potatoes and green beans.

Teriyaki fish with noodles

Impress your friends with this deceptively easy meal. The aromatic flavors of teriyaki sauce are a popular and delicious combination with sweet, thick fish fillets.

The fish

Cod loins, or thick fillets of salmon or mahi mahi

• **PREP** 10 mins • **COOK** 15 mins • **SERVES** 4

Ingredients

4 cod loins, about 5½oz (150g) each, scaled and pinboned

9oz (250g) thick or medium udon noodles, or thin rice noodles

4 scallions, sliced

handful of cilantro, leaves only

lime quarters, to serve

For the teriyaki sauce

1–2 tbsp dark soy sauce

1 tbsp honey

1in (2.5cm) fresh ginger, peeled and grated

pinch of sugar

1 tbsp mirin or dry sherry

1 Preheat the oven to 400°F (200°C). Mix the ingredients for the teriyaki sauce in a bowl. Pour over the fish, and leave for 10 minutes.

2 Sit the fish and sauce in a roasting pan, and bake for 15 minutes, until cooked through.

3 Meanwhile, prepare the noodles according to the package instructions. Leave for a few minutes, then drain and toss with the scallions and cilantro. Serve with the fish and lime.

Skewered swordfish with caperberries

A very easy, yet satisfying and piquant dish. You'll need 12–15 short wooden skewers, or toothpicks.

The fish

Swordfish, or tuna, mahi mahi, or marlin

• **PREP** 15 mins • **COOK** 10 mins • **SERVES** 4

Ingredients

1lb (450g) swordfish steaks, cut into bite-sized pieces

salt and freshly ground black pepper

3 tbsp olive oil

1 tbsp white wine vinegar

2 tbsp caperberries

2 garlic cloves, finely sliced

splash of chili oil, to serve

1 If using wooden skewers, soak them in cold water for 30 minutes before using. Preheat the oven to 400°F (200°C). Thread 3 pieces of swordfish on to each skewer. Place in a baking dish and season with salt and pepper.

2 Mix the oil, vinegar, caperberries, and garlic in a small bowl, crushing half the caperberries with the back of a fork. Pour evenly over the swordfish and bake for 10 minutes. Serve with a splash of chili oil and fresh crusty bread.

Pike with herb crust

This recipe works well with many fish that have a reputation for a slightly earthy taste. Pike has lots of large pinbones so make sure you take care to remove them all.

The fish

Pike, or walleye, freshwater perch, carp, gray mullet, or trout

- **PREP** 15 mins ▪ **COOK** 12–15 mins
- **SERVES** 4

Ingredients

4 pike fillets, about 6oz (175g) each, pinboned and skinned

3 tbsp butter

1 tbsp chopped flat-leaf parsley

juice of ½ lemon

salt and freshly ground black pepper

sprigs of sage, to garnish

lemon wedges, to garnish

For the crust

8 tbsp fresh breadcrumbs

2 tbsp melted butter

1 tbsp chopped sage

1 tbsp chopped chives

grated zest of ½ lemon

1 Preheat the oven to 400°F (200°C). Arrange the fish on a baking sheet.

2 Mix the butter, parsley, and lemon juice, and season with salt and plenty of pepper. Spread a thin layer of butter over each fish.

3 Mix together the breadcrumbs, melted butter, sage, chives, and lemon zest, season lightly, and sprinkle over the fish, pressing to stick to the butter.

4 Roast in the oven for 12–15 minutes or until the fish is cooked—it will be white, firm, and opaque.

5 Transfer to a warmed serving dish, garnish with the sage and lemon wedges, and serve with green beans.

Sea bass in a salt crust

This classic North Italian dish is usually served with aïoli or mayonnaise. It is one of the very few recipes where the fish is not scaled before cooking, as the scales help to prevent the fish from absorbing the salt.

The fish

Sea bass, or sea bream or gray mullet

- **PREP** 25 mins ▪ **COOK** 22–25 mins
- **SERVES** 4

Ingredients

1 whole sea bass, about 3–4½lb (1.35–2kg), trimmed

2¼lb (1kg) coarse sea salt

1–2 egg whites

1 Preheat the oven to 425°F (220°C). Gut the fish through the gills (see page 266). Clean well and rinse, but do not scale.

2 Spread a layer of salt on to a large piece of foil on a baking sheet. Arrange the fish on top. Moisten the remaining salt with the egg whites, adding a splash of water if necessary. Pack this mixture on the fish to completely encase it.

3 Bake in the preheated oven for 22–25 minutes. Transfer the fish on to a serving dish. At the table, carefully chip off any remaining salt crust. Peel away the skin and serve the fish straight from the bone with aïoli or mayonnaise.

PIKE FLAVOR PAIRINGS: The fine flavor of pike is flattered by unsalted butter, pungent sage, cream, and bay leaf. Any earthy taste can be cut with lemon and white wine.

Mackerel roasted with harissa and lime

Hot harissa paste and citrus are perfect partners for mackerel, which takes assertive flavors well.

The fish

Mackerel, or herring or trout

- **PREP** 10 mins • **COOK** 30 mins • **SERVES** 4

Ingredients

4 large or 8 small mackerel, scaled, gutted, and washed

3–4 tsp harissa paste

1½ tbsp olive oil

2 limes, quartered

2½lb (1.1kg) baby new potatoes, halved if large

handful of fresh cilantro, finely chopped

1 Preheat the oven to 400°F (200°C). Lay the mackerel in a roasting pan, then mix the harissa paste with half the oil. Drizzle this over the fish, making sure the mackerel are covered inside and out. Add the limes to the pan, then toss the potatoes with the remaining oil and add them to the pan, too.

2 Roast in the oven for 20–30 minutes, or until the potatoes and fish are cooked through. Scatter with the cilantro, and serve with a crisp green salad.

Halibut with chunky romesco

Romesco is a classic sauce from Catalonia, Spain, made from tomatoes, garlic, onion, peppers, almonds, and olive oil.

The fish

Halibut, or swordfish or mahi mahi

- **PREP** 10 mins • **COOK** 30 mins • **SERVES** 6

Ingredients

3 tbsp extra virgin olive oil, plus extra for greasing

2¼lb (1kg) halibut fillets, ¾in (2cm) thick, scaled

salt and freshly ground black pepper

2 garlic cloves, grated or finely chopped

2½oz (75g) almonds, coarsely chopped

4½oz (125g) breadcrumbs

3 tbsp chopped flat-leaf parsley

For the romesco sauce

12oz (350g) jar roasted red peppers, rinsed, patted dry, and coarsely chopped

1 tbsp sherry vinegar

¼ tsp cayenne pepper

pinch of smoked paprika

1 Preheat the oven to 450°F (230°C). Brush the bottom of an ovenproof dish with olive oil, and add the fish, skin-side down. Season to taste.

2 Heat 2 tbsp oil in a heavy frying pan. Add the garlic, almonds, and breadcrumbs, and fry over medium heat, stirring, for 6–8 minutes, until just golden. Do not let the nuts burn. Stir in the parsley, then spoon the mixture over the fish.

3 Bake the fish uncovered for 5 minutes, then loosely cover with foil, and bake for 15 minutes, or until just cooked through. The fish will flake easily when it is ready. Remove from the oven and sprinkle with the remaining olive oil.

4 Meanwhile, to make the romesco sauce, combine all the ingredients. Either serve the fish topped with the sauce, or serve the romesco separately in a bowl.

Prepare ahead

The romesco sauce can be made, covered, and refrigerated for 2 days. The flavors will deepen. The nut and breadcrumb topping can be made 6 hours ahead and stored in an airtight container at room temperature.

Mackerel with garlic and tomatoes

A very speedy superfood supper.

The fish

Mackerel, or sardines, herring, or trout

- **PREP** 10 mins ▪ **COOK** 25 mins ▪ **SERVES** 4

Ingredients

24 cherry tomatoes on the vine

4 garlic cloves

few sprigs of thyme

grated zest of 1 lemon

pinch of red pepper flakes

1–2 tbsp olive oil

salt and freshly ground black pepper

4 mackerel fillets, about 4–5½oz (115–150g) each, scaled

1 Preheat the oven to 400°F (200°C). Put the tomatoes, garlic, and thyme in a roasting pan. Sprinkle over the zest and pepper flakes. Drizzle with oil, and season. Roast in the oven for 10 minutes, until the tomatoes soften and shrivel.

2 Remove from the oven, sit the mackerel on the tomatoes, then cover with foil. Return to the oven for a further 10–15 minutes, until the fish is cooked through. Serve hot with salad and fresh crusty bread.

Roasted squid and potato with spiced cilantro pesto

Herby and immensely satisfying, this is a different way to cook squid.

The fish

Squid, or tuna, swordfish, or scallops

- **PREP** 10 mins ▪ **COOK** 20 mins ▪ **SERVES** 4

Ingredients

2½lb (1.1kg) waxy potatoes, cut into chunks

2 tbsp olive oil

salt and freshly ground black pepper

12oz (350g) squid, gutted, cleaned, and scored (see page 282)

pinch of red pepper flakes (optional)

For the pesto

large handful of cilantro leaves

large handful of basil leaves

2 garlic cloves, chopped

large handful of pine nuts

2oz (60g) Parmesan cheese, grated

pinch of red pepper flakes

⅔ cup extra virgin olive oil

1 Preheat the oven to 400°F (200°C). To make the pesto, put the herbs, garlic, pine nuts, most of the Parmesan, and the red pepper flakes in a food processor, and whizz to grind. Slowly add the olive oil in a stream, until it forms a smooth paste. Stir in the remaining Parmesan.

2 Put the potatoes in a roasting pan. Drizzle over half the oil, and toss. Season, and roast in the oven for 15–20 minutes until golden.

3 Meanwhile, mix the squid with the remaining oil and pepper flakes. Add to the potatoes for the last 10 minutes of cooking. Toss everything together, and serve with the cilantro pesto.

Prepare ahead

Make the pesto up to 3 days ahead, cover with a film of extra virgin olive oil, seal, then refrigerate. (If not completely covered with oil, it will discolor and begin to stale.)

Roast cod with garlic

Cooked at a very high temperature, the flour seasons the fish well.

The fish

Cod, or any firm, meaty white fish, such as pollock, haddock, ling, snapper, or Patagonian toothfish

- **PREP** 5 mins ▪ **COOK** 15 mins ▪ **SERVES** 4

Ingredients

5 tbsp extra virgin olive oil

2 sprigs of rosemary

4 garlic cloves, unpeeled

4 cod loins, about 6oz (170g) each, skin on, scaled and pinboned

2 tbsp seasoned flour (see page 55)

1 Preheat the oven to 450°F (230°C). Put the olive oil in a large, heavy-duty, flameproof roasting pan, add the rosemary and garlic and cook in the oven for 2–3 minutes. Remove from the oven.

2 Dry the cod with paper towels. Dust with the seasoned flour and shake to remove excess.

3 Put the fish skin side down in the hot oil, place the roasting pan over medium heat and fry for 2–3 minutes or until the skin is crisp. Turn the fish over and put in the oven. Roast for 6–7 minutes or until just cooked—the flesh should be white and flake easily—and the garlic is soft. Serve straight away.

Roast gurnard with bacon

This fish has a very special flavor, and is best cooked on the bone.

The fish

Gurnard, or monkfish

- **PREP** 5 mins ▪ **COOK** 7–10 mins
- **SERVES** 4

Ingredients

4 small to medium gurnard, scaled, gutted, and trimmed

salt and freshly ground black pepper

4 smoked bacon strips, cut in half

4 sprigs of thyme

1 tbsp extra olive oil

lemon wedges, to serve

flat-leaf parsley, to serve

1 Preheat the oven to 400°F (200°C). Arrange the fish on a baking sheet and season.

2 Stretch each strip of bacon with the back of a kitchen knife.

3 Arrange a sprig of thyme over each fish and drape with 2 half strips of bacon; do not tuck them under the fish. Drizzle with olive oil and roast in the oven for 7–10 minutes or until the bacon is brown and the fish cooked; it should be white and opaque.

4 Lift on to a warmed plate and serve with lemon wedges and parsley.

GURNARD FLAVOR PAIRINGS: Sweet-tasting gurnard is great with plenty of olive oil, or with pancetta, bacon, or chorizo—salty flavors that will flatter the fish and keep it moist during cooking.

Monkfish wrapped in prosciutto

This popular meaty fish takes robust flavors well and is also low in fat.

The fish

Monkfish, or catfish or salmon

- **PREP** 5 mins ▪ **COOK** 12–15 mins ▪ **SERVES** 2

Ingredients

2 monkfish fillets, about 5oz (140g) each, trimmed of membrane (see page 270)

splash of olive oil

½ tbsp chopped flat-leaf parsley

½ tbsp chopped basil

4 slices of prosciutto or pancetta

freshly ground black pepper

1 Preheat the oven to 425°F (220°C). Arrange the monkfish on a lightly oiled baking sheet, sprinkle with the herbs, and drape the prosciutto slices over the top. Brush with more olive oil and season with pepper.

2 Roast in the oven for 12–15 minutes or until the fish is firm and opaque and the prosciutto is crisp. Serve with a green salad.

MONKFISH FLAVOR PAIRINGS:

This sturdy, firm, sweet fish stands up as well to punchy chorizo, sage, and arugula, as it does to basil and prosciutto. Or try it rubbed with spices.

Baked salt cod

Salt fish including cod and Alaskan pollock are excellent staples to have on hand for fishcakes and baked dishes.

The fish

Salt cod, or salt pollock or salt ling

- **PREP** 40 mins, plus overnight soaking
- **COOK** 40 mins ▪ **SERVES** 4

Ingredients

1lb (450g) strips of boneless, skinless salt cod

3 tbsp extra virgin olive oil

1lb (450g) potatoes, peeled and diced

1 large onion, finely sliced

2 garlic cloves, crushed

2 red bell peppers, thickly sliced

freshly ground black pepper

1¼ cups fish stock

handful of black olives

2 tbsp chopped flat-leaf parsley

1 Soak the salt cod in several changes of water for 24 hours.

2 Preheat the oven to 375°F (190°C). Heat the oil in a large flameproof casserole over medium heat, add the potatoes, and stir for 5–6 minutes or until beginning to brown. Add the onion and cook for another 3–4 minutes. Stir in the garlic and red peppers. Season with pepper, pour in the stock, cover, and bake in the oven for 15 minutes.

3 Tuck the salt cod into the potatoes and red peppers and return to the oven for another 15–20 minutes, or until the salt cod is white and flakes easily.

4 Remove from the oven and stir in the olives and parsley. Serve with a green salad.

Prepare ahead

While the salt cod must be soaked 24 hours in advance of cooking, the potato base made in Step 2 can also be made 1 day ahead, cooled, covered, and refrigerated. Reheat in the oven for 10 minutes before continuing.

Hungarian roast carp

The world's most extensively farmed fish, carp is popular in countries with no easy access to the coast, including Hungary and China.

The fish

Carp, or sea bass, sea bream, or freshwater perch

- **PREP** 25 mins, plus soaking ▪ **COOK** 30 mins
- **SERVES** 4

Ingredients

2¾lb (1.25kg) carp, scaled, gutted, and trimmed

3 tbsp white wine vinegar

2 tbsp seasoned flour (see page 55)

1 tsp paprika

For the topping

1lb (450g) floury potatoes, peeled and cut into ¾in (1.5cm) cubes

salt and freshly ground black pepper

splash of vegetable oil

3¾oz (110g) chopped bacon

3 tbsp coarsely chopped gherkins or dill pickles

2 tbsp chopped flat-leaf parsley

1 Preheat the oven to 375°F (190°C). Put the carp into a sink of cold water with the vinegar for 10 minutes. Transfer to a cutting board and pat dry with paper towels.

2 Mix the seasoned flour and paprika and dredge over the fish to coat evenly. Arrange on a baking sheet and cook in the oven for 15 minutes.

3 Meanwhile, blanch the potatoes in boiling salted water for 3–4 minutes. Drain and reserve 1 cup of the cooking water.

4 In a separate frying pan, heat the oil and cook the potatoes until beginning to brown. Add the bacon and cook for another 2–3 minutes. Add the gherkins and parsley, and season well.

5 Spoon this mixture over the carp and pour in the reserved potato liquid. Return to the oven for 15–20 minutes or until the carp is completely cooked: the flesh should be white and opaque and will easily pull away from the bone. Serve with roasted red peppers.

Simple Italian roast lobster

This Neapolitan dish is easy to prepare and makes an excellent celebration dish.

The fish

Lobster, or Dublin Bay prawns or shrimp

- **PREP** 15 mins ▪ **COOK** 15 mins ▪ **SERVES** 4

Ingredients

2 cooked lobsters, preferably rock lobsters, split and prepared (see pages 290–291)

4 tbsp Italian extra virgin olive oil

4 tbsp finely chopped flat-leaf parsley, plus extra sprigs, to serve

2 garlic cloves, crushed

3–4 tbsp fresh breadcrumbs

salt and freshly ground black pepper

lemon wedges, to serve

1 Preheat the oven to 375°F (190°C). Place the split lobsters on a large baking sheet or baking dish.

2 Heat the olive oil in a small saucepan, add the parsley and garlic, and sizzle for 30 seconds, then stir in the breadcrumbs and season well.

3 Spoon the mixture over the cut lobster flesh. Bake in the oven for 7–10 minutes, or until the lobsters are piping hot. Remove from the oven and arrange on a large, warmed serving dish with lemon wedges.

CARP FLAVOR PAIRINGS: This fish is best with central European tastes of paprika, butter, capers, dill, garlic, parsley, and cornmeal, or fresh ginger, rice wine, and sesame.

Poached and Steamed

Sole bonne femme

A delicious old-fashioned recipe.

The fish

Dover sole, or any flat fish

- **PREP** 30 mins · **COOK** 30 mins · **SERVES** 4

Ingredients

1 tbsp butter, plus extra for the baking dish

3½ cups mushrooms, sliced

salt and freshly ground black pepper

2 shallots, finely chopped

2 Dover sole, about 2¼lb (1kg) each, filleted, heads and bones reserved

For the fish stock

1 onion, sliced

3–5 sprigs of flat-leaf parsley

1 tsp peppercorns

1 cup dry white wine or juice of 1 lemon

For the velouté sauce

2 tbsp butter

2 tbsp all-purpose flour

3 tbsp heavy cream

3 egg yolks

juice of ½ lemon, or to taste

1 Put the fish heads and bones in a saucepan. Add the sliced onion, 2 cups water, parsley, peppercorns, and wine. Simmer for 20 minutes.

2 Preheat the oven to 350°F (180°C). Melt the butter in a pan, add the mushrooms, salt, and pepper. Cook for 5 minutes. Set aside.

3 Butter a baking dish and add the shallots. Fold each fillet in half, skinned side in, and put on top. Half-cover with stock. Top with foil. Poach in the oven for 15–18 minutes. Drain, reserving the liquid, and keep warm.

4 Add the cooking liquid and shallots to the remaining stock; boil down to 1½ cups. Melt the butter in a separate saucepan. Whisk in the flour. Cook for 1–2 minutes, strain in the reduced stock, then simmer for 5 minutes. Remove from the heat and add the mushrooms.

5 Whisk the cream and egg yolks in a small bowl. Whisk in a little hot sauce, then stir it all back into the sauce. Stir over low heat for 2–3 minutes. Add lemon juice, salt, and pepper.

6 Preheat the broiler. Arrange the fillets on flameproof plates. Ladle the sauce over the top, broil for 1–2 minutes, then serve at once.

Sole veronique

This dish, with white grapes, is part of the classic French repertoire.

The fish

Lemon sole, or petrale sole, halibut, or turbot

- **PREP** 30 mins · **COOK** 20 mins · **SERVES** 4

Ingredients

4 lemon sole, skinned and filleted

½ onion, thinly sliced

6 black peppercorns

1 bay leaf

½ cup dry white wine

6oz (175g) seedless white grapes

For the sauce

4 tbsp butter

1 rounded tbsp all-purpose flour

5 tbsp warm milk

5 tbsp heavy cream

salt and freshly ground white pepper

1 Preheat the oven to 350°F (180°C). Fold the sole fillets into 3, skinned-side in. Arrange in an ovenproof dish and sprinkle around the onion, peppercorns, and bay leaf. Mix the wine with ½ cup water, pour in, and cover with buttered parchment paper.

2 Poach in the oven for 10–12 minutes or until the fish is cooked; it will be white and opaque. Remove the fish and keep warm. Strain the cooking liquor into a saucepan and boil rapidly to reduce to 1 cup. Peel the grapes (a paperclip assists greatly), and set aside.

3 In another saucepan, melt half the butter, remove from the heat, and stir in the flour. Cook over low to medium heat for 30 seconds. Remove from the heat and blend in the milk, then the fish liquor. Return to low heat and bring to a boil, stirring. Stir in the cream, remove from the heat, and whisk in the remaining butter. Season, add the grapes, and heat through.

4 Transfer the fish on to warmed plates. Carefully spoon over the sauce to serve.

Prepare ahead

Peel the grapes up to 4 hours in advance, cover, and chill. Return to room temperature before adding to the sauce.

PETRALE SOLE FLAVOR PAIRING:

A fine, sweet fish, lovely when bathed in a cream sauce, or try it more simply with butter and lemon, or even deep-fried.

Truite au bleu

For this recipe, you need to use just-caught, unwashed trout, gutted through the gills. The trout's blue color is a result of the reaction between the vinegar and the slime on the skin.

The fish

Trout, or any freshwater fish, such as carp or perch

- **PREP** 10 mins ▪ **COOK** 35 mins ▪ **SERVES** 2

Ingredients

1 cup white wine vinegar

1 onion, sliced

1 carrot, sliced

2 bay leaves

4 sprigs of thyme

4 sprigs of flat-leaf parsley

6 black peppercorns

2 small trout, freshly caught, unwashed, scaled, and gutted through the gills (see page 266)

4 tbsp butter, to serve

salt and freshly ground black pepper, to serve

squeeze of lemon juice, to serve

1 Pour 1 quart water, ½ cup of the vinegar, the onion and carrot, half the herbs, and the peppercorns into a saucepan. Simmer for 15 minutes. Strain this court bouillon into a clean saucepan and return to a boil.

2 Prepare the trout and place in a flameproof roasting pan. Bring the remaining vinegar to a boil and pour directly over the fish, then pour in the court bouillon. It should be just covered. Add the remaining herbs.

3 Bring to a boil and poach for 12–15 minutes or until the fish is cooked. The eye of the fish will be white and the dorsal fin will peel away easily. The flesh will be flaky and a delicate pink. Remove the fish from the roasting pan and allow to drip dry for a moment or two, then transfer to a serving dish.

4 Heat the butter in a separate saucepan with a little salt and pepper, allow the milk solids in the butter to brown, and immediately add the lemon juice; it will sizzle. Now pour straight over the trout, and serve with roast potatoes and a simple salad.

Poached turbot with champagne and oysters

Rich and decadent, this is an all-time Escoffier classic from the French culinary repertoire.

The fish

Turbot, or halibut or flounder, and oysters, or mussels or scallops

- **PREP** 35 mins ▪ **COOK** 30 mins ▪ **SERVES** 4

Ingredients

4 turbot fillets, about 6oz (175g) each, scaled

1¼ cups Champagne

½ cup fish stock

1 tsp black peppercorns

2 sprigs of thyme

1 bay leaf

sprigs of flat-leaf parsley

4 tsp Sevruga caviar (optional), to garnish

For the sauce

2 tbsp butter

1 tbsp all-purpose flour

⅔ cup heavy cream

salt and freshly ground black pepper

2 tbsp snipped chives

6 oysters, preferably native, removed from the shell

1 Skin the turbot and fold in half. Put the Champagne, stock, peppercorns, and herbs into a large sauté pan, bring to a boil, and simmer for 1 minute. Remove from the heat.

2 Put the turbot into the hot liquid, cover with buttered parchment paper, and slowly bring to a boil. Reduce the heat until it just quivers and poach for 6–7 minutes, or until opaque.

3 Melt the butter in a small saucepan, remove from the heat, and blend in the flour.

4 When the fish is cooked, lift it from the liquid and keep warm. Add a splash of the liquid at a time to the butter and flour over low heat, stirring constantly. Once it has all been added, bring to a boil, stirring. Simmer for 4–5 minutes until thickening. Blend in the heavy cream and simmer until the sauce coats the back of a spoon. Season.

5 Add the chives and oysters, and poach for 1 minute or until the oysters are firm. Arrange the turbot on a warmed plate and coat with the sauce and oysters. Top each fillet with a small spoon of caviar, if using.

TURBOT FLAVOR PAIRINGS: The fine, firm flesh of turbot is delicious with wild mushrooms, cream, Gruyère or Parmesan cheeses, and butter, or a sauce made from shellfish stock with lemon.

Skate with beurre noire and capers

Skate is subject to overfishing so choose a sustainable smaller, fast-growing species, such as spotted or cuckoo ray, for this recipe. It is poached in a lightly acidulated court bouillon in this classic French dish.

The fish

Skate, or any flat fish

- **PREP** 15 mins - **COOK** 30 mins - **SERVES** 2

Ingredients

1 onion, sliced

1 carrot, sliced

1 celery rib, sliced

1 cup medium white wine

1 bay leaf

2 skate wings, about 6oz (175g) each, skinned (see page 277)

4 tbsp unsalted butter

2 tbsp white or red wine vinegar

2 tsp capers

2 tsp chopped flat-leaf parsley

1 Put 3 quarts of water, the onion, carrot, celery, white wine, and bay leaf into a large sauté pan, bring to a boil, and simmer for 15 minutes. Remove from the heat and cool for a few minutes.

2 Lower the skate into the court bouillon, bring to a boil, reduce the heat, and poach for 10–12 minutes. It is cooked when the thick part of the cartilage at the "shoulder" of the wing will pull away easily. Lift on to a plate and pat dry with paper towels.

3 Melt the butter in a large frying pan, allow it to sizzle, and then keep cooking until it is nut brown, but not smoking. Add the vinegar, capers, and parsley, and pour the furiously sizzling sauce over the skate wings to serve.

Prepare ahead

Make the court bouillon up to 2 days ahead, cover, and refrigerate. Return to just under a simmer before continuing.

Bourride

Rich, creamy, and served in many French restaurants, this recipe uses mussels, but other fish are great here, too.

The fish

Mussels, or haddock, cod, or Patagonian toothfish

- **PREP** 35 mins - **COOK** 20 mins - **SERVES** 4

Ingredients

4$\frac{1}{2}$lb (2kg) mussels, prepared (see page 278)

2 tbsp unsalted butter

2 shallots, finely chopped

3 garlic cloves, crushed

large pinch of saffron

1 tsp medium curry powder

2–3 strips of orange zest

$\frac{2}{3}$ cup dry white wine

$\frac{2}{3}$ cup mayonnaise

2 tbsp chopped flat-leaf parsley

squeeze of lemon juice

salt and freshly ground black pepper

warm baguette, to serve

1 Check to be sure the mussels are all closed; discard any that are broken or will not shut when sharply tapped.

2 Melt the butter in a very large saucepan or flameproof casserole over very low heat, add the shallots and 1 garlic clove, and cook for 1–2 minutes to soften. Add the saffron, curry powder, and orange zest, stir, then pour in the wine. Bring to a boil and simmer for 1–2 minutes.

3 Add the mussels. Cover with a well-fitting lid and steam for 4–5 minutes, or until they are fully opened. Lift the mussels into a large soup tureen or divide between 4 individual bowls and keep warm.

4 Bring the cooking liquor to a boil and reduce to half the original quantity by boiling rapidly over high heat. Mix 3–4 tbsp of the liquid into the mayonnaise and stir in the remaining garlic, the parsley, lemon juice, and seasoning. Whisk the mayonnaise back into the hot cooking liquid, set over low heat and stir until it comes to just under a boil. (Do not boil or it will separate). Spoon over the mussels and serve with the baguette.

SKATE FLAVOR PAIRINGS: Sharp, piquant tastes match deliciously with skate. Try vinegar, capers, parsley, and lemon juice, and marry those flavors with butter.

Poached salmon with dill butter

Poaching is one of the simplest methods of cooking salmon, and it produces a succulent result.

The fish
Salmon, or char, trout, or pollock

- **PREP** 10 mins ▪ **COOK** 10 mins ▪ **SERVES** 4

Ingredients
4 skinless salmon fillets or steaks, about 6oz (175g) each, scaled and pinboned

2 cups court bouillon (see page 302)

4 tbsp butter, softened

2 tbsp finely chopped dill

grated zest and juice of ½ lemon

salt and freshly ground black pepper

sprigs of dill, to serve

lemon wedges, to serve

1 Put the salmon into a sauté pan. Add the court bouillon with some water to ensure the fish is just submerged. Bring slowly to a boil, reduce the heat, and cook over low heat so that the liquid just simmers. Cover and cook for 4–6 minutes or until the fish has lost its translucency and is pale pink in color.

2 Meanwhile put the butter, dill, and lemon zest into a small bowl and beat until smooth. Then gradually beat in the lemon juice and season well.

3 Remove the fish from the court bouillon and pat dry with paper towels. Melt the dill butter in a frying pan and add the fish, turning it once to ensure it is evenly coated. Lift on to a warmed serving dish and drizzle with the remaining butter. Garnish with dill and lemon wedges, and serve with new potatoes and steamed asparagus.

Variation

Poached salmon with cilantro and lime butter
Make as above, but mix the butter with a large handful of chopped fresh cilantro, and 2 peeled, segmented, and coarsely chopped limes, instead of the dill and lemon. Serve hot with new potatoes.

Whole poached and dressed salmon

A classic for cold buffets, traditionally served with hollandaise sauce.

The fish
Salmon, or sea trout, large brown trout, or large rainbow trout and shrimp

- **PREP** 40 mins ▪ **COOK** 45 mins
- **SERVES** 8–10

Ingredients
4½–6½lb (2–3kg) salmon, scaled, gutted through the gills (see page 266), and trimmed

3–4 quarts court bouillon (see page 302)

For decoration
1 cucumber, thinly sliced

24 unpeeled, cooked shrimp, deveined (see page 285)

handful of sprigs of dill

1¼ cups aspic jelly (optional)

To serve
grated zest of 1 lemon, and a squeeze of juice

1¼ cups mayonnaise

1 Make sure the fish is clean and the bloodline has been removed. Trim the tail into a "V" shape with scissors.

2 Arrange the fish in a suitable flameproof baking tray or on the trivet of a fish kettle. Pour in the court bouillon. Cover and bring to a boil, then reduce the heat so the liquid barely quivers. Cook for 15 minutes, then remove from the heat and leave the fish in the liquid for another 15 minutes. Remove from the fish kettle and allow to cool completely.

3 Very carefully peel away the top skin of the fish, carefully turn, and remove the skin from the other side. Slide on to a serving dish. Arrange slices of cucumber over the fillets and decorate with shrimp and dill. If it is not to be served within an hour or two, a coating of aspic can keep it glossy. Follow the package instructions to make the aspic, cool completely, then spoon over the top of the garnish and fish.

4 Mix the lemon into the mayonnaise and serve separately, with potato and side salads.

Prepare ahead
Poach the fish up to 6 hours ahead, cover, and refrigerate. Return to room temperature before garnishing and serving.

CHAR FLAVOR PAIRING: Excellent poached with butter and dill, or highlight the taste with white wine vinegar and lemon, or even pair with toasted hazelnuts and almonds in a sauté.

Steamed halibut with dill butter sauce and cucumber

There is a good supply of farmed Atlantic halibut and excellent supplies of Pacific halibut (often frozen).

The fish
Halibut, or turbot or salmon

- **PREP** 40 mins, plus soaking ▪ **COOK** 20 mins
- **SERVES** 4

Ingredients
2 tbsp sea salt

4 halibut steaks or thick-cut fillets, about 6oz (175g) each, scaled

For the dill butter sauce
8 tbsp unsalted butter, plus 2 tbsp to serve, plus extra for steaming

1 shallot, finely chopped

⅔ cup fish stock

5 tbsp dry white wine

2 tbsp aquavit or vermouth

2 tbsp chopped dill

squeeze of lemon juice

freshly ground black pepper

1 large cucumber, peeled, seeded, and thinly sliced

1 Heat the salt and 1¼ cups of water over medium heat, stirring until dissolved. Cool.

2 Put the halibut into a deep dish, pour in the cold salt solution, and soak for 15 minutes.

3 Remove the fish from the liquid and arrange in a steamer lined with buttered parchment paper (you may need 2 steamers). Steam for 10–12 minutes or until white and opaque.

4 Melt 1 tbsp of the butter in a small saucepan and add the shallot; cook over low heat for 3–4 minutes. Add the stock, wine, and aquavit, bring to a boil, and simmer until the liquid has reduced by one-third. Pull the pan a little off the heat and beat in the butter, a tablespoon at a time, until the sauce is creamy and buttery. Add the dill, lemon, salt, and pepper. Set aside.

5 In a frying pan, melt the 2 tbsp butter until beginning to brown, add the cucumber, and toss for 1–2 minutes until very hot.

6 Spoon the cucumber on to a large dish and arrange the fish on top. Spoon the dill butter sauce over the top to serve.

Sea bass with black bean sauce

A wonderful combination. The well-flavored bass works well with the saltiness of the sauce.

The fish
Sea bass, or sea bream, pomfret, or snapper

- **PREP** 25 mins ▪ **COOK** 30 mins ▪ **SERVES** 4

Ingredients
3 tbsp black fermented Chinese beans

2 tbsp sunflower oil

2 scallions, finely chopped

2in (5cm) fresh ginger, cut into matchsticks

1 garlic clove, very finely sliced

3 tbsp soy sauce

2 tbsp Chinese rice wine or dry sherry

1 tsp superfine sugar

1 cup fish stock

1 tsp cornstarch

4 sea bass fillets, about 6oz (175g) each, scaled and pinboned

sprigs of cilantro, to garnish

splash of sesame oil

1 Rinse the black beans very thoroughly under cold running water. Heat the oil in a large frying pan over low heat. Add the scallions and ginger, and cook over low heat until aromatic. Add the garlic and stir-fry for another minute.

2 Remove from the heat and add the soy sauce, rice wine, and sugar; bring to a boil. Add three-quarters of the stock and return to the heat. Bring to a boil and simmer for a couple of minutes. Mix the cornstarch with the remaining stock in a small bowl.

3 Arrange the fish on a bamboo steamer and cook for 7–8 minutes, covered, over a large saucepan of simmering water.

4 Meanwhile, stir the cornstarch mixture into the hot stock with the beans, stir to a boil, and simmer for 2–3 minutes until thickened slightly.

5 Arrange the fish on a platter with the cilantro. Spoon the sauce over the top and drizzle with sesame oil. Serve with rice.

Prepare ahead
The black bean sauce can be made 1 day ahead, covered, and refrigerated. Return to a simmer before continuing. Add a splash of water, until the consistency is as you prefer.

SEA BASS FLAVOR PAIRINGS: Chinese flavors are great with sea bass, but also try Mediterranean tomatoes, garlic, olive oil, and red bell peppers, or even Pernod.

Steamed carp in beer sauce

If you would like a spicier dish, add a few juniper berries, peppercorns, or cloves to the fish before steaming.

The fish

Carp, or sea bass, sea bream, scallops, or monkfish

- **PREP** 10 mins ▪ **COOK** 15 mins ▪ **SERVES** 4

Ingredients

1 carp, about 3lb (1.35kg), filleted, pinboned, and skinned

11fl oz (330ml) sweet malt or dark beer, or wheat beer

1 onion, finely sliced

1 celery stalk, finely sliced

1 carrot, finely sliced

4–5 thick flat-leaf parsley sprigs

1 bay leaf

1 tsp salt

8 tbsp unsalted butter

½ cup gingerbread crumbs

2–3 tsp cornstarch (optional)

freshly ground black pepper

2 tbsp chopped flat-leaf parsley

1 Cut any large carp fillets into portion-sized pieces. Arrange the fillets on a steamer.

2 Put the beer, onion, celery, carrot, parsley sprigs, bay leaf, and salt into a large saucepan. Bring to a boil and simmer for 2–3 minutes. Arrange the steamer over the bubbling beer. Steam for 7–10 minutes or until the carp is cooked: it will be firm and opaque.

3 Lift the carp from the steamer and keep warm. Strain out and discard the vegetables from the beer, then return it to the heat. Whisk in the butter a little at a time. Stir in enough of the gingerbread crumbs to form a smooth and creamy sauce. (If you prefer, you can sieve the sauce.) If the sauce seems too thin, mix the cornstarch with enough water to make a paste, and slowly whisk it into the sauce, over low heat, until it thickens. Season to taste with pepper.

4 Arrange the carp in a deep-sided dish, pour over a little sauce, and sprinkle with parsley. Serve the remaining sauce on the side.

Chinese-style steamed bass

An impressive but easy dish that brings out the clean, delicate flavors of the sea bass.

The fish

Sea bass, or snapper or bream

- **PREP** 15 mins ▪ **COOK** 20–24 mins
- **SERVES** 4

Ingredients

8 tbsp dark soy sauce

8 tbsp Chinese rice wine or dry sherry

6 tbsp shredded fresh ginger

4 small sea bass, scaled, gutted, and rinsed

2 tbsp sesame oil

1 tsp salt

4 scallions, trimmed and shredded

8 tbsp sunflower oil

4 garlic cloves, grated or finely chopped

2 small red chiles, seeded and shredded

finely grated zest of 2 limes

1 Prepare a steamer, or position a steaming rack above a wok containing water. Bring to a boil.

2 Stir together the soy sauce, rice wine, and 4 tbsp ginger, and set aside. Using a sharp knife, make slashes in the fish, 1in (2.5cm) apart and not as deep as the bone, on both sides. Rub the fish inside and out with the sesame oil and salt.

3 Scatter one-quarter of the scallions over a heatproof serving dish that will hold 2 fish and fit in the steamer. Place 2 fish on the dish and pour over half the sauce.

4 Place the dish in the steamer, cover, and steam for 10–12 minutes, or until the fish flakes easily when tested with a knife. Remove the fish, cover, and keep warm. Repeat with the remaining fish.

5 Meanwhile, heat the sunflower oil in a small saucepan over medium-high heat until it shimmers. Scatter the fish with the remaining scallions and ginger, the garlic, chiles, and lime zest. Drizzle the oil over the fish and serve.

Steamed trout filled with herbs

The flavor of trout pairs well with the fresh herbs and acidity of the wine in this recipe.

The fish
Trout, salmon, char, or mackerel

- **PREP** 5 mins · **COOK** 15–20 mins
- **SERVES** 2 generously

Ingredients
1 trout weighing about 2¼lb (1kg), scaled and gutted

sea salt and freshly ground black pepper

small bunch of herbs including flat-leaf parsley, dill, chervil, and sage

⅔ cup medium white wine

2 tbsp unsalted butter, melted

lemon wedges, to serve

1 Wash the fish well and check the belly cavity shows no traces of blood. Season the cavity, and fill with the herbs.

2 Pour 2in (5cm) of water into a large saucepan, add the wine, and bring to a boil. Arrange the fish on a large plate or steamer. Cover with a tight-fitting lid and steam for 15–20 minutes or until the eye has turned white and you can feel the fish flake when you press the skin.

3 Lift the fish on to a warmed plate and spoon the melted butter over the top. Serve with lemon wedges and slow-roasted red bell peppers for a lovely summer lunch.

Prepare ahead
Stuff the fish with herbs up to 12 hours in advance, cover, and refrigerate. The herb flavors will permeate the flesh.

Steamed trout in lettuce

Steaming is the ultimate way of enjoying very fresh trout, as well as keeping it low in fat. Cooked lettuce is a slightly bitter revelation.

The fish
Trout, or monkfish or gurnard

- **PREP** 15 mins · **COOK** 10 mins · **SERVES** 2

Ingredients
8 large Iceberg lettuce leaves

4 trout fillets, pinboned and skinned

salt and freshly ground black pepper

1 tbsp sunflower oil

4 scallions, finely sliced

8 shiitake mushrooms, finely sliced

2 tbsp chopped tarragon

splash of lemon juice

For the dressing
⅔ cup Greek-style yogurt

1 tbsp chopped capers

2 tbsp chopped parsley

1 shallot, finely chopped

1 Blanch the lettuce leaves in boiling water for 20–30 seconds. Rinse under running cold water and pat dry with paper towels. Trim out the thick center veins so it is possible to lay the leaves flat. Overlap 2 leaves together, arrange a trout fillet on each, and season.

2 Heat the oil in a small saucepan, add the scallions and mushrooms, and fry over brisk heat for 3–4 minutes until cooked. Add the tarragon and lemon juice, then cool.

3 Divide the mushroom mixture over each trout fillet. Fold the lettuce over to encase.

4 Lift the trout on to a large bamboo steamer. Do not allow the parcels to touch. Steam for 5–6 minutes, until the fish flakes to the touch.

5 Meanwhile, mix the yogurt, capers, parsley, and shallot together and season lightly. Lift the fish parcels on to a large serving dish and serve the dressing separately.

Prepare ahead
Assemble the trout parcels, cover, and refrigerate for up to 1 day. Bring to room temperature before continuing.

Steamed lobster with herbed lemon butter

Lobster is often included in a steamed clam bake. This is a quick version.

The fish

Lobster, or mussels or clams

- **PREP** 5 mins ▪ **COOK** 10 mins ▪ **SERVES** 2

Ingredients

salt and freshly ground black pepper

1 live lobster, about 2¼lb (1kg)

4 tbsp butter, softened

grated zest and juice of ½–1 lemon, to taste

2 tbsp chopped flat-leaf parsley, plus extra sprigs to serve

2 tbsp chopped tarragon

1 Put the lobster in the freezer to render it unconscious (see page 290). Fill a very large pot three-quarters full with water, and salt well. Bring to a boil. Cook the lobster in the boiling water for 5 minutes. Split the lobster in half and remove the digestive tract.

2 Arrange the lobster halves, cut side up, in a steamer over a large saucepan of simmering water. Cover with a well-fitting lid and steam for a further 5 minutes.

3 Meanwhile, put the butter, lemon zest and juice in a bowl, and add the herbs. Season lightly with pepper.

4 Lift the lobster on to a warmed serving dish and spoon some of the butter over the top. Serve with warm crusty bread and the parsley.

Prepare ahead

You can make the herbed lemon butter up to 2 days in advance. Wrap in parchment paper, and refrigerate until needed.

Leaf-wrapped Asian sole

Wrapping fish in leaves helps it to retain moisture. Add a little chile for more heat.

The fish

Lemon sole, or red mullet or halibut

- **PREP** 15 mins ▪ **COOK** 10 mins ▪ **SERVES** 4

Ingredients

4 lemon sole fillets, about 6oz (175g) each, scaled

4 tsp lemon juice

4 tsp dark soy sauce

2 tsp grated fresh ginger

¼ tsp ground white pepper

sesame oil, to drizzle

16–20 large bok choy leaves, tough stalks removed

1 Drizzle each sole fillet with the lemon juice, soy sauce, ginger, pepper, and a light, even drizzle of sesame oil. Gently roll the fillets lengthwise and arrange on a heatproof plate.

2 Fill a large saucepan fitted with a steamer with 1in (2.5cm) water, bring to a boil, then reduce the heat to a simmer.

3 Blanch the bok choy for 30 seconds in boiling water, then refresh in ice water. Drain.

4 Wrap each fillet in 4–5 leaves, securing with toothpicks if necessary. Set on a plate, then place on the steamer rack, cover, and steam for 8–10 minutes, or until the fish is opaque. Serve with stir-fried vegetables, or boiled white rice.

Prepare ahead

Assemble the fish parcels 1 day in advance, cover, and refrigerate. Bring back to room temperature before continuing.

Variation

Spinach-wrapped sole

Use spinach instead of bok choy without blanching it. Replace the soy sauce, ginger, and sesame oil with a little butter over the fillets, and sprinkle with dried mixed herbs.

Garlic and rice wine steamed razor clams

Take care not to overcook razor clams. As soon as the shells open, lift them on to a serving dish.

The fish
Razor clams, or scallops, sea bass, sea bream, or monkfish

- **PREP** 5 mins - **COOK** 10 mins - **SERVES** 2

Ingredients
2¾lb (1.25kg) razor clams

2 tbsp sunflower oil

2 garlic cloves, chopped

1 red chile, seeded and finely chopped

1 tbsp grated fresh ginger

4 tbsp rice wine

salt and freshly ground black pepper

2 tbsp roughly chopped cilantro

1 Wash the razor clams and check that they are alive: the shell will either be tightly shut or will shut if you run a knife along the open edge. Discard any that are cracked or broken.

2 Heat the oil in a large casserole, add the garlic, chile, and ginger, and stir over low heat for 2–3 minutes. Add the rice wine, bring to a boil and add the clams. Cover with a well-fitting lid and cook over medium heat for 2–3 minutes or until the clams have opened.

3 Lift the clams on to a large, warmed serving dish. Reduce the cooking liquid by boiling for 1 minute, season to taste and add the cilantro. Spoon over the razor clams to serve.

Steamed fish with warm vinaigrette

The three different-colored skins of the snapper, lemon sole, and mackerel look beautiful together in this recipe.

The fish
Red snapper, lemon sole, and mackerel, or salmon, lemon sole, and plaice

- **PREP** 35–40 mins - **COOK** 20–30 mins
- **SERVES** 6

Ingredients

For the bouillon
1 bouquet garni

6 peppercorns

2 cloves

1 carrot, quartered

1 onion, quartered

For the fish
13oz (375g) red snapper fillets, with skin, scaled

13oz (375g) lemon sole fillets, with skin, scaled

13oz (375g) mackerel fillets, with skin, scaled

salt and freshly ground black pepper

For the vinaigrette
½ cup red wine vinegar

2 tsp Dijon mustard

2 shallots, very finely chopped

⅓ cup olive oil

¾ cup vegetable oil

leaves from 5–7 sprigs of tarragon or thyme, finely chopped, plus more to garnish

leaves from 7–10 sprigs of flat-leaf parsley or chervil, finely chopped, plus more to garnish

1 Combine 4¼ cups water, the bouquet garni, peppercorns, cloves, carrot, and onion in a pan over which you can fit a large steamer. Bring to a boil and simmer for 20–30 minutes.

2 Trim the fish fillets so they are roughly the same length. Cut each into 6 strips. Transfer to the steamer and sprinkle with salt and pepper. Set the steamer over the bouillon. Cover and steam for 8–10 minutes, until the fish just flakes easily.

3 In a small saucepan, whisk together the vinegar, mustard, and shallots, then the oils. Heat gently until warm, whisking constantly. Remove from the heat and whisk in the herbs and salt and pepper to taste. Spoon on to 6 warmed plates and put the fish on top. Garnish with the herb sprigs.

Variation

Steamed fish with warm sherry vinaigrette
Make the bouillon. Cut the fish into even diamonds. Steam for 5–7 minutes, depending on thickness. Prepare the warm vinaigrette, substituting sherry vinegar for red wine vinegar and walnut oil for olive oil. Spoon a little over the fish and serve the remainder separately.

Broiled and Grilled

Grilled swordfish

Meaty fish is best grilled, rather than broiled. They need fierce heat to color the exterior.

The fish

Swordfish, or tuna, marlin, or mahi mahi

- **PREP** 5 mins ▪ **COOK** 5 mins ▪ **SERVES** 2

Ingredients

2 swordfish steaks, about 5oz (140g) each, about 1in (2.5cm) thick is best

splash of olive oil

salt and freshly ground black pepper

1 Preheat a well-seasoned ridged grill pan until it is just beginning to smoke. Meanwhile, brush the swordfish with olive oil and season.

2 Press the steaks on to the hot pan with a palette knife. Allow to cook for 1–2 minutes, or until the steak will lift cleanly off the pan. Flip over and press flat with the palette knife. Cook for another 1–2 minutes, or until they will lift cleanly from the pan. Reduce the heat and turn again, trying to position them so that the grill marks are at an angle with those of the first cooking. Cook for another 1 minute before turning on to the second side.

3 Avoid turning the steaks a third time, but cook until firm to the touch. Leave to rest for 1 minute before serving with a simple salad or a flavored butter.

Grilled snapper in banana leaves

Grilling fish in banana leaves allows the fish to steam in its own moisture. The leaves also give a wonderful smoked flavor.

The fish

Red snapper, or mahi mahi, black sea bass, or Patagonian toothfish

- **PREP** 20 mins, plus marinating
- **COOK** 20 mins ▪ **SERVES** 4

Ingredients

1 red snapper, about 3lb 3oz (1.5kg), scaled and gutted

2–3 large banana leaves

1 tsp sesame oil, plus more for the banana leaves

lime wedges, to serve

For the marinade

2 tbsp coarsely chopped cilantro

1/2 tbsp grated ginger

2 garlic cloves, chopped

2 tbsp soy sauce

1 tbsp rice wine vinegar

grated zest of 1 lime

1 red chile, seeded and chopped

salt and freshly ground black pepper

1 Make 3–4 slashes on each side of the fish, nearly to the bone.

2 Put the marinade ingredients into a blender, and chop. Press into the slashes in the fish, and the cavity. Set aside for 15–20 minutes.

3 Blanch the banana leaves in boiling water for 30 seconds to soften. Remove with tongs and rinse under cold running water. Cut the thick vein from the center, and arrange them overlapping on a large cutting board, shiny side down. Brush with sesame oil. Put the fish on the leaves and wrap to encase the body (the head and tail can be visible). If necessary, secure the leaves with cocktail sticks.

4 Preheat the grill until glowing red and the coals are ash gray. Cook the fish, turning often, to prevent the leaves from burning. It will take around 18–20 minutes. Insert a metal skewer into the center of the fish, through the leaves, for 30 seconds. If the fish is cooked, the skewer will emerge piping hot.

5 Transfer to a serving dish and garnish with lime wedges. Unwrap at the table, and serve with warm rice.

SWORDFISH FLAVOR PAIRINGS:

This substantial fish is great simply grilled, or try it smoked over mesquite fries (see page 307), or rubbed with spices such as paprika, ground cumin, and ground coriander.

Griddled swordfish with fennel and sun-dried tomatoes

Beautifully scented with aniseed from the fennel and Pernod, this is an elegant dish for a party.

The fish

Swordfish, or tuna, marlin, or mahi mahi

- **PREP** 25–30 mins, plus marinating
- **COOK** 55 mins ▪ **SERVES** 4

Ingredients

leaves from 2–3 sprigs of thyme

2 tbsp vegetable oil, plus extra for the griddle

juice of ½ lemon

salt and freshly ground black pepper

4 swordfish steaks, about 9oz (250g) each, skinned

4 tbsp butter, plus extra for the foil

3 fennel bulbs, sliced

2oz (60g) sun-dried tomatoes in oil, drained and chopped

1–2 tbsp Pernod, or other aniseed liqueur

1 Put the thyme, oil, and lemon juice into a shallow, non-metallic dish. Season the swordfish and coat in the marinade. Cover and refrigerate for 1 hour.

2 Melt the butter in a saucepan, add the fennel, season, and press a piece of buttered foil on top. Cover and cook over low heat until very soft; it will take 40–45 minutes.

3 Stir in the sun-dried tomatoes with the Pernod. Cook for about 10 minutes, then season to taste.

4 Heat a griddle pan. Brush the griddle with oil, and add the swordfish. Brush with the marinade, and cook for 2–3 minutes, without turning, until a steak comes away from the griddle without tearing. Turn, brush with the remaining marinade, and griddle for 2–3 minutes more. Serve with the fennel mixture on the side.

Prepare ahead

Make the fennel mixture up to 2 days ahead, cover, and refrigerate. Reheat very gently.

Trout with orange-mustard glaze

Broiled whole fish is a dream for the cook, as it is quick to prepare, and easy to present.

The fish

Trout, or snapper or sea bass

- **PREP** 15–20 mins ▪ **COOK** 20–30 mins
- **SERVES** 6

Ingredients

6 trout, each weighing 13oz (375g), scaled and gutted through the gills (see page 266)

leaves from 6–8 sprigs of tarragon

3–4 tbsp vegetable oil, for the broil pan

3 large sweet onions, thickly sliced

9oz (250g) mushrooms, trimmed

3 ripe tomatoes, cored and halved

For the orange-mustard glaze

4 tbsp Dijon mustard

2 tsp honey

juice of 2 oranges

4 tbsp vegetable oil

salt and freshly ground black pepper

1 Slash the fish diagonally 3–4 times on both sides. Tuck a tarragon leaf into each slash. Set aside.

2 Whisk the mustard, honey, and orange juice. Gradually whisk in the oil, until thickened. Season to taste.

3 Preheat the broiler on its highest setting. Brush the rack with oil. Arrange the onion, mushrooms, and tomatoes on the rack. Brush with glaze and season. Broil, brushing with glaze and turning, allowing 3 minutes for mushrooms, and 5–7 minutes for onions and tomatoes; they should char. Keep warm.

4 Broil the fish for 4–7 minutes, until brown. Carefully turn, and brush generously with glaze. Broil until the flesh flakes easily (it should take 4–7 minutes more). Serve with the vegetables and any remaining glaze.

Prepare ahead

The glaze can be made 1 week ahead and kept, covered, in the refrigerator. Whisk before use.

Variation

Broiled cod steaks with maitre d'hotel butter

Omit the glaze. Cream 5 tbsp butter. Mix in 1 finely chopped shallot and a large handful of finely chopped parsley, the juice of ½ lemon, salt, and pepper. Shape into a roll; chill until firm. Brush 6 scaled cod steaks with olive oil, and broil for 3–5 minutes each side. Set a slice of the butter on top and serve.

Broiled sea bream with spice rub

The firm flesh of bream is wonderful with the strong flavors in this recipe.

The fish

Sea bream, or sea bass, rainbow trout, or snapper

- **PREP** 15 mins ▪ **COOK** 6–8 mins ▪ **SERVES** 4

Ingredients

4 sea bream fillets, about 5½oz (150g) each, scaled and pinboned

lemon wedges, to serve

For the spice rub

3 tbsp walnut or olive oil

4 tbsp chopped cilantro leaves

2 garlic cloves, crushed

1 tsp crushed coriander seeds

1 tsp lemon juice

1 small green chile, very finely chopped

salt

For the tomato salad

1 tbsp walnuts

4 plum tomatoes, chopped

1 tbsp chopped cilantro leaves

1½ tsp walnut or olive oil

sea salt and freshly ground black pepper

1 Mix all the ingredients for the spice rub together and season with salt. Preheat the broiler on its highest setting.

2 Line a baking sheet with foil and place the fish fillets on it, skin-side down. Brush the spice rub over the fish. Place under a hot broiler for 6–8 minutes, until cooked through and lightly golden. Remove from the heat and keep warm.

3 Meanwhile, toast the walnuts by stirring them in a dry frying pan over medium heat for 2–3 minutes, then remove and lightly crush. Mix with all the other ingredients for the tomato salad and season. Serve the fish with the salad and lemon wedges.

Prepare ahead

Make the spice rub and toast the walnuts up to 6 hours ahead and store in separate airtight containers at room temperature.

Herrings in oatmeal with gooseberry sauce

Gooseberry sauce is traditional with broiled mackerel but is served here with herring.

The fish

Herring, or mackerel

- **PREP** 10 mins ▪ **COOK** 15 mins ▪ **SERVES** 4

Ingredients

4 herrings, scaled, gutted, and trimmed

4½oz (125g) fine oatmeal

For the gooseberry sauce

12oz (350g) fresh or frozen gooseberries

2 tbsp butter

2 tbsp sugar

¼ tsp nutmeg, freshly grated

salt and freshly ground black pepper

1 Cook the gooseberries in a pan with 1–2 tbsp water and cook for 4–5 minutes, or until tender.

Purée in a food processor, add the butter, sugar, and nutmeg, and season.

2 Cut off and discard the herring heads and slit the fish along the belly right down to the tail. Open the herrings out flat and place, skin-side up, on a chopping board. Press firmly all along the backbone with the heel of your hand. Turn over and pull away the backbone, snipping it off at the tail with scissors. Remove any bones left behind with a pair of fishbone pliars.

3 Preheat the broiler on its highest setting. Spread the oatmeal on to a large plate and season well. Press the herrings firmly into the oatmeal. Arrange them in a broiler pan and broil for 6–8 minutes, or until tender and flaky, turning once.

4 Meanwhile, gently reheat the sauce over a very low heat, and serve with the herrings. Serve with a green salad.

Prepare ahead

Make the sauce several hours in advance, or freeze for up to 6 months.

SUSTAINABILITY CHOICE

Buy line-caught fish

Line-fishing, when baited lines are placed in the water, is a more selective method of fishing that produces a much smaller bycatch than other methods, such as trawling and beam trawling. The most sustainable forms of line-fishing are rod and handline. Handline fishing from small boats (shown here) is particularly sustainable, as only a few fish, such as mackerel and sea bass, are caught. The fish are often in premium condition, as each fish is individually landed. Handlined fish will usually be labeled as such but you can also identify them by damage to their jaw.

GIANT BLACK TIGER PRAWN FLAVOR PAIRINGS:

These are hardy enough to stand up to fierce heat and Asian flavors, or sharpen the sweet flesh with lemon juice and capers.

Sesame grilled prawns

Meaty prawns are excellent for grilling, but are best left in the shell to protect them from the fierce heat. You'll need 8 wooden skewers, soaked in water for 30 minutes.

The fish
Tiger prawns, or scallops

- **PREP** 40 mins, plus marinating
- **COOK** 10 mins ▪ **SERVES** 4

Ingredients
16 large raw unpeeled tiger prawns, about 1¾oz (50g) each

handful of cilantro, to serve

lime wedges, to serve

For the marinade
2 tbsp sunflower oil

2 tsp toasted sesame oil

2 tbsp soy sauce

1 tbsp honey

2 tsp Thai fish sauce

1 large red chile, seeded and chopped

1 tbsp grated fresh ginger

1 garlic clove, crushed

salt and freshly ground black pepper

2 tbsp sesame seeds

1 Snip off the small legs and feelers from the prawns. Snip down the back of the shell and remove the digestive tract if visible (sometimes it isn't, especially if the prawns are farmed).

2 Put all the ingredients for the marinade except the sesame seeds into a small blender and process until smooth. Stir in the sesame seeds. Put the prawns in a non-metallic dish and pour the marinade over; marinate for 30 minutes.

3 Preheat the grill until the coals are glowing and gray in appearance.

4 Thread 2 prawns on each skewer. Grill, brushing with marinade, for 2–3 minutes each side. Pile on to a large plate and garnish with the cilantro and lime wedges. Serve with a dressed salad of bitter green leaves such as arugula and watercress.

Prepare ahead
Make the marinade up to 2 days in advance, cover, and refrigerate. Only marinate the prawns for 30 minutes, or the texture will change.

Grilled prawn satay

You'll need 8 wooden skewers, soaked in water for 30 minutes.

The fish
Tiger prawns, or snapper

- **PREP** 40 mins, plus marinating
- **COOK** 20 mins ▪ **SERVES** 4

Ingredients
16 large raw unpeeled tiger prawns, about 1¾oz (50g) each

lime wedges, to serve

For the marinade
2 garlic cloves, crushed

1 tbsp grated fresh ginger

1 large red chile, seeded and chopped

2 tbsp tamarind paste

2 tbsp kecap manis

salt and freshly ground black pepper

For the satay sauce
1 tbsp vegetable oil

1 small onion, finely chopped

1 garlic clove, chopped

2 tbsp grated fresh ginger

1 tsp shrimp paste

½ cup smooth peanut butter

⅔ cup coconut milk

2–3 tsp dark brown sugar

1 tbsp kecap manis

1 Snip off the small legs and feelers from the prawns. Snip down the back of the shell and remove the digestive tract if visible (sometimes it isn't, especially if the prawns are farmed).

2 Place the ingredients for the marinade into a small blender and process until smooth. Put the prawns in a non-metallic dish and pour the marinade over; marinate for 30 minutes.

3 Heat the oil in a saucepan, add the onion, garlic, and ginger, and cook over low heat for 3–4 minutes. Add the shrimp paste, peanut butter, coconut milk, and sugar. Stir over low heat until you have a smooth paste. Add the kecap manis and season. Remove from the heat.

4 Preheat the grill until the coals are glowing and gray in appearance. Thread 2 prawns on each skewer. Grill, brushing with marinade, for 2–3 minutes each side. Pile on to a platter with the lime wedges. Serve the sauce separately.

Marinated sweet and hot tuna steaks

Juicy, healthy, quick, and wonderfully moreish.

The fish
Tuna, or swordfish or salmon

- **PREP** 10 mins, plus marinating
- **COOK** 5 mins • **SERVES** 4

Ingredients
2 tbsp dark soy sauce

2 tbsp olive oil

juice of 2 limes

2 garlic cloves, grated

1in (2.5cm) fresh ginger, grated

2 tbsp dark brown sugar

1 tsp cayenne pepper

salt and freshly ground black pepper

4 skinless tuna steaks, about 7oz (200g) each

1 Put the soy sauce, oil, lime juice, garlic, ginger, sugar, and cayenne pepper in a bowl. Season with salt and pepper, and mix together well. Put the tuna steaks in a plastic freezer bag, add in the marinade, and seal. Massage the fish through the bag, making sure it is well coated. Marinate in the refrigerator for 30 minutes.

2 Heat the barbecue, or a charcoal grill or griddle pan, until hot. Griddle the tuna steaks over high heat for 2 minutes on each side. Remove to a plate, and rest in a warm place for 2 minutes. Serve with a fresh green salad.

Griddled shrimp with hot pepper sauce

You can make this dish even more quickly by substituting a pinch of red pepper flakes for the fresh chile.

The fish
Shrimp, or squid or scallops

- **PREP** 10 mins • **COOK** 4 mins • **SERVES** 4

Ingredients
9oz (250g) large raw shrimp, unpeeled

2 tbsp olive oil

1 hot red chile, seeded and finely chopped

For the hot pepper sauce
1 garlic clove, grated or finely chopped

1 tsp hot chili powder

1 tsp paprika

pinch of ground cumin

juice of 1 lime

4–5 tbsp mayonnaise

salt and freshly ground black pepper

1 Put the shrimp in a bowl, and combine with half the oil and the chile. Toss well. Set aside.

2 To make the hot pepper sauce, stir together the remaining oil, garlic, chili powder, paprika, cumin, lime, and mayonnaise. Taste, and adjust the seasoning.

3 Heat a large, heavy frying pan or ridged cast-iron grill pan over high heat. Add in the shrimp, and cook for about 2 minutes on each side until they turn pink. Serve with the hot pepper sauce, salad, and fresh crusty bread.

Prepare ahead
Make the hot pepper sauce up to 6 hours ahead, cover, and refrigerate. It will get spicier. Return to room temperature before serving.

Variation
Skewered shrimp with hot pepper sauce
Thread the shrimp on to skewers, and serve 2 or 3 per person. (If using bamboo skewers, soak them in water for 30 minutes first.)

Grilled sardines with salsa verde

A quick and very healthy recipe with a sparkling, piquant Italian herb dressing.

The fish

Sardines, or sprats

- **PREP** 20 mins • **COOK** 6–8 mins • **SERVES** 4

Ingredients

1 bunch of watercress

3 sprigs of flat-leaf parsley

2 sprigs of marjoram

1oz (30g) breadcrumbs

½ cup olive oil

3 tbsp lemon juice

1 tbsp capers in vinegar, rinsed

salt and freshly ground black pepper

8 large sardines, scaled and gutted

1 Trim the coarse stalks from the watercress. Place in a blender with the parsley, marjoram, breadcrumbs, oil, lemon juice, and capers. Blend until the mixture forms a sauce, scraping down the sides as necessary. Season to taste.

2 Place the sardines on a sheet of foil on the broiler rack. Broil for 3–4 minutes on each side until sizzling brown and cooked through. Serve with the salsa verde spooned over.

Prepare ahead

Make the salsa verde up to 3 hours in advance, coat with a film of oil to prevent discoloration, cover, and refrigerate.

Variations

Barbecued mackerel, or herring, with salsa verde

Put mackerel or herring in a hinged wire rack and cook them over a preheated barbecue; the coals should be white-hot. The fish will need to cook for 5–8 minutes on each side. Serve with the salsa verde.

Oysters with salsa verde

The salsa is also good spooned over oysters just before eating.

Mediterranean-style broiled sardines

Popular all over southern Europe, this is the way to enjoy these oily fish at their very best.

The fish

Sardines, or small mackerel and herring, or sprats

- **PREP** 15 mins, plus marinating
- **COOK** 4–6 mins • **SERVES** 4

Ingredients

8 large sardines, scaled and gutted

8 sprigs of thyme or lemon thyme, plus extra to garnish

4 lemons

3 tbsp olive oil

2 garlic cloves, crushed

1 tsp ground cumin

1 Rinse the sardines inside and out, and pat dry. Put a sprig of thyme inside each fish, and place them in a shallow non-metallic dish.

2 Grate the zest and squeeze the juice from 3 of the lemons and place in a small bowl. Add the oil, garlic, and cumin, and whisk together. Pour this mixture over the sardines, cover, and refrigerate for at least 2 hours.

3 Preheat the broiler on its highest setting. Put the sardines in a broiler pan, allowing space between each fish, and grill for 2–3 minutes on each side, basting with the marinade.

4 Cut the remaining lemon into wedges. Place the sardines on a warmed serving plate and serve with lemon wedges and sprigs of thyme.

Prepare ahead

The sardines will benefit from marinating for 2–4 hours before cooking. Cover, and refrigerate.

Broiled halibut with beurre blanc

Halibut has a delicate flesh that is low in fat. Simple flavors suit its texture and flavor well.

The fish

Halibut, or cod, salmon, or turbot

- **PREP** 5 mins ▪ **COOK** 15 mins ▪ **SERVES** 2

Ingredients

2 halibut steaks, about 5oz (140g) each, scaled

8 tbsp unsalted butter, plus extra, melted, for the fish

1 shallot, finely chopped

5 tbsp fish stock

1 tbsp white wine vinegar

salt and freshly ground black pepper

lemon juice, to taste

1 Preheat the broiler, or heat a ridged grill pan over high heat. Brush the halibut steaks with the melted butter. Cook for 3–4 minutes on each side.

2 Cut the remaining butter into small chunks. Melt 2 tbsp in a small saucepan, add the shallot, and cook for 2–3 minutes, or until soft. Add the stock and vinegar, bring to a boil, and simmer until the liquid has reduced to about 3 tbsp.

3 Reduce the heat to very low and add the remaining butter, a few pieces at a time, whisking vigorously between each addition. It is important to keep the stock hot, but don't allow it to boil. Once all the butter has been added, the sauce should be creamy and fairly thick. Remove from the heat, season, add lemon juice to taste, and serve, poured over the halibut, with peas.

Grilled sea bass with roast artichokes and fennel

Some of the best globe artichokes are grown in Lazio, Italy, and they make an excellent combination with sea bass.

The fish

Sea bass, or bluenose, black sea bream, mahi mahi, or catfish

- **PREP** 45 mins ▪ **COOK** 25 mins ▪ **SERVES** 4

Ingredients

6 tbsp extra virgin olive oil

4 sea bass fillets, scaled and pinboned

salt and freshly ground black pepper

8 small or 3–4 large artichoke bottoms

squeeze of lemon juice

1 large fennel bulb, finely sliced

3 garlic cloves, finely sliced

large handful of basil, shredded

1 Preheat the oven to 400°F (200°C). Brush a ridged grill pan with 2 tbsp of the oil. Slash the skin of each fillet 3 times, and season. Set aside.

2 Cut the artichoke bottoms into quarters and blanch in boiling water with the lemon juice for 3–4 minutes. Drain and put into a large roasting pan with the fennel and garlic. Toss with the remaining olive oil. Season generously and roast in the oven for 15–18 minutes, or until the fennel is roasted and the artichokes are soft.

3 Heat the pan until just smoking, add the fish, skin side down, and cook for 2–3 minutes on each side: the skin will be charred and the flesh white and firm.

4 Toss the basil into the roasted artichokes and pile on to a serving dish. Arrange the sea bass on top and serve.

Prepare ahead

Roast the vegetables up to 6 hours ahead and keep, covered, at room temperature. Reheat gently before continuing.

BLACK SEA BREAM FLAVOR PAIRING:

Delicious with braised fennel, or complement it with Pernod, or spice the fish up with saffron, cilantro, and plenty of garlic.

Jerk salmon

Jerk seasoning is Jamaican in origin. Traditionally used to marinate both poultry and meat, it works well with fish, too.

The fish

Salmon, or mahi mahi, snapper, tuna, or swordfish

- **PREP** 20 mins, plus marinating
- **COOK** 10 mins ▪ **SERVES** 4

Ingredients

4 thick salmon fillets, about 6oz (175g) each, with skin, scaled and pinboned

1–2 tbsp sunflower oil

For the jerk seasoning

1 tbsp ground allspice

½ tsp ground cinnamon

½ tsp freshly grated nutmeg

2 tbsp dark brown sugar

4 garlic cloves, chopped

2 Scotch bonnet chiles, seeded

½ tbsp thyme leaves

4 scallions, white part only, coarsely chopped

2 tbsp lime juice

1 tbsp sunflower oil

salt and freshly ground black pepper

1 Put the ingredients for the jerk seasoning together in a small blender and process until well chopped. Rub some of the seasoning on to the fish; you may decide not to use it all.

2 Brush a ridged grill pan with the sunflower oil and heat until smoking. Add the fish and reduce the heat. Grill for 3–4 minutes on each side until charred on the outside and the flesh is cooked: it will flake and be paler in appearance with no sign of translucency.

Prepare ahead

Make the jerk seasoning 1–2 weeks in advance and store in a sealed jar in the refrigerator.

Grilled tuna steaks with salsa

Always be careful with tuna to keep the center of the fish moist and slightly rare.

The fish

Tuna, or swordfish or mahi mahi

- **PREP** 25–30 mins, plus marinating
- **COOK** 4–6 mins ▪ **SERVES** 4

Ingredients

4 skinless tuna steaks, about 9oz (250g) each

salt and freshly ground black pepper

4 tomatoes, peeled, seeded, and chopped (see page 112)

7oz (200g) canned corn, drained

leaves from 1 bunch of cilantro, finely chopped

1 onion, chopped

1 red bell pepper, diced

2 limes

For the marinade

2–3 sprigs of thyme

2 tbsp vegetable oil

juice of ½ lemon

1 For the marinade, strip the thyme leaves into a non-metallic dish with the oil and lemon juice. Season the tuna, then add to the dish. Cover and marinate for 1 hour, turning once.

2 Put the tomatoes, corn, cilantro, onion, and pepper in a bowl. Squeeze 1 of the limes into the mixture and season. Leave to stand.

3 Heat a ridged grill pan. Cook the tuna for 2–3 minutes, turn, and brush with marinade. Cook for 2–3 minutes more. The tuna should be rare in the center.

4 Put the tuna on to 4 warmed plates. Serve the salsa and lime wedges on the side.

Prepare ahead

Make the salsa 1 day in advance, cover, and refrigerate. Serve at room temperature.

Variation

Grilled swordfish with fennel and sun-dried tomatoes

Marinate 4 swordfish steaks, 9oz (250g) each. Slice 3 fennel bulbs. Melt 4 tbsp butter in a saucepan, add the fennel, and cook until soft. Stir in 2oz (60g) chopped sun-dried tomatoes with 1–2 tbsp Pernod. Cook for 10 minutes. Grill the swordfish and serve with the fennel.

MAHI MAHI FLAVOR PAIRING:

This dense, meaty fish takes equally well to chile heat and Caribbean spices, and to Asian fish sauce, lime, garlic, and cilantro.

Broiled halibut with anchovy butter

Halibut has a sweet flavor that works very well with the salty anchovy butter.

The fish

Halibut, or turbot, lemon sole, or flounder

- **PREP** 15 mins ▪ **COOK** 4–6 mins ▪ **SERVES** 4

Ingredients

4 halibut fillets, about 6oz (175g) each, skinned

butter, for greasing

4oz (115g) arugula, to serve

lemon wedges, to garnish

For the butter

4 tbsp unsalted butter, softened

2 salted anchovy fillets, rinsed and patted dry

1 tsp anchovy paste

squeeze of lemon juice

freshly ground black pepper

1 Preheat the broiler. Put the fish, skinned side down, on a large sheet of lightly buttered foil on a baking sheet.

2 Put the butter, anchovies, and anchovy paste into a mortar and pestle or small food processor. Work together until well combined. Beat in the lemon juice and season with pepper.

3 Broil the halibut for 2–3 minutes, turn, and spread each fillet with a generous layer of anchovy butter. Return to the broiler on a lower shelf and broil for another 2–3 minutes or until golden brown on top.

4 Arrange the arugula on a large serving dish and arrange the broiled fish on top. Garnish with the lemon wedges.

Prepare ahead

The anchovy butter can be made, wrapped in parchment paper, and refrigerated 1–2 days in advance.

Broiled herring with mustard butter

Many breakfast herring recipes use bacon and oatmeal, but the mustard here makes this recipe a great way to start the day.

The fish

Herring, or sprats, mackerel, sardines, or trout

- **PREP** 10 mins ▪ **COOK** 4–6 mins ▪ **SERVES** 4

Ingredients

8 herrings, scaled, gutted, and trimmed, heads removed

1 tbsp vegetable oil

salt and freshly ground black pepper

4oz (115g) bunch of watercress, to garnish

lemon wedges, to garnish

For the butter

5 tbsp butter, softened, plus extra for broiling

1 tbsp wholegrain mustard

1 tsp thyme leaves

splash of lemon juice

1 Preheat the broiler. Pat the herrings dry with paper towels, brush with oil, and season lightly. Place on a large sheet of lightly buttered foil on a baking sheet.

2 Mix the butter, mustard, and thyme together. Add a little lemon juice and season.

3 Broil the herrings for 2–3 minutes on each side or until cooked; it will be firm to the touch.

4 Transfer the herrings on to a large, warmed serving dish and dot with the mustard butter to melt over the fish. Garnish with watercress and lemon wedges.

Prepare ahead

The mustard butter can be made, wrapped in parchment paper, and refrigerated 1–2 days in advance.

HALIBUT FLAVOR PAIRINGS: The fine, firm flesh of halibut is a treat with a buttery sauce, or a sauce made from white wine or Champagne and cream, or wild mushrooms and Parmesan cheese.

Lobster Thermidor

Another version of this classic recipe is where the raw lobster is split along the center (see page 290) and roasted then broiled, with the sauce poured over.

The fish

Lobsters, or Dublin Bay prawns

- **PREP** 20 mins ▪ **COOK** 10–15 mins ▪ **SERVES** 4

Ingredients

2 lobsters, about 1½lb (675g) each, cooked

paprika, to garnish

lemon wedges, to serve

For the sauce

2 tbsp butter

2 shallots, finely chopped

½ cup dry white wine

½ cup fish stock

⅔ cup heavy cream

½ tsp ready-made English mustard

1 tbsp lemon juice

2 tbsp chopped flat-leaf parsley

2 tsp chopped tarragon

salt and freshly ground black pepper

2½oz (75g) Gruyère cheese, grated

1 Cut the lobsters in half lengthwise. Remove the meat from the claws and tail, along with any roe or meat from the head (see page 291). Cut the meat into bite-sized pieces. Clean out the shells and reserve.

2 To prepare the sauce, melt the butter in a small saucepan, add the shallots, and cook gently until softened but not browned. Add the wine and boil for 2–3 minutes, or until reduced by half.

3 Add the stock and cream and boil rapidly, stirring, until reduced and slightly thickened. Stir in the mustard, lemon juice, and herbs, then season to taste. Stir in half the cheese.

4 Preheat the broiler. Add the lobster meat to the sauce, then divide among the lobster shells. Top with the remaining cheese.

5 Place the lobsters on a foil-lined broiler pan and broil for 2–3 minutes, or until bubbling and golden. Sprinkle with a little paprika and serve hot with lemon wedges.

Grilled sardines in harissa

Very fresh sardines, still stiff with rigor mortis, have a sweet and delicate flavor.

The fish

Sardines, or mackerel, sprats, or herrings

- **PREP** 25 mins ▪ **COOK** 2–3 mins ▪ **SERVES** 4

Ingredients

12–16 sardines, scaled, gutted, and trimmed

1–2 tbsp olive oil

salt and freshly ground black pepper

1 tsp ground coriander

For the harissa dressing

2 tbsp extra virgin olive oil

2 tbsp harissa paste

2 tsp honey, to taste

grated zest and juice of 1 lime

For the salad

large handful of cilantro

2 Little Gem lettuces, finely sliced

grated zest and juice of 1 lemon

pinch of sugar

3 tbsp extra virgin olive oil

1 Preheat a grill until the coals are glowing and gray in appearance.

2 Cut 3 slashes in either side of each sardine. Brush with olive oil and season generously with salt, pepper, and ground coriander. Set aside.

3 To make the dressing, whisk together the oil, harissa, honey, and lime zest and juice, season, and add more honey if necessary to balance the acidity of the lime. Set aside.

4 Prepare the salad: toss the cilantro with the lettuce and pile into a large, flat serving dish. Whisk together the lemon zest, juice, sugar, and olive oil. Season and drizzle over the salad.

5 Cook the sardines on the grill (or under a preheated broiler) for 2–3 minutes or until the flesh is white and opaque. Brush with the harissa paste and grill the other side for another 30 seconds. Pile on to the cilantro salad and serve with warm crusty bread.

Prepare ahead

Make the harissa dressing 1 day ahead, cover, and refrigerate. The flavors will deepen.

SARDINE FLAVOR PAIRINGS: The definite tastes of oil-rich sardines can take almost any strong flavors. Try it with harissa, or Sicilian olive oil, garlic, golden raisins, pine nuts, and oregano.

TECHNIQUES

Tools

Stock your kitchen with this kit, which includes the essentials you need for preparing all manner of seafood. After using your tools, rinse and scrub them thoroughly in cold running water to remove any trace of scale and flesh. Follow this with a thorough hot, soapy wash. Handles and chopping boards should then be rinsed in a sterilizing solution (baby bottle sterilizer is a good option) and dried. This will keep your equipment scrupulously clean and odor-free.

Fish scaler
A fish scaler makes scaling fish easy and the scales tend to collect in one place. There are several varieties around; choose one that feels comfortable to grip. In the absence of a scaler, use the back of any kitchen knife but take care, as the scales tend to flick further around the kitchen. For scaling fish, see page 264.

Carving knife
A carving knife is a long-bladed, rigid knife (around 12in/30cm) that is excellent for cutting through bones, and so perfect for carving large fish (see pages 270 and 275). It is also good for skinning larger fillets. If you do not have a carving knife, you can use a large chef's knife in its place.

Filleting knife
A flexible knife with a 6–8in (15–25cm) blade is essential for filleting. Choose a knife that has good flexibility without being too bendy. Use the tip to slip under fillets, and the mid-section to cut through skin and to make the long cuts required to remove the fillet. The mid-section can also be used to skin small fillets. Apply pressure to the heel, the least flexible part of the knife, to cut through bones.

Steel
Knives require steeling on a regular basis in order to keep them sharp. Once blunt, it is virtually impossible to sharpen the blade yourself. To steel a knife, place the tip of the steel on a work surface and hold it firm. Run the blade from the heel to the tip, at a 30° angle. It should feel gritty when being drawn over the steel.

Scissors
A good, sturdy pair of kitchen scissors makes light work of some tough jobs, such as removing the head from a flat fish, trimming fins, and cutting through soft bones. Many fishmongers generally use a knife for these jobs, but scissors make easier work of it.

Claw crackers

These can be very helpful when dressing a lobster or crab, or if you have guests over for dinner and need to crack the claws at the table—in which case, you'll need more than one set. In their absence, use a heavy-based pan in the kitchen to shatter the claw.

Lobster pick

Use a lobster pick along with claw crackers when extracting the meat from lobsters (and crabs). The length of a lobster pick allows you to easily extract the meat from the legs.

Seafood fork

Use this to extract meat from crustacean legs, or to pull the meat from gastropods, such as whelks and periwinkles. You need several pairs; one for each guest. Shown here are a bamboo fork (top) and a steel fork (bottom).

Fish kettle

A long fish kettle is extremely helpful, although not essential, for the poaching of large, round fish, such as salmon and trout. It contains a trivet that lifts the fish from hot liquid (see page 302). In the absence of a fish kettle use a large flameproof baking tray, or wrap large fish in foil and bake in the oven. Many fishmongers will loan you a fish kettle.

Whole round fish can sit snugly inside long fish kettles for poaching.

Fishbone pliars

Use these to remove fine pinbones that run through the fillets of round fish. Choose wide-headed varieties, as these grip the top of the pinbone well. A pair of household tweezers is a good alternative. For pinboning, see page 271.

Oyster knife

There are several kinds of oyster knife. Those with a pointed blade make light work of prying the oyster shells apart (see page 278), but they can damage easily so may need to be replaced. A blade that is too flimsy will break easily, so choose a knife that feels firm to grip.

Choosing and storing

Choosing

Sight, smell, and touch are used to assess the quality of all seafood. Fish and shellfish should be bought and cooked as fresh as possible, preferably when in season. Choose the freshest, best-looking fish available—one that has bright eyes and smooth, glistening skin. There are particular signs of quality all over the body of a fish and a shellfish (shown here are a brook trout and a Dungeness crab) that are worth knowing before you buy.

Fish

Most fish can be assessed in the same way. Round fish have a round body and produce a fillet either side of the backbone. Flat fish start life as small round fish, turning on to their side as they grow. Fish can also be categorized by their texture: white or oil-rich. White fish have low-fat flesh that turns white and opaque when cooked, and the liver contains most of the oil. The flesh can be very dense and meaty, as with monkfish, or flaky, as with cod and snapper. Oil-rich species have fat distributed throughout their body and have high levels of omega-3 fatty acids. These include mackerel, herring, trout, and salmon.

Scales
On a whole fish these should be bright and glistening and firmly attached to the skin. Dull and dry scales that detach easily indicate the fish is not fresh.

Skin
Look for fish with bright skin with evenly distributed surface slime that appears clear and colorless. The fish's color fades as it decomposes and the slime becomes sticky and discolored.

Feel
A fresh fish may still show signs of rigor mortis (be stiff and rigid), indicating that it has been out of the water for no more than 24–48 hours. Once there are no signs of rigor, a good-quality fish should feel firm and elastic and the flesh should be firmly attached to the backbone. Press down along the fish's back to assess firmness.

Eyes
These should be bright, convex, and black with a translucent cornea. As a fish loses condition the eyes look sunken, the pupil appears gray or milky, and the cornea opaque.

Gills
A fresh, gutted fish has bright red gills. As the fish loses condition the color fades to brown and the mucus becomes sticky.

Smell
Fresh fish should either have no smell at all or should smell pleasantly of the sea, with no underlying offensive aroma. Fish that are beginning to decompose will smell stale and sour.

Shellfish

The term "shellfish" refers to many edible species that are covered by a shell. Crustaceans are a group of mainly aquatic shellfish, such as lobsters and prawns, that have segmented bodies, no backbone, jointed legs/claws, two antennae, and that can move independently. Molluscs are soft-bodied invertebrates with a hard shell. They can be subdivided into many groups as follows: gastropods/univalves, typically found in one coiled shell, include whelks, periwinkles, snails, and conch; bivalves or filter feeds, typically found in two hinged shells, include oysters, clams, mussels, and scallops; cephalopods are a group of invertebrates, such as octopus, squid, and cuttlefish, that have tubular heads and many arms with suckers.

Look
All live shellfish should show signs of life, most obviously movement. Never buy dead, uncooked molluscs, as decomposition begins immediately after death (see box, page 279). The tubular part of octopus, cuttlefish, and squid should be white in appearance; avoid flesh that has become pink.

Smell
Cooked shellfish should have a fresh smell with the sweet aroma of sea ozone. Avoid any that smell stale, musty, and of ammonia, as they are beginning to decompose and are not safe to eat.

Feel
When cooked or raw, the limbs of crabs and lobsters should hold firmly and snap back into position if extended. Floppy or loose limbs may indicate the crab is dead or dying, and so may not be safe to eat.

Shell
The shell should feel heavy and should not be seeping water; a crab or lobster that feels light may have recently shed its shell, and may lack brown meat. Shells should be hard and dry.

Refrigerating

Try to buy seafood on the day you intend to cook it, but if you have to store it for a short period of time you must ensure it is safe to eat. Ideally, fish should be stored at 32°F (0°C) (40°F/5°C cooler than a domestic fridge). Ice helps to create a cooler environment. Refrigerate shellfish at 37°F (3°C) or under, for the timings given below. Never submerge any shellfish in water and always check molluscs for signs of life before cooking (see page 279).

Whole fish

Surround whole fish with ice and place it in the coldest part of the refrigerator (the lowest shelf). Fishmongers pack whole fish directly over ice and you can replicate this using ice or ice packs. Storage times vary between species, but all fish is best eaten within 24–36 hours.

Fillets

Ensure the fillet's flesh side doesn't come into direct contact with ice, as this will give the fish bleached patches. Either store the fillets skin side in contact with ice, or in a plastic container, loosely covered with plastic wrap, with ice packed around it. Best eaten within 24–36 hours.

Shellfish

Refrigerate mussels and clams in a covered bowl for 36 hours. (Oysters and scallops may last for 1 week, stored round side down.) Live lobsters and crabs, wrapped in a damp cloth, will keep for 48 hours. Cooked or raw shrimp will keep for 24 hours. Squid and cuttlefish will store for 3 days.

Freezing

If you intend to use fish after 24 hours of purchase, freeze it as soon as you get it home. Freezing fresh fish slows the changes that occur as spoilage takes place and, if carefully done, it can be impossible to tell the difference between fresh and frozen. First, pat the fish (fillets, steaks, or whole fish) dry with paper towels. If freezing whole fish, remove the scales, guts, and fins before freezing. To defrost fish, remove it from the freezer bags and place in a colander set over a plate. Place the fish in the refrigerator and allow to defrost very slowly—rapid defrosting can result in loss of moisture, ruining the texture of the fish. For home-freezing, only freeze cooked shellfish.

Whole fish and fillets

To freeze surplus fresh fish at home, pack fillets, steaks, or small whole, gutted fish individually (or no more than two at a time), in a double layer of plastic freezer bags. Then exclude the air and freeze. Freeze for up to 6 weeks.

Shellfish

Once cooked and cold, wrap the shellfish in a double layer of plastic wrap and then a freezer bag, and label. Freeze for up to 6 weeks. Cooked lobster and shrimp, and cooked mussels, whelks, and periwinkles (removed from the shell) can be frozen in this way.

Cuts of a large round fish

Most round fish are cut into two long fillets, which run along either side of the backbone. These are portioned into individual servings. Large round fish (over 3lb 3oz/1.5kg), such as salmon (shown here), cod, pollock, and saithe can be divided into other cuts as well as fillets. Some species, including snapper, breams, and mahi mahi, have a laterally compressed body, which is best simply filleted.

Tail fillet ▼

This thin triangular fillet spans from the base of the tail to the base of the anal fin. It does not contain pinbones and rarely takes more than 5 minutes to pan-fry, bake, grill, roast, or poach. For a more unusual dish, skin the fillet and lightly pound it out between two pieces of parchment paper. It can then be rolled with a stuffing to cook as paupiettes (rolls of tail fillet).

The thin flesh around the belly is sometimes sold separately.

Steaks ▶

Steaks (or darnes) are cross sections, about 1–1¾in (2.5–4cm) thick, that contain a section of backbone. The bone helps the flesh retain moisture when cooked, and, in turn, lengthens the cooking time slightly. Broil, pan-fry, braise, microwave, or grill steaks in oil or an herb butter.

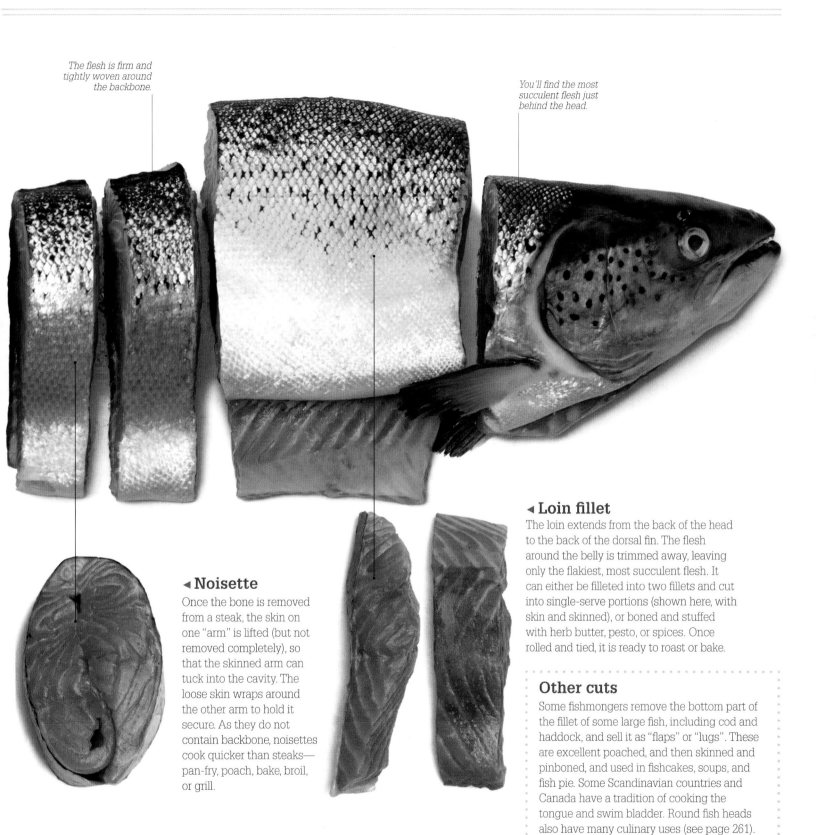

The flesh is firm and tightly woven around the backbone.

You'll find the most succulent flesh just behind the head.

◄ Loin fillet

The loin extends from the back of the head to the back of the dorsal fin. The flesh around the belly is trimmed away, leaving only the flakiest, most succulent flesh. It can either be filleted into two fillets and cut into single-serve portions (shown here, with skin and skinned), or boned and stuffed with herb butter, pesto, or spices. Once rolled and tied, it is ready to roast or bake.

◄ Noisette

Once the bone is removed from a steak, the skin on one "arm" is lifted (but not removed completely), so that the skinned arm can tuck into the cavity. The loose skin wraps around the other arm to hold it secure. As they do not contain backbone, noisettes cook quicker than steaks—pan-fry, poach, bake, broil, or grill.

Other cuts

Some fishmongers remove the bottom part of the fillet of some large fish, including cod and haddock, and sell it as "flaps" or "lugs". These are excellent poached, and then skinned and pinboned, and used in fishcakes, soups, and fish pie. Some Scandinavian countries and Canada have a tradition of cooking the tongue and swim bladder. Round fish heads also have many culinary uses (see page 261).

Cuts of a large flat fish

The shape of flat fish is better suited to filleting rather than other methods of cutting. However, large flat fish of over 3½lb (1.7kg), such as halibut (shown here) and turbot, are thick enough to be cut into single steaks (taken from one side of the backbone) or double steaks (where the cut spans the width of the fish). Unlike those taken from a round fish, flat fish fillets do not contain pinbones; filleted correctly and carefully, they are bone free.

Single fillets ▼

Flat fish can either be filleted into four quarter-cross fillets, where the fillet is taken from either side of the backbone on both sides of the fish (one of these is shown below), or as "cross-cut" or double fillets, one on each side of the fish (see page 274). The fillets can be skinned and portioned or just portioned; a large fish produces thick, boneless fillets, great for pan-frying, broiling, and baking.

Tail fillet ▲

The triangular tail fillet extends from the anal fin to the base of the fish. It is best to fillet the tail, as it is too thin for steaks. The tail end piece of the fillet can be skinned or left as it is for quick pan-frying or baking. As with all fish, the tail fillet contains no pinbones and is quick to cook.

Their scale covering is much more modest than that of round fish.

A fillet is taken from each quarter of the fish.

Steaks ▶

Usually 1–1¾in (2.5–4cm) thick, steaks are cut up to two-thirds along the body. Flat fish steaks are more triangular than those taken from a round fish because the guts of a flat fish sit just behind the head area, rather than along the fish's body. The skin protects the flesh during cooking, but pulls away easily once the fish is cooked. Large flat fish offer meaty, dense steaks that are suitable for grilling, pan-frying, microwaving, or broiling.

Fish heads

The head contains the cheek or "pearl", which is worth removing, either before or after cooking. It is considered a delicacy in Scandinavia, North America, Southern Europe, and some other parts of the world where it is deep-fried, poached, or pan-fried. Use the head to make fish head curry and to flavor fish stock, or simply poach and remove the flesh to use in fishcakes and pies. If using the head in this way, remove the gills and rinse the head first to wash away any traces of blood.

The cheeks are extracted from larger fish and are particularly delicious. Ask your fishmonger for them.

Dense cheeks are removed from both sides of the head of a large flat fish.

Portions of a cooked crab

All species of crab are comprised of the same parts: two claws, eight legs, a carapace, and the main body. Shown below is a brown edible crab and the sections where you will find the brown and the white meat. Start by removing the claws and the legs and then pull the main body away from the carapace. Make sure you remove all of the inedible parts, all of which are easily identified (see box, below). For more information on how to dress a crab, see pages 288–289.

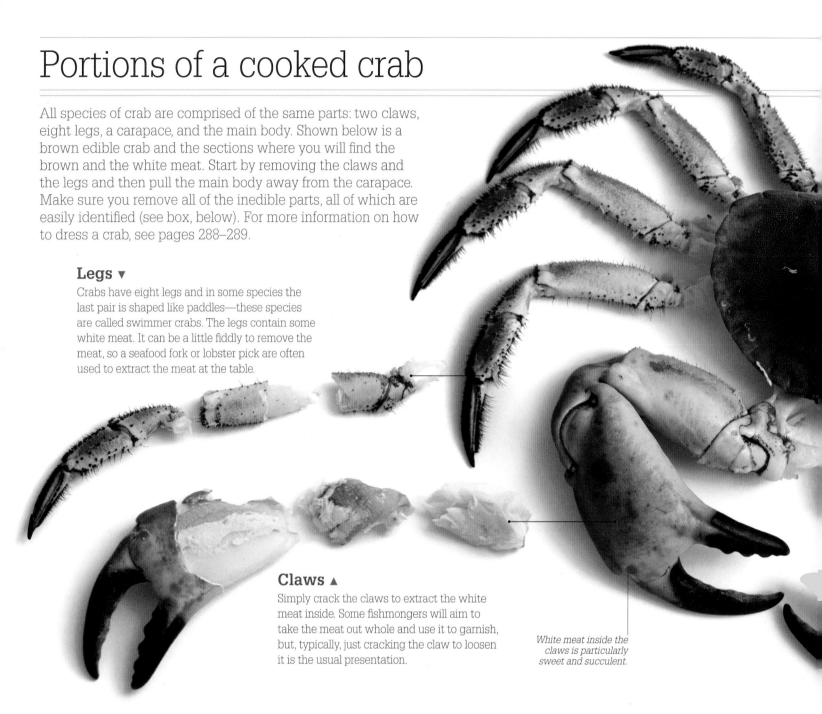

Legs ▼

Crabs have eight legs and in some species the last pair is shaped like paddles—these species are called swimmer crabs. The legs contain some white meat. It can be a little fiddly to remove the meat, so a seafood fork or lobster pick are often used to extract the meat at the table.

Claws ▲

Simply crack the claws to extract the white meat inside. Some fishmongers will aim to take the meat out whole and use it to garnish, but, typically, just cracking the claw to loosen it is the usual presentation.

White meat inside the claws is particularly sweet and succulent.

Inedible parts

The gills, or "dead man's fingers", are attached to the main body, but a few may be left in the carapace during preparation. Their dry, spongy texture makes very unpleasant eating. The mouth and stomach sac are found in the carapace and also need to be removed. The crab's tail, or apron, located on the underside of the main body, is inedible. Male crabs have thin aprons, while hens have wider, more rounded aprons (see page 378). Shards of shell can ruin white meat. To locate any, put the meat into a metal bowl and shake it around. Listen for the shell pinging against the side of the bowl.

Apron   *Mouth*   *Stomach sac*   *Gills*

Remove the apron—the crab's tail—which is located on the underside of the main body.

The inedible gills grow either side of the main body.

◄ Main body

Firmly embedded inside the carapace, the main body consists of lots of chambers that contain a surprising quantity of white meat. Once the body is removed and the gills discarded, split it into quarters so that it is easier to access the white meat inside. There is a residue of brown meat left from the carapace.

Carapace ▼

This large shell contains the brown meat (offal). The crab sheds the carapace at various stages of its lifecycle, enabling it to take in water and form a larger shell, into which it grows.

Remove the stomach sac and mouth, which are found just behind the eyes.

Using the meat

White meat

The main body, legs, and claws contain white meat, which has a sweet, seafood taste and is very juicy and tender. Remove it carefully, making sure you don't take any shell with it and serve unadulterated in salads or sushi, or use in crab cakes or curry.

Brown meat

The carapace contains the earthy-tasting brown meat. Its quantity and consistency depends on the season and whether or not the crab has recently shed its shell—if it has, the meat may be runny; use soft breadcrumbs or matzo meal to help bind it together. Season to serve, as preferred (see page 70).

Preparing round fish

Scaling and trimming

Always remove the scales if you intend to cook fish with its skin, so they don't spoil the dish. Scaling is messy, so put the fish (salmon is shown here) in a plastic bag or in a sink to stop the scales flicking around the kitchen. Trimming the fins neatens the fish. Fins also stick to a baking sheet or foil, making it hard to release a fish intact after cooking.

1 Holding the fish by the tail, run a scaler or the back of any kitchen knife along its length, from tail to head, to lift off the scales. Don't forget to scale the back and the belly as well as the side flanks of the fish.

2 Use scissors to trim the fins close to the body. In some cases, this should be done before scaling, as the fins can get in the way. Some species have sharp fins, so it is best to remove them before scaling.

Removing the gills

If you plan to cook a fish with the head on (mackerel is shown here), remove the gills as soon as possible, as they contain bacteria, which cause the fish to decompose. It is best to cook fish whole, as bones retain moisture and flavor, and prevent the fish from drying out. Remove the bones, head, and tail once the fish is cooked, if you prefer.

1 Firmly lift the gill flap with your thumb and forefinger and cut the throat with the tip of a sharp filleting knife. Lifting the gill makes it easier to get a clean cut through the fish.

2 Insert a thumb and index finger around the gills, and pull. They should come out fairly easily. If not (they can be tough on large fish), cut through the gills where they attach to the head, then pull them out.

Removing the head

There is no real reason to remove the head of a fish before cooking, but many people prefer to. It's important to cut into the fish on a sharp diagonal behind the fins to avoid wasting any of the flesh, which is at its most succulent just behind the head and nearest to the bones. Use the head to flavor soups and stews.

1 Using a sturdy, sharp knife, make cuts on a sharp diagonal behind the fins and into the back of either side of the head. This ensures maximum flesh stays on the fish.

2 Make a cut underneath the head, behind the ventral fins, to join up with the two head cuts. This also removes the ventral fins that would otherwise be trimmed away before cooking.

3 Firmly gripping the fish body in one hand and the head in the other, bend the head backward away from the belly. Be quite forceful; you should be able to hear a few distinct cracks.

4 Turn the fish around, and swiftly and firmly bend the head back in the opposite direction, toward the belly of the fish. You should now be able to pull the head clear from the body.

Gutting through the stomach

You need to remove the guts (the internal organs) of the fish because they quickly decompose. Once you have removed the guts, loosen and remove the dark bloodline running along the spine near the head, then thoroughly rinse the belly cavity to remove any remaining traces of blood or viscera. A mackerel is shown here.

1 Insert a slim filleting knife into the vent (you will see a small hole), and with a single stroke cut along the belly to the chin.

2 Lift the belly flap with your thumb and cut all the way down into the fish until you reach the dark-colored bloodline near the spine.

3 With the back of the knife, release the bloodline (see page 272), then scrape it away with the guts. Rinse, then firmly wipe the belly cavity clean.

Gutting through the gills

This technique is far trickier than gutting through the stomach, but is great for recipes where it is important to keep the fish as intact as possible, such as for Whole Poached Salmon (see page 224). It is also the ideal way to gut any round fish that you plan to cut it into steaks. A rainbow trout is shown here.

1 Cut the gills with scissors at the base of the head, and pull them out. Take care as these can be sharp.

2 Using an index finger, hook the entrails through the hole left by the gills and pull to release them from the body cavity.

3 Snip the vent end, and pull out the remaining guts. Run a finger inside the fish to loosen the bloodline, then rinse the cavity well to remove it.

Boning through the back

Often referred to as "canoeing", this technique keeps the fish in shape so it can take flavoring or stuffing before cooking. It removes the backbone, dorsal fin, and some pinbones. Once boned, remove the guts and pull away the gills. Finally, rinse the fish only briefly, as the delicate flesh absorbs water easily. A black sea bass is shown here.

1 With a filleting knife, cut along the back of the fish on one side of the backbone. Using a long, sweeping action, run the knife over the bones.

2 Turn the fish and do the same on the other side, keeping the knife flat over the bones. If the knife is angled, you could cut through to the second side.

3 Once the fillets are released, snip the backbone at the head and tail and pull it free. Pinbone the fillets (see page 271).

Boning through the stomach

If you intend to stuff a fish, this is the ideal method of boning. It is also the usual technique used to prepare herrings (shown here) for Rollmops (see page 297), and for baking fish. A fish that has been boned through the stomach will lie flat during cooking and will need to be turned only once, so is great for pan-frying and grilling.

1 Remove the head and guts. Lie the fish on its back and run a filleting knife along one side of the backbone from top to tail.

2 Run the knife along the other side of the bone and release the second fillet, keeping the knife flat to the bone to avoid wasting too much flesh.

3 Carefully pull away the backbone and snip it free at the tail with scissors, or cut it with a sharp knife. Pinbone the fillets (see page 271).

Classic filleting

A round fish such as red mullet (shown here) is typically cut into two fillets. A sharp, flexible filleting knife and good control of the blade are vital. Keep the blade flat against the bone and use long, sweeping cuts to prevent damage to the fillet. Use this technique to remove the head and bones. Fillets are quick to cook, but overcook easily.

1 Release the fillet close to the head: using a sharp, flexible filleting knife, insert the blade at an angle into the head to prevent losing too much flesh. Make a cut until you reach the bone.

2 With the knife flat, stroke the blade along one side of the backbone to open up the skin and reveal the backbone underneath. One or two strokes are all that are needed.

3 Keeping the knife flat, cut over the rib cage and out the other side of the fish. Using stroking, sweeping cuts of the knife, continue to the tail end to release the whole fillet.

4 Turn the fish over and do exactly the same on the other side. Support the fish with your free hand and remember to keep the knife flat, and the cuts firm, but long and stroking. Pinbone the fillets (see page 271).

Block filleting

Fishmongers use this technique to remove both fillets at the same time, leaving the rib cage behind on the bone. It is achievable at home and, although a little wasteful, gives a particularly neat fillet as well as a "cage" (carcass), which is great for fish stock. This technique works best on small, round fish such as whiting (shown here).

1 Starting from the belly, lay a sharp, flexible filleting knife flat against the ribcage and—using the ribcage as a guide—cut in a sweeping action from head to tail, keeping the tip of the blade on the backbone.

2 Turn the fish over and repeat on the other side, holding the released fillet with your other hand. Keep the blade of the knife flat against the bones to avoid too much wastage, and use long, sweeping strokes.

3 Run the tip of the knife along the back of the fish. Pull the two fillets from the bones with your free hand. With scissors, snip the backbone close to the tail to free the fillets. Pinbone the fillets (see page 271).

The double fillet achieved by the block technique gives you the chance to work with a large, neat amount of boneless fish. Try baking with an herb stuffing for an unusual, impressive dish.

Filleting a monkfish tail

Monkfish is usually sold by the tail. Once filleted, monkfish is boneless and the flesh is sweet and dense. Although a fishmonger will often skin the fish, there will be a couple of layers of gray-brown membrane under the skin that you will need to remove. If left attached, they shrink around the fish during cooking, making it a little tough.

1 Lay the monkfish tail on its belly. Using a sharp, flexible filleting knife, cut along one side of the backbone with long, sweeping strokes, straight through to the belly. Turn the fish and repeat on the other side.

2 Lay the fillet on a board, membrane down. With the knife at a sharp angle, cut between membrane and fillet. Grip the end of the membrane firmly, and continue to cut it away from the length of the fillet.

Cutting steaks

Steaks are cut straight through the fish and have bone in the center. The bone retains flavor and moisture in the fish during cooking. If the fish is large, with dense bones, hit the back of the knife with a wooden mallet to break the backbone. This prevents the flesh from being crushed under too much pressure. A salmon is shown here.

1 Remove the head of the gutted fish by cutting with a sturdy, sharp knife at a diagonal behind the fins. Repeat on the other side, hitting the back of the knife with a mallet to break through the neck.

2 Using a large, sharp chef's knife, score the skin at 1in (2.5cm) intervals along the length of the fish to ensure even steaks. Once marked, cut the steaks straight through the fish. Wipe the knife between each cut.

Pinboning and skinning a fillet

When skinning, keep the knife flat against the board, or you will leave too much flesh on the skin. You don't always have to skin a fillet, as the skin helps to retain moisture during cooking. It also looks attractive, and will peel away easily once the fish is cooked. A salmon fillet is shown here. Always pinbone fish fillets, to avoid choking hazards.

1 Run your thumb along the pinbones to make them stand out. Grasp the bone with fishbone pliars and pull it out toward the head. Pinbones are usually found at the thickest part of the fillet, and not at the tail end.

2 Choose a knife that is long and flexible enough to work up the whole fillet. Starting at the tail (the thinnest part of the fillet), and keeping the knife close to the skin, make a cut between the flesh and the skin.

3 Grip the flap of skin with your free hand. Keeping the skin taut, and the knife at a 30° angle to—and in contact with—the board, saw and push the knife toward the head. Discard the skin.

Traces of iridescent "silverskin" left on a fillet is the clearest sign that you have skinned it well, as the wastage of flesh is negligible.

Preparing flat fish

Removing the gills

Before handling flat fish, rinse them under cold, running water, as they are often slimy, making them slippery to handle. If necessary, use a brush to scrub off the slime.

If the head is to be left on for cooking, the gills need to be removed as one of their roles was to trap bacteria, which would now cause the fish to spoil. A plaice is shown here.

1 Lift the gill flap with your finger and cut behind the gills with the tip of a sharp, slim knife. Pull the gills up, and run the knife around their base. Release them by making one small cut with the tip of the knife.

2 Pull the gills free with your fingers, remove, and discard. Rinse the fish briefly under cold running water, checking to ensure all traces of blood from the gills have disappeared.

Removing the bloodline

As flat fish are gutted once caught, the only viscera you need to remove is the bloodline, which is the main artery, and runs down the backbone. Fish blood has an unpleasant, bitter taste, and it should be banished from the cavity. When rinsing fish, do so as briefly as possible, or the delicate flesh will begin to absorb the water.

1 Insert the tip of a sharp, slim knife to break the membrane holding the bloodline in place. This is found in a small pocket at the head of the fish, attached to the thickest part of the backbone.

2 Pull or scrape away the dark, congealed bloodline, checking carefully that you have removed it entirely. Finally, rinse the cavity of the fish briefly under cold running water.

Trimming

Some flat fish need scaling (see page 264). If you are unsure whether a fish needs scaling, scrape a sharp knife from tail to head. If nothing much comes off, scaling isn't necessary.

Although a flat fish's fins and tail tend to be wider and less obvious than those of a round fish, they are no less inedible for that, and need trimming.

1 Cut away the fins with scissors, working from tail to head. Removing fins makes the fish look neat. If you leave them attached, they can be pulled away after cooking.

2 Trim away the tail; this is both to make the fish neat and because it will stick to whatever the fish is cooked on. Removing the tail means you will be able to lift the fish easily from a baking sheet or broiler pan.

Removing the head

Most fishmongers would offer to remove the head of a flat fish as part of trimming, so the fish is ready to cook. If you are attempting the job yourself, it is important to aim for

minimum waste. With a sharp knife, score a guiding mark around the back of the head, close to the bone, to avoid wasting the thick piece of fillet nearest the head.

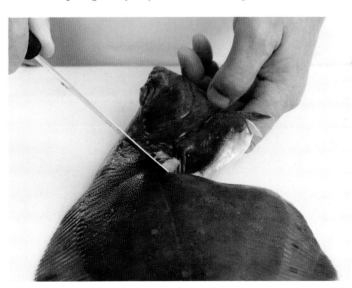

1 Lift the head from the board with your free hand, being careful to tuck your fingers away from the blade. With a sturdy, sharp knife, cut across the fillet where the fish has been gutted.

2 Following the natural boneline of the head, mark the flesh by scoring with a knife close to the bone. Using sturdy scissors, snip through the fish, following the guide mark, to remove the head.

Cutting two fillets

Fillets are great for pan-frying, roasting, baking, broiling, steaming, or grilling. Remember that flat fish fillets are thin and delicate and can overcook easily. When filleting small flat fish, use this technique of "cross-cut"—or double—filleting, to transform the fillets into more substantial portions. A lemon sole is shown here.

1 Remove the head. Lift it with your hand, and score around it with a sharp knife close to the head, for minimum wastage. Using the scoring mark as a guide, cut the head off with sturdy scissors.

2 Turn the fish over. Insert a long, flexible filleting knife between flesh and one side of the backbone in the center of the fish, keeping it close to the bone. With a sawing action, cut to the edge of the fillet.

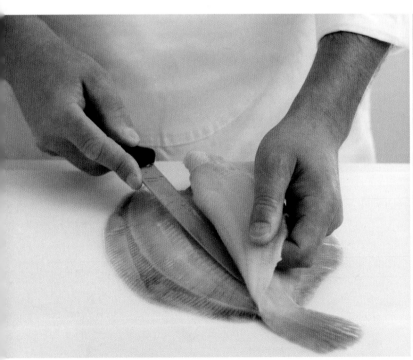

3 Holding the released fillet gently with one hand, run the knife in a long, sweeping action from the tail to the head, until you come into contact with the backbone.

4 Release the fillet at the backbone. Continue to use a long, stroking action with the knife, to release the fillet at the opposite fins. Turn the fish over and repeat on the other side.

Cutting four fillets

This is the easiest technique for filleting flat fish and the most commonly used. There are two key points to remember: first, keep the knife as close to the bone as possible (you should hear the blade "pinging" against the bones); second, use long, sweeping strokes to prevent damage to the delicate fillet. A turbot is shown here.

1 Using a long, flexible filleting knife, cut down the center of the fish to the bone, using the whole length of the blade. Work on the dark side first.

2 Using the tip of the knife, release the fillet along the backbone. With long, sweeping strokes, remove the fillet from the bone right to the edge of the fish.

3 Repeat on the second half of the dark side. Turn the fish over, and remove the two fillets from the white side in the same way.

Steaking a flat fish

Steaks are an easy way to get the most from a large flat fish. Each has a small piece of bone in the middle, so the flesh retains moisture and will easily lift from the bone once cooked. Using a heavy mallet to push the blade through the central bone prevents damage to the delicate flesh. Wipe the blade between cuts. A turbot is shown here.

1 Trim the fish and, using a sharp, sturdy knife, remove the head (see page 273). Remove the bloodline (see page 272).

2 Split the fish with a sharp, sturdy steaking knife down both sides of the backbone. Rinse the cavity briefly to remove traces of blood.

3 Score the fish into steaks using the tip of the knife, then cut them out. A mallet will help to push the knife through the bone.

Skinning and boning sole

This technique is almost impossible to do well with very fresh fish because the skin will not separate easily from the flesh, which will tear. So choose a fish that is a few days old and can "kiss its tail" (where the fish can be bent so its mouth reaches its tail), because it will be far easier to skin, and the flesh will be firmer and tastier.

1 Cut the skin from the flesh at the tail, with a sharp, slim knife. Peel back 1in (2.5cm) of skin. You may need to grip it with a cloth.

2 Insert a finger under the skin at the edge of a fillet and gently but firmly run it up to the head. Repeat with all four fillets.

3 Grasp the skin firmly in one hand (use a cloth if it is slippery), and pull the skin toward the head slowly to avoid ripping the flesh.

4 Cut down the middle of the fish with a filleting knife. Cut the fillets away with long, sweeping strokes. Turn the fish and repeat.

5 Using sturdy scissors, and keeping close to the edge of the fillet, cut the main bone from the fish. It can be used for fish stock (see page 310).

The boneless sole can be reassembled simply by folding back the bottom and top fillets. It will be very quick to cook, but take care not to dry it out.

Skinning and filleting a skate wing

Skate "wings" are the large fins of various species of ray. The rest of the body is usually discarded, except the round, tasty skate "knobs", found just behind the wings, which are similar to scallops in shape and sweetness. The skin of these cartilaginous fish can be rough so, to protect your hands, you may prefer to use a cloth when removing skin.

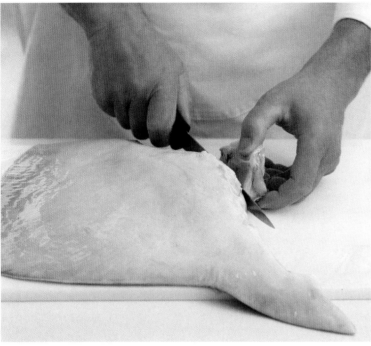

1 Cut the bony "knuckle" off at the thickest end of the fillet, using a chef's knife. This makes it far easier to see where the top of the cartilage begins, so making it simpler to fillet.

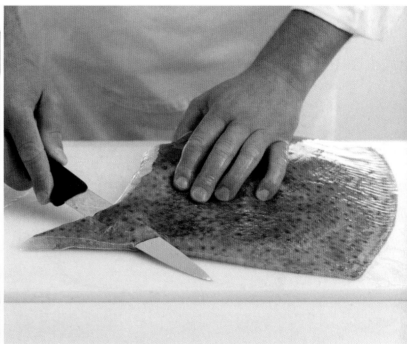

2 Trim the edges of the skate with a sharp, heavy knife, or with sturdy scissors. Insert a sharp, slim filleting knife between the top of the fillet and the skin, and move the knife across the flesh to the edge.

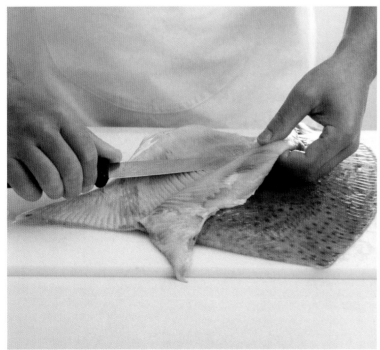

3 To remove the skin completely, move the knife to the thickest part of the wing. Using a sweeping action and cutting away from yourself, sweep the knife across the fillet to the edge to release the skin.

4 Starting at the thickest part, insert the tip of the knife between the flesh and the central cartilage. Release the fillet, keeping the knife close to the cartilage and using a long, sweeping action. Turn, and repeat.

Preparing shellfish

Cleaning and de-bearding mussels

Mussels need more preparation than other bivalve molluscs. If dredged they have a coating of barnacles that you need to scrape off with a knife. The byssus thread ("beard") needs to be removed, too. Prepare mussels just before cooking. If you need to prepare them earlier, always check when ready to cook that the shells will still close.

1 Scrub the mussels with a stiff brush under cold running water, to remove any stubborn grit, sand, or seaweed, that will spoil the finished dish. Check each mussel for signs of life (see box, facing page).

2 Remove the hairy "beard" from each mussel by pulling it away sharply with your fingers, and discard. If it is thin, grasp it close to the mussel shell, to prevent it from snapping in two.

Opening oysters

Despite their reputation, oysters are easy to open, or "shuck", if you use a good, firm oyster knife. Oysters are traditionally served in the half shell and should be enjoyed immediately, either cooked or simply raw. You can open them from the round end, too, using a type of pincer that cracks the shell easily, but shards of shell may break off.

1 Hold the oyster firmly in a thick cloth to protect your hand. Insert the tip of an oyster knife at the hinge end of the oyster. Twist the knife to get a good hold in the shell, release pressure, and pry off the top shell.

2 Discard any chips of the shell that have fallen inside the oyster. Run the knife under the oyster to release it from the shell, taking care not to spill any of the juices.

Opening clams

Clams are most often served raw or cooked (steamed or baked) directly in the shell. Served from the shell they are as easy to eat as mussels. If you want to eat raw clams, or if you're removing the meat to make chowders or stuffings, you need to pry the shell apart. Check the shell is tightly closed before doing this; if not, discard the clam.

1 Hold the clam in a thick cloth to protect your hands. Insert the tip of a narrow, pointed oyster knife into the shell, opposite the hinge. Twist the knife to separate the shells.

2 Once pried open, pull back the top shell, and carefully release the clam from the bottom shell using the tip of the knife, trying to ensure that you do not cut into the flesh.

Opening razor clams

Razor clams are often steamed or broiled in their shells, but the delicate meat is also excellent raw in a ceviche. Like all bivalves, they must be alive at the time of shelling.

1 Run a sharp, thin-bladed knife along the shell opening and pry the clam apart with your thumb. Take care, as the shell is sharp.

2 Remove the clam from the shell and separate the white muscle from the intestine. The muscle can be either thinly sliced or left whole for cooking.

Mollusc safety

All bivalve molluscs, such as oysters, clams, mussels, and scallops, must be alive at the time of cooking, or removing from the shell, otherwise they may not be safe to eat.

Always check the shells are tightly closed before cooking, and discard any that are chipped or damaged. Mussels, clams, oysters, and scallops may gape; give them a sharp tap to see if they close and discard any that remain open.

In all cases, discard any that remain shut after cooking, and warn your guests to do the same.

Opening scallops

Once the scallop is removed, both parts of the shell (valves) can be boiled for a few minutes and used as a container in which to cook the scallop. You can broil scallops on the rounded shell or seal the two shells together with pastry and either bake or grill them. Lightly rinsed, both roe and muscle can be cooked: pan-fry, poach, broil, or grill.

1 With the round shell down, run a sturdy knife around the shell's groove to release it, keeping the knife close to the round shell.

2 Discard the rounded shell, or reserve it for cooking. Use a sharp knife to remove the skirt (or frill), located around the muscle, and discard.

3 Remove the black stomach and intestines. Using the tip of the knife, remove the small sac of mud attached to the thick white muscle.

4 Hold the shell at an angle, and cut away the scallop, keeping the knife as close to the shell as possible to minimize waste.

5 Cut away the thick white piece of muscle on the edge of the scallop and discard. This is firmer and can be tough when cooked.

Freshly prepared scallops look luscious when returned to their cooked shell. Simply slice off the roe, if preferred.

Removing whelks and periwinkles from their shells

You can buy whelks and periwinkles live or cooked. To cook them at home, wash them in several changes of water, soak in a little salt water for a few minutes, then boil until cooked. Periwinkles will only take 3–5 minutes, while whelks require 12–15 minutes. Once cooked, they are very easy to extract from the shell with a small seafood fork or pin.

Whelks

1 Insert a seafood fork into the meat and gently twist the shell to extract all the meat. Avoid pulling, or some of the meat will be left behind.

2 Peel back the muscle at the top of the whelk to reveal a small piece of tough, inedible meat. Gently pull this away.

Periwinkles

Insert a clean pin into the meat and gently twist it from the shell. Remove the operculum (the horny "foot") before eating.

Opening sea urchins

It is worth wading your way through the prickly shell of a sea urchin to locate the creamy roe (or uni), which has an intensely salty and seaweedy flavor. Serve it raw, poach, or purée to add to a cream-based sauce and serve with grilled fish or pasta. Look out for sea urchins in spring and in autumn when they are in season.

1 Hold the sea urchin in a towel, prickles down, and locate the small hole on the underside. Insert sturdy scissors into this hole and snip around the underside of the sea urchin. Discard the cut-away shell.

2 Using a teaspoon, lift out the orange-colored sacs of roe, which are attached to the top of the shell, and collect them in a bowl. Take care not to break them, as they are very delicate.

Cleaning and preparing squid

The edible parts of squid are the tube, tentacles, and wings, and they are eaten all over the world. Over high heat, they cook in just seconds, becoming translucent; overcooked they become rubbery. Squid also suits slow and gentle cooking. The texture of slow-cooked squid is wonderfully different from the quick-seared version.

1 Hold the mantle (body) in one hand and gently pull the tentacles away from it to separate them. The eyes, some viscera, and beak (mouth-piece) will come away with the head.

2 Cut the tentacles with a small, sharp knife just below the eyes to separate the viscera and trim the two long arms level with the remaining tentacles. Discard the head, beak, eyes, and viscera.

3 Locate the hard quill attached to the inside of the mantle and pull it away. Pinch the two fins (wings) together and pull away, with the purple membrane. Pull the membrane from the wings and discard.

4 Leave the tube whole for stuffing, cut into rings for deep-frying, or open flat (as shown), and lightly score with a sharp knife. This enables heat to travel quickly to the center and prevents overcooking.

Cleaning and preparing cuttlefish

Once skinned of its thick membrane, a cuttlefish's white flesh can be opened out flat and scored in the same way as squid. Either cook it as a whole "steak" or slice it very thinly and flash-fry, poach, or deep-fry. The tentacles are often very tough and don't respond well to quick methods of cooking, but are best casseroled or braised.

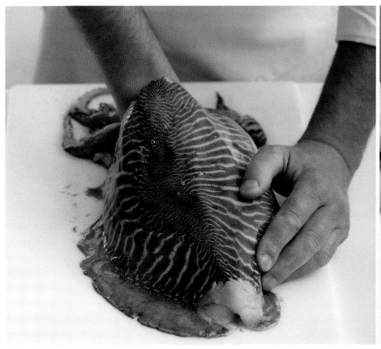

1 Insert your hand inside the head, gently grasp the viscera, and pull away with the tentacles. Avoid breaking the pearly-gray ink sac, as the ink will stain. You can use the ink to flavor and color many dishes.

2 Cut the head away from the tentacles below the eyes with a sturdy, sharp knife, and discard, then cut off and discard the hard beak from the middle of the tentacles. Trim the two long arms level.

3 Nick the membrane, stand the cuttlefish head upright, and press down firmly to release the internal shell (quill), peeling back the outer skin. It should come out cleanly. Discard the shell.

4 Peel away the thick, inedible membrane from the body, by virtually turning it inside out. Discard the membrane and prepare the flesh for cooking as for squid tubes (see facing page).

Cleaning and preparing octopus

Unlike squid and cuttlefish, octopus has no internal shell (quill). Baby octopus can be simply fried and served whole. Larger specimens are better suited to longer methods of cooking; although the head can cook quickly, the tentacles need to be slow-cooked to become tender. Octopus makes a wonderful rich stew when cooked in its own ink.

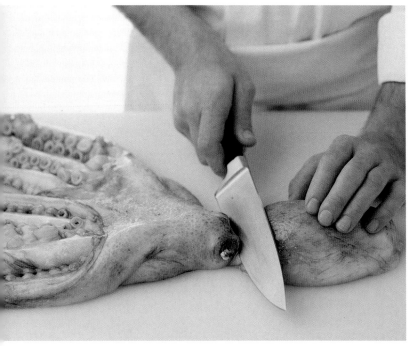

1 With a sharp, heavy chef's knife, cut the head from the body above the eye. The head can be opened out, gutted, skinned of its membrane, and cooked along with the tentacles.

2 Remove the beak (mouth-piece) from the center of the tentacles, using a small, sharp knife. Wash the tentacles thoroughly in two or three changes of water to remove any traces of mud or grit.

3 Cut off the individual tentacles and—for a larger octopus—cut the tentacles into short sections, or leave them whole until after cooking (see box, right). Trim off and discard the hard parts of the suction pads.

Tenderizing octopus

To cook a large octopus, you have to tenderize it by very slowly simmering in a court bouillon (see page 302), adding enough water to cover the octopus, and simmering gently in a very large saucepan for 15 minutes.

Weigh the cleaned octopus. Add the octopus to the pan, return the liquid to a boil, reduce the heat, and gently simmer for about 50 minutes for an octopus weighing less than 3lb 3oz (1.5kg). A larger octopus may take longer; simmer until tender. Leave in the liquid until completely cool.

Remove the octopus from the liquid, and drain on paper towels. Cut into chunks, and dress with olive oil, lemon juice, and white wine vinegar. Frozen octopus will have been further tenderized by freezing.

Cleaning and preparing shrimp

All shrimp have a black intestinal vein, which should be discarded, without removing the shell if need be. If the shrimp is to be broiled or grilled, leave the shell on to protect it from the heat. Opening the shrimp out across its back is called butterflying. In farmed shrimp, often the intestinal vein is so insignificant it is invisible, so will not need to be removed, but always check. The same technique can be used for Dublin Bay prawns.

Peeling and deveining

1 Pull the head from the shrimp, then carefully peel away the shell, starting from the underside, without damaging the flesh. Both head and shell can be used for stock. Leave the tail on, if preferred.

2 To remove the vein, lay the shrimp flat and, using a small, sharp knife, make an incision down the back of the shrimp less than a quarter inch deep. Pull out the black vein.

Deveining without cutting

Butterflying

You will see the beginning of the black vein where the head once was. Using a toothpick, stab the vein and very gently pull it out, to avoid it breaking and remaining inside the shrimp.

To butterfly a shrimp, make a deep cut into the back three-quarters of the way through to the belly, using a small, sharp knife. The shrimp will open up attractively during cooking.

Picking cooked crawfish

Crawfish and other similar crustaceans—including slipper lobsters and Dublin Bay prawns—are most often served directly in the shell with a finger bowl of hot water and lemon. They are boiled in a court bouillon, fish stock, or salted water for 6–8 minutes. The heat-sensitive pigment in the shell turns them an intense color.

1 Twist the head away from the body shell and remove. In the head of all crustaceans there are sweet juices and trimmings of meat that can be extracted with a small teaspoon.

2 The tail shell is sharp so, to help remove it, pinch the shell between your thumb and index finger until it snaps. Peel it away carefully to prevent tearing the meat.

Cleaning a live soft-shelled crab

All crabs molt their hard shell (carapace) at various stages of their life, enabling the main body to grow. It is at this stage that they are called "soft-shelled". The whole crab is eaten and the slightly crunchy carapace is particularly good. When using a live crab, chill it in the freezer for at least an hour before preparing, to render it dormant.

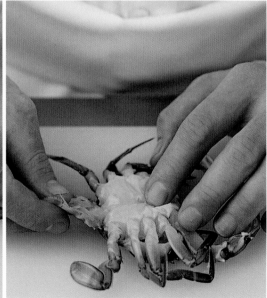

1 Using sturdy kitchen scissors, cut across the front of the crab to remove the eyes and mouth, and discard.

2 Pull back the soft carapace to reveal the gills (dead man's fingers), snip these away, and discard. There are around four gills each side of the body.

3 Turn the crab on to its back and pull away the tail flap (apron). The guts should come out with the apron. The crab is now ready to cook.

Cleaning a live crab

Crabs that have not molted their hard carapace can be slightly more tricky to clean. When using a live crab, chill it in the freezer for at least an hour before preparing, to render it dormant. It is unsafe to cook a dead crab unless you know exactly when it died. Once dormant, a crab is much easier to prepare than you might imagine.

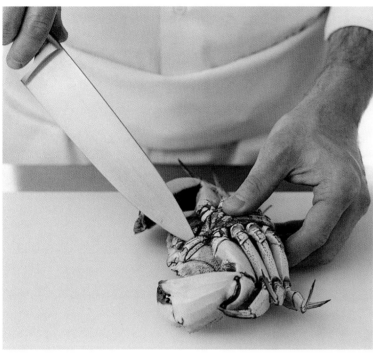

1 Lay the dormant crab on its back. With a very sturdy, sharp knife, pierce the crab firmly through the mouth, between and below the eyes, bringing the knife sharply down to the board.

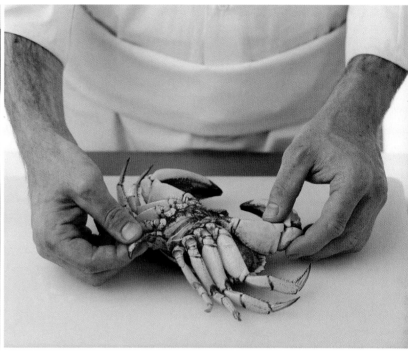

2 Lift up and pull off the triangular tail flap (apron). Hen crabs have rounded aprons; the male apron is long and thin. It is useful to know if you have a hen, so you can watch out for any roe (a delicacy) later.

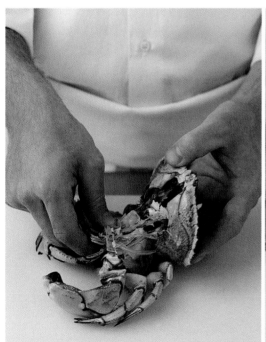

3 Turn the crab on to its front. At the head end, firmly press down on the shell, then pull the shell up and away from the legs and body.

4 With sturdy scissors, trim off the gills (dead man's fingers) from the body. Locate and discard the spongy bag (the stomach) behind the eyes.

5 With a very sturdy, sharp knife, cut the crab body into halves or quarters, depending on size and the cooking method.

Removing the meat from a cooked crab

Whatever the species of crab, the same parts need to be located and removed during the "dressing" process. As the meat is pre-cooked (see box, facing page), any reheating needs to be done with care to prevent losing the sweet flavor. Collect the white and brown meat in separate bowls and return to the cleaned shell to enjoy as dressed crab.

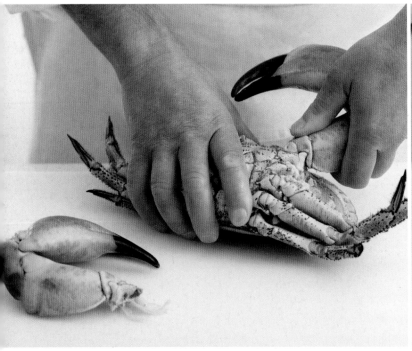

1 Lay the crab on its back on a chopping board and firmly grip a claw. Twist it away from the main body cleanly and forcefully. Repeat with the other claw, and with the legs. Set aside.

2 Set your thumbs between the carapace and main body at the head of the crab. Firmly lever the main body away from the carapace. It should come away cleanly in one piece. Pull away the tail (apron) from the body.

3 Pull away the gills (dead man's fingers) from the main body and discard any that have been left behind in the carapace.

4 Cut the main body into halves or quarters. Using the back of a small teaspoon or a seafood fork, pick the white meat from the body chambers.

5 Gently press the mouth shell down to break it from the carapace. Pull away the mouth and the stomach sac should come with it.

6 Position a large, sharp knife on the groove on the underside of the carapace and carefully crack the edges. Remove the excess shell.

7 Scoop out the brown meat from the carapace with a teaspoon. Watch out for buttery tomalley (liver) or yellow roe, as they are both delicacies.

8 Use the back of a heavy knife to crack the legs at their narrowest point. Pick away the white meat with a seafood fork.

9 Crack the claws using a heavy implement, or claw crackers. Take care not to use too much force, as this will damage the delicate meat.

10 Remove the piece of thick cartilage from the claws with your fingers and extract the white meat with a seafood fork.

Boiling crab

Boil the crab for 15 minutes per 1lb 2oz (500g) in a very large saucepan with enough heavily salted water or court bouillon (see page 302) to cover. Ensure the liquid is rapidly boiling when you add the crab and start timing when the liquid returns to the boil. Large crabs may take longer to cook, as they have a thicker carapace.

Once cooked, if the crab is to be eaten cold it should be cooled rapidly, not only for safety reasons but also to help the meat draw away from the shell, making it easier to remove. Place the cooked crab in the bottom of the refrigerator, well away from other perishables.

Preparing a live lobster for broiling

For broiling, use a raw lobster. Reheating cooked lobster toughens and dries the meat and it loses flavor. When using a live lobster, chill it in the freezer for at least an hour before preparing, to render it dormant. It is unsafe to cook a dead lobster unless you know exactly when it died. This is one of the techniques suitable for Lobster Thermidor.

1 Place the dormant lobster on a chopping board and hold the tail with one hand. Using a large, heavy chef's knife, cut down the center of the head shell to cut it in half. For a better grip, secure the tail with a cloth.

2 Turn the lobster around and split the tail shell right to the bottom, keeping the knife in as straight a line as possible, so that the lobster is cut in half evenly.

3 Locate the intestine that runs along the back, and remove. In the center of a female lobster, there will be a dark green roe. The pale green-brown tomalley (the liver) can also be left in place, and broiled.

4 Remove the stomach sac, situated behind the eyes. It is not necessary to remove the gills. These are located close to the carapace and you'd need to remove the upper part of the shell to dislodge them.

Removing the meat from a cooked lobster

Unlike crab, a lobster contains essentially only white meat, found in the tail and the claws. If purchasing a boiled lobster, you need to make sure it was cooked when fresh. Pull open the tail shell: it should snap back into position. If the shell stays floppy, it indicates that the lobster has been dead for some time prior to cooking, and should be avoided.

1 Twist the tail away from the main carapace. The carapace can be used for stock, but scoop out any grayish-green tomalley (the liver) first.

2 Using sturdy kitchen scissors, cut open the tough tail shell on the underside, being careful of your fingers because it is sharp.

3 Open up the shell and carefully extract the meat in one piece. Remove the dark intestine, which runs along the back of the tail meat.

4 Using a heavy implement, or claw crackers, split the claws. Take care not to use too much force, because this will damage the delicate meat.

5 Open the claws and extract the meat carefully from the shell, removing the piece of thick cartilage. Locate any shards of shell and discard.

Boiling lobster

Boil the lobster for 10–12 minutes per 1lb 2oz (500g) in a very large saucepan with enough heavily salted water or court bouillon (see page 302) to cover. Ensure the liquid is rapidly boiling when you add the lobster and start timing when the liquid returns to the boil. Large lobsters have thicker shells and may need longer in the boiling pot.

Leave the lobster to cool rapidly in the refrigerator once cooked.

Sushi techniques

Slicing fish fillets

Always use supremely fresh fish that has been commercially frozen specifically for sushi and sashimi. Freezing kills parasites that are present in raw fish. Oil-rich species, such as mackerel and tuna are sliced slightly thicker than other fish used for sushi, such as lemon sole, brill, snapper, and sea bass, because they have a softer texture. When preparing salmon, remove the dark muscle close to the skin. Use a long, flexible sashimi knife or a very sharp smoked salmon knife.

Using a long stroking action, slice the fillet into ¼in (5mm) slices on the angle through the bias (diagonally). Don't apply too much pressure or the flesh will tear. These are ideal for Nigiri Sushi (see page 48).

Slice a fillet into slices (see left), then slice again into even ½in (1cm) wide sticks using the tip of the knife. These are ideal to place inside Nori Maki Sushi (see page 48).

Make wafer-thin ⅛in (3mm) cuts across the top of the fillet, keeping the blade parallel to the board. Drape over Nori Maki Sushi, or scatter into Chirashi Sushi (see pages 48–51).

Cut the trimmed fillet into even slices, each about ½in (1cm) thick. Use the slices to top Nigiri Sushi, scatter into Chirashi Sushi, or use for Sashimi (see pages 48–53).

Preparing fish steaks

Steaks require boning and skinning before using for sushi and sashimi. Trim away any fatty tissue from the boned and skinned steaks to form a neat block. Cut the block into slices of around ½in (1cm) to use in Chirashi and Nigiri Sushi, or Sashimi, (see pages 48–53). Cut these strips in half again to form small finger-sized strips, useful for all rolled sushi, such as Nori Maki Sushi (see page 48). A salmon steak is shown here.

1 Lay the steak on its side and slice it in half: work the knife into the steak just under the main backbone and through the other side. Keep the blade flat, and avoid too much pressure on the blade in case it slips.

2 Turn the fish over and make a second cut underneath the backbone in one action, you will feel the knife cut through pinbones. Remove the pinbones and skin the fish as necessary (see page 271).

Sushi rice

Make fresh rice to accompany sushi and serve it at room temperature. For best results use a rice cooker, but this method also works well. This recipe makes enough for 10 sushi rolls.

1 Put 1lb 5oz (600g) Japanese short-grain sushi rice in a sieve and lower it into cold water, rinse thoroughly, and discard the water. Repeat until the water runs clear.

2 Put the rice and 2¼ cups water in a very heavy-bottomed pan. Add 2 small strips of kombu (dried seaweed) and cover with a tight-fitting lid. Slowly bring to a boil and, once bubbling, reduce the heat and simmer for 11–12 minutes. Remove from the heat, leaving the lid on, and leave to steam for 10 minutes. Remove the kombu.

3 Put 8 tbsp Japanese rice vinegar, 4 tbsp sugar, and 1 tsp salt into a saucepan, and heat slowly until the grains have dissolved.

4 Turn the rice on to a large shallow dish or plastic tray. Drizzle the warmed vinegar mixture over and turn to coat until all the grains look glossy. Fan the rice as you go (ideally with an electric fan). Once cool, it is ready to use.

Turn the rice with a wooden spatula to make sure it is evenly coated with the vinegar mixture. Try to keep the rice quite thin so it cools quickly.

Curing fish fillets for sushi

Small fish fillets with a high oil content and soft flesh, such as mackerel (shown here), benefit from marinating before use in sushi. The fish is salted, then marinated briefly in rice wine vinegar, firming up the flesh and creating an added dimension to the taste. It is excellent used to top Nigiri Sushi (see page 48).

1 Place 4 mackerel fillets in a bowl and rub with 8 tbsp coarse sea salt. Arrange in a bamboo strainer. Leave for 30 minutes.

2 Rinse the fillets and pat dry. Submerge them in 2 cups rice wine vinegar mixed with 2 tbsp mirin, and 2 tsp salt, and marinate for 1–2 hours.

3 Remove the fillets from the vinegar, and pat dry. Slowly peel off the papery thin outer skin. Place the fillets on a board, and pinbone (see page 271).

Tenderizing skin

The skin of some species, such as snapper (shown here), sea bass, and bream, is tough and difficult to remove even after scaling. This technique is very quick, so it is important to have boiling water and a bath of ice water to hand. The blanching can start to cook the flesh if it isn't chilled and refreshed immediately after contact with boiling water.

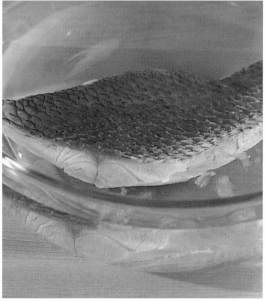

1 Arrange a scaled and pinboned fillet, skin side upward, on an upturned bamboo strainer set over a shallow dish.

2 Cover the fillet with cheesecloth or a dish towel. Using a ladle, splash a small amount of boiling water on to the skin.

3 Immediately remove the cheesecloth and lower the fish into the ice bath. Drain, pat dry, and proceed to slice as preferred (see page 292).

Preparing shrimp for sushi

Large warm water shrimp are hugely popular in Japan for use in sushi, sashimi, and tempura. They do require cooking, unlike many other species. For Nigiri Sushi, or whenever the shrimp is to be presented flat, they need preparation before cooking to prevent them curling into their natural shape during the initial poaching.

1 Insert a wooden skewer through the center of a raw shrimp to hold it flat. Put into a large pan. Pour over boiling water and poach for 2–3 minutes.

2 Carefully pull away the head of the shrimp, keeping the tail flesh intact, and discard, or use to make fish stock (see page 310).

3 Starting on the underside of the shrimp, peel the body shell away. Some chefs prefer to leave the tail shell in place.

4 Lay the shrimp flat on its back and make a neat incision along the center, nearly through to the back, enough to show any digestive tract.

5 Remove the digestive tract with a toothpick or your fingers, being firm but careful that it does not break, and discard.

6 If the tail shell has been left on, trim it to make a neat "V". Japanese food is all about attention to detail.

Preserving

Curing in salt

Gravadlax, which means "buried salmon" in Swedish, is a classic recipe. Salmon is swathed in a blanket of salt, dill, and sugar that draws out moisture. You can also use sea bass and trout. The curing takes 48 hours and leaves the fish firm. Serve with a sweet dill mustard sauce. Refrigerate and eat within 3–4 days, or freeze for up to 2 months.

1 Combine 3oz (85g) caster sugar, 1oz (30g) chopped dill, 1 tbsp lemon juice, 2½oz (75g) fine sea salt, and 1 tsp freshly ground black pepper in a small bowl. Mix all the ingredients together well.

2 Lay one thick, scaled and pinboned fillet of salmon (approx 1lb 2oz/500g), skin side down, in a clean, non-metallic shallow dish or tray. Spread all the curing mix evenly over the whole fillet.

3 Place another fillet on top. Wrap tightly in cling film and weigh them down with a plate and cans of food. Refrigerate for 48 hours.

4 Turn the fish every 12 hours to compress each side, and to drain the fluid so the fillets firm up. Remove, unwrap, and pat dry with kitchen paper.

Use a sharp knife to slice the salmon at an angle from the tail end into thin slices, discarding the skin.

Curing in vinegar

Pickling fish in vinegar, or citrus, in effect "cooks" the flesh and dissolves tiny bones. Here, vinegar is used to make classic rollmop herrings. Seafood Ceviche (see page 60) uses citrus as the pickling element. Feel free to experiment with either recipe, making the flavorings as mild or as sharp as you want, using your favorite spices.

1 Put 6oz (175g) sea salt and 3 cups water into a pan, bring to a boil, and stir until dissolved. Cool completely. Pour over four scaled and filleted herrings, to submerge. Cover and refrigerate for 24 hours.

2 Put 1 quart (1 liter) distilled malt vinegar, 4 black peppercorns, 4 allspice berries, 1 mace blade, 3 bay leaves, and 1 dried chili into a large saucepan, bring to a boil, then simmer for 5 minutes. Cool.

3 Rinse the herrings and pat dry. Lay on a board, skin side down, and arrange a few fine slices of red onion and a pickled gherkin over the top of each. Roll up and secure with a cocktail stick.

4 Pack the rollmops into a small plastic or glass container, and pour the cold spiced vinegar over to cover. Refrigerate for a minimum of 12 hours, or up to two or three days.

Cooking

Baking

Baking is great for fish fillets, some fish steaks (including salmon, snapper, halibut, and turbot), and whole fish. You can bake fish in a paper case, in a salt crust, in banana leaves, and in pastry; all seal in flavor and moisture. The fish can also be baked with the skin on, skin side up, which protects it from the oven heat. If it's skinned, the fish needs a coating of butter or oil to protect it. Baking is usually done at 350°F (180°C).

Fillets

1 Lay the fish fillets in a lightly buttered ovenproof dish or baking tray. Season with salt, finely ground black pepper, and chopped herbs (optional). Brush with melted butter and place in a preheated oven.

2 Bake for 6–8 minutes, until opaque, and the flakes separate when lightly pressed. Some fish also become a lighter color once cooked. If the fish still has its skin, it will peel away easily once cooked.

Whole fish

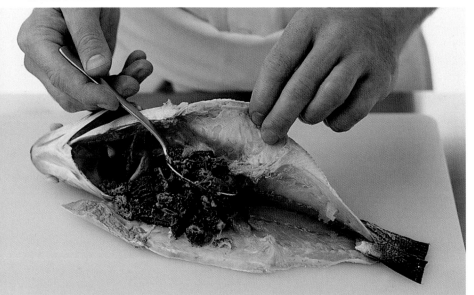

If fish is to take a marinade, slash the sides into the flesh. This allows flavors to penetrate. Place aromatics in the gut cavity and wrap in aluminum foil. Bake until the eye turns white, and, if you press the skin, you can feel the flakes separate.

Baking times

Fish is very quick to bake, but it is hard to give a specific time as the thickness and density of different fish varies so greatly.

Small, low-fat, flaky fillets such as whiting will take just a few minutes to bake, while a thick salmon steak takes up to 12 minutes and a whole sea bass may take 35 minutes. Once cooked, the fish loses translucency, becomes paler in appearance, and the flakes separate easily.

When any fish is cooked, protein comes to the surface: look for a white curd. If you baked the fish with its head on, one of the most reliable signs that it is ready is that the eyes have turned white.

Baking en papillote

Cooking fish in paper produces succulent, moist flesh and, if no oil or butter is used, is low in fat. Use aromatics and vegetables to flavor the fish as you wish. Serve the parcel, still wrapped, to be opened at the table to release all of its wonderful aromas. Make the parcel with parchment paper so you can see the fish cook inside. While preparing the fish, preheat the oven to 450°F (230°C) with a baking sheet placed inside to heat up.

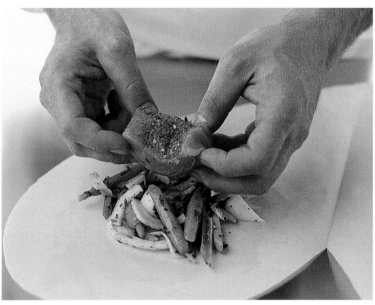

1 Cut out a large heart shape from parchment paper, big enough to enclose the fish plus a border. Arrange the fish on sautéed vegetables, or simply add a sprig of herbs and a squeeze of citrus juice.

2 Fold the paper over the top, and pleat the edges tightly to seal, twisting the end. Make sure it is wrapped well, but has space inside so hot air can circulate around the fish in the oven.

3 Place on the hot baking sheet and bake for 10–15 minutes. Don't open the parcel, but insert a metal skewer through the paper into the fish for 15 seconds. The tip should be piping hot when removed.

4 Lift the parcel on to a serving dish and present it to your guests. They should open the parcel at the table to enjoy the fabulous aroma released with the first breath of steam.

SUSTAINABILITY CHOICE

Buy pot-caught shellfish

This is a relatively unobtrusive fishing method where sturdy pots are placed on the seabed for a few days. The pots are baited with pieces of fish that entice the selected species, such as crab, prawns, crawfish, and lobster, into the pot through a hole. Once in the pot the creature finds it virtually impossible to escape. This method is very selective and has the advantage that if the shellfish is undersized or carrying roe, it can be returned to the water. Other selective methods of shellfish fishing include diver-caught scallops, where divers search for individual scallops.

Poaching

This gentle method of cooking produces succulent flesh. The fish is submerged in liquid and cooked over low heat, or covered, and oven-poached at 350°F(180°C).

The liquid barely simmers throughout the process, which prevents the fish from breaking up. Skate wings (shown here) are excellent poached, as the fish retains moisture.

1 To make a court bouillon, put 4¼ cups water, ½ cup white wine vinegar, sliced onions and carrots, fresh herbs, and a few black peppercorns into a saucepan. Simmer for 15 minutes.

2 Arrange the fish in a suitable flameproof baking tray or fish kettle. Ladle over enough hot court bouillon to cover the fish. It should be completely submerged, so top up with hot water, if necessary.

3 Set over low heat (you may need two burners). Bring to a boil. Reduce the heat until bubbles blip the surface. Cover, ensuring the liquid doesn't boil.

4 After 10–15 minutes, check the fish is cooked. It will flake easily. (For skate wings, the thick shoulder cartilage will pull away easily).

5 Lift the fish from the liquid and drain. Pat dry. Slide on to a serving dish and spoon over some of the cooking aromatics.

Microwaving

A fish fillet or steak can be cooked in a microwave in a very short time. It cooks in its own juices, just like steamed fish. Don't season with salt, as the flavor becomes intense very easily. The microwaving technique works very well with small fish fillets or steaks, white, textured species, and salmon (shown here).

1 Season the fish with black pepper and place in a microwaveable dish. Brush with oil, add 1–2 tbsp water, cover with plastic wrap and microwave according to the manufacturer's instructions (usually 2–3 minutes).

2 Allow the fish to stand for 1 minute once it is cooked, then remove the plastic wrap, being careful of your hands, as the steam is very hot. Lift on to a serving dish.

Braising

Braising is a mix of steaming and baking. It's best to leave the fish whole or in one large piece, and arrange it on aromatic herbs and vegetables. Add liquid, and cook the dish, covered, at a low temperature (325°F/160°C). Braising is ideal for whole fish including salmon, trout, and skate wings, and for the monkfish tails shown here.

1 Lay sliced vegetables in a large casserole or roasting pan. Cut the vegetables thinly if you are cooking a smaller piece of fish, as they need to cook simultaneously. Add herbs, such as rosemary, sage, or tarragon.

2 Arrange the fish on top and spoon over hot stock just to cover the vegetables. Cover and cook in the oven for 12–15 minutes, or until the center of the fish is white. Serve with the reduced cooking juices.

Steaming

Steaming is ideal for small fish such as snapper, and for seafood including clams, both shown below. It is a fast, but gentle technique that is very low in fat. Fish is arranged in a steamer over boiling liquid, or in a saucepan with a very small amount of liquid. You can also use another technique called "indirect steaming", as used in Steamed Trout in Lettuce, (see page 229), when the fish is placed in a dish or bowl within a steamer, so it cooks entirely in its own juices.

Shellfish in a pan

1 Pour in enough water to cover the base of a large saucepan with about ¼in (0.5cm) of liquid. Add a splash of lemon juice or wine, and finely chopped aromatic herbs, such as oregano and parsley. Bring to a boil.

2 Add the seafood, cover, and cook over medium heat until the shells have opened (2–3 minutes). Shake the pan occasionally, and avoid lifting the lid so the steam doesn't escape.

Whole fish in a steamer basket

1 Choose a saucepan or wok with a well-fitting lid. Pour in enough water to come just below the base of the steamer. Add preferred aromatics, such as lemongrass and cilantro. Arrange the fish in a steamer basket.

2 Place over medium heat and bring to a simmer. Place the steamer over the liquid, cover, and keep the liquid at a boil for 7–8 minutes. Don't lift the lid, as this allows the steam to escape.

Making seafood quenelles

A quenelle is a classic fish recipe: a dumpling made with cream and egg white. It is poached in stock or court bouillon. Although whiting and pike are traditional, you can use most fish or seafood. Always use fresh fish, as defrosted fish gives a coarse texture. All the ingredients must be cold. In fact, quenelles are often prepared in a bowl set directly over ice and water, as shown here. Do not overwork the mixture, because the cream may split.

1 Work 1lb 2oz (500g) chilled seafood in a food processor until smooth (scallops trimmed of roe are shown here). Chefs use a fine-meshed sieve for this, which is hard work, but does produce a particularly fine result.

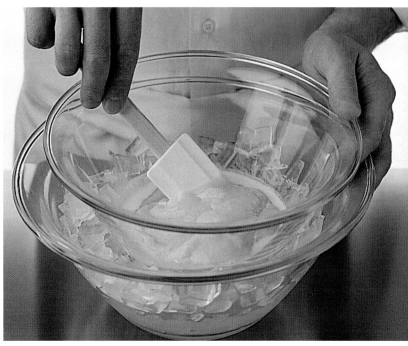

2 Put the puréed fish into a glass bowl over a bowl of ice. Start stirring in 2 cups cream and then fold in 3 whisked egg whites. Do not overwork, because the mixture can curdle easily.

3 Dip two dessert spoons into hot water, scoop out a spoonful of the mixture, and shape into lozenges, to give three sides to each quenelle. Dip the spoons in hot water after forming each one.

4 Lower the quenelles into simmering water. Initially they sink to the bottom. Once cooked, in about five minutes, the quenelles rise to the surface and feel firm to touch. Serve with a cream or white wine sauce.

Broiling

Fish becomes golden and succulent under the heat of a broiler. This technique is great for steaks, fillets, such as the red mullet shown here, and small whole mackerel and herring. Make sure the broiler is red-hot and the broiler pan preheated. Leave the skin on the fish, to protect it. You'll need to turn the whole fish halfway through; fillets won't need turning, as they are thin, but it helps to slash the skin. The side you cook last should be uppermost on the plate.

1 Arrange the fish on a pre-heated broiler pan, skin side up. Brush generously with seasoned melted butter or oil. Arrange under the broiler and cook for 3–4 minutes.

2 Check the fish is cooked: the skin will become loose, and the flesh lose its translucency and become white. Lift on to a serving dish and pour some of the cooking juices over the top.

Grilling

This technique is good for many types of robustly textured fish, including tuna, halibut, swordfish, marlin, and salmon, and shellfish, such as squid and scallops (shown here). More delicate fish are not suitable, as they will break easily. Both the grill and grill pan must be very hot (charcoal should be glowing and gray). Fish often benefits from a marinade to prevent it from drying out. You can also brush the fish with oil to stop it sticking to the grill pan or rack.

1 Marinade prepared scallops in oil, herbs, and seasoning. If using citrus, marinate for only 30 minutes, or the texture will change.

2 Thread the scallops on to skewers. This aids in turning the fish. If using wooden skewers, soak in water for 30 minutes first, to prevent scorching.

3 Place on a grill pan. Turn after 2–3 minutes. Once cooked, scallops will be bar-marked and the fish firm. Drizzle with a splash of lemon to serve.

Hot-smoking

This simple technique imparts a subtle smokey flavor into fish. Use hardwood shavings, such as oak or fruit, and add other aromatics to give flavor. Add a little water or wine to create a moist atmosphere and stop scorching. Small fish, such as rainbow trout (shown here) and mackerel, steaks, thick fillets, and many types of seafood, including shrimp and mussels, are ideal for home-smoking. This is best done on a grill outside, as the smoke is very invasive.

1 Line a wok that has a well-fitting lid with aluminum foil, being sure to cover the whole inside of the pan, and fold the foil tightly over the sides. Sprinkle over some wood shavings and add a splash of water or wine.

2 When smoking whole fish, score them through the skin nearly to the bone with a sharp knife. This enables the fish to take on all the flavors of the smoke well. Place the fish on a trivet that fits inside the wok.

3 Light the shavings with a long match, splash with water or wine, add the fish, and cover. Seal with a foil collar to trap the smoke, and place over medium heat; whole fish will take 15–18 minutes.

Hot-smoked fish are a glorious golden brown, with a deep, satisfying flavor, and excellent in salads, pies, or mousses.

Deep-frying

There are a few rules for perfect deep-fried fish. It should be coated in batter or breadcrumbs to protect it from the heat. Once cooked, drain on paper towels and season with salt. The frying pan must not be more than half-filled with oil. Once the pan is on the heat, keep a lid at hand to cover it, in case of fire. Never leave a deep-fat fryer unattended.

1 Dip the seafood in well-seasoned flour and shake off the excess. Now dip it in beaten egg to coat it evenly.

2 Roll in breadcrumbs. These are often dried and sieved to make sure that they are fine and also that they give an even coating.

3 When the oil reaches 350°F (180°C), add the seafood and cook for about 2 minutes, or until golden brown. Do not overcrowd the pan.

Pan-frying

Small whole fish, fillets, steaks, and some shellfish are ideal for pan-frying. It is not suitable for large fish, as they must fit into the frying pan. The fish can be rolled in seasoned flour, breadcrumbs, or cornmeal before cooking to create a golden brown crust. If you're not using a coating, pan-fry the skin first and serve skin-side up.

1 Roll the fish in a coating, ensuring it is evenly covered. If using flour, do this just before frying the fish or it will become soggy.

2 Lower the fish into hot oil, and cook for several minutes until the flesh is opaque (see box, right). Carefully turn with tongs halfway through cooking.

Heating the oil

For deep-frying, the oil must be at the correct temperature, usually 350°F (180°C). If it is too hot, the coating will turn brown before the fish is cooked. If it is too cool, the coating will soak in oil, making it soggy, and the fish will not brown.

If you don't have an oil thermometer, use a cube of bread to test the oil: if it turns golden brown within 60 seconds, it is hot enough. If it browns much more quickly, the oil is too hot; if it does not brown within a minute, it's too cool.

For pan-frying, heat the oil or butter (butter gives an excellent flavor), until hot. When the oil is hot, it expands in the pan and becomes free-running just before it starts to smoke. Butter will foam and sizzle as it melts. When it stops sizzling and begins to brown, it is hot enough.

Pan-frying fish in oil that is too cool stops the fish browning well and can make it pale and unappetizing.

Frying information

Deep-frying

Fish	Cut	Frying time	Coating
Large, flaky fish, such as cod, haddock, saithe, pollock, and hake	Fillets	6–8 mins	Breadcrumbs, batter
Small, flaky fish, such as tilapia, sea bass, and river cobbler	Fillets	4–6 mins	Breadcrumbs, cornmeal, batter
Scallops	Prepared out of the shell; white muscle only	1–2 mins	Tempura batter, breadcrumbs
Tiger prawns	Deveined (with or without shell)	1–2 mins	Tempura batter, breadcrumbs
Squid, small octopus, and cuttlefish	Thin slices	1–2 mins	Tempura batter, breadcrumbs

Pan-frying

Fish	Cut	Frying time	Flavoring
Large, flaky fish, such as, cod, haddock, saithe, pollock, salmon, halibut, and turbot	1in (2.5cm) bone-in steaks (large fish only)	3–4 mins per side	Brush with oil. Add dill, or tarragon, capers, and lemon juice at the end of cooking. Treat both steaks and fillets in the same way.
	Fillets	2–3 mins per side	
Small, flaky fish, such as sea bass, bream, snapper, carp, gurnard, and John Dory	Fillets	3–5 mins per side (adjust depending on size of fish)	Roll in seasoned flour or brush with oil. Finish with herb butter, soy sauce, sesame oil, and rice wine or citrus juice.
	Small, whole, gutted fish	3–5 mins per side	Slash the fish, roll in flour or brush with oil. Finish with citrus juice, fish sauce, soy sauce, and rice wine.
Firm-textured fish, such as tuna, swordfish, and mahi mahi	1in (2.5cm) boneless steak	2–4 mins per side. Thicker steaks and denser textured fish will require longer	Brush with seasoned oil. Deglaze the pan after cooking with soy sauce, sesame oil, and rice wine or sherry.
Flat fish, such as sole, plaice, and flounder	Skinned fillets	30 secs–1 min per side	Roll in seasoned flour. Deglaze the pan after cooking with lemon, parsley, and capers.
Small oil-rich fish, such as trout, mackerel, anchovies, sardines, and herring	Small, whole, gutted fish	3–5 mins per side (adjust depending on size of fish)	Roll in seasoned flour. Deglaze the pan after cooking with lemon, parsley, capers, and add slivered or chopped nuts.
Skate and rays	Wing	4–6 mins per side (adjust depending on size of fish)	Roll in seasoned flour. Wipe pan clean after cooking and add extra butter, heat until it turns brown or nutty, and add capers, lemon, and parsley.
Scallops	Prepared out of the shell. Cook the roe separately, as it "pops" or bursts easily, over a high heat	30 secs–1 min per side	Roll in seasoned flour or brush with oil. Finish with citrus juice, or soy or Worcestershire sauces.
Tiger prawns	Deveined (with or without shell)	In the shell: 2–3 mins per side Shelled: 1–2 mins per side	Brush with oil or dust in dry spice mix. Finish with citrus juice, soy sauce, or rice wine vinegar.
Squid, small octopus, and cuttlefish	Thin slices	30 secs–3 mins, or until opaque	Brush with oil and seasoning or dust with cornstarch. Finish with sesame oil, citrus juice, soy sauce, or fish sauce.

Making fish stock

Homemade fish stock is far better than store-bought, and freezes well. You can make a basic stock with the raw bones of white, non-oily fish. Classically, the bones of flat fish are used, but salmon (shown here) makes excellent stock. Shellfish stock requires raw shrimp shells, or cooked crab or lobster shells. Reduce stock by rapid boiling after straining, to intensify the flavor. Stock will keep in the refrigerator for a few days, or freeze for up to 3 months.

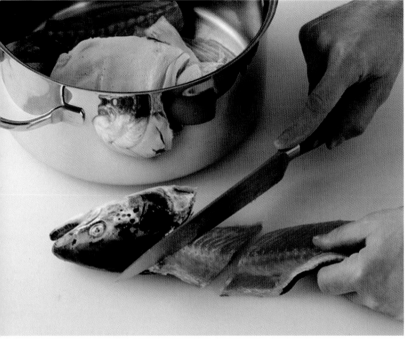

1 Break the fish frames (bones with fillets removed) into pieces. If using fish heads, remove the gills and rinse well to wash off any traces of blood, which will make the stock bitter.

2 Add a balanced selection of sliced root vegetables, such as onion, carrot, leek, and celery, and bay leaves, parsley sprigs, and thyme, and peppercorns. Don't add salt, as the flavor will intensify during cooking.

3 Cover the ingredients with cold water and bring to a boil, then use a skimmer or flat spoon to remove the scum from the surface (this is just fat and impurities that need to be removed).

4 Reduce the heat and allow the stock to simmer for 25–30 minutes. Do not boil. Remove the stock from the heat and allow it to cool for a few minutes before straining.

Serving whole cooked fish

Serving fillets is easy, but a whole fish is more challenging. If serving a large fish to more than one person, you'll need to remove the flesh to share. Fillets can be removed just as cleanly from a cooked fish as they can from a raw fish.

If the fish is skinned before cooking, remove the fillets in the same way as the technique below. Don't forget the delicious morsels of flesh located inside and just behind the head. Red snapper and Dover sole are shown here.

Round fish

1 Remove any untrimmed fins and gently peel away the skin; discard. If the skin won't peel away easily, it could indicate that the fish isn't quite cooked. Return the fish to the oven and cook for a few minutes more.

2 Run a table knife along the center of the fish to separate the two fillets, then slide it under to lift them off. Snip the backbone at the head with scissors, then lift the bone free to reveal the fillets beneath.

Flat fish

1 Run a table knife around the edge of the fillet and firmly push away the loose fin bones. Slide the knife under the fillet, above the rib cage, and lift it away from the bone.

2 Pull the bone away. This should be easy, because the flesh releases from the bone once it is cooked. The head should also come away with the bone. Push away any fin bones from the bottom fillet, and serve.

FISH GALLERY

Cod *Gadidae*

Fished throughout the cold waters of the Atlantic, Pacific, and Arctic oceans by both line and trawl, cod is one of the most important commercial fish in the Northern Hemisphere. Members of the cod or Gadidae family can be identified by a distinct three-fin-dorsal pattern. They are "white" fish, with the main concentration of oil being found in the liver, so the flesh is low in fat. The flesh color varies, but cod is renowned for having well-flavored flesh that, when cooked, offers succulent and sweet flakes.

SUSTAINABILITY Cod, especially Arctic cod, is endangered in some parts of the world. For many members of this group there is a maximum catch quota in place and landed fish must be of a minimum size to preserve stocks. Sustainability issues are a cause for concern, so cod farming has recently begun to develop as an industry. The following fish are good alternatives to cod: haddock, pollock, saithe (coley), whiting, and pouting. Pacific cod is a suitable alternative to Arctic cod.

CUTS Whole (gutted, with head on or off), fillets, steaks; Atlantic cod: head, cheek, tongue, roe, liver, swim bladder/"sounds."

EAT Cooked: Deep-fry or pan-fry in batter or breadcrumbs, bake, poach in stock or milk, use chopped flesh for soup or chowder, broil fillets or whole fish. **Preserved:** Cold smoked (dyed and undyed), salted, dried.

FLAVOR PAIRINGS Dill, parsley, bay leaf, lemon, olive oil, tomatoes, olives, capers, garlic, breadcrumbs, butter.

CLASSIC RECIPES Deep-fried fish and chips; brandade de morue; taramasalata; cod in parsley sauce.

Poor cod ▶
Trisopterus minutus capelanus
Also known as pelan, poor cod can grow to 16in (40cm) and is fished commercially across the Eastern Atlantic as far as the Atlantic coast in the Mediterranean. It is popular in southern Europe. Much like whiting, it is soft, white, and delicate, with a low fat content. Good pan-fried, steamed, or baked.

Look out for the three-fin dorsal pattern that is typical of the Gadidae family.

This fish is distinguished by an olive-green skin and yellow freckling with a white lateral line.

Atlantic cod ▲
Gadus morhua
Also known as codling, sprag, or scrod, Atlantic cod is one of the largest members of the Gadidae family. It is identified by a white lateral line, green-yellow marbled skin that fades to white on the belly, and a square tail. This species can grow to 5ft (1.5m). Atlantic cod is fished extensively by North America, many European countries, and Scandinavia. This fish has white, chunky flakes with a sweet seafood taste. Commonly used deep-fried in fish and chips, but excellent poached for fish pie or baked with a crust.

Atlantic cod has white flesh with a firm texture that chunks and flakes well.

Firm, sweet, and well flavored, Pacific cod is a popular fish for cooking.

Belly flaps are often trimmed away from large members of the cod group and sold separately for use in fish pies and fishcakes.

Pacific cod
Gadus macrocephalus
Also known as Alaskan cod, gray cod, true cod, or treska brown, Pacific cod has dark mottled skin and a pale belly. It can grow to over 6ft 6in (2m) and is found in the North Pacific and Pacific Rim. It is fished by the US, China, Japan, Canada, and Korea, is exported to Europe, and is enjoyed in North and South America and the Caribbean. Excellent for fish and chips, poaching, and broiling. Pacific cod is a good alternative to Arctic cod, which has been heavily over-fished.

Saithe *Gadidae*

The cheeks, considered a delicacy, are sold ready prepared and can be poached or fried.

Saithe is also known as coley, coalfish, black cod, green cod, and sometimes as pollock in the US. This key member of the cod family is considered an inexpensive alternative to cod but for many years has been viewed as good only for cat food, as it is only palatable if eaten very fresh. Young fish live in the top layers of the sea and swim deeper as they mature. Saithe is caught in the Northern Atlantic, both in the US and Europe, and is available all year round, though it is not at its best during the summer months.

CUTS Whole (gutted, with head on or off), fillets.
EAT Cooked: Deep-fry, pan-fry in batter or breadcrumbs, bake, poach in a court bouillon, steam, use poached flesh for fish pie and fishcakes. Inexpensive addition to fish soups. **Preserved:** Cold and hot smoked (dyed and undyed), dried, salted, cured, smoked.
FLAVOR PAIRINGS Butter, milk, beer, parsley, chives.
CLASSIC RECIPES Norwegian fish soup; *frikadeller* (fish rissoles).

Fresh saithe will have firm and tightly knitted flakes.

Saithe
Pollachius virens
The flesh of this fish has been described as coarse, but it has been undervalued. It looks gray-pink when raw but, on cooking, whitens well and becomes flaky and well flavored. It works in a fish casserole or curry, as it takes robust flavors well.

Saithe has a heavily scaled iron-gray or black back with a thick, white lateral line.

The lower jaw protrudes slightly, and the fish has a large prominent eye.

Haddock *Gadidae*

Fishmongers refer to haddock, from the Gadidae family, as ping, chat, kit, gibber, and jumbo (in ascending order of size). Haddock is found in the Northeast Atlantic and neighboring seas. It is second to cod in popularity, particularly when it is smoked.

SUSTAINABILITY There is a maximum catch quota in place and landed fish must be of a minimum size, so that stocks remain sustainable.

CUTS Whole (gutted, with head on or off), fillets, roe.

EAT Cooked: Deep-fry or pan-fry in batter or breadcrumbs (considered sweeter than cod), broil, bake, poach in stock or milk, steam.
Preserved: Hot smoked (Arbroath smokies), cold smoked (undyed and dyed fillet), traditional Finnan haddock.
FLAVOR PAIRINGS Parsley, milk, bay leaf, dulse seaweed, Cheddar cheese.
CLASSIC RECIPES Haddock Mornay; kedgeree; haddock and chips; Cullen skink.

Haddock
Melanogrammus aeglefinus
Haddock has a black lateral line on a gray back and a silver flank. Traditionally used for fish and chips, and preferred in this dish in Scotland, but also poached for fish pie and baked for Haddock Mornay. It is creamy-white, and has a delicate, sweet flavor.

Quality haddock has creamy-white flesh.

Haddock has a black spot on the shoulder known as St. Peter's mark or thumbprint.

The thick, scaly skin is easy to remove, but can be left on while poaching and removed afterward.

Pollock and Alaskan pollock *Gadidae*

Pollock, also known as green pollock and lythe, rivals cod in flavor and texture. Not of great importance commercially, it is a sport fish for recreational sea anglers. It is caught in the coastal waters throughout the North Atlantic and extensively spans the coast from Newfoundland right down to the Iberian Peninsula. It is often found in shallow inshore waters and grows up to 3ft 3in (1m) in length. With an olive-green back fading to a silver belly, pollock has a fine lateral line that has the appearance of being stitched in place, as it is slightly puckered. Alaskan pollock, a related species, is similar to cod in color (with yellow speckles on the skin) and in the texture of the fillets (lean, snow white, and succulent). Found in the North Pacific and caught by Alaska, Russia, and Japan, it is prolific in the Bering Sea.

CUTS Whole (gutted, with head on or off), fillets.
EAT Cooked: Roast, deep-fry, bake, poach, steam. **Preserved:** Salted, smoked.
FLAVOR PAIRINGS Tomatoes, chile, pancetta, basil.
CLASSIC RECIPE Fish and chips.

Alaskan pollock
Theragra chalcogramma
Also known as Pacific pollock and walleye pollock, this fish is the largest food-fish resource in the world, and is thought to make up nearly half of all white-fish stocks. It is white and firm with a medium texture. Excellent for deep-frying as well as poaching to put into fish pie.

Fresh pollock has a very firm texture and cooks to a white, delicate sweetness.

If cooking with the skin on, remove the heavy layer of scales first.

Ling and Tusk *Gadidae*

These fish are two similar members of the Gadidae family. Ling is a highly commercial fish found in temperate waters spanning the Northwest and Northeast Atlantic, and the Northwest Mediterranean. It has a long body, reaching a maximum of 6½ft (2m). The skin can be marbled reddish-brown along the back and flanks, fading to a white belly. There is a distinct black spot at the back of the first dorsal fin. Ling has a long history, particularly as a salted fish to add to pies and soup. It is at its best when line caught. Tusk, also known as torsk and cusk, is found in the temperate waters of the Northwest and Northeast Atlantic. It can be 4ft (1.2m) long, but is mostly found at around 20in (50cm). It varies from dark red-brown to olive green along the back with a pale yellow belly.

SUSTAINABILITY For both ling and tusk, there's a maximum catch quota in place and landed fish must be of a minimum size.
CUTS Whole, fillets, steaks.
EAT Cooked: Steam, pan-fry, broil, bake. **Preserved:** Dried, salted.
FLAVOR PAIRINGS Olive oil, cream, potatoes, garlic.
CLASSIC RECIPE Salted ling with mashed potatoes.

Ling
Molva molva
Also known as lingcod, it is excellent in fish pies, soups, and stews. This white fish cooks to an excellent firm and white, textured, sweet flesh. Salt ling is a traditional Irish feast.

Australian whiting *Sillaginidae*

A wide range of important whiting from the Sillaginidae family are caught in the waters surrounding Australia, Tasmania, and New Zealand. These fish are long and tapered in shape, with two dorsal fins, each with a differing number of spines and soft rays. They are unrelated to the whiting from the Gadidae family (see page 318). Various methods of fishing are used to harvest these fish commercially, and they all have differing habitats. All members have a bony structure and white, flaky, textured flesh.

CUTS Whole (gutted); fillets (single and block/butterfly).
EAT Cooked: Steam, pan-fry, broil, bake. **Preserved:** Smoked, dried, salted.
FLAVOR PAIRINGS Olive oil, butter, milk, parsley, chervil.
CLASSIC RECIPE Fish pie.

School whiting
Sillago bassensis
There are several "school whiting" caught in the waters around the Australian coast. They are similar in appearance, each with some distinguishing marks on a silver skin. They have a delicate, sweet flavor, similar to other whiting, and are low in fat, with a fine texture. Best when fresh, and excellent when steamed, poached, or pan-fried.

School whiting has firm flesh and a subtle flavor.

The skin is a coffee brown with a delicate lateral line that curves over the shoulder of the fish.

Sand whiting has a dark area at the base of the pectoral fin, and the anal and ventral fins are yellow in color.

Sand whiting
Sillago ciliate
Also known as silver or summer whiting, this elegant fish is being considered for aquaculture. It is caught along the east coast of Australia by beach seine, haul nets, and gill nets, and is a highly regarded angling fish.

The flesh of a sand whiting is firm, flaky, and well flavored.

Whiting

Whiting is the name used to describe several species from a variety of unrelated groups of fish, including the Gadidae, Merlucciidae, and Sillaginidae families. The taste of the fish varies from one species to the next, but the flesh of whiting is always white. The Gadidae whiting is found in the North Atlantic and surrounding seas, and the related southern blue whiting is caught in the Southwest Atlantic. Both these species have an easily digestible flesh. Hake (Merlucciidae family) is sometimes referred to as whiting. The fish is undervalued by many, as it has a delicate taste (it becomes almost tasteless when the fish is past its best). It is often popular with fish sellers, because it tends to be less expensive than some other members of the cod group. The skin of a whiting is particularly thin and care should be taken when skinning the fish, although leaving the skin on, particularly for broiling, protects the delicate flesh.

CUTS Whole (gutted); fillets (single and block/butterfly).
EAT Cooked: Steam, pan-fry, broil, bake. **Preserved:** Smoked, dried, salted.
FLAVOR PAIRINGS Olive oil, butter, milk, parsley, chervil.
CLASSIC RECIPE Fish pie.

Pout whiting ▼
Trisopterus luscus
Also known as bib, pout, or pouting, this fish is found as far south as the Mediterranean and up to the North Sea. It has a delicate texture, and spoils easily, so should be eaten very fresh.

Soft and delicate, pout whiting has a subtle texture and is low in fat.

Pout whiting is identified by a black spot behind the pectoral fins.

Whiting flesh is delicate and should be enjoyed very fresh, as it deteriorates quickly.

Atlantic whiting ▼
Merlangius marlangus
Whiting can grow up to 28in (70cm), although its usual size is around 10–12in (25–30cm). It has a light yellow-brown back, sometimes with hues of blue and green, and a gray to silvery-white belly. It has a light and delicate texture and is very low in fat.

Hake *Merlucciidae*

Although hake is often associated with cod and the Gadidae family, it comes from the Merlucciidae family. It is caught in many waters around the world, but particularly in the Atlantic and Northern Pacific. Silver hake (also known as Atlantic hake or New England hake) is caught in the Northwest Atlantic. European hake is fished throughout Europe, but is particularly popular in Spain. Often regarded as a "cod-like" fish, the white flesh is very similar to cod, but the bone, fin pattern, and skeleton all differ. This species of fish is deceptively soft—in many other fish, soft, delicate flesh would indicate bad quality, but hake cooks to a firm and meaty texture.

SUSTAINABILITY Some areas have been over-fished and strict catch quotas—and even bans—are in place in some countries. Other members of the cod family can be used interchangeably.
CUTS Whole, fillets, steaks.
EAT Cooked: Pan-fry, roast, poach, sauté, broil. **Preserved:** Dried, smoked.

FLAVOR PAIRINGS Olive oil, garlic, smoked paprika, butter, lemon.
CLASSIC RECIPE Hake in green sauce with clams (Basque recipe).

European hake
Merluccius merluccius
Also known as hake, colin, or in France, merluche, this species comes from North Africa, the Mediterranean, and as far north as Norway. A large, deep-water fish, it has been greatly affected by over-fishing.

Morid cod and Blue cod

There are a few types of morid cod, including New Zealand red cod and ribaldo, found in waters around South and Southeastern Australia, and New Zealand. They have a long dorsal fin running the length of the back, and the fillet tapers toward the caudal fin. Their size ranges from 16in to 5ft (40cm to 1.5m). They have white, textured, soft flesh. Like whiting, these fish are best eaten very fresh. Sandperch or blue cod (from the Pinguipedidae family) are temperate marine fish found in the Atlantic and along the coasts of South America

and Africa. They are also found in the Indo-Pacific, from Hawaii to New Zealand, and off Chile. New Zealand blue cod are part of this group.

SUSTAINABILITY Both morid cod and blue cod are endangered in some parts of the world. Use Pacific cod as an alternative.

CUTS Whole (gutted), fillets (single and block/butterfly).

EAT Cooked: Steam, bake, en papillote, poach, fry, microwave.
Preserved: Smoked.

FLAVOR PAIRINGS Batter, capers, pickles, parsley, soft-leaf herbs.

New Zealand blue cod
Parapercis colias
Other names for this fish include Boston blue cod, sandperch, and, in Maori, rawaru or pakirikiri. It is a species that is exclusive to New Zealand and is commercially harvested by the South Island. This is a white, textured fish with similarities to other white fish from the true-cod group, but slightly more coarse in texture. Good for deep-frying, broiling, steaming, and roasting.

White, sweet, and succulent, New Zealand blue cod is a popular fish.

Adult blue cod have a blue-green back, fading to white on the belly. Young fish are dappled.

Roughy *Trachichthyidae*

Roughy refers to an unusual family of fish (*Trachichthyidae*) that include several roughys, slimeheads, and sawbellys. They have a wide global distribution and are landed by many countries. Orange roughy is the main species to receive international acclaim and it has been marketed intensely as an alternative to cod. Also known as sea perch or deep-sea perch, orange roughy is

an important commercial fish in Australia, where it is found around the south coast of the continent, and New Zealand. The layer of oil under the skin is routinely used in the cosmetics industry.

SUSTAINABILITY Orange roughy was fished extensively until it was discovered that they mature and develop slowly. They have become seriously threatened and are

endangered in some parts of the world. Pacific or Atlantic cod can be used as alternatives.

CUTS Occasionally whole, commonly skinned fillets.

EAT Cooked: Pan-fry, broil, deep-fry, bake.

FLAVOR PAIRINGS Olive oil, chile, lime, butter, beer batter, crème fraîche, cream.

Orange roughy
Hoplostethus atlanticus
The soft, moist, white, textured flesh of orange roughy has a sweet flavor. It is usually "deep skinned", to remove the skin, and also the layer of fat directly under the skin.

Hake has a deep blue or steel-gray back and silvery skin. Its lateral line has black edging.

The flesh of this fish is soft, moist, and white, with a sweet, mild taste.

Bream *Sparidae*

The extensive bream family (Sparidae) is distributed globally in temperate and tropical seas. The members of this group (known as porgies in the US) are important commercial fish for many countries. Most bream have a round, deep, laterally compressed body with a long, single, spiny dorsal fin. They have a good covering of large scales across the body and head. Different species are identified by the teeth as a general rule. Many are marine fish, but some dwell in estuarine brackish waters or fresh water. Most are fairly small, about 16–28in (40–70cm) in length. They require careful trimming and scaling. Their white, well-textured flesh, is at its best when simply pan-fried.

SUSTAINABILITY There is a minimum landing size in place for many species around the world, which varies from region to region. Alternatives can be responsibly farmed bream or sea bass.

CUTS Whole, fillets, often with skin on (after scaling), thick steaks (larger species).

EAT Cooked: Pan-fry, broil, bake, stuff.

FLAVOR PAIRINGS Fennel, Pernod, cilantro, lemon, saffron, parsley, garlic.

CLASSIC RECIPES Bream en papillote; *besugo al horno* (a classic festive Spanish dish).

Yellow fin sea bream ▶
Acanthopagrus latus
Found in the Indo-West Pacific, yellow fin sea bream dwells in fresh, brackish, and marine waters. It is used in Chinese medicine and is popular for recreational fishing.

Firm and sweet, gilt-head bream is very popular in many Mediterranean countries.

The sharp points on the dorsal and anal fins should be trimmed before scaling, as they are sharp.

Black sea bream ▼
Spondyliosoma cantharus
Also known as old wife, the black sea bream is common to Northern Europe and the Mediterranean, where it is fished extensively. Like other members of the bream family, it is a shoaling fish. It is silver in color with black markings across the body. Considered to be one of the finest of the bream family, it can be cooked whole or filleted: roasting, pan-frying, or broiling the fillets. Its firm, white, textured flesh is admired in many Mediterranean countries.

As with the gilt-head bream, the cheeks of the black sea bream are sought after.

Gilt-head bream ▲
Sparus aurata
Gilt-head is the most popular bream in Europe and is farmed extensively throughout the Mediterranean. It has a lightly scaled, silvery skin with a spiny dorsal fin, and a deep body with a distinctive gold band across the brow. Farmed fish has white, firm flakes, with a medium texture.

Common pandora
Pagellus erythrinus
Also known as Spanish sea bream, this fish is found in the East Atlantic from Norway to the Mediterranean, Madeira, and the Canary Islands. An hermaphrodite, it changes from female to male on reaching a certain size. It grows up to 24in (60cm) in length but the usual landed size is around 12in (30cm). It is a popular game fish and like many of its group, it has an excellent flavor, slightly herbaceous with firm fillets. It is delicious roasted, broiled, and en papillote.

The lateral line of this species slightly rises over the shoulder of the fish.

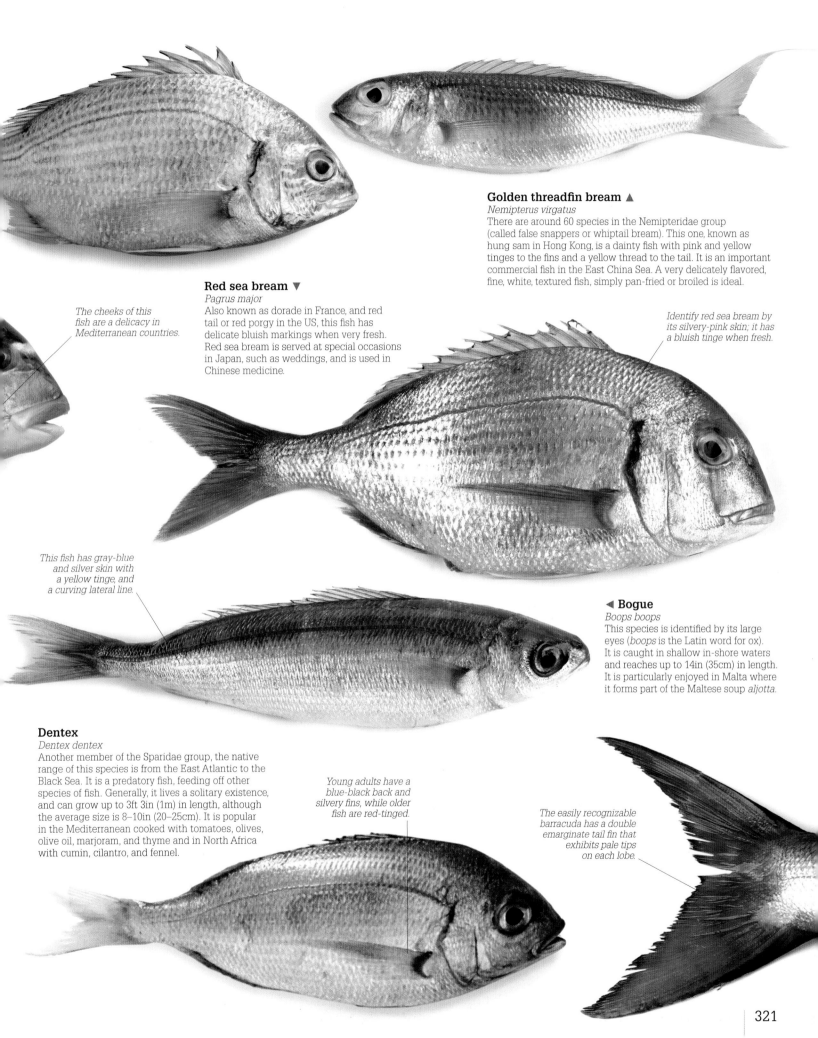

The cheeks of this fish are a delicacy in Mediterranean countries.

Golden threadfin bream ▲
Nemipterus virgatus
There are around 60 species in the Nemipteridae group (called false snappers or whiptail bream). This one, known as hung sam in Hong Kong, is a dainty fish with pink and yellow tinges to the fins and a yellow thread to the tail. It is an important commercial fish in the East China Sea. A very delicately flavored, fine, white, textured fish, simply pan-fried or broiled is ideal.

Red sea bream ▼
Pagrus major
Also known as dorade in France, and red tail or red porgy in the US, this fish has delicate bluish markings when very fresh. Red sea bream is served at special occasions in Japan, such as weddings, and is used in Chinese medicine.

Identify red sea bream by its silvery-pink skin; it has a bluish tinge when fresh.

This fish has gray-blue and silver skin with a yellow tinge, and a curving lateral line.

◄ Bogue
Boops boops
This species is identified by its large eyes (*boops* is the Latin word for ox). It is caught in shallow in-shore waters and reaches up to 14in (35cm) in length. It is particularly enjoyed in Malta where it forms part of the Maltese soup *aljotta*.

Dentex
Dentex dentex
Another member of the Sparidae group, the native range of this species is from the East Atlantic to the Black Sea. It is a predatory fish, feeding off other species of fish. Generally, it lives a solitary existence, and can grow up to 3ft 3in (1m) in length, although the average size is 8–10in (20–25cm). It is popular in the Mediterranean cooked with tomatoes, olives, olive oil, marjoram, and thyme and in North Africa with cumin, cilantro, and fennel.

Young adults have a blue-black back and silvery fins, while older fish are red-tinged.

The easily recognizable barracuda has a double emarginate tail fin that exhibits pale tips on each lobe.

Emperor bream *Lethrinidae*

Emperor bream or emperor fish are also called scavengers, rudderfish, and porgies. They are members of the Lethrinidae family, a relatively small group with 39 known species located in tropical reef seas of the Indo-Pacific through to Australia, and also off the west coast of Africa. They are carnivorous, feeding off the bottom of the sea. Most of the species are esteemed food fish and are recognized by their two dorsal fins with 10 spines. Emperor bream has a beige back with brown lines along the flanks and an orange mark around the gill flap. The lateral line curves over along the body to the forked tail or caudal fin. The flesh is white, full flavored, and firm textured.

CUTS Usually whole.
EAT Cooked: Pan-fry, bake, roast; it takes robust flavors well.
FLAVOR PAIRINGS Asian flavors: chile, lemongrass, coconut.

Red spot emperor bream
Lethrinus lentjan
This exotic fish has a firm texture and slightly sweet flavor. It works well with Indo-Pacific flavors such as ginger, chile, and cilantro.

The fish is densely scaled and needs trimming and scaling, prior to cleaning or filleting.

Gray mullet *Mugilidae*

The dashing, sleek, silver-gray mullets of the Mugilidae family are found near the shore, in brackish and fresh water, and in tropical, subtropical, and temperate seas worldwide (in the Atlantic, Pacific, and Indian oceans). Gray mullet is very common and is a popular food fish, which is highly commercial in many countries. They are also used in Chinese medicine. There are around 75 species, which have silver-gray, elongated bodies with no visible lateral line. They are noted for their small mouths and, sometimes, thick lips. In Southeast Asia, gray mullet is cultivated in ponds. It can have a slightly earthy taste, but soaking it in a little acidulated water before cooking improves the flavor.

CUTS Whole; fillets (scaled, but skin on).
EAT Cooked: Pan-fry, roast, bake. The roe is used fresh and smoked.
Preserved: Dried and salted.
FLAVOR PAIRINGS Citrus flavors, Moroccan spices, garlic, chile.
CLASSIC RECIPES Taramasalata; *besugo al horno*.

The flesh is pink in color, cooking to an off-white, and is firm and meaty.

Common gray mullet
Mugil cephalus
Its numerous names include black true, flathead, or striped mullet, harder, and, in Australia, poddies or hardgut mullet. Its olive-green back has silver shading to the sides.

Goatfish and Red mullet *Mugilidae*

Members of the Mugilidae family, include goatfish and red mullet. Many of the 55 species are beautifully colored. Caught in warm-temperate and tropical seas in the Indo-Pacific, Atlantic, Pacific, and Indian oceans, they are sometimes found in brackish waters. They have thick scales (which should be removed before cooking), forked caudal fins,

and a distinct pair of chin barbells, used to detect food and, in the case of males, attract a female. Most are sold at around 6–8in (15–20cm), although many reach around 12in (30cm) in length. The red mullet's liver is considered fine eating and should be left intact.

SUSTAINABILITY There are some sustainability issues in relation to

the method of fishing. Sustainably farmed bream or sea bass are good alternatives.

CUTS Whole (gutted and scaled, with liver intact), fillets.

EAT Cooked: Pan-fry, broil.

FLAVOR PAIRINGS Citrus flavors, tarragon, cream, garlic.

CLASSIC RECIPES Provençal fish soup with rouille; *fritura malagueña*.

This highly prized fish is dark pink, becoming white when cooked. It has a delicate flavor.

Red mullet
Mullus surmuletus
This fish is a particularly fine eating fish. It has many bones, so it is best to cook it whole so they can be located easily. Red mullet works well with citrus flavors, and herbs such as chervil and tarragon complement it nicely.

Indian goatfish
Mullus indicus
Indian goatfish is popular in Oman and East and South Africa, where it is landed. Its firm, white flesh is slightly earthier in flavor than its close relative, the red mullet.

This well-flavored fish has a flaky texture, which is slightly coarser than that of red mullet.

Barracuda *Sphyraenidae*

Also known as sea pike and giant pike, barracuda are aggressive predators with plenty of sharp teeth. They are found in several oceans but are essentially warm-water marine dwellers known to frequent tropical reef areas. Species include the great barracuda of the Western Pacific, and the Eastern Pacific and Atlantic species. They vary in size, but only

smaller specimens should be eaten because the toxins that can cause ciguatera poisoning affect larger fish. (This affects a handful of fish that live in some reef areas. Ciguatera poisoning has no effect on the fish, but it can cause extremely unpleasant symptoms in those who consume it, and has been fatal in a small number of cases.) Avoid

marinating this fish for too long—particularly in an acidic juice—as the flesh will change texture and can become dry when cooked.

CUTS Fresh or frozen: whole fish or fillets.

EAT Cooked: Pan-fry, broil, deep-fry, roast. **Preserved:** Smoked.

FLAVOR PAIRINGS Olive oil, garlic, paprika, spices, coconut.

With a firm, meaty texture and excellent taste, this fish takes robust flavors well.

Their large pointed heads contain a jaw lined with two layers of razor sharp teeth.

Barracuda
Sphyraena sphyraena
The elongated fillets are dense, meaty, and succulent. This fish works well with many flavors and is an excellent dish when it is broiled with olive oil and herbs.

Dory

There are several varieties of dory that come from two fish groups. The six species belonging to the Zeidae family are found worldwide in temperate waters. These solitary fish have a wide, compressed body, a dramatic display of dorsal fins, and retractable jaws (so they are able to vacuum up their prey). The group from the Oreosomatidae (oreo) family include the smooth oreo and black oreo dories. With similarities to the dories of the Zeidae group, they have extremely large eyes set in a big head, a compressed body, and gray and black skin. These fish are found in waters around Australia and New Zealand, where they are fished commercially. They are thought to be slow-growing, living up to 100 years. They reach 28–35in (70–90cm) in length. Silvery John Dory (*Zenopsis conchifer*) is also known as the American John Dory, sailfin dory, or buckler dory in Australia. It is caught in the Western Indian Ocean and the Atlantic, and is popular in Japan. The mirror dory (*Zenopsis nebulosa*) is a similar species found in Indo-Pacific waters.
CUTS Whole (usually gutted), fillets.
EAT: Pan-fry, broil, steam, bake.
FLAVOR PAIRINGS Red peppers, garlic, olives, capers, tomatoes, mushrooms, robust, creamy sauces.
CLASSIC RECIPE Bouillabaisse.

These extremely sharp barbs make filleting hazardous: trim them off with scissors first.

This species bears a black mark, encircled with a gold band, on each side of the body.

John Dory
Zeus faber
John Dory is highly prized for its excellent eating quality. Sharp barbs around the fish need to be trimmed before filleting. The skin is delicate and can be left on if cooking the fish whole, or it can be skinned, revealing the fillet's three natural sections. The fish's wonderfully sweet and firm texture is often matched with rich, creamy sauces, wild mushrooms, sage, capers, lemon, and crème fraîche.

The best part of this fish is the loins (the thickest part of the fillet and excellent for barbecuing and pan-frying).

Gurnard *Triglidae*

Also known as sea robin in the US, varieties of gurnard (from the Triglidae family) found in the Atlantic, Pacific, and Indian oceans have only recently gained a reputation as being worth cooking. However, gurnard is part of the traditional cuisine of the South of France (where *grondin* is the common name), of which the classic Provençal stew bouillabaisse is a fine example. This fish has a triangular-shaped bony head, a tapering body, and noticeable pectoral fins. Several species are sold in Europe, including yellow, red, and gray gurnard, and tubs. Some species are available in the US and Australia.

Usually 10–16in (25–40cm) long, they can reach 23½in (60cm). Over 40 percent of their weight is made up of bone. The head (with gills removed), bones, and skin make good fish stock. Gurnard has many pinbones and is tricky to prepare, because it has sharp dorsal spines and spiny barbs at each gill flap. The head can be removed and the fillets lifted off either side of the "tail".
CUTS Usually whole (ungutted).
EAT Cooked: Roast, pan-fry, broil.
FLAVOR PAIRINGS Bacon/pancetta, thyme, sage, rosemary, olive oil, Moroccan spice, lemon.

The fish is often best cooked on the bone and the tail is sweet and flaky.

Red gurnard
Aspitrigla cuculus
Also known as cuckoo gurnard and soldier, this is one of the most readily utilized of the species in Europe. It is caught around the coast of Britain and further south to the Mediterranean. Look for brightness of color (the deep red or orange color begins to fade as the fish loses condition).

Gray gurnard
Eutrigla gurnardus
This member of the group is also found in the Eastern Atlantic from Norway to Morocco, Madeira, and Iceland. Gurnard are distinctive in appearance and therefore easy to identify on the fishmonger's slab. The sweetly flavored flesh can be roasted or grilled; it requires a little olive oil or a pancetta or chorizo jacket to help prevent it from drying during cooking.

Toothfish *Nototheniidae*

The group of fish known as toothfish and rock cod are all found in cold water, particularly in the Antarctic, but also in the Southeast Pacific and Southwest Atlantic. They can reach considerable lengths, but most landed fish are around 28in (70cm) long. Toothfish are often marketed under the name of sea bass, but are not related to that group.
SUSTAINABILITY Toothfish are endangered in some parts of the world. As it is a slow-growing fish, there have been concerns, but the MSC (Marine Stewardship Council) has certified the South Georgia Patagonian Toothfish Longline Fishery as sustainable. The white flesh has a dense texture and sweet flavor to rival other white fish, so there are no immediate alternatives, but any firm, white, textured fish, such as cod, sea bass, or pollock, can be used instead.
CUTS Steaks, fillets (usually frozen and occasionally fresh).
EAT Cooked: Pan-fry, grill, broil, crust, sauté, roast, bake.
Preserved: Cold and hot smoked.
FLAVOR PAIRINGS Smoked bacon, garlic, chile, soy, sesame oil.

Patagonian toothfish
Dissostichus eleginoides
The popularity of some toothfish species has grown in recent years, because they are considered fine eating. This species (also known as Chilean sea bass, Australian sea bass, and Antarctic ice fish) has become a favorite with Californian chefs.

Fillets are dense with a gentle sweetness that works well with piquant flavors.

Wolf fish *Anarhichadidae*

The wolf fish group is a small number of related species found in both Atlantic and Pacific waters. Aggressive in appearance with a mouth with lots of uneven teeth, wolf fish resemble an eel in shape but have a thick-set body. Also known as seawolf, ocean catfish, and wolf eel (the common name for the Pacific species), they vary in color from a simple brown to sporting strips or spots. The flesh is firm, white, and meaty with a good flavor.

SUSTAINABILITY Wolf fish are endangered in some parts of the world. They have been subject to over-fishing and there are concerns over rapidly depleting stock. Alternatives include Pacific cod and barracuda.

CUTS Skinned fillets (fresh or frozen).
EAT Cooked: Steam, fry, broil, poach, bake.
FLAVOR PAIRINGS Butter, garlic, cream, tomatoes.

Rabbit fish and Surgeon fish *Siganus*

Also known as spinefoots or ratfish, there are around 28 species of rabbit fish. Caught in the Indo-Pacific and the Eastern Mediterranean, several species are fished for food. Many species are colorful and some are also very decorative, which makes them popular in aquariums. They grow to around 16in (40cm) long and are easily identified by their small, slightly pouting lips over obvious front teeth, giving the fish a rabbit-like appearance—hence the name. The dorsal fin is spiky and particularly hazardous, and it needs to be trimmed away before cooking. There are around 80 species of surgeon fish found in marine tropical waters worldwide, often around a reef. The Latin name of the surgeon fish means "thorn tail", but it is also known as doctorfish and unicornfish. Each of these fish has a sharp barb, like a scalpel, on either side of the tail, that the fish can flex to protect itself from other predators.

CUTS Whole (ungutted and uncleaned), fillets.
EAT Cooked: Broil, pan-fry, bake, add to curries and stews.
FLAVOR PAIRINGS Thai and African-Caribbean flavors of coconut, cilantro, and spices.

Mild and delicate, the fillets need combining with robust flavors.

The yellow band around the shoulder makes this fish easy to identify.

Rabbit fish
Siganidae
Dark khaki-colored skin with lines running laterally along the body. The flesh is white with a subtle flavor, but dries easily and becomes quite tasteless. It is a good addition to curries and stews that have robust or Asian flavors.

Remove the sharp spines before gutting or filleting. The smooth skin needs little preparation.

The dorsal fin on the wolf fish runs the length of the body and leads into a seal-like tail.

Atlantic wolf fish
Anarhichas lupus
Also known as rock fish, sea leopard, and sea cat, this is the largest of the wolf fish group, measuring up to 5ft (1.5m) long. The fish inhabits very cold water and is able to produce anti-freeze to keep its blood fluid.

A diet of spiny sea urchins and crab may account for wolf fish's sweet, meaty, and succulent flesh.

Easily recognizable by its fierce appearance, the wolf fish has a plain, dark brown, reddish skin with vertical black bands.

The barb is ½in (1cm) from the tail and needs careful removal, as it is as sharp as a surgeon's scalpel.

Surgeon fish
Acanthuridae
This species is particularly popular in African and Caribbean communities, who use it in curries and other spicy dishes. The flesh is delicate, so it can dry out and lack flavor if overcooked.

Redfish *Scorpaenidae*

Redfish are a selection of fish that include rockfish, the spiny scorpion fish (including the rascasse, one of the key ingredients in bouillabaisse), some ocean perch, and also rose fish. Found in temperate waters worldwide, some species are commercially significant. Norway haddock is an important member of this group; it is located in the North Atlantic coasts of both Europe and North America. Younger redfish have brown skin, but as an adult the back develops a deep red color that fades to a paler red-orange on the flanks. The fish have a large mouth and prominent eyes and can grow up to 3⅓ft (1m) in length; however, the normal market size tends to be around 12–18in (30–46cm). This fish has one long dorsal fin and a spiny, sharp front section, so it needs to be handled with care.

SUSTAINABILITY Redfish are endangered in some parts of the world. Alternatives include members of the cod group.
CUTS Whole (fresh and frozen), prepared (head off and gutted), fillets.
EAT Cooked: Pan-fry, bake, broil.
FLAVOR PAIRINGS Cream- and dill-based sauces, tomatoes, peppers, chile.

Redfish
Sebastes marinus
The names redfish and Norway haddock are interchangeable. The fillets are white, flaky, and delicately flavored, and are particularly enjoyed in Scandinavia and Eastern Europe. It is harvested, frozen in fillets, and then exported.

Only 50 percent of this fish produces fillets, as it has a heavy head and plentiful fins.

Grouper and Rock cod *Serranidae*

There are several hundred members of the Serranidae group, including groupers, gropers, rock cod, sea perch, and some fish called sea bass. The grouper family includes Jewfish, and the coral trout that is popular in Australia. They are often labeled by their Creole names, such as croissant and vieille rouge. This diverse family are tropical water dwellers and are found in the Atlantic, Pacific, and Indian oceans. The skin of a grouper is thick and slightly rubbery, and underneath it is a layer of fat that can cause stomach irritation. It is therefore advisable to skin the fish deeply prior to cooking.
SUSTAINABILITY Many of these species are important commercial fish and have been exploited to the point of collapse. Alternatives include cod, mahi mahi (dolphin fish), and barramundi from sustainable sources.
CUTS Fresh and frozen, whole, fillets, steaks.
EAT Cooked: Broil, pan-fry.
Preserved: Salted.
FLAVOR PAIRINGS Soy sauce, sesame, Parmesan, olive oil, butter, lime, red chile, cilantro, ackee.
CLASSIC RECIPE Jamaican jerk fish.

Coral trout
Plectropomus leopardus
Also known as leopard coral grouper, footballer cod, and lunartail rockcod (Australia), this brightly colored fish is listed as endangered, but it is carefully managed in Australian waters. It has also been associated with ciguatera poisoning. Firm, white, and sweet-flavored flesh, it is great for pan-frying, grilling, and roasting.

The white flesh has an excellent flavor that is popular with chefs, particularly in Australia.

Red grouper
Epinephelus morio
This marine and subtropical species is often located near a reef in the West Atlantic. It is fished to unsustainable levels in some areas. Generally the fillets of these fish are white and the flavor is not dissimilar to cod, but less sweet.

All members of this group have handsome heads and prominent jaws.

Jewfish
Epinephelus itajara
This important game fish is found in subtropical marine waters and close to reefs of the Western and Eastern Atlantic and in the East Pacific. An aggressive fish, it feeds on crustaceans, which may account for its firm texture and sweet flavor. Confusingly, Jewfish is also the name for a member of the Sciaendidae group—(kob, see page 334). It is good for baking and pan-frying, usually as steaks.

These fish have a thick, rough skin that requires deep-skinning before cooking.

Bass *Moronidae*

Confusingly, sea bass is a name used to identify several species of fish, but the group from the Moronidae family include several bass and perch, found in the temperate waters of the East and West Atlantic. They are mainly marine fish; in the wild they often locate to brackish and sometimes fresh water, specifically the American striped bass, which is a popular fish for recreational fishing. All members have sharp spines and a thick covering of scales that need to be removed prior to cooking. Bass is often compared to sea bream, and although in Northern Europe sea bass is popular, in the Mediterranean bream is generally the favorite.

SUSTAINABILITY Its flavor and popularity has led to over-fishing that has threatened stocks of these species. In some areas, landed fish must be of a minimum size, while other areas have a closed season for recreational fishing. Sea bream is an appropriate alternative.

CUTS Whole unprepared fish, trimmed whole fish, fillets. Fish is scaled and rarely skinned.

EAT Broil, bake, pan-fry, en papillote.

FLAVOR PAIRINGS Asian flavors such as fermented black beans, sesame, dark soy, and ginger. Mediterranean flavors including tomatoes, garlic, olive oil, and red peppers. Pernod and other ingredients that have a hint of licorice.

CLASSIC RECIPE Branzino in salt.

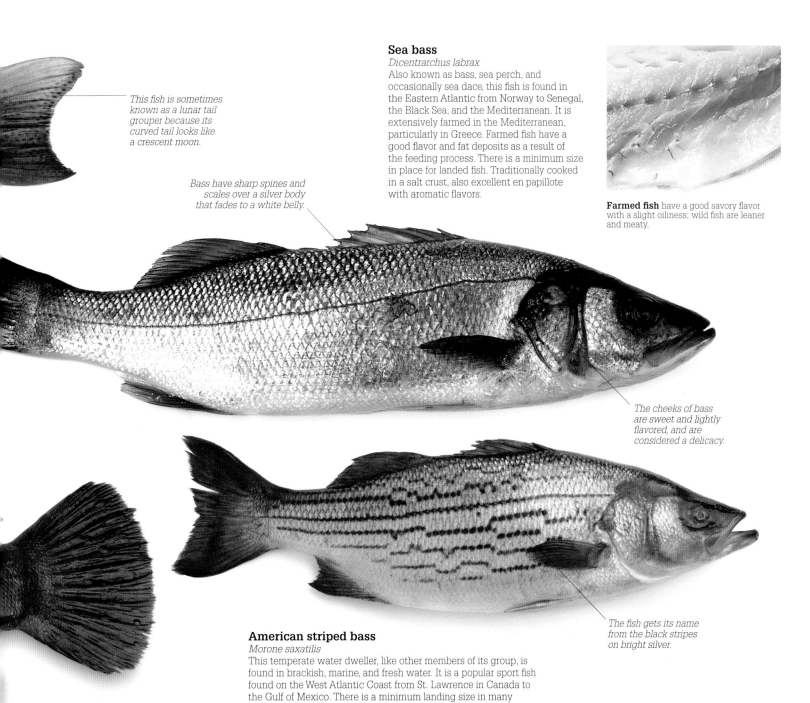

This fish is sometimes known as a lunar tail grouper because its curved tail looks like a crescent moon.

Bass have sharp spines and scales over a silver body that fades to a white belly.

Sea bass
Dicentrarchus labrax
Also known as bass, sea perch, and occasionally sea dace, this fish is found in the Eastern Atlantic from Norway to Senegal, the Black Sea, and the Mediterranean. It is extensively farmed in the Mediterranean, particularly in Greece. Farmed fish have a good flavor and fat deposits as a result of the feeding process. There is a minimum size in place for landed fish. Traditionally cooked in a salt crust, also excellent en papillote with aromatic flavors.

Farmed fish have a good savory flavor with a slight oiliness; wild fish are leaner and meaty.

The cheeks of bass are sweet and lightly flavored, and are considered a delicacy.

American striped bass
Morone saxatilis
This temperate water dweller, like other members of its group, is found in brackish, marine, and fresh water. It is a popular sport fish found on the West Atlantic Coast from St. Lawrence in Canada to the Gulf of Mexico. There is a minimum landing size in many areas and some quantities are responsibly farmed. Good cooked en papillote with black beans, chile, lemongrass, olive oil, and soy.

The fish gets its name from the black stripes on bright silver.

Jack, Pompano, and Scad *Carangidae*

The Carangids are a large group of over 150 species of fish that includes some very notable members. Found in the Atlantic, Indian, and Pacific oceans, most members are voracious predators. Their body shape is not dissimilar to the mackerel group, having deeply forked tails, although they have a different fin structure. Many of these species are highly commercial and are used extensively across the world, although in some species there have been reports of ciguatera poisoning in endemic areas. The flesh varies between species, but generally the fillets are a pink that lightens to white on cooking, with firm, white flakes. Exotic species have a delicate sweetness and most take robust flavors well.

CUTS Depending on the fish—but generally whole, fillets, and steaks. Fillets can be large on some species so these will be taken as a shoulder, loin, and tail cut.
EAT Cooked: Grill, broil, pan-fry.
FLAVOR PAIRINGS Red and green chile, ginger, soy, warm spice mixes, coconut milk, tomatoes.

Crevalle jack
Caranx hippos
Crevalle jack, jack, or jackfish is found in subtropical marine and brackish areas of the East and West Atlantic. The flesh dries easily so it needs careful cooking; it is good pan-fried or broiled with flavored butter or brushed in oil.

The flavor and texture of this group varies, but the fillets are usually pale and delicate.

Greater amberjack
Seriola dumerili
The largest member of the Carangidae group is found in many subtropical areas of the Mediterranean, Atlantic, Pacific, and Indian oceans. Fast and powerful in the water, this pelagic fish is a voracious predator. It looks similar to the kingfish and has silver-blue skin with a delicate gold lateral line. Meaty steaks make excellent eating.

Laterally compressed, it has a silver body and yellow fins.

Mahi mahi *Coryphaenidae*

Mahi mahi, meaning "strong strong" is the Polynesian name for this fish. Other names include dolphin fish and *lampuga* (in Malta). This warm-water, marine, and brackish dwelling fish is caught in the tropical and subtropical waters of the Atlantic, Indian, and Pacific oceans. It grows rapidly, often to over 6½ft (2m), but is more commonly seen just under 3ft (1m). A striking fish, it has a domed head (particularly noticeable on a mature male) and a long, single dorsal fin running from head to tail. Mahi mahi has a dense, meaty texture that takes robust flavors, particularly spices, very well.
CUTS Whole, fillets (fresh and frozen).
EAT Cooked: Pan-fry, grill, char-grill.
FLAVOR PAIRINGS Caribbean: cardamom, allspice, fennel, cilantro, curry, cayenne, and ginger; Asian: chile, garlic, nam pla, lime.
CLASSIC RECIPE Lampuga.

Mahi mahi
Coryphaena hippurus
There is some aquaculture of these prized, premium fish, and there have been reports of ciguatera poisoning in endemic areas. It requires careful cooking, as the flesh surprisingly takes a little longer to cook than flaky fish, and it can dry out in the process.

The color becomes a rich yellow toward the tail.

The flesh of this fish is pink and dense.

Trevally has a curved dorsal fin, yellow fins and tail, and golden hues above a greeny-blue and silver belly.

It has a silver-colored skin with a yellow tail.

Soft fillets with a low oil content; the flesh is a marbled pink that cooks to delicate white.

Trevally
Carangue australienne
Also known as silver trevally, sand trevally, skipjack trevally, and skippy, this fish is found worldwide in waters including the East and West Atlantic, Indo-Pacific, South Africa, Japan, and Australia. The flavor is herbaceous and takes Asian and bold ingredients well, including chile, ginger, and sesame.

Scad
Trachurus trachurus
A member of the Carangidae family also known as horse mackerel, jack, and chinchard in France. This particular species is found in the Northeast Atlantic, but others are found in global waters. It has a similar texture to mackerel, but many bones. Landed fish must be of a minimum size.

It has sharp spines and a row of bony scutes running along its flank to the tail.

Florida pompano
Trachinotus carolinus
Also known as butterfish, this species is found in the marine subtropical waters of the West Atlantic. A premium fish in the US, it often fetches a high price. It is endangered in some areas, but tilapia is a good alternative. It has a pink, buttery-flavored flesh that takes spicy and strong flavors well.

Adult males have a vertical head profile with the development of a bony crest.

It has a yellow back with iridescent metallic blue and green along the body and a golden belly.

Snapper *Lutjandae*

This group has over 100 members, some of which are known as jobfish. Found in most tropical waters worldwide, many are key commercial fish. All vary in size, from a plate-sized lane or yellowtail snapper at 10in (25cm) up to the large red snapper mostly marketed at around 18in (46cm). Smaller members of the group, including yellowtail and lane snappers, can be streamlined, but the larger members, specifically the Malabar, cubera, bourgeois, and true red snappers, have a laterally compressed body. As with many fish of this type, they have a generous layer of thick scales and sharp spines on the fins. A fish sold whole should be trimmed, scaled, and gutted before cooking. The flesh of most is slightly off-white, lightening to white on cooking.

SUSTAINABILITY Some members are known to be fished beyond a sustainable level, but a level of aquaculture is developing that will support these important fish. There is a minimum landing size in place to preserve stocks. Alternatives include responsibly sourced sea bass.

CUTS Whole, fillets, steaks.
EAT Cooked: Steam, pan-fry, broil, bake, stir-fry.
FLAVOR PAIRINGS Sesame oil, soy, ginger, garlic, cilantro, palm sugar, nam pla.
CLASSIC RECIPES Blaff (Martinique fish stew); Cajun blackened snapper.

A beautifully flavored fish with sweet-tasting, white flesh when cooked.

Red snapper
Lutjanus camperchanus
Many of the snapper group are a deep pink color and are mistakenly labeled as red snapper, but this one is the true red snapper. Also known as pargo, this reef marine fish is found in the Gulf of Mexico and the Southeastern Atlantic coast of the US. It has a dark, red back fading to a lighter red on the flank. It is good cooked with just a squeeze of lemon, and spices. It can be broiled, pan-fried, roasted, and wrapped in banana leaves as en papillote.

Lane snapper
Lutjanus synagris
A smaller member of the group, with fish from 6in (15cm) upward. It has a delicate pink skin with pink and yellow stripes on its side and a pink tail. Caught in the West Atlantic, it is mostly exported by Brazil. It can be broiled or baked whole with coconut, lime, and lemongrass.

Its sweet, pink meat becomes white when cooked.

Firm pink flesh, excellent for pan-frying, broiling, or baking.

Yellowtail snapper
Ocyurus chrysurus
A striking snapper with a deep pink, scaly skin, a strong yellow stripe along the flank, and a yellow tail. This is commercially caught for the table on the West Atlantic coast of the US, and it is abundant in Florida, the West Indies, and Brazil. Good marinated in warm spices such as cumin and ground coriander.

The shiny golden stripe on deep pink makes this a striking member of the snapper group.

Pomfret

Confusingly, the name pomfret is used to describe various fish from several different fish families. Pomfrets come from the Carangidae, Stromateidae, and Bramidae groups, which are found in the East and West Pacific, and some parts of the Atlantic. These fish share several attributes, including their deep and laterally compressed bodies. Their fillets are handled in much the same way as those of flat fish. The firm, white, sweet-flavored flesh is good for pan-frying and broiling. The Atlantic pomfret (Brama brama) is a member of the Bramidae group and is also known as ray's bream, angelfish, aral bream, bowfish, and carp bream. It has a steel-colored, almost black body, and a large eye, and offers a well-flavored, meaty, textured, white fillet.

CUTS Whole, fillets (fresh and frozen).
EAT Cooked: Pan-fry, bake, broil, grill.
Preserved: Some species are dried and salted.

FLAVOR PAIRINGS Middle Eastern/North African: couscous, orange, lemon, parsley, cilantro, *ras el hanout* spice mix, chermoula.

Black pomfret ▼
Formio niger
A member of the Carangidae family, this fish is found in both marine and brackish tropical waters of the Indo-Pacific. It is a shoaling fish, often reaching 12in (30cm) in length. It has a sweet flavor and firm texture and is available fresh, dried, and salted.

The sandy appearance of the fish is off-set by fins that vary in color from black to sea green.

This laterally compressed fish is filleted in much the same way as a flat fish.

Silver pomfret ▶
Pampus argenteus
A member of the Stromateidae family, this pomfret is found in the subtropical waters of the Indo-Pacific from the Persian Gulf to Indonesia to Japan. The usual market size is around 12in (30cm). It has sweet and dense white fillets, and is excellent wrapped in foil and grilled. It also works well with couscous and sweet, dried fruit, including apricots and almonds.

Straight from the sea, this fish is a beautiful silver color with blue hues that are rubbed off once landed to show darker markings.

The dorsal and anal fins are preceded by 5–10 blade-like spines, and the body has a scattering of black spots.

Cuskeel *Ophidiidae*

Cuskeels are distributed in shallow and deep water worldwide. They have an unusual shape similar to that of an eel, with their elongated bodies tapering to the tail. Both the dorsal and anal fins run along the fish and meet at the tail end. Cuskeels are shy marine-reef dwellers that hide during the day and appear at night to feed. There are over 200 species in the Ophidiidae group, but one particularly notable species is the fabulously flavored kingclip, whose meaty flesh is reminiscent of lobster. It is found in the Southeast Atlantic off the West African coast from Namibia to South Africa.

CUTS Long, slender fillets.
EAT Cooked: Grill, pan-fry, roast, broil.
FLAVOR PAIRINGS Butter, citrus flavors, chorizo, pancetta, bay, rosemary.

Long and eel-like with a pointed head and pink-marbled skin.

Meagre, Grunt, and Drum *Sciaendidae*

Found extensively in freshwater, brackish, and marine waters around the globe, this large group of fish includes meagres, grunt, and drums. They take their name from the noise that they make by vibrating their swim bladders; it creates a croak or drumming noise that can be heard from some distance. A notable member of the family is the kob or mulloway (Aboriginal for "the greatest one"). This is a popular fish caught around South Africa, Madagascar, and South Australia. Mulloway is considered a great catch by recreational anglers.

CUTS Whole, fillets.
EAT Cooked: Broil, steam, bake.
FLAVOR PAIRINGS Chile, lime, orange, white wine vinegar, olive oil, dill.
CLASSIC RECIPES Ceviche; escabeche.

Meagre
Argyrosomus regius
Also known as croaker and corvina, it is distributed around the coasts of some subtropical waters along the East Atlantic and Mediterranean. The off-white fillets cook to a luscious and dense white. It can be broiled, roasted, or wrapped for the grill.

This fish has succulent, sweet, and meaty white fillets or steaks.

A firm-textured fish, the striking scales need removing prior to cooking.

The pale pink flesh can be cut into steaks for baking or broiling.

Kob
Argyrosomus hololepidotus
Hugely popular in South Africa, kob is also known as mulloway, butterfish, kingfish, or jewfish in Australia. It is a marine, demersal fish found in coastal and estuarine waters. There is a minimum catch size in place to preserve stocks. It is a sashimi-grade fish that is sold to the European sushi market.

Mulloway has a stunning metallic silver-blue-and-bronze-colored skin with a spiny dorsal fin.

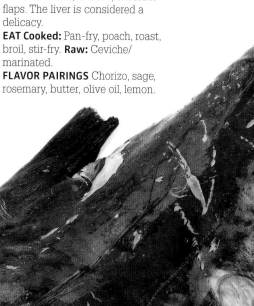

Kingclip
Genypterus capensis
This species can reach over 6ft (1.8m) long. It is rated very highly as an excellent table fish, and is featured particularly in menus across South Africa. Typical South African recipes suit the cooking of kingclip, which, along with other fish, can be added to make the traditional stew, potjie.

This fish produces succulent, sweet, and meaty white fillets or steaks.

Monkfish *Lophidae*

One of a small group of related species from the Lophidae family, which includes the East Atlantic monkfish caught in European waters and the West Atlantic goosefish caught in North American waters. These demersal fish are extraordinary in appearance, with flattened, long, tapering bodies below wide heads and huge mouths with inwardly pointing teeth. The thick, shiny skin is easily pulled back to reveal a meaty tail. Underneath the skin are several layers of membrane; these need to be removed, as they shrink during cooking and toughen the exterior of the fish. The flesh has no pin bones and a firm texture that holds its shape well in cooking. The cheeks are sweetly flavored and perfect for stir-frying and grilling.

SUSTAINABILITY Some stocks of monkfish are depleting. Alternatives include prawns and scallops, as they have textures similar to monkfish. Responsibly sourced huss is also a good option.

CUTS Whole, head on or off, skinned and unskinned; cheeks; shoulder flaps. The liver is considered a delicacy.
EAT Cooked: Pan-fry, poach, roast, broil, stir-fry. **Raw:** Ceviche/marinated.
FLAVOR PAIRINGS Chorizo, sage, rosemary, butter, olive oil, lemon.

The "tail" is the part that is eaten—this runs from the shoulder to the base of the tail fin.

Monkfish have mild-flavored, slightly chewy, white flesh.

The cheeks on a monkfish are harvested and sold separately.

The head of a monkfish is most often removed on harvesting, as it weighs a lot.

Monkfish
Lophius piscatorius
Also known as angler fish, this fish is found in Eastern Atlantic waters and has gained popularity over recent years. It has folds of brown and black mottled skin, which are perfect for successful camouflage.

Tuna *Scombridae*

Easily identifiable by their bullet-shaped bodies that taper to a pointed snout and deeply forked tails, these fish can swim fast—speeds of around 43mph (70kph) have been recorded. Although they come from temperate and cold waters, many are able to adapt to tropical and subtropical waters. High levels of myoglobin give the flesh a pink to deep red color, earning tuna the

nickname the "rose of the sea." Although a deep color, the flesh has a subtle flavor and, once filleted, no bones. It is often likened to a beef fillet steak in texture and flavor. The southern bluefin tuna (*Thunnus maccoyii*) is caught in the temperate and cold seas of the Atlantic, Indian, and Pacific oceans, but it migrates to tropical seas during spawning. These fish are particularly sought-

after in Japan, where they can fetch an extremely high price. Northern bluefin tuna (or giant bluefin tuna) is native to the Western and Eastern Atlantic oceans, the Mediterranean, and the Black Sea, and are also commercially cultivated off the Japanese coast. This species is popular for the sushi trade.

SUSTAINABILITY The extensive desire for this fish has led to severe overexploitation of the species. Some stocks are well-managed globally, but there are many that are not. Choose tuna that comes from a sustainable source that is either pole- or line-caught. Both southern bluefin tuna and northern bluefin tuna are critically endangered and

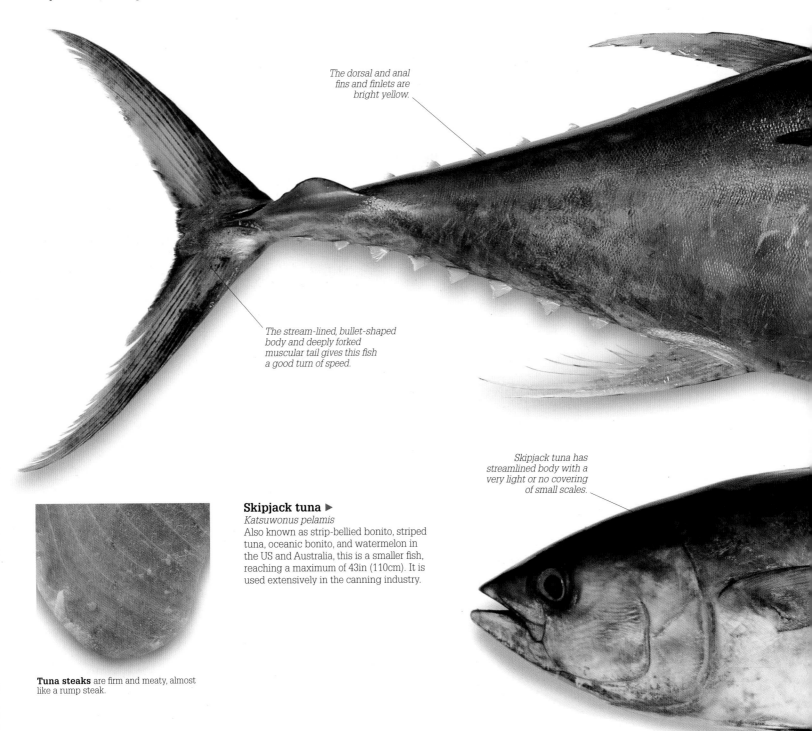

The dorsal and anal fins and finlets are bright yellow.

The stream-lined, bullet-shaped body and deeply forked muscular tail gives this fish a good turn of speed.

Skipjack tuna has streamlined body with a very light or no covering of small scales.

Skipjack tuna ▶
Katsuwonus pelamis
Also known as strip-bellied bonito, striped tuna, oceanic bonito, and watermelon in the US and Australia, this is a smaller fish, reaching a maximum of 43in (110cm). It is used extensively in the canning industry.

Tuna steaks are firm and meaty, almost like a rump steak.

are close to collapse, so avoid purchase. Responsibly sourced swordfish is a suitable alternative.
CUTS Whole, in sections: loins, steaks, belly.
EAT Cooked: Loins: chargrill, pan-fry.
Preserved: Dried, smoked, salted. Tuna roe is also sold dried.
Raw: Sushi and carpaccio.
FLAVOR PAIRINGS Japanese: shoyu, sesame, teriyaki, shiso leaf, Japanese rice wine vinegar, wasabi. Mediterranean: tomatoes, garlic, olives.
CLASSIC RECIPES Salade Niçoise; tuna sashimi/sushi; carpaccio of tuna with salsa verde; tuna teriyaki.

Yellowfin tuna
Thunnus albacares
Caught in all tropical and subtropical seas, this species is also known as yellowfin tunny and Allison's tuna. It is overfished in some areas, particularly if it has been net-caught. Pole-caught is a more selective method of capture. It is a big fish that can reach up to 8ft (2.5m) long. The meat taken from the back or loin of the tuna is lean, meaty, with a slight flavor of rump steak. The belly meat is much higher in fat and is popular in Japanese cuisine.

The back is black metallic turning to dark blue along the flanks.

The yellow to silver belly often has broken, practically vertical lines running along it.

The powerful, shapely tail is a rusty orange color.

Mackerel and Bonito *Scombridae*

The Scombridae family has around 54 members found in all oceans worldwide. It includes the mackerel, bonito, wahoo, kingfish or king mackerel, and tuna fish groups—all extremely important commercially for many countries. These oil-rich species contain high levels of omega-3 essential fatty acids; the oil is located throughout the body and not just in the liver. All members of this group should be stored at a constant low temperature. High levels of histadine naturally occur in their flesh, and if not stored at a low enough temperature, this converts into histamine, which can cause scombroid poisoning (symptoms of which are upset stomach and diarrhoea). Rather confusingly, the names "mackerel" and "bonito" are used interchangeably. For example, horse mackerel and frigate mackerel are often labeled as bonito.

SUSTAINABILITY Many species from the mackerel and bonito group have a maximum catch quota in place, and landed fish must be of a minimum size. Opt for line-caught specimens, as they are the more sustainable.

CUTS Whole and ungutted, fillets, steaks of the larger bonito, kingfish, and wahoo.

EAT Cooked: Grill, bake, broil, roast.
Preserved: Canned, smoked, dried, or salted.
Raw: Cured and used in sushi and sashimi.

FLAVOR PAIRINGS Japanese: shoyu, sesame seeds, mirin, rice vinegar, cucumber and daikon, chile and cilantro; Mediterranean: basil, olive oil, garlic.
CLASSIC RECIPES Soused mackerel; mackerel with gooseberry sauce; smoked mackerel pâté; mackerel with rhubarb; gravad mackerel; marmite (Basque fisherman's bonito dish).

The Atlantic mackerel is identified by the bar or scribble markings along its back.

The fins can fold flat against the body to give a streamlined shape that enables it to swim fast.

Damage to the jaw may indicate that it has been line-caught (preferable) rather than netted.

Atlantic mackerel
Scomber scombrus
This commercially important pelagic species is the most northerly member of the family. It is found extensively in the North Atlantic, with smaller pockets in the Mediterranean. It can grow up to 2ft (60cm) long. Look for mackerel that are still stiff with rigor mortis and cook as soon as possible. Grilling, broiling, and roasting make the most of the creamy textured flakes.

Wahoo steak has a dense and meaty texture.

Wahoo
Acanthocybium solandri
The wahoo has an iridescent bluish-green back, and silver flanks striped with cobalt blue. It can reach 8ft (2.5m), although is more commonly landed at around 5½ft (1.7m). It is found in the Atlantic, Indian, and Pacific oceans, including the Caribbean and Mediterranean seas. An often solitary fish, it sometimes forms small groups rather than shoals. Superb to eat, with a firm, meaty texture and a delicate, sweet taste. In the Caribbean, slices of wahoo are cured in spices.

King mackerel
Scomberomorus cavalla
Also known as kingfish, the king mackerel is found in the Western Atlantic from Canada to Massachusetts, US, to São Paulo, Brazil; also in the Eastern-central Atlantic. It reaches a maximum length of 6ft (1.8m), although it is usually found at about 28in (70cm). It lives near reefs, and in some areas may feed on plankton that cause ciguatera poisoning in humans. The meat is full-flavored, and great for chargrilling or grilling.

Deep silvery-gray skin with a long tapering fillet to the tail.

The cheeks of many fish, including the bonito, are considered to be a delicacy.

Bonito
Sarda sarda
A selection of fish come under this heading: the belted bonito, horse mackerel, short-finned tunny, pelamid, and strip-backed pelamis. The bonito has an extensive range: it is caught in the Eastern Atlantic from Norway to South Africa; the Mediterranean and Black Sea; in the Western Atlantic, from Nova Scotia to Colombia, Venezuela, and northern Argentina. It can reach up to 35in (90cm), but is most commonly found at around 20in (50cm). Dried flakes of bonito are used in dashi, a Japanese soup stock. Bonito is perfect for grilling or broiling with a robust-flavored baste or marinade.

Dark, rich, and meaty, bonito has a firm texture; the flesh lightens during cooking.

Chub mackerel is good for sashimi, where the fillets are cured briefly to firm up the texture.

Chub mackerel
Scomber colias
Also known as Spanish mackerel, thimble-eyed mackerel, and southern mackerel, this close relation of the Atlantic mackerel has similar bar markings, but they are not so defined. The chub mackerel grows to about 20in (50cm) long. It prefers warm waters, and is found in the East and West Atlantic. Its related species in the Indo-Pacific, *Scomber japonicus*, grows to 8–14in (20–35cm).

The chub mackerel has a lightly speckled underside.

The king mackerel is an impressive-looking fish with a slim, silver body and dark bars along its back.

Escolar *Gempylidae*

The escolar, or snake mackerel, is a member of the Gempylidae group that also includes gemfish, snoek, and barracouta. It has a fierce appearance, with an elongated body and head, and jaws lined with menacing sharp teeth. It is often associated with the barracuda group and is a voracious predator to smaller species including mackerel, flying fish, and squid. Escolar are located in tropical marine waters worldwide, but some are found in temperate locations. They favor mid-water depth as immature fish, moving to deep water as they mature. Although Gempylidae members are found globally, most are landed as part of a catch of other more valuable species, including tuna. The oil-rich flesh of the escolar is enjoyed in Europe, the US, and Asia, where it may be served as sushi and sashimi. In the US, it is sometimes called "white tuna". In Japan, escolar is often used in fishcakes and sausages; it is also popular in Hawaii and South Africa.
CUTS Whole and frozen fillets.
EAT Cooked: Broil, roast, pan-fry, deep-fry, bake. **Preserved:** Smoked and canned.
FLAVOR PAIRINGS Chile, sesame, coconut, and Asian spices and herbs.
CLASSIC RECIPES Grilled escolar with chile dressing; teriyaki.

Escolar
Lepidocybium flavobrunneum
This fish has several names: snake mackerel, black oil fish, butterfish, castor oil fish, and rudderfish in Australia. It varies in size but can grow to well over 6½ft (2m) long. It has a well-flavored but very oily flesh (containing a wax ester), and can cause stomach irritation, so eat only small quantities at a time. "Deep-skinning" will remove most of the wax; broiling also helps to release it. Thick, succulent, escolar steaks can be brushed with oil and pan-fried or roasted.

Steaks of escolar are thick and oily.

Scabbard fish *Trichiuridae*

The scabbard fish or cutlass fish is closely related to escolar and shares similar characteristics. There are over 40 members of this group. It is also known as the sabre fish, hairtail, ribbon fish, and frostfish. It gets its name from a very long, thin body, and the color varies, but most species sport a steely-blue or silver skin. They have fang-like teeth set in a long jaw, which are coated in a powerful anticoagulant, and so need to be handled with care. Scabbard fish are found in many waters globally, and fished on both sides of the Atlantic. Black scabbard fish is a delicacy in Madeira; it has to be eaten very fresh and does not store well, so is not usually exported fresh. These fish are extremely palatable, with a delicate texture and almost buttery flavor. It may appear difficult to prepare.
CUTS Whole fish, long and thin fillets, usually skinned. Cut into wide steaks.
EAT Cooked: Broil, pan-fry, bake, smoke on a grill.
FLAVOR PAIRINGS Cumin, coriander, orange, cinnamon, and North African/Italian flavors.
CLASSIC RECIPES *Filetti di spatola al pane* (Italian breaded recipe); *espada preta vinho e alhos* (Madeiran recipe for cooking in wine).

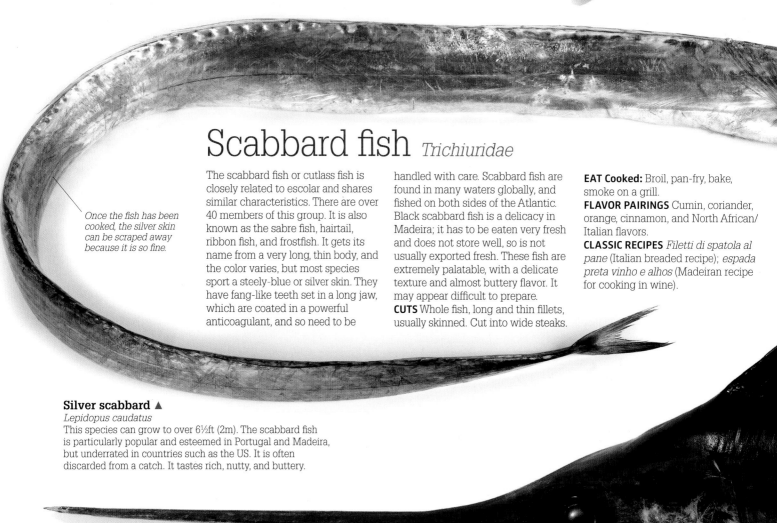

Once the fish has been cooked, the silver skin can be scraped away because it is so fine.

Silver scabbard ▲
Lepidopus caudatus
This species can grow to over 6½ft (2m). The scabbard fish is particularly popular and esteemed in Portugal and Madeira, but underrated in countries such as the US. It is often discarded from a catch. It tastes rich, nutty, and buttery.

Swordfish
Xiphias gladius
The swordfish grows to a maximum of about 14¾ft (4.5m) long and is found in the Atlantic, Pacific, and Indian oceans and in the Mediterranean Sea. Its flesh color varies according to its diet and habitat; the meaty-tasting steaks vary from white to a pinkish tinge. It has the longest bill of all the fish in the group, and is aggressive, often attacking before being attacked, and using its sword to slash and tear its prey.

Puffer fish *Tetraodontidae*

This highly poisonous fish must be treated with extreme care, although it is considered a great delicacy. When threatened by a predator, the puffer fish fills its stomach with water or air and enlarges itself to many times greater than its body size. It is found in marine, fresh, and brackish waters globally. The Japanese enjoy fugu, a delicacy, made from puffer fish of the genus *Takifugu, Sphoeroides*, and *Lagocephalus* (they also call the fish fugu). Thousands of tons of fugu are consumed in Japan every year. The fugu is notorious, as certain parts of it contain tetrodotoxin and are poisonous. Despite this it is a highly sought-after and very expensive fish. The skin may be used in salad, stewed, or pickled.

CUTS Fillets; must be prepared extremely carefully by a licensed chef.
EAT Cooked: Fry. **Raw:** As fugu.
FLAVOR PAIRINGS Pickled ginger, soy sauce, wasabi, sake.
CLASSIC RECIPES Sashimi; fugu kara-age (deep-fried); hire-zake (fried; served with sake).

Puffer fish
Takifugu, several species
The toxin in parts of the fish causes paralysis and asphyxiation—there is no antidote; the safe preparation of fugu, by specially trained chefs, is very time-consuming. Fugu sashimi is a very popular fugu dish. Wafer-thin slices are typically arranged in a chrysanthemum pattern, which symbolizes death in Japanese culture.

The puffer fish has a rounded body. When it is prepared for sashimi, fillets are cut so thinly that the slices are almost transparent.

Swordfish and Marlin

The billfish family includes swordfish and marlin. These fish have a long bill or spear. They produce meaty, dense steaks. Billfish are found in most warm and tropical oceans worldwide. Most are slow-growing species that take years to reach maturity. The swordfish, also known as the broadbill, resembles other members of the Istiophoridae family, but belongs to the Xiphiidae group. There are four main species of marlin that belong to the Istiophoridae family. They can grow to over 1 ton in weight. The Atlantic sailfish (*Istiophorus albicans*) is closely related to the marlin, and is found in the Atlantic and the Caribbean Sea. Some billfish have a high metal content, particularly traces of methylmercury. Pregnant women and small children should avoid eating it. But, it is argued, the health benefits of eating it—for the general population—outweigh the possibility of consuming too much mercury, as it contains omega-3 essential fatty acids.

SUSTAINABILITY These big, impressive fish are of great commercial importance. They have been hunted mercilessly and are seriously endangered in some countries. Many are harvested from the Pacific every year, but are carefully managed. Systems are in place in the North Atlantic to protect juvenile fish. Alternatives include sustainably and responsibly caught tuna.
CUTS Fresh: Sometimes whole, steaks, or whole loins.

EAT Cooked: Grill, pan-fry.
Preserved: Smoked. **Raw:** Sushi, sashimi, marinated raw.
FLAVOR PAIRINGS Basil, rosemary, cilantro. Warm spice mixtures including cumin, paprika, coriander. Citrus flavors, olive and sesame oils, mesquite smoking chips.
CLASSIC RECIPES Smoked marlin with scrambled egg (Latin American); grilled swordfish with salsa verde.

Loins are taken from each side of the backbone and cut into thick, succulent steaks, ready for pan-frying or grilling.

Herring and Sardine *Clupeidae*

With over 50 species, the Clupeidae group of fish includes the herring, shad, sardine/pilchard, sprat, hilsa, and menhaden. Anchovies (see opposite) are closely associated with this group. The species are mostly marine, but some are freshwater. These shoaling, pelagic fish feed on plankton and grow rapidly. They are an important food source for large predatory fish. Herrings are an oil-rich fish, caught extensively worldwide, and form a key low-cost food for many countries. They are one of the most abundant species in the world, although, as with many other fish, some stocks around the world are currently overexploited. Landed in huge quantities, the fish spoil quickly and if eaten fresh, need to be cooked while they are as close to rigor mortis as possible. This fact has led them to be processed into various products, from salted (in times past) to canned (for today's market). A whole herring, split and salted or pickled and then smoked, is called a kipper.

SUSTAINABILITY Some stocks are threatened but others are well managed. Their landing sizes vary and controls are in place in many areas to protect stocks.

HERRING
CUTS Whole, gutted, or filleted, frozen, and canned. Roes, both hard and soft (milt), are available. Female roe is a less expensive alternative to other caviars and is a delicacy in Japan. Small, immature herring members are harvested and marketed as whitebait (but are overexploited).
EAT Cooked: Pan-fry, grill, broil, roast, souse. **Preserved:** Smoked, salted, marinated, cured, canned.

See pages 384–389: kippers, bloaters, buckling, and maatjes herring.
FLAVOR PAIRINGS Sour cream, dill, oatmeal, bacon, horseradish, lemon, capers, parsley.
CLASSIC RECIPES Herrings in oatmeal; herrings with bacon; rollmops; jugged kippers; devilled whitebait.

SARDINE
CUTS Whole, gutted, or filleted.
EAT Cooked: Pan-fry, grill, broil.
Preserved: Smoked, marinated, cured, and canned (in olive oil or different kinds of prepared sauces, such as tomato).
FLAVOR PAIRINGS Mediterranean: olive oil, garlic, lemon, golden raisins, pine nuts, parsley, oregano, thyme.
CLASSIC RECIPES Broiled sardines with Greek salad; grilled sardines with oregano and lemon.

SPRAT
CUTS Whole (you will usually need to gut the fish yourself).
EAT Cooked: Broil, bake, pan-fry.
Preserved: Smoked, canned, salted.
FLAVOR PAIRINGS Beet, white wine and red wine vinegar, flat-leaf parsley, cilantro, coriander seeds.
CLASSIC RECIPE Pan-fried sprats with lemon.

The twaite shad has a bright silver body with a covering of scales.

European sprat
Sprattus sprattus
Also known as bristling or brisling, this small member of the herring family is found in European marine waters from the Northeast Atlantic (North Sea and Baltic Sea) down to the Mediterranean, Adriatic, and Black seas. Its flesh appears gray, but changes to off-white when cooked. It has a smooth, oily texture and it can grow up to 6½in (16cm), but 5in (12cm) is more usual.

Sprats are a startlingly bright silver, with a small head and a beady black eye.

Sardine or Pilchard
Sardina pilchardus
Pilchards are known as sardines if they are less than 6in (15cm) in length. This fast-growing fish is immensely important to many countries. It is a rounded, oil-rich fish, high in omega-3 essential fatty acids. It has a greeny-blue back, with bright, silvery sides and belly, and loose scales. The fish can grow to 8–12in (20–30cm) in length. Sardines have a lot of bones, a coarser texture, and are meaty with a robust flavor.

It is best to gut sardines and cook them on the bone, as the fine bones are easier to locate when the fish is cooked. The loose scales also need removing with the back of a knife.

These fish have shiny, loosely scaled skin and swim in shoals.

Atlantic herring
Clupea harengus

Also known as sild, yawling, digby, and mattie, Atlantic or sea herring are found on both sides of the Atlantic. This pelagic species forms huge schools of billions of fish. They can grow up to 18in (45cm) long, but 12in (30cm) is more usual. They were overfished during the 1990s, but today there are some well-managed, sustainable stocks. Fresh herring is at its best simply broiled with a slice of lemon. It is high in omega-3 essential fatty acids; if eaten extremely fresh, the flakes are fine and sweet, and not overly oily in texture. Lots of pinbones make this fish a challenge for some to eat.

Atlantic herrings have a bluish-green back, bright silver flanks, and loose scales.

Twaite shad
Alosa fallax

The twaite shad is found along the west coast of Europe, in the Eastern Mediterranean, and in some large rivers along these coasts. It has declined in many parts of Europe over recent years. With a similar appearance to a herring, this fish is generally larger, with a more delicate taste. It produces decent-sized fillets and has a delicate, grassy, and milky taste. If cooked well, it has lovely succulent flakes, but lots of pinbones.

Anchovy *Engraulidae*

Anchovies are from the Engraulidae family group of about 140 species, and resemble herrings in many ways. They are a small, oil-rich, saltwater fish, and are found in the Atlantic, Indian, and Pacific oceans. They are generally concentrated in temperate waters and are rare in very cold or very warm waters. Huge schools of anchovies are usually found in the shallows in estuarine waters and bays. The small, greenish fish have a hint of iridescent blue to their skin. They vary in size dramatically, from ¾in (2cm) to 16in (40cm) long. Body shape varies according to species, but on the whole it is a long, slender fish. Once landed, anchovies need to be cooked quickly—because they do not keep well—or preserved by curing in vinegar or salting. Sometimes they are available fresh from the boat.

SUSTAINABILITY Anchovies are overfished in some areas. Sprats make a good alternative.
CUTS Whole.
EAT Cooked: When available fresh, pan-fry. **Preserved:** In jars as salted, cured, or marinated/brined fish. Also made into anchovy paste. **Raw:** Traditionally marinated and enjoyed in a raw state.
FLAVOR PAIRINGS Sherry vinegar, white wine vinegar, shallots, marjoram, oregano, sage, thyme, parsley, Mediterranean olive oil.
CLASSIC RECIPES *Boquerones en vinagre* (Spanish marinated anchovies); deep-fried anchovies with sage; *alici ripiene; alici al limone;* salsa verde; salade Niçoise. Dried: *Bagna caoda; asparagi in* salsa; *polenta nera; puntarelle in salsa di alici* (Italy); *anchoïade* (France).

European anchovy
Engraulis encrasicolus

This fish is abundant in the Mediterranean and is caught off the coasts of Sicily, Italy, France, and Spain, where it is sold straight from the boat. It is also found along the coast of North Africa, and can extend as far north as the south of the Atlantic. It grows to a maximum of 8in (20cm). Salty anchovies make a classic partner to chargrilled beef steaks. They also make an excellent butter, which is delicious with broiled white fish such as brill and Dover sole.

Nile perch, Barramundi, and Murray cod

Several key species of freshwater fish are found in the warmer waters of Africa, Asia, and Australasia. Nile perch (*Lates niloticus*) is also known as Victoria perch and capitaine. It is a predatory fish living mainly in fresh, but some brackish, waters. It was introduced to Lake Victoria in Africa, where it has caused much damage by virtually wiping out other species of fish. It is an important commercial fish, harvested for export and sold at a good price. It is mostly wild, but some aquaculture has been established. The barramundi (*Lates calcarifer*) is found from the Persian Gulf to China, Asia, and Australia. It inhabits creeks, rivers, and estuarine waters. In Australia, it is farmed as a highly commercial species, and is a

major export. It is very similar in taste and texture to Nile perch. The Maccullochella genus of predatory freshwater fish is native to Australia and known as "cod". A few species are found in the river systems, including the Murray cod (*Maccullochella peelii peelii*) and the trout cod (*M. macquariensis*). Murray cod is renowned for its flavor.

SUSTAINABILITY Many of these species are now listed as critically endangered. Murray cod is seriously threatened, though it is farmed in Victoria. All Murray cod on sale or served in restaurants is from this source. Commercial fishing of Murray cod is banned in Australia. Responsibly sourced snapper and coral trout are suitable alternatives.

CUTS Whole, fillets, steaks.
EAT COOKED: Pan-fry, grill, broil, poach, steam.
FLAVOR PAIRINGS Nile perch and barramundi: bok choy, lime, chile, fresh herbs, white wine. Murray cod: butter, white wine, beer, white wine vinegar, orange, mild to medium spices.

Nile perch is usually sold ready prepared: the neat, creamy-white fillets are excellent pan-fried, battered, or cooked in breadcrumbs. The fillets taste like barramundi and can be cooked in similar ways.

Nile perch ▲
Lates niloticus
The Nile perch is native to the River Nile and other major West African freshwater rivers. It has been introduced to lakes in East Africa and North Africa, and in North America. It may grow to over 6½ft (2m) long. It is most often cut into fillets, which are firm, white, and succulent. As a freshwater fish, it can have a slightly earthy taste. New-style Asian flavors complement it well, such as steamed bok choy with shiitake mushrooms.

Murray cod
Maccullochella peelii peelii
Murray cod is known to be the largest of Australia's freshwater fish, measured by weight, rather than length. It is a slow-developing species that lives for over 30 years. It weighs in at 44lb (20kg); the largest recorded specimen was 247lb (112kg). The flesh of this fish is considered excellent, producing large, thick, white steaks with a delicate texture. It is a versatile fish that suits many methods of cooking and flavor combinations. It can also be cooked over an open fire; good, too, for escabeche.

Murray cod is farmed to a suitable size for individual portions.

The firm and meaty flesh of the Murray cod works well with Asian flavors and is equally good served battered, with chips.

It is light to dark green in color. The underside is a creamy white

Barramundi
Lates calcarifer
Juvenile fish are brown and mottled; adult fish grow to 4ft (1.2m) long. They have a pointed head and large jaw, and light-silver skin with a heavy armoring of scales. This fish has a succulent, flaky, white flesh with a low oil content, although there can be a tendency toward an earthiness, depending on where it is caught. Farmed fish are rarely much bigger than plate size; they differ in flavor from wild fish. Barramundi was popular with the native Aboriginal people, who would cook a whole large "barra" by wrapping the fish in wild ginger leaf and cooking it in the embers of a fire. The cheek (or pearl) of a barramundi is a particular treat: this is juicy and sweet flavored. Barramundi is excellent broiled, steamed, and grilled. The large fish can be filleted. For small fish, scale, gut, and cook whole.

The scales of the barramundi are notoriously well attached to the flesh; the best way to remove them is with a scaler, running from tail to head.

Catfish and River cobbler

Catfish from various families have been caught in the wild and farmed on most continents for hundreds of years. They live in fresh inland and coastal waters. Many are nocturnal, bottom-feeding, and predatory. Catfish are considered a delicacy in many parts of the world, particularly in Central Europe and Africa. Migrants from these areas took catfish to the US, where it is now a popular part of traditional Southern food. Different species are common to each continent. Channel catfish and blue catfish (from the Ictaluridae family) are native to the US, living in freshwater streams, rivers, and creeks. The "channel cat" is farmed in an industry worth millions of dollars. River cobbler or basa (Pangasiidae) is native to Vietnam and Thailand, and has recently become valuable in the international market.

CUTS Live, whole, fillets (fresh or frozen).
EAT Cooked: Pan-fry, broil, bake, poach, deep-fry. **Preserved:** Smoked, dried, salted.

FLAVOR PAIRINGS Cornmeal, sesame seeds, sour cream, mushrooms, scallions, parsley, bay leaf, thyme.
CLASSIC RECIPES Southern deep-fried catfish with cornmeal; *pecel lele*; *ikan kele*, blackened catfish.

Catfish skin is thick and slippery like an eel, and requires some effort to remove it with pliers.

African sharptooth catfish ▲
Clarias gariepinus
This air-breathing freshwater catfish lives in rivers, lakes, and swamps. It is farmed in Africa, Europe, and the US. Farmed and wild catfish grow to a weight of 4½lb (2kg). It is hugely popular in the US and Africa. Catfish is moist and succulent, and as with many other freshwater species, it has a distinct taste of the river. The flesh is white and firm-textured, and suits various methods of cooking; it combines well with Asian flavors, including ginger and chile.

Tilapia *Cichlidae*

There are around 100 species in the Cichlidae family and tilapia (also known as St. Peter's fish) is their common name. These fish are found in warm areas of fresh water, where they can grow to 16in (40cm) long. Tilapia are second only to carp in their production through aquaculture, and some species are extensively farmed in many areas of the world. They are omnivorous, and aquatic vegetation makes up an important part of their diet, which makes them environmentally friendly to produce, as they do not need the extensive quantity of fish meal that other species demand. Many different hybrid species of tilapia are now farmed to produce sweet-flavored, firm-textured white flesh. Tilapia are invasive and have become problematic in some areas where they have been introduced.

CUTS Fresh: Whole (unprepared and gutted), fillets. **Preserved:** Salted, dried.
EAT Cooked: Pan-fry, deep-fry, steam, bake, broil, grill.

FLAVOR PAIRINGS Thai: bird's eye chile, palm sugar, nam pla, shrimp paste, cilantro, coconut, galangal.
CLASSIC RECIPE *Pla tub tim tod samrod.*

Trim away the tilapia's fins prior to cooking.

Take care to avoid spines when preparing the fish: there are some sharp ones that can cause a nasty wound.

River cobbler or basa is available ready processed into neat, white, frozen fillets.

River cobbler
Pangasius bocourti
The river cobbler is a member of the shark catfish family, and is also known as basa, bocourti, pangasius, and panga. It grows to 10–12in (25–30cm) when farmed and is now one of the most extensively farmed species worldwide (along with carp and tilapia). Its availability takes pressure off the threatened wild stocks of some species of catfish, and it is easy and environmentally friendly to farm. The river cobbler has very little flavor, but cooks to a flaky texture; it is ideal for deep-frying or taking strong flavors to help enliven it.

Tilapia scales are firmly attached to the body and require a scaler to remove them successfully. The skin of the fish is also cured and used for leatherwork.

Red tilapia
Oreochromis niloticus
Tilapia varies in color from species to species, in much the same way as koi carp. Red tilapia are pinkish in hue; prepare and cook in exactly the same way as gray tilapia.

Fillets of tilapia are white and densely textured. They hold together well, so are suitable for pan-frying and broiling.

The fins are notoriously thick and dense, and require a good pair of scissors to cut through.

The sturgeon fish's tail is distinctive, as it's sickle-shaped and the upper fin is longer than the lower fin.

◀ Tilapia
Oreochromis niloticus
In Thailand, tilapia is known as pomegranate fish and cooked in a variety of ways. This hybrid tilapia, which is gray with a darker gray banding, is underused, but becoming steadily more accepted and important. The fish produces very firm, white fillets with a sweet flavor, which lend themselves to various methods of cooking, and take many flavors well. Farmed species are usually marketed at 8–10in (20–25cm) long.

Carp *Cyprinidae*

There are over 2,500 members of the Cyprinidae family including the carp, minnow, tench, roach, bream, dace, chub, and bitterling, as well as aquarium species, such as the koi and goldfish. As a group, most are native to North America, Africa, and Eurasia. They have no stomach or teeth and feed mainly on vegetation and some invertebrates. The species vary in size from less than an inch to 5ft–6½ft (1.5–2m) long. The carp, as head of this family, was one of the earliest farmed species. It is still the top farmed species in the world today. Although extensively used and farmed in China, carp are not so popular in many cultures. This is because they tend toward an earthy, slightly muddy flavor (dependent on habitat), and have lots of fine bones. Some species are farmed for the Chinese, Eastern European, and kosher markets as well as land-locked countries that have no access to marine fish. Angling for coarse fish is a popular hobby and members of the carp family are particularly sought after. They have acute hearing, making them quite a challenge for fishing.
CUTS Fresh: Usually whole, or live.
EAT Cooked: Steam, roast, pan-fry, pané (cook in breadcrumbs), bake.

Use carp frames for stock and soup.
Preserved: Carp roe, and smoked and salted.
FLAVOR PAIRINGS Paprika, butter, capers, dill, garlic, parsley, cornmeal, ginger, rice wine, sesame.
CLASSIC RECIPES *Carp au bleu*; roast Hungarian carp with paprika sauce; gefilte fish; carp in fennel sauce.

Grass carp
Ctenopharyngodon idella
Farmed extensively in China, this fish is also known as white amur in the US. It has been introduced to the US and New Zealand for sport, and to help maintain aquatic vegetation, although its presence can be destructive to certain plant life and aquatic species. It grows up to 4ft (1.2m) long. It has a herbaceous taste and benefits from the addition of robust flavors. In Eastern Europe it is served at feasts and festivals.

The grass carp is olive, shading to brownish-yellow, with a white underside.

Sturgeon *Acipenseridae*

The sturgeon is probably best known for the exquisite delicacy of its roe, marketed as caviar. Ultrasound is used to check for eggs in females. It also produces dense fillets with an excellent flavor. There are around 25 sturgeons in the Acipenseridae group, found in the northern hemisphere. Some live in brackish and fresh waters, while other species are anadromous (migratory fish that enter fresh water to spawn, then return to the sea). This unusual species looks quite prehistoric. Only some of its bones are calcified and bony; the skull and most of the vertebrae are made of cartilage. It has an elongated body with rows of scutes along the length of its back. Most species have sensitive barbels on the chin, which they use to suck food from the mud and into their mouth. Sturgeons grow slowly, and can live to be 100 years old. Well-known species prized for their roe include beluga (*Huso huso*); osetra (*A. gueldenstaedtii*), sevruga (*A. stellatus*), and sterlet (*A. ruthenus*). The freshwater Siberian sturgeon (*A. baerii*) is farmed, primarily to raise female fish for their roe, but male fish are used for their meat.
SUSTAINABILITY Due to the price that caviar can reach, these fish have been relentlessly overexploited and some are now seriously endangered. For the flesh, alternatives include carp and pike, for the roe, try lumpfish or salmon roe.
CUTS Fresh: Whole fish, steaks, and fillets, female roe.
EAT Cooked: Bake, pan-fry, steam.
Preserved: Smoked.
FLAVOR PAIRINGS Horseradish, sour cream, beets, vinegar, butter, citrus.
CLASSIC RECIPES Caviar.

Take care when preparing a sturgeon whole: the scutes are sharp.

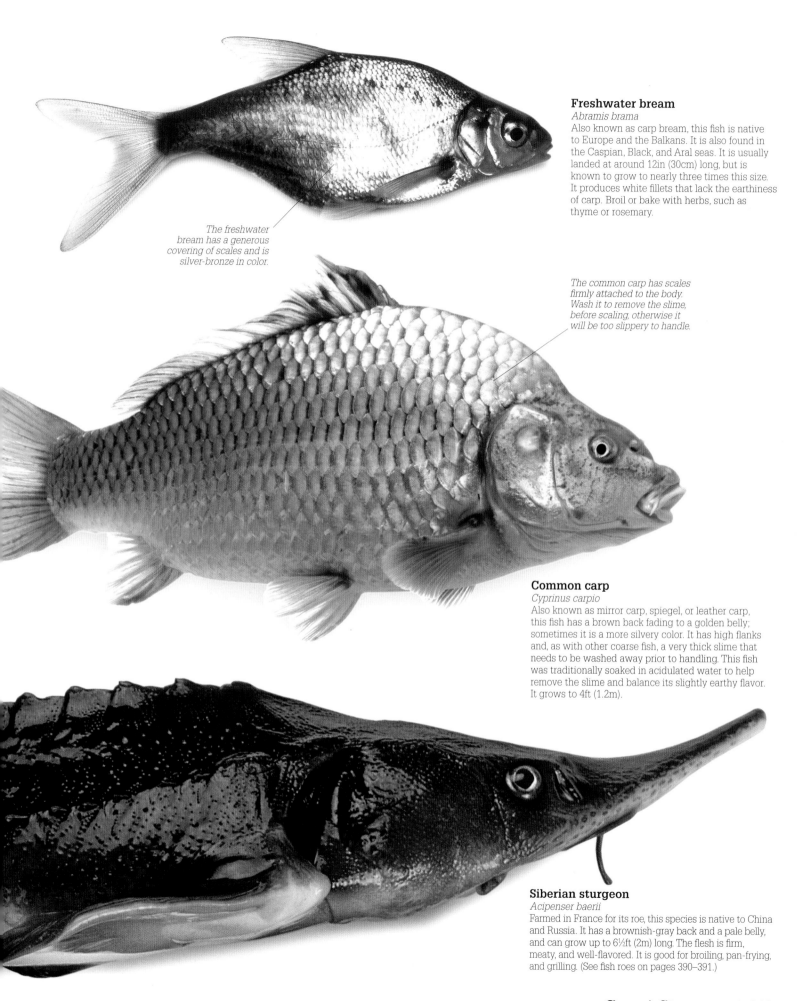

Freshwater bream
Abramis brama
Also known as carp bream, this fish is native
to Europe and the Balkans. It is also found in
the Caspian, Black, and Aral seas. It is usually
landed at around 12in (30cm) long, but is
known to grow to nearly three times this size.
It produces white fillets that lack the earthiness
of carp. Broil or bake with herbs, such as
thyme or rosemary.

*The freshwater
bream has a generous
covering of scales and is
silver-bronze in color.*

*The common carp has scales
firmly attached to the body.
Wash it to remove the slime
before scaling, otherwise it
will be too slippery to handle.*

Common carp
Cyprinus carpio
Also known as mirror carp, spiegel, or leather carp,
this fish has a brown back fading to a golden belly;
sometimes it is a more silvery color. It has high flanks
and, as with other coarse fish, a very thick slime that
needs to be washed away prior to handling. This fish
was traditionally soaked in acidulated water to help
remove the slime and balance its slightly earthy flavor.
It grows to 4ft (1.2m).

Siberian sturgeon
Acipenser baerii
Farmed in France for its roe, this species is native to China
and Russia. It has a brownish-gray back and a pale belly,
and can grow up to 6½ft (2m) long. The flesh is firm,
meaty, and well-flavored. It is good for broiling, pan-frying,
and grilling. (See fish roes on pages 390–391.)

Pike *Esocidae*

A member of the Esocidae family, the pike is a predator that feeds on other pike, smaller fish, birds, snakes, and mammals (including mice and rats). It is a freshwater fish, caught commercially and by recreational fishermen. The pike is also known as the pickerel (usually used to describe smaller species), snoek, and jackfish. Pike are found in the rivers of North America, Western Europe, Siberia, and Eurasia. There are several species, including the muskellunge pike (*E. masquinongy*), grass pickerel pike (*E. americanus vermiculatus*), and the northern pike (*E. lucius*). It is famously used in France for *quenelles de brochet*, a mousseline of sieved pike flesh with cream and egg white. Pike has a fine flavor, but contains many small bones. This recipe makes the best of the flesh, as the bones are dealt with prior to serving.

CUTS Whole; fillets.
EAT Cooked: Pan-fry, broil, steam, poach, roast. **Preserved:** Smoked, salted, dried, roe.
FLAVOR PAIRINGS Unsalted butter, sage, lemon, cream, bay leaf, white wine.
CLASSIC RECIPES *Quenelles de brochet* (pike quenelles); traditional roast pike.

Zander, Walleye, Perch, and American yellow perch *Percidae*

The Percidae family of freshwater fish is found globally. Once eaten by those with no access to the coast, many species are now less frequently used for the table. They remain popular with recreational fishermen; commercial fishing and aquaculture are still viable in some cases. Percids share the same fin pattern: the first dorsal fin is spiny (the number of spines varies), the second is soft. The family includes the zander, perch, ruffe, American yellow perch, silver perch, sauger, and walleye. The largest is the zander, a predatory fish found in fresh water; some are caught in brackish water. Native to Eastern Europe, it has also been introduced to Western Europe and the US. The perch (also known as the European perch or English perch), native to Europe and Asia, has been introduced to South Africa, New Zealand, and Australia. It is deep green with some stripes, scaly, and has red fins. In cool European waters, it rarely reaches more than 16in (40cm); it can reach a greater size in Australia. Another sought-after species, the walleye, is closely related to zander. It is native to Canada and the northern US. The walleye is not farmed, but for decades has been used to replenish stocks in some river systems.

CUTS Usually whole fish.
EAT Cooked: Pan-fry, broil, bake.
FLAVOR PAIRINGS Butter, herbs including chives, sage, rosemary, thyme, and bay leaf, lemon and white wine vinegar, cream, eggs.
CLASSIC RECIPES Perch: water souchy (fish soup); Zander: matelote (fish stew from the Loire). All these fish could be used for quenelles and gefilte fish.

Walleye
Sander vitreus
Chefs often say that the walleye has the best flavor of any freshwater fish. It grows to about 3ft (92cm) long and its color depends on its habitat. The meat has few bones and is light and flaky, with a mild taste.

Remove the generous layer of scales prior to gutting and cooking.

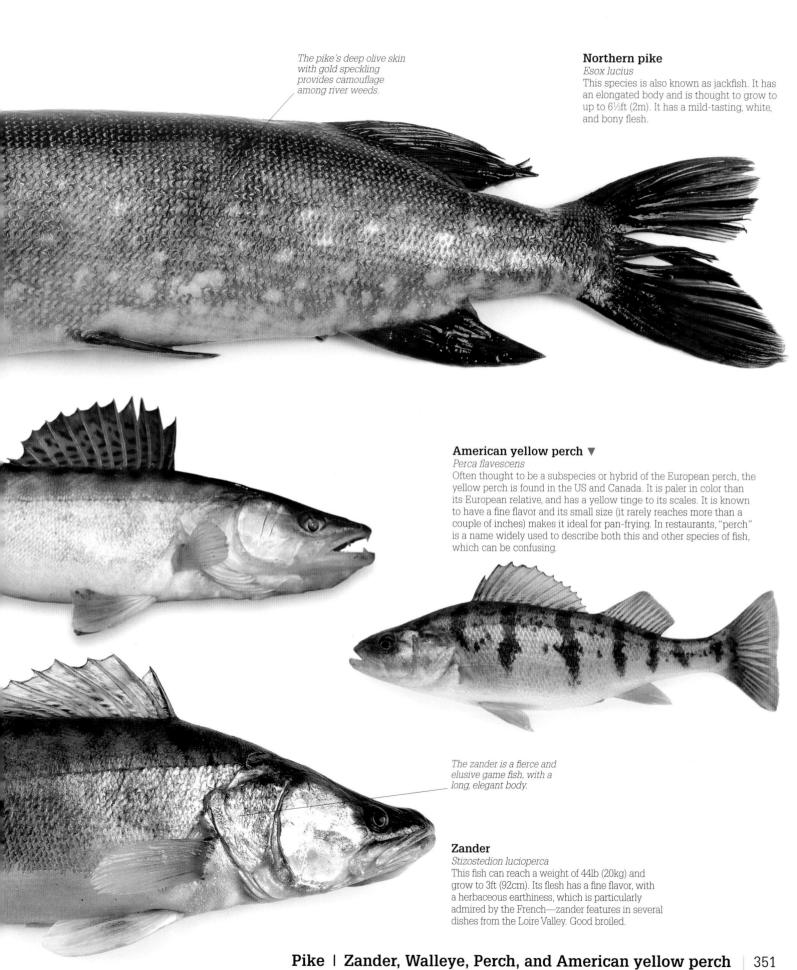

The pike's deep olive skin with gold speckling provides camouflage among river weeds.

Northern pike
Esox lucius
This species is also known as jackfish. It has an elongated body and is thought to grow to up to 6½ft (2m). It has a mild-tasting, white, and bony flesh.

American yellow perch ▼
Perca flavescens
Often thought to be a subspecies or hybrid of the European perch, the yellow perch is found in the US and Canada. It is paler in color than its European relative, and has a yellow tinge to its scales. It is known to have a fine flavor and its small size (it rarely reaches more than a couple of inches) makes it ideal for pan-frying. In restaurants, "perch" is a name widely used to describe both this and other species of fish, which can be confusing.

The zander is a fierce and elusive game fish, with a long, elegant body.

Zander
Stizostedion lucioperca
This fish can reach a weight of 44lb (20kg) and grow to 3ft (92cm). Its flesh has a fine flavor, with a herbaceous earthiness, which is particularly admired by the French—zander features in several dishes from the Loire Valley. Good broiled.

SUSTAINABILITY CHOICE

Buy farmed mussels

The development of some shellfish farming, particularly mussels, has been very positive. Set a small distance from the shore, the mussels grow like bunches of grapes on ropes or wooden stakes placed in the water. After around three years the mussels are harvested—a process that causes minimal harm to the environment. Fish meal is not used, because the mussels feed on naturally occurring nutrients in the water to develop a wonderful sweet flavor. As a species that are at the bottom of the food chain, they are one of the world's most sustainable seafoods.

Trout, Char, and Grayling *Salmonidae*

This group of fish is extensive and an important food globally. The species are all rich in oil. The pink color of the flesh is the result of a diet of crustaceans that have a naturally occurring caryatid pigment. Farmed fish are sometimes given a chemical substitute to replicate this. Some species of trout are used for aquaculture or to stock trout lakes. Most trout spend their lives in fresh waters around the world; others are anadromous and migrate to the sea,

returning to their natal river to spawn. Trout can have an earthy taste, because they feed over muddy riverbeds. Farmed fish may be reared with a gravel bed and then purged in clean water prior to harvest, in order to prevent this. Indigenous North American trout include the rainbow, Dolly Varden, and brook trout. Other popular species include lake trout (*Salmo trutta lacustris*), golden trout (*S. aguabonita*), and the cut-throat trout (*S. clarki*). The char is similar

in size and appearance to trout. Lake char (*Salvelinus namaycush*) reach around 9lb (4kg) in weight; the Arctic char can reach over 13lb (6kg). The grayling (*Thymallus thymallus*) is a popular game fish in Europe and North America. It has a distinct aroma of fresh thyme when landed. It is not harvested commercially.
CUTS Whole, gutted, fillets, roe.
EAT Cooked: Pan-fry, bake, broil, roast. **Preserved:** Hot- and cold-smoked, salted roe.

FLAVOR PAIRINGS Classical French: white wine vinegar, butter, lemon, chives, almonds, hazelnuts.
CLASSIC RECIPES Trout in breadcrumbs; trout with Serrano ham; trout with almonds; *truite au bleu* (poached immediately on capture in an acidulated bouillon, and turns blue); potted char.

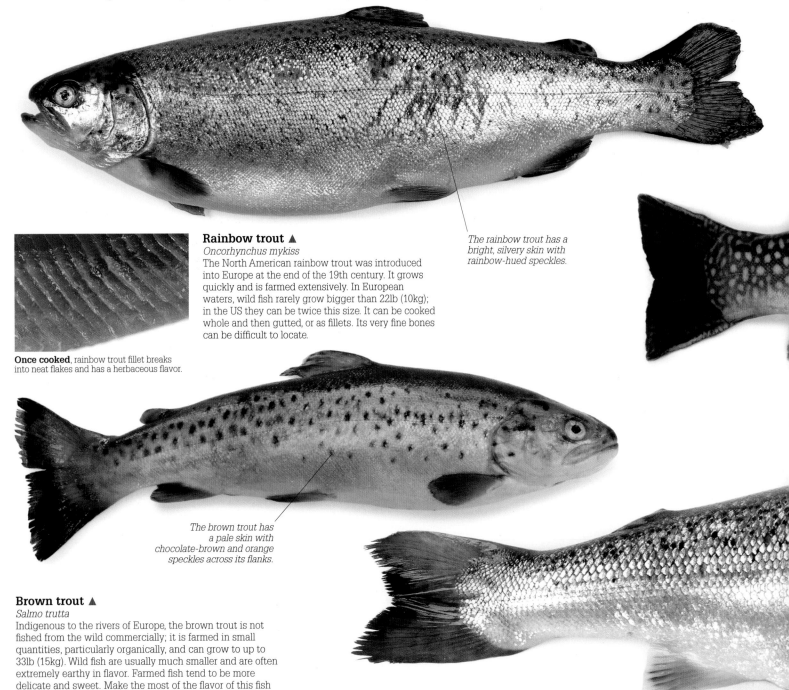

Rainbow trout ▲
Oncorhynchus mykiss
The North American rainbow trout was introduced into Europe at the end of the 19th century. It grows quickly and is farmed extensively. In European waters, wild fish rarely grow bigger than 22lb (10kg); in the US they can be twice this size. It can be cooked whole and then gutted, or as fillets. Its very fine bones can be difficult to locate.

The rainbow trout has a bright, silvery skin with rainbow-hued speckles.

Once cooked, rainbow trout fillet breaks into neat flakes and has a herbaceous flavor.

The brown trout has a pale skin with chocolate-brown and orange speckles across its flanks.

Brown trout ▲
Salmo trutta
Indigenous to the rivers of Europe, the brown trout is not fished from the wild commercially; it is farmed in small quantities, particularly organically, and can grow to up to 33lb (15kg). Wild fish are usually much smaller and are often extremely earthy in flavor. Farmed fish tend to be more delicate and sweet. Make the most of the flavor of this fish by wrapping it with bunches of mixed herbs and grilling it.

The Arctic char has light spots on a dark background; its color varies according to habitat and time of the year.

Arctic char
Salvelinus alpinus
These fish are also known as mountain trout and salmon trout. Some are landlocked in deep glacial lakes, specifically the Lake District in the north of England, where they were trapped at the end of the last ice age. Farmed fish are harvested at about 6½lb (3kg) in weight. The flesh is less earthy than that of trout, with an aroma of thyme and cut grass. Excellent poached and potted with butter, mace, and citrus; serve on Melba toast.

Robust herbs, such as sage, rosemary, and parsley marry well with the sweet, flaky texture of Arctic char.

Brook trout
Salvelinus fontinalis
Also known as brook char, speckled trout, red trout, and squaretail. Its color is green to brown with a distinctive marbling. It grows up to 25½in (65cm), and its white-to-yellow meat is very tasty.

The shiny silver skin of sea trout is interspersed with black and green dots toward the fish's back.

Sea trout
Salmo trutta
Sea trout, also commonly known as salmon trout, is the migratory form of the brown trout. It has a particularly sweet and fine flavor that is not as intense as that of salmon. Poach it whole or in fillets, and serve with hollandaise sauce and lemon.

Atlantic salmon *Salmonidae*

Salmon are found in both Atlantic and Pacific waters. The salmon is anadromous, spending part of its life cycle in fresh water, and part in the sea. Only one species is found in the Atlantic. Most Atlantic salmon is now farmed in Scotland and Norway. Japan consumes one-third of the world's salmon, but it is also enjoyed in many European countries and worldwide. Wild salmon and farmed species are quite different. Farmed fish can be of excellent quality and flavor, with a good balance of oil.
SUSTAINABILITY The high demand for the "king of fish", the wild Atlantic salmon, has led to overexploitation and many fishing bans are now in place. Once prolific, a wild specimen of Atlantic salmon has become a rare sight and it subsequently fetches a very high price. The aquaculture of the Atlantic salmon became a big commercial enterprise during the 1980s and it caused much controversy at its inception, as there were many environmental issues to overcome.

Alternatives to Atlantic salmon include organically farmed or responsibly sourced trout or a Pacific salmon species, such as sockeye.
CUTS Whole, fillets, steaks, head, roe.
EAT Cooked: Pan-fry, poach, broil, bake. Head often used as a base for soup. **Raw:** Frozen and sold for sushi and sashimi. **Preserved:** Hot- (kiln-roasted salmon) and cold-smoked. Salted roe used as keta, a caviar substitute.
FLAVOR PAIRINGS Lemon, butter, dill, samphire, tarragon, ginger, sorrel, kecap manis.
CLASSIC RECIPES Poached salmon with hollandaise sauce; gravadlax; salmon coulibiac (Russia); traditional poached and dressed whole salmon.

Atlantic salmon ▲
Salmo salar
Salmon may be described as fry, smelt, parr, grilse, or kelt, depending on the stage of its life cycle and whether it's in fresh water or the sea. Farmed fish are sold at 8–10lb (3.5–4.5kg). The flesh is firm, moist, and oily with a delicate flavor. To cook a whole salmon, measure the thickest part of its girth with a piece of string. For each 1in (2.5cm), calculate 4 minutes cooking time at 450°F (230°C). It will be sweet and succulent.

Atlantic salmon fillets are particularly good roasted, grilled, or pan-fried.

Pacific salmon *Salmonidae*

There are several species of Pacific salmon, including the chinook (king), sockeye, chum, coho, pink, and Japanese cherry salmon. They are prolific species and although there is some farming, they are caught commercially by many countries of the Pacific Rim, particularly Alaska and Canada. Unlike the Atlantic salmon, which can return to the river after spawning, Pacific species die. The chum salmon (*Oncorhynchus keta*) (MSC certified) is also known as dog salmon, keta salmon, qualla, calico salmon, hum, and fall salmon. It is abundant in the North Pacific, in the waters of Korea and Japan, and the Bering Sea. It is also found in Arctic Alaska and south to San Diego in California. The flesh is canned, dried, and salted; the roe is also used. Pink salmon (*O. gorbuscha*) is also known as humpback salmon and gorbuscha. This is the smallest Pacific salmon (it averages 5lb/2.25kg) and is found in the Arctic and Northwest to Eastern Central Pacific Ocean. Coho (*O. kisutch*) (MSC certified) is also known as silver salmon, blueback, medium red salmon, jack salmon, and silverside. Growing to around 43in (110cm), it is found in the North

Pacific from the Anadyr River in Russia, south toward Hokkaido in Japan; from Alaska to Baja California and Mexico. It has a fine-textured flesh and full flavor. The Japanese cherry salmon (*O. masou*) is also known as masu. It is caught in the northwest Pacific, the Sea of Okhotsk, and the Sea of Japan.
CUTS Whole, fillets, steaks.
EAT Cooked: Poach, pan-fry, microwave, broil, bake, steam.
Preserved: Smoked, roe, dried, salted, frozen, canned.
FLAVOR PAIRINGS Asian flavors: cilantro, soy sauce, sesame, chile, lime. Excellent for plank cooking.
CLASSIC RECIPES Salmon coulibiac (Russia); salmon sashimi; poached and dressed salmon; squaw candy.

Chinook salmon
Oncorhynchus tshawytscha
Also called the king, Pacific, spring, black, quinnat, and chub salmon. It can grow to 5ft (1.5m); the usual size is 27in (70cm). It is caught in the Arctic, and Northwest to Northeast Pacific from Alaska down to California and Japan. This fish has a similar oil-rich texture and flesh to Atlantic salmon and suits the same methods of cooking.

In the sea, the chinook salmon has a greeny blue back with lots of small, dark spots.

A wild Atlantic salmon has iron-gray skin along the back with black specks and well-developed fins. Farmed fish are likely to be more speckled and often have malformed fins.

Sockeye ▶
Oncorhynchus nerka
Also known as red and blueback salmon. Caught in the North Pacific, this is one of the most commercially important species and can grow up to 33in (84cm). It can take a little longer to cook than an Atlantic fish; the lack of fat also means that it can dry out: baste or use a marinade to keep it moist.

The chinook salmon is a little leaner than the Atlantic salmon. It is succulent and sweet, and good for broiling, pan-frying, and baking.

The sockeye's closely knit, lean, meaty, dense flesh is a deep orange from the crustaceans in its diet.

A chinook resembles the Atlantic salmon more closely than any of the other Pacific species.

Needlefish and Flying fish

The billfish family of needlefish (also known as garfish) is related to that of the flying fish. The needlefish (from the Belonidae family) are slender, elongated fish found in fresh water, brackish, and marine environments, with around 45 species in all. It has a long beak containing many sharp teeth for a jaw, and is found in temperate and tropical waters worldwide. It makes small jumps out of the water to escape predators. It is often caught at night, when it is attracted to the surface by lanterns and flashlights. The flying fish, a member of the Exocoetidae family, is a marine fish with around 64 species. It is found mainly in tropical and subtropical waters of the

Atlantic, Pacific, and Indian oceans. It uses its long pectoral fins, which are similar to a bird's wing, to escape predators by leaping out of the water up to 164ft (50m). It can leap much further if there is updraft on a wave and the fish vibrates its tail. An ingenious way of fishing for it is by holding nets in the air. These fish have long, slim fillets that are generally pale gray with a sweet taste and delicate texture.

CUTS Whole, fillets, roe (tobiko).
EAT Cooked: Pan-fry. **Preserved:** Dried. **Raw:** Sushi.
FLAVOR PAIRINGS Okra, corn meal, chile, onion, garlic, peppers.
CLASSIC RECIPES Cou cou (national dish of flying fish from Barbados).

Atlantic needlefish ▼
Strongylura marina
Caught in the Western Atlantic from Maine to the Gulf of Mexico and Brazil. It grows to 4ft (1.2m) and has a sweet, succulent, white flesh.

In fresh water, eels are a deep emerald green; in brackish water they revert to dark brown and silver.

European eel
Anguilla anguilla
This species usually grows to about 31½in (80cm). Eels are popular for eating at various stages in their life. Bootlace eels or elvers are usually deep-fried—a delicacy in parts of Europe. Smoked eel is also a delicacy and the eel's very oily flesh is especially suitable for hot-smoking. For cooking fresh, eels are usually skinned as soon as they have been killed, then gutted and cut into steaks or fillets. For smoking, they are often left whole. They have a very distinctive firm, slightly rubbery, and oil-rich texture.

Eel *Anguillidae*

There are 22 known members of the eel group. They have a long, slithering, snake-like body. The eel is a catadromous fish: it is spawned in the sea and moves to fresh water to mature, then returns to the sea to spawn, after which it dies. Eels live in temperate, tropical, and subtropical waters worldwide. They have a distinct spawning ground, depending on the species. Eels have firm and rich-tasting flesh, and an oily texture.
SUSTAINABILITY There has been a massive decline in eels over recent years, which is attributed not only to overfishing but also to pollution. They are listed as critically endangered. Some species are extensively farmed in Northern Europe and Asia, to try to take the pressure off the wild

stocks, but this has done little to halt the decline. There is no close alternative, but you could use an oil-rich species such as mackerel.
CUTS Live, whole; smoked whole and in fillets.
EAT Cooked: Broil, pan-fry, bake, poach (for jellied eels).
Preserved: Smoked, dried.
FLAVOR PAIRINGS Bay leaf, vinegar, apples, red and white wine, allspice berries, cloves, mint, parsley, cream.
CLASSIC RECIPES Jellied eels; *matelote d'anguille* (France); deep-fried elvers; *anguilla allo spiedo* (Italy); eel and bay leaf kebabs; *bisato sull'ara*; fried eel; *capitone marinato* (Italy).

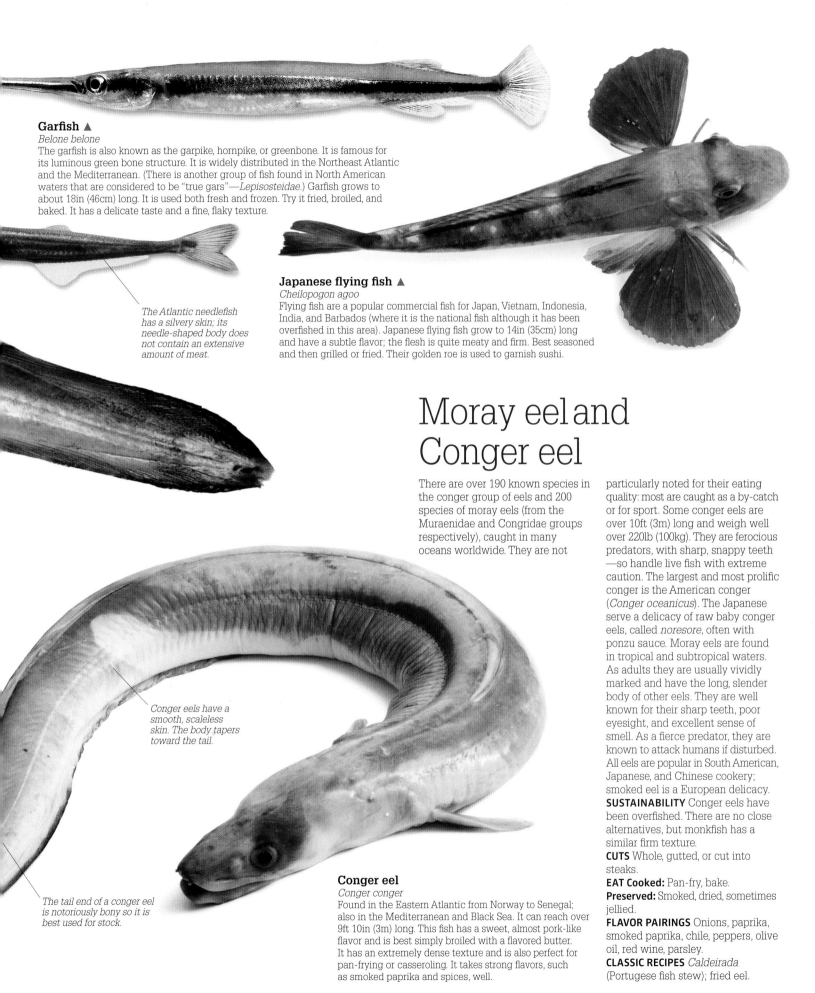

Garfish ▲
Belone belone
The garfish is also known as the garpike, hornpike, or greenbone. It is famous for its luminous green bone structure. It is widely distributed in the Northeast Atlantic and the Mediterranean. (There is another group of fish found in North American waters that are considered to be "true gars"—*Lepisosteidae*.) Garfish grows to about 18in (46cm) long. It is used both fresh and frozen. Try it fried, broiled, and baked. It has a delicate taste and a fine, flaky texture.

The Atlantic needlefish has a silvery skin; its needle-shaped body does not contain an extensive amount of meat.

Japanese flying fish ▲
Cheilopogon agoo
Flying fish are a popular commercial fish for Japan, Vietnam, Indonesia, India, and Barbados (where it is the national fish although it has been overfished in this area). Japanese flying fish grow to 14in (35cm) long and have a subtle flavor; the flesh is quite meaty and firm. Best seasoned and then grilled or fried. Their golden roe is used to garnish sushi.

Moray eel and Conger eel

There are over 190 known species in the conger group of eels and 200 species of moray eels (from the Muraenidae and Congridae groups respectively), caught in many oceans worldwide. They are not particularly noted for their eating quality: most are caught as a by-catch or for sport. Some conger eels are over 10ft (3m) long and weigh well over 220lb (100kg). They are ferocious predators, with sharp, snappy teeth —so handle live fish with extreme caution. The largest and most prolific conger is the American conger (*Conger oceanicus*). The Japanese serve a delicacy of raw baby conger eels, called *noresore*, often with ponzu sauce. Moray eels are found in tropical and subtropical waters. As adults they are usually vividly marked and have the long, slender body of other eels. They are well known for their sharp teeth, poor eyesight, and excellent sense of smell. As a fierce predator, they are known to attack humans if disturbed. All eels are popular in South American, Japanese, and Chinese cookery; smoked eel is a European delicacy.

SUSTAINABILITY Conger eels have been overfished. There are no close alternatives, but monkfish has a similar firm texture.

CUTS Whole, gutted, or cut into steaks.

EAT Cooked: Pan-fry, bake.

Preserved: Smoked, dried, sometimes jellied.

FLAVOR PAIRINGS Onions, paprika, smoked paprika, chile, peppers, olive oil, red wine, parsley.

CLASSIC RECIPES *Caldeirada* (Portugese fish stew); fried eel.

Conger eels have a smooth, scaleless skin. The body tapers toward the tail.

The tail end of a conger eel is notoriously bony so it is best used for stock.

Conger eel
Conger conger
Found in the Eastern Atlantic from Norway to Senegal; also in the Mediterranean and Black Sea. It can reach over 9ft 10in (3m) long. This fish has a sweet, almost pork-like flavor and is best simply broiled with a flavored butter. It has an extremely dense texture and is also perfect for pan-frying or casseroling. It takes strong flavors, such as smoked paprika and spices, well.

Shark, Skate, and Ray

Several thousand species of shark, from many families, are found globally, from the Great White to the dogfish. They often find their way to fish and chip shop menus in the UK, where they are sold as rock salmon, flake, and in the EU, huss. They are available whole, skinned, and boned. Skates and rays belong to the Rajidae family and are related to the sharks. They are found in all oceans from the Arctic to the Antarctic. They are flat and their large pectoral fins or "wings" give them a rhomboid shape. The mouth and gills are on the underside of the body and the eggs are laid in a leathery capsule known as a mermaid's purse. Their skin can be challenging to remove without pliers and gloves. Such species expel their urea through the gills and if incorrectly stored, smell strongly of ammonia. If a fish smells of ammonia, do not buy it. The wings of skates and rays take longer to cook than most thin white fillets. They have an unusual fibrous texture and taste herbaceous. A thick piece of cartilage at the shoulder end of the fillet comes loose when the fish is cooked.

SUSTAINABILITY There has been a decline in the stocks of some shark species, which like the Great White, are now protected. They have been overfished for their use in Chinese medicine, and the Chinese classic, shark fin soup. Skates have also been overexploited in many areas. They are subject to a fishing quota and the landing of some species in designated areas is banned. Alternatives include responsibly sourced monkfish.

CUTS Shark: Fresh and frozen, fillets, whole. Skate: Wings, "knobs" (muscles taken from the back of the fish).

EAT Cooked: Shark: Pan-fry, broil, roast, deep-fry. Skate: Pan-fry, deep-fry, poach, roast.

Preserved: Shark: Smoked and dried.

Thornback ray
Raja clavata
Also known as roker, thorny, and maiden ray, the thornback ray is caught in the Eastern Atlantic, from Iceland, Norway, the North Sea and the Baltic, south to Morocco and Namibia, including the Mediterranean and the Black Sea. Most thornback rays grow to 33½in (85cm). The back of the fish is different shades of brown with variegated dark spots. There are some responsibly sourced rays available. It has a strong taste and is best poached, baked, or dusted with seasoned flour and pan-fried. The dense flesh of a ray wing takes 10–12 minutes to poach.

FLAVOR PAIRINGS Shark: Beer batter, tartar sauce, soy, sesame oil, ginger, and chile. Skate: Vinegar, capers, parsley, lemon juice, butter.
CLASSIC RECIPES Skate with beurre noisette; skate with beurre noir and capers.

Smoothhound
Mustelus mustelus
Also known as flake and rock salmon, smoothhound, from the Triakidae family, is very similar to dogfish and huss. This small shark variety usually grows to around 20in (50cm) and lives in coastal waters worldwide. Once the shark is fully mature, it ventures out into deeper water. The variety has been heavily overfished and there is a strict catch quota in place. The flesh is firm and meaty with a very distinctive, almost pork-like taste. It is great deep-fried, pan-fried, or used in stir fries.

Ray, like sharks, are cartilaginous with only a central cartilage and no bone.

Plaice and Sole *Pleuronectidae*

The Pleuronectidae group (the name means "side swimmers"—these are flat fish) includes plaice, some flounders, halibut, and some types of sole, such as lemon sole (*Microstomus kitt*), petrale sole (*Eopsetta jordani*), rex sole (*Glyptocephalus zachirus*), and North Pacific sole (*Eopsetta grigorjewi*). True sole belong to the *Soleidae* group. All are demersal fish and have white flesh; the main concentration of oil is in the liver. They are fished in Europe, North America, and in the northern Pacific. When a flat fish hatches, it is a tiny, round fish; as it grows, it turns on to its left or right side and the eyes move to one side of the head. Most flat fish are dextral, with eyes on the right side. The fish use the seabed to hide and have highly camouflaged skin on the upper body to enable them to blend into their habitat. The underside of a wild fish is pearlescent white, helping it to blend in with its environment if viewed from underneath. These fish have a delicate taste and texture. They are usually gutted on landing, enabling the fish to retain quality. Most flat fish have a heavy coating of slime that is usually clear. As the fish loses condition, the slime becomes sticky and discolored and this indicates that it is past its best.

SUSTAINABILITY All of these species are heavily targeted in many countries and are subject to a legal-minimum landing size. There are some MSC-certified sources.

CUTS Usually gutted on landing. Sold whole (head on or off), cross-cut and quarter-cross fillets, skin on or off.

EAT Cooked: Pan-fry, poach, deep-fry, bake.

FLAVOR PAIRINGS Seasoned flour, butter, lemon, parsley, breadcrumbs, sage, chestnut mushrooms, lingonberry, potato.

CLASSIC RECIPES Plaice/lemon sole meunière; sole Véronique.

Lemon sole
Microstomus kitt

Also known as smear dab and Scottish sole, lemon sole is caught in shallow seas in Northern Europe. Its usual size is 10–12in (25–30cm). A very fresh fish has a heavy coating of creamy slime, unlike other fresh, flat fish, which have a clear slime. It has a sweet, mild taste and delicate texture.

Lemon sole is good simply rolled in flour and pan-fried, broiled, or poached.

Lemon sole can be identified by lemon piping (a strip of yellow flesh) around the gill flap.

Plaice
Pleuronectes platessa

This plaice is common in European waters, and is the most popular flat fish in Europe, with a mild taste and fine texture. It has a distinct "wrist" at the tail and a bony ridge from the head to the gills. The underside is white with chevron markings that indicate the pattern of muscle bands. It can grow to 24in (60cm), but this is rare. It is best from May to December/January.

Some species have a weak electrical organ in their long, slender tail.

Plaice have a greenish-brown skin and orange or rusty-green spots.

Plaice and Sole *Continued*

Petrale sole ▶
Eopsetta jordani
The petrale sole is also known as Pacific coast sole and regarded as one of the finest sole in that region. It is usually caught at around 12in (30cm). It is found in the Eastern Pacific, from the coast of Alaska to northern Baja California and Mexico. It is usually skinned and filleted for sale. It has a sweet flesh that is best pan-fried.

The upper surface of the petrale sole is a uniform light to dark brown.

Petrale sole's head is deep with large eyes on the right side. The fish is white in color on the blind side.

White, flaky fillets of petrale sole can be deep-fried, pan-fried, or broiled.

The skin of the Atlantic halibut is a uniform dark brown to black; young fish are often marbled.

▲ Witch
Glyptocephalus cynoglossus
Also known as gray flounder and occasionally marketed as Torbay sole. The witch is found in the Eastern Atlantic, from Northern Spain to Northern Norway, and in the Western Atlantic from Canada to North Carolina in the US. It grows up to 2ft (60cm) long and has a subtle flavor. Best baked whole; or filleted, rolled in seasoned flour, pan-fried in butter and then finished with a splash of lemon.

The witch produces very slim fillets. It's best to trim the head and fins when cooking whole.

Dab ▶
Limanda limanda
Dabs are found in abundance in the Northeast Atlantic. It is one of the smaller flat fish and can grow to around 16in (40cm), but 12in (30cm) is more common. The white flesh of a dab is best eaten fresh, but has very little flavor. It is small, so is usually trimmed and cooked whole on the bone. Also sold dried, salted, and smoked.

Dabs are usually pale brown with darker colored blotches.

Halibut *Pleuronectidae*

Sometimes called the "Cow of the Sea", this fish is the largest of all the flat fish. A handful of halibut species are caught in Atlantic and Pacific waters, and are highly regarded. As with all flat fish, halibut vary in color depending on the seabed that they inhabit; the top side provides camouflage. A wild fish can reach mammoth proportions: some specimens have been recorded as weighing over 700lb (330kg). However, most landed today would not exceed 24–30lb (11–13.5kg). This fish has a dense, white, firm-textured flesh and has become so sought after that it is now extensively farmed to meet high demand.

SUSTAINABILITY Halibut mature slowly, making them very susceptible to overfishing. Wild Atlantic halibut has been overexploited and there is a minimum landing size and strict regulations for catch quota in many areas. It is better to choose the farmed or Pacific species as an alternative.

CUTS Large fish: steaks/cutlets; Small fish: whole, fillets, also called fletches.

EAT Cooked: Steam, pan-fry, broil, poach, bake. **Preserved:** Dried, salted, cold-smoked.

FLAVOR PAIRINGS Butter, seasoned flour, nutmeg, pickles, capers, lemon.

CLASSIC RECIPES Poached halibut with hollandaise sauce; broiled halibut with beurre blanc.

Atlantic halibut ▼
Hippoglossus hippoglossus
This fish can reach up to 15ft (4.5m) in length. It is found in the Eastern and Western Atlantic, and is extensively farmed. The fish is moist and very lean with a sweet, mild taste; the lack of fat makes it easy to over-cook, as it dries easily.

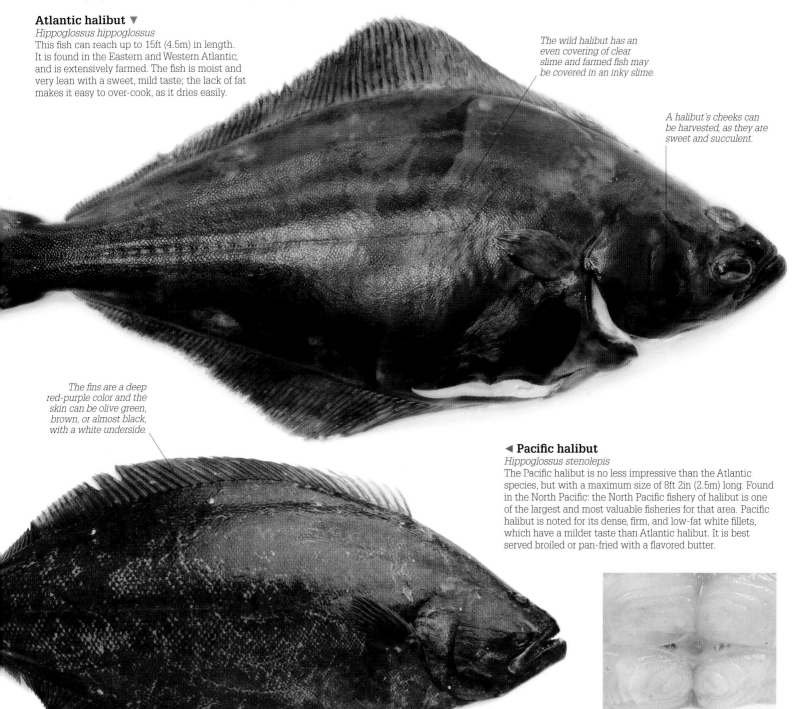

The wild halibut has an even covering of clear slime and farmed fish may be covered in an inky slime.

A halibut's cheeks can be harvested, as they are sweet and succulent.

The fins are a deep red-purple color and the skin can be olive green, brown, or almost black, with a white underside.

◄ Pacific halibut
Hippoglossus stenolepis
The Pacific halibut is no less impressive than the Atlantic species, but with a maximum size of 8ft 2in (2.5m) long. Found in the North Pacific: the North Pacific fishery of halibut is one of the largest and most valuable fisheries for that area. Pacific halibut is noted for its dense, firm, and low-fat white fillets, which have a milder taste than Atlantic halibut. It is best served broiled or pan-fried with a flavored butter.

Pacific halibut produces thick, white, flaky fillets with a light flavor.

Sole *Soleidae*

Found in waters worldwide, the "true" sole includes around 165 species. They have a long, slipper-shaped body with small eyes, mouth, and tail. Some members have attractive markings and patterns; most have a unique coarse skin texture—similar to a cat's tongue—if stroked from tail to head. The maximum length is around 27½in (70cm). These species of fish are dextral, with eyes on the right side of the head. The white flesh has a subtle and distinctive flavor.

SUSTAINABILITY Dover sole is popular in Europe, in the restaurant trade. This has lead to overfishing. A strict size for landed fish is in place, as is a catch quota. Look for MSC-certified fishery Dover sole or try responsibly sourced turbot, lemon sole, or plaice as alternatives.

CUTS Usually gutted and sold whole, trimmed and skinned, and in fillets.

EAT Cooked: Broil, pan-fry.

FLAVOR PAIRINGS Lemon, butter, seasoned flour, cucumber, mint, shiitake mushrooms, mushrooms, truffle oil, capers, parsley.

CLASSIC RECIPES Sole colbert; lemon sole Doria; broiled Dover sole with anchovy butter; sole Véronique.

Dover sole
Solea vulgaris
Also known as common sole, tongue, or slip sole (a small specimen), Dover sole can be expensive. It grows up to 27½in (70cm) and is caught in the Eastern Atlantic and farmed on a small scale. It has very firm and slightly rubbery white flesh; full-flavored. It is best when well past rigor mortis, as flavor and texture develop properly.

Turbot, Brill, and Megrim *Scophthalimidae*

The family includes turbot, brill, megrim, and a species called topknots. They are found in many temperate seas of the Atlantic and Pacific oceans. Turbot and brill are a valuable species and highly commercial. They are sinistral fish, with their eyes on the left side of the head. They can have a similar colored skin, but there are differences. Turbot is almost circular in shape and the dark eye-side has no scales but large, sharp tubercles. It is farmed extensively. Although the flesh has a flaky texture, it holds its shape well and so is versatile. Brill is oval in shape and has scales, but no tubercles. Like many other species, it adapts its color to its habitat. The megrim is noted for its large mouth that extends into a tube. It is a popular food in southern Europe, particularly Spain. Megrim is best eaten very fresh; it needs seasoning, and butter or olive oil to prevent it from drying out.

SUSTAINABILITY Turbot and brill have a maximum catch quota in place, and landed fish must be of a minimum size. Alternatives can be responsibly sourced lemon sole, plaice, and responsibly farmed or sourced halibut.

CUTS Whole and head on; trimmed; fillets (depending on species). Large turbots may be cut into steaks.

EAT Cooked: Steam, pan-fry, crust, bake, roast, broil.

FLAVOR PAIRINGS Wild mushrooms, champagne, cream, butter, shellfish stock, lemon, Gruyère cheese, Parmesan.

CLASSIC RECIPE Poached turbot with oysters and champagne.

Turbot
Psetta maxima
Also known as britt, butt, breet, it's one of the most expensive of all flat fish and highly sought after. It is found in the northeast Atlantic, throughout the Mediterranean and along the European coasts to the Arctic Circle. It grows up to 3ft (1m) long. The flesh is meaty and, unlike other white fish, holds together well enough for stir-frying. It's also good for poaching, pan-frying, and broiling. It's often sold cut into thick steaks with the backbone running through the steak. It has a rounded and recognizable, very fine and sweet flavor.

Turbot is firm, white, dense and suitable for various cooking methods.

Wild turbot varies from dark mottled brown to gray; farmed fish are light gray-green to dark gray-black.

The megrim has a glassy, light brown skin and a white underside.

Megrim
Lepidorhombus whiffiagonis
Also known as meg, sale fluke, Scarborough sole, or whiff, megrim is a deep-water fish living in the Northeast Atlantic. It is commonly found at 10in (25cm) long. Best trimmed and cooked whole on the bone; it has a similar flavor to plaice and is flaky, delicate, and low in fat. Suits subtle flavors such as butter and mild herbs.

Sand sole
Pegusa lascaris
Also known as snouted sole, lascar, and Atlantic sole, sand sole is found in the North and Southeastern Atlantic, the Mediterranean, and the Black Sea. It lacks the superior flavor of the Dover sole. It is of minor commercial importance, but is available. Skin the fish whole and cook on the bone.

The sand sole has yellow-brown skin with pale blotches and looks similar to the Dover sole.

The fish has an oval body up to 16in (40cm) in length with smoothly curving dorsal and anal fins.

Brill has a superb fine, white, flaky texture. It is best pan-fried, broiled, or roasted.

Brill ▼
Scophthalmus rhombus
Also known as kite and pearl. Brill reaches a maximum length of 30in (75cm). It lives in the Eastern Atlantic, from Iceland to Morocco, throughout the Black Sea and the Mediterranean. At one time it was underrated, now it's well regarded. It has an equally fine, sweet flavor to turbot, but is more flaky.

A turbot has a lot of sharp nodules on its skin, known as turbercles.

Brill is a sandy, greenish-brown. The young fish are dark brown. It is often flecked with white.

Abalone *Haliotidae*

Abalone is considered a rare delicacy and gourmet food. It is harvested from the wild and from aquaculture in many coastal waters in oceans worldwide. There are about 100 species of this sea snail, which vary greatly in size. The well-flavored meat is found in an ear-shaped shell. Abalone is also known as ormer, sea-ear, ear-shell, Venus's ears, perlemoen (South Africa), muttonfish (Australia), and paua (New Zealand). Abalone attach to rocky surfaces using a very strong suction action, and live off green algae.

SUSTAINABILITY Some abalone grow slowly; overharvesting has reduced some stocks and increased prices. Although abalone's texture is somewhat unique, whelks and limpets are similarly chewy.

AVAILABILITY Fresh: Sold in the shell. **Preserved:** Frozen meat/steaks (ready tenderized), canned, dried (used for flavoring soups), salted.

EAT Tenderize by pounding before cooking. Sauté or fry very briefly, as it toughens easily. Add dried abalone to soup and simmer for a long period of time to add flavor.

FLAVOR PAIRINGS Asian: Chinese ear mushrooms, sesame, soy sauce, ginger, garlic, butter.

CLASSIC RECIPE Abalone with oyster sauce.

Red abalone
Haliotis rufescens
This species is the most readily available, and the largest of the abalone group. Found in the Pacific from Oregon to Baja California, and Mexico; harvested with restrictions. Sear briefly: if overcooked, it becomes tough. It has a sweet, meaty, and strong seafood flavor.

The foot or muscle is the main part eaten. Remove the meat from the shell and pound it before searing briefly.

Conch *Strombidae*

The queen conch (*Strombus gigas*) is one of many species of saltwater gastropods. It is also known as the pink or Caribbean conch (pronounced conk). The main suppliers and consumers are Jamaica, Honduras, and the Dominican Republic. Conch has an intense flavor.

SUSTAINABILITY Although this species was once abundant, commercial harvesting is now banned in the US. Alternatives include responsibly sourced abalone or whelks and limpets, which are much cheaper alternatives.

AVAILABILITY Wild: Frozen, chopped, ground. **Farmed:** Fresh, prepared, frozen. Farmed conch are generally more tender.

EAT Wild conch needs to be sliced thinly, then tenderized with a mallet.
Cooked: Roast, broil, pan- and stir-fry, sauté, steam. **Raw:** Marinate in lime juice and chile as ceviche.

FLAVOR PAIRINGS Onion, garlic, peppers, tomato, jalapeño, hot sauce, cilantro, cayenne.

CLASSIC RECIPES Conch fritters; conch chowder.

The meat, which has a dark membrane, is prized from the shell as a whole piece and can be up to 12in (30cm) long. Good-quality conch is creamy white with hints of pink and orange; if it is discolored, gray, and smells strongly, do not buy it.

Queen conch
Eustrombus gigas
This conch is farmed in the Calicos Islands making it more available year round. In the Caribbean, dried or ground conch is used in fritters, pan-fried for salads, and as a base for chowder. The taste is sweet with a rubbery, jellied texture.

Once extracted from the decorative shell, conch meat can be marinated and eaten raw, or cooked by various methods.

Periwinkle, Whelk, and Murex

Sea snails in the form of periwinkles, whelks, and murex are found in waters worldwide. They are considered to be a delicacy by a small number of consumers, but the limited sales have led some to decline in availability. Periwinkles, or winkles (from the Littorinidae group), and whelks are enjoyed in northern Europe and form a part of a traditional Sunday dinner in London's East End. There are around 180 species, but only a few of these are eaten. In the UK, whelk refers to species from the Buccinidae family. Whelks are also popular in North America, where species from the Melongenidae group are harvested. Whelks have a distinct salty, seafood taste and are often likened to clam meat. They are tough and very meaty. Murex are another family of small sea snails from the Muricidae group. They are only found in the coastal areas and specialist fish markets of Mediterranean countries. Murex taste similar to whelks but the meat is reputedly tougher.

AVAILABILITY In the shell, both raw and cooked. Winkles: fresh, frozen, shucked; pickled in vinegar and canned. In the US, they are sold cooked, shucked, and trimmed.

EAT Rinse in salt water before boiling. Cook periwinkles for 3–5 minutes in the shell, whelks for 12–15 minutes, murex for 10–12 minutes (see page 281). The operculum (the horny "foot") is not eaten: trim this off. If desired, coat in crumbs and pan-fry.

FLAVOR PAIRINGS Chili vinegar, malt vinegar, salt, lemon juice.

CLASSIC RECIPES Periwinkles in the shell with malt vinegar and salt; periwinkle and watercress sandwiches.

To enhance the color of the greenish-black shell, roll periwinkles in a little oil before serving to give the shell a gloss.

Angulate periwinkle
Littorina angulifera
These tiny snails are popular in Europe and often harvested by hand, ensuring that little damage is done to their habitat. It is traditionally served as part of a seafood platter and its intense flavor combines sweet and salty tastes. It's prone to be gritty, so rinse well.

Murex shells are often collected because of their beauty: they are fat and spiny, tapering to a tail-like point.

Murex ◀▶
Murex brandaris
The Mediterranean murex has been a popular delicacy for many centuries; it was also collected to harvest a rare purple dye. The flavor is similar to that of a whelk; it needs gentle cooking, as it can be tough. In the South of France, murex make a classic addition to a *fruits de mer* platter.

Many gastropods have a horny foot that needs to be trimmed away or removed after cooking.

Common northern whelk
Buccinum undatum
The whelk group of shellfish has hundreds of members in waters worldwide. They are carnivores and scavengers. In Europe, the common northern whelk, found in the North Atlantic, is eaten. It is 2–4in (5–10cm) long and caught year-round in baited pots. This species is best during the summer.

Clams and Cockles

There are hundreds of types of clam and cockles found in waters worldwide. They are a well-utilized food source and create an important income for many countries. Clams are particularly popular in parts of Europe, the US, and Asia. The Veneridae group has hard, tough shells, and names for the species include Venus clam, carpetshell clam, hard-shell clam, and quahog. The Myidae group have a soft, thin, and brittle shell structure. Species are found in both the Pacific and Atlantic oceans. The species include steamer clam, soft-shell clam, and Ipswich clam. The geoduck (pronounced gooeyduck) clam is also known as the piss clam (due to its long siphon) or horse clam. It is the largest clam in the world, and is also thought to be the longest-living animal in the world. Surf clams come from the Mactridae group, and there are several related species. The Solenidae group includes razor or jackknife clams that are harvested worldwide. They resemble a cut-throat razor and have a razor-sharp edge. The amande comes from the Glycimeridae group.

AVAILABILITY Fresh: Live in the shell, shucked as prepared meat. **Preserved:** Frozen, brined, canned.

EAT Large clams: Chopped or minced in chowder; Smaller specimens: shucked and enjoyed raw. Hard-shell: Raw or steamed open to add to soups. Soft-shell: Siphon sliced or minced for chowder, or thinly sliced for sushi. Body meat sliced, tenderized, and pan-fried or sautéed. In the shell: Steamed. Removed from shell: Served raw with lemon juice, also for chowder. Razor clams: In the shell, broiled, or steamed. Removed from shell, raw in ceviche, or pan-fried.

FLAVOR PAIRINGS Cream, onion, herbs, white wine, tomatoes, garlic, parsley, bacon, chiles.

CLASSIC RECIPES Manhattan clam chowder (tomato-based); New England clam chowder (cream-based); linguine alle vongole; stuffed clams.

The shell of a cockle is corrugated. Use them as soon as possible, as they can't be stored for long.

Cockle
Cerastoderma edule
Cockles are usually sold at around 1¼in (3cm). Wash, and then steam open over simmering stock or wine. Extract from the shell to serve. Excellent in salads or as a starter with a simple dressing. They have a sweet taste of the sea and can be a little gritty, but are a real treat when freshly cooked.

Check that the shells are tightly closed, as this indicates that they are still alive.

The glossy brown shell of the razor clam is brittle and needs careful handling, as it has a razor-sharp edge.

Geoduck clam ▼
Panopea abrupta
Also known as Pacific geoduck or king clam, this clam is usually sold at 4–6in (10–15cm) in diameter. The siphon can be up to 27½in (70cm) long, when fully extended. The geoduck can live to over a 100 years old. It can grow much bigger and weigh as much as 15½–17½lb (7–8kg). The meat can be tough, but the flavor is intense. They are particularly popular in Japan.

Razor clam
Ensis ensis
These are usually harvested at 5in (12cm) or larger. Check that the clam is alive immediately prior to cooking: the shell should close tightly if tapped. Best steamed, or broiled (but toughens easily). Extract the sweet and tender muscle from the shell and discard the stomach contents (see page 279). Slice thinly for a marinated dish such as ceviche. The taste is not dissimilar to that of a scallop.

Surf clam ▼
Spisula solidissima
These are also known as trough, bar, or hen clam, and are found on the eastern coast of the US, where they are highly valued and used for clam chowder. Small related species are found in Europe. Surf clams are good for steamed clam dishes. Check that they are alive prior to cooking, rinse, then steam open over stock and white wine. They have a delicate, sweet flavor with a salty aftertaste.

Hard-shell clam ▶
Mercenaria mercenaria
These are also known as quahog, round, or Venus clam. Small, young clams may be called littleneck clams, while a half-grown clam is called a cherrystone and considered a delicacy (eaten raw or cooked). Small hard-shell clams can be enjoyed raw, but the larger ones are often used in clam chowder. The shells are quite heavy, but open to reveal a sweet, tender, and pleasantly salty clam meat.

Surf clams have a smooth beige shell. They usually grow to 1½–2in (4–5cm) in diameter, but can reach 6in (16cm).

Hard-shell clams are 3–5in (8–12cm) wide.

Amande ▼
Glycymeris glycymeris
Also known as the dog cockle, the amande is caught around European coasts. Its shell can grow up to 3in (7cm) across. It has a firmer texture than most clams, so is good for chowders and stuffing although it is enjoyed raw in Europe. Sweet, meaty, and a little chewy.

The amande is round, with a chocolate zigzag pattern on a cream shell. It is harvested at about 1½in (4cm) in diameter.

The siphon of the geoduck clam is edible, but the thick skin needs to be removed first and the meat cooked slowly until tender.

Scallops *Pectinidae*

Escallops are commonly known as scallops and are a popular shellfish. They are harvested in oceans worldwide and found deeper than most shellfish. There are over 500 species, coming from three groups; some are an important commercial food source, harvested from the wild, or farmed. Scallops are harvested by dredging or gathered by hand. (The latter is considered a more responsible method. The scallops are often larger than dredged ones and fetch a high price.) They are hermaphrodites and comprise a powerful adductor muscle (the white section), coral or roe containing the eggs (the orange section), and milt (the cream section). This swells and bursts in the water, mixing with the eggs for fertilization. This is the only bivalve that is sold raw in a prepared state. The main part of the scallop that's eaten is the sweet, succulent adductor muscle. The coral is also eaten in Europe, but is discarded in the US. The coral may be dried in a low oven and pulverized to add to shellfish sauces, to provide a greater depth of flavor. Scallops have a sweet seafood taste and tender, succulent texture. The roe has a richer and more intense flavor.

SUSTAINABILITY There is a minimum landing size for the king scallop caught off the coast of the UK and many other areas. Try to buy responsibly sourced specimens. Razor clams have a similar texture.

AVAILABILITY Fresh: Live in the shell, prepared on the half-shell, prepared and trimmed (processed). **Preserved:** Frozen with roe both on and off, canned, smoked, some species are dried.

EAT Cooked: Pan-fry, steam, poach, broil, grill; pan-fry smoked meat. **Raw:** Ceviche and sushi (white meat only).

FLAVOR PAIRINGS Bacon, chorizo, red bell peppers, red onions, olive oil, sesame oil, black beans, scallions, ginger, chile.

CLASSIC RECIPES Scallops in bacon; scallops with black bean sauce or soy and ginger; scallop gratin; Coquilles St. Jacques.

Bay scallop
Argopecten irradians
This scallop is found in the western North Atlantic, and is harvested along the coast of the US. Sear in hot butter for a few seconds on both sides to make the most of the tender, sweet meat.

Do not overcook bay scallops, as they will shrink and dry out.

The shell can reach over 8in (20cm) in diameter. It is cream with brown markings; it has a flat bottom shell and a concave top shell.

The mantle and dark stomach sac are removed when a scallop is sold on the shell.

Sea scallop ▶
Pecten maximus
This scallop is caught in the deep waters of northern Europe, and enjoyed in many European countries. The shell is corrugated, which prevents it from closing very tightly, unlike other bivalves. Sea scallops are at their very best pan-seared, although intense heat makes the roe pop. Care needs to be taken not to overcook them—cook for about a minute on either side in a hot pan.

Queen scallops do not usually grow to more than 2½in (6cm) across.

The adductor muscle allows the shell to open and close, giving the scallop mobility.

◀ Queen scallop
Aequipecten opercularis
"Queenies" are rarely sold live in the shell. They are either extracted or trimmed, and sold on the half-shell. They have a sweet, delicate taste. They are best used in a stir-fry or in a fish stew—they overcook very easily and shrink. If served on the shell, they are good with a little flavored butter and a few seconds under the broiler.

Mussels *Mytilidae*

Mussels live in cool waters all over the world. They are abundant and are harvested from the wild by dredging and hand-gathering. They are also farmed in large quantities (see page 300–301). Mussels are one of the most sustainable seafoods available. There are various species.

AVAILABILITY Fresh: Live in the shell, cook fresh. **Preserved:** Frozen meat, canned in brine or vinegar, smoked. Often included in frozen seafood mix. Green-lipped mussel: usually cooked on the half-shell and frozen.

EAT Cooked: Steam, roast, broil. Green-lipped mussel: Topped and réchauffé as baked and broiled. Remove the shell if adding to a sauce or stew.

FLAVOR PAIRINGS White wine, butter, garlic, cream, ginger, lemongrass, spices, parsley, cilantro, dill, rosemary, fennel, Pernod.

CLASSIC RECIPES Moules marinières, moules frites, paella, moules à la crème, moules farcies, mouclade.

The shell of this variety is smooth and glossy and it has uniform angles.

This variety is identified by its distinctive green lip inside its shell.

Green-lipped mussel
Perna canaliculus
Also known as the New Zealand mussel, or green mussel, this may grow to 9½in (24cm) long. It is of economic importance around the New Zealand coastline, where it is harvested abundantly. It has a dark brown shell with a vivid green lip. It is very meaty—almost chewy—and intensely flavored.

Rope-grown mussels are smooth, blue/black, and glossy in appearance. They require minimal preparation.

You can work out a mussel's age by counting the number of circles on its shell.

Common mussel
Mytilus edulis
Also known as the blue mussel, the common muscle is found in temperate and polar waters worldwide. The shell varies from brown to a bluish-purple. The mussels attach themselves to rocks, or when farmed, to rope, by a strong thread called the byssus thread (or beard), a protein they secrete. They taste slightly salty, with an intense flavor of the sea.

Oyster *Ostreidae*

Eating oysters is a global pastime, and a well-documented gourmet delight. Like other bivalve (two-shell) molluscs, an oyster lives inside its shell, which it opens and closes with a strong muscle. The shell is oval, either cupped or flat, and covered in frilly, rock-like crevices. Fresh oysters are tightly closed, and hard to open without a shucking knife. Mostly found in temperate coastal waters, oysters are harvested from both wild and farmed beds worldwide. Two main genera are gathered: *Ostrea*, native to Europe, and the west coast of the US; *Crassostrea*, native to Asia, Japan, the east coast of the US, and Australia. Once harvested, the fish are purified and graded by size. An all-time favorite is the creamy Pacific oyster *(Crassostrea gigas)*, originally from the coast of Japan, but farmed in northern Europe, the Northwest Pacific, where it is famously cultivated along the coastal waters of British Columbia, and the states of Washington, Oregon, and California in the US. Equally popular is the small, buttery Kumamoto oyster (from Japan), widely regarded as one of the world's finest oysters. A more salty Atlantic choice is the Blue Point oyster *(C. virginica)*, native to the East Atlantic coast, and Gulf states, but cultivated in beds all along the east coast of the US. Oysters harvested in different waters differ subtly in flavor and shell color. Oyster-tasting is an art, much like wine-tasting, with many gourmet terms for the varied flavors, including tangy, metallic, nutty, grassy, ozone, sweet, cucumber, fruity, iodine, earthy, and coppery. One topic still hotly debated is whether to eat oysters cooked or raw, *au naturel,* or dressed. Eat wild oysters during late spring or early summer, when they are not spawning. Farmed oysters can be eaten all year round.

AVAILABILITY In the shell, smoked, canned.
EAT Cooked: Deep-fry, pan-fry, poach, broil, bake. **Raw:** In the half shell.
FLAVOR PAIRINGS Cooked: Anchovy paste, butter, spinach. **Raw:** Red wine vinegar, Tabasco, lemon juice.
CLASSIC RECIPES Oysters in the half shell with shallot vinegar; oysters Rockefeller; oyster po-boys.

Native oyster
Ostrea edulis
Also called the European flat oyster, it is often served raw on a bed of crushed ice, dressed with lemon juice, Tabasco, and shallot vinegar. Graded by size, from 1 to 4, the largest "royals" can reach 4in (10cm).

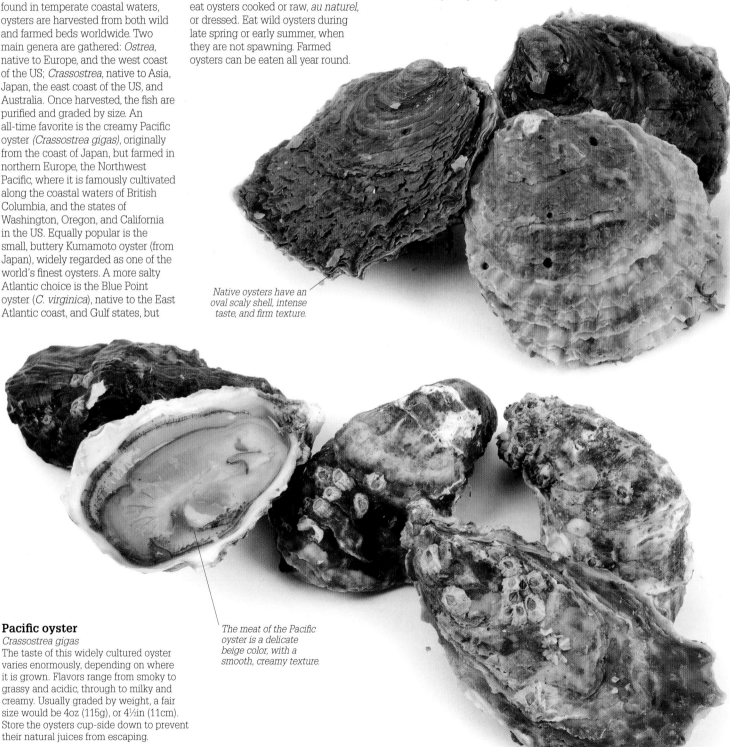

Native oysters have an oval scaly shell, intense taste, and firm texture.

The meat of the Pacific oyster is a delicate beige color, with a smooth, creamy texture.

Pacific oyster
Crassostrea gigas
The taste of this widely cultured oyster varies enormously, depending on where it is grown. Flavors range from smoky to grassy and acidic, through to milky and creamy. Usually graded by weight, a fair size would be 4oz (115g), or 4½in (11cm). Store the oysters cup-side down to prevent their natural juices from escaping.

The head is wide, but it is the meaty tail that is eaten, either pulled off the cooked fish, or preserved in brine.

The large, robust, smooth claws are orange on the underside.

Once immersed in boiling water, the heat-sensitive pigment in the brownish green shell turns a bright cardinal red.

Freshwater crawfish *Astacidae*

Also called crayfish (in the UK), écrevisse (France), and camarón (Spain), the crawfish is a freshwater crustacean related to the lobsterette (see below). Caught mainly in fresh waters, many species are harvested in the US, where they feature in the Cajun cuisine of Louisiana. They also thrive in the lakes and rivers of New Zealand, East Asia, and Europe and are popular in France and Scandinavia. Most crawfish have a segmented body, varying in color from chocolate-brown to sandy-yellow. Equally variable in size, crawfish range from 3–12in (7.5–30cm), depending on the species. They are quite feisty, but it is impractical to band their claws. Handle carefully to avoid a sharp nip. Many crawfish caught in the wild are hand-gathered by turning over rocks in streams and farm dams.

SUSTAINABILITY Some Australian cousins, including the West Australian marron (*Cherax tenuimanus*) and the yabby (*C. destructor*), have been farmed for an overstretched market. The crawfish found in the UK faced sustainability issues because of a virus. The American signal crawfish was introduced but it's a very invasive species. Alternatives include responsibly sourced langoustine.

AVAILABILITY Whole, most often live; frozen tails; cooked.

EAT Cooked: Boil and sauté.

FLAVOR PAIRINGS Butter, garlic, lemon, cream, tomatoes, parsley.

CLASSIC RECIPES Crawfish jambalaya; crawfish étouffée.

Signal crawfish
Pacifastacus leniusculus
This crawfish is native to North America, where it thrives in freshwater ponds, lakes, rivers, and streams. It is a robust creature and easy to farm. As the crawfish are not huge, just 4–6in (10–15cm), serve around 12 to 15 per person, with lots of melted butter and bread.

Lobsterette *Nephropidae*

Lobsterettes are mini-lobsters, much like prawns, but with minuscule claws. Many species live on the muddy or sandy sea floor of the world's oceans. Commonly known as Italian scampi, popular varieties include the Dublin Bay prawn (*Nephrops norvegicus*), and Florida lobsterette (*Nephropsis aculeata*). They are caught commonly along the West Atlantic and East Atlantic coasts, from Iceland in the north to Morocco in the south. For the European market, especially France and the Mediterranean, where they are a popular seafood, lobsterettes are harvested around the British Isles, and then exported. Much like prawns in appearance, most live lobsterettes are amber-rose, or coral-colored. Unusually, they do not change color much when cooked, which can be confusing. Look instead at the tail, which curls under the body; and at the flesh on the underside, which turns from translucent to opaque.

SUSTAINABILITY There is a minimum landing size in place to prevent overuse. Look for responsibly sourced Dublin Bay prawns.

AVAILABILITY Fresh: Whole live, raw, cooked. **Frozen:** Whole, raw, cooked; also tails, breaded for scampi.

EAT Cooked: Boil, roast, pan-fry or as scampi, deep-fry, poach.

FLAVOR PAIRINGS Lemon, basil, sage, butter, garlic.

CLASSIC RECIPES Scampi Provençale; deep-fried scampi and chips.

Dublin Bay prawn
Nephrops norvegicus
Also known as nephrop, Norway lobster, and langoustine, this prawn has recently become prized for its sweet, tender meat, and now fetches a high price. Whole langoustine can pose a challenge on the dinner plate. Traditionally, the claws are cracked and opened, then the meat prized out with a lobster pick. As the tail can be sharp, it is best pinched until the underside cracks, exposing the meat.

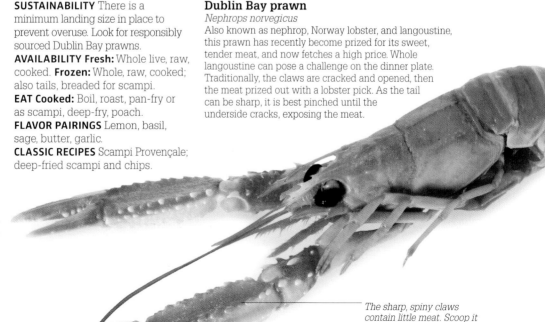

The sharp, spiny claws contain little meat. Scoop it out with a toothpick, and break up the claws for stock.

Rock lobster *Palinuridae*

Unlike "true" clawed lobsters, rock lobsters (also known as spiny lobster) lack claws. Instead they have a rocky carapace (head), and short, sharp spines running the length of their body. Some species also have a distinctive orange-brown shell, flecked with green, yellow, and blue spots, which intensify in color when cooked. Also known as crawfish or crayfish, especially in Australasia, rock lobsters thrive along rocky coasts below the tidal zone, hiding in crevices and caverns. Typically found in the Western Atlantic, from North Carolina to Brazil, and in the Gulf of Mexico and the Caribbean Sea, most are caught in the tropical and subtropical waters of the northern hemisphere and in some cold waters of the southern hemisphere. They are harvested and sold to around 90 countries worldwide, and valued as a delicacy in their own right. Although some taste less sweet than true lobster, many have particularly succulent and dense tail meat. If overcooked, however, they can become tough and fibrous.

AVAILABILITY Fresh and frozen, whole and tails.

EAT Cooked: Whole tails: Boil, steam, deep-fry, broil. Tail meat: Dice and stir-fry, add to soups and stews.
FLAVOR PAIRINGS Chile, garlic, lemon, olive oil, butter.
CLASSIC RECIPES Boiled with lemon and garlic; grilled rock lobster.

Rock lobster
Palinurus elephas
Although fairly large, about 16in (40cm), these shellfish lack the fleshy claws of true lobsters. Instead, the dense, sweet meat typical of the species is concentrated in the tail shell, although some meat can be extracted from the legs.

The legs of a lobster contain sweet juice that can be sucked from the shell.

The claws do not contain as much white meat as those of clawed lobsters.

A lobster uses its long antennae to navigate its way around the murky ocean floor.

The carapace is slightly compressed in this variety.

American lobster ▶
Homarus americanus
Also known as the Atlantic or Maine lobster, this traditionally large and meaty shellfish can grow to at least 2ft (60cm), and take seven years to reach 1lb (450g). An ideal weight for a main dish is 1lb 10oz (750g) or 2¼lb (1kg), before the shell grows too thick and heavy.

Lobster

Lobster is prized worldwide as a luxury food. Many lobster families populate the oceans of the world. Classified as invertebrates, with a hard, protective shell, lobsters live in burrows, or crevices in rocks, mud, and sand, feeding on molluscs and other crustaceans. A lobster's body is made of several sections: a carapace (head), and tail shell with legs, swimlets, and, in some species, claws. Like crabs and other arthropods, lobsters molt their shells in order to grow. For the chef, lobsters come in two main types: clawed (see below) and clawless (see facing page). Among the Nephropidae family several members are clawed, including the European, American, and Canadian lobsters, and the Dublin Bay prawn (or langoustine). Both the European and American varieties are extensively farmed and harvested from the wild to feed the appetites of Europe, the US, and

Canada. Most are caught by one-way baited traps and pots. Many American lobsters are exported to Japan where they are also prized as a delicacy. The European lobster, rather less abundant than its American cousin, is usually more expensive. It is often wondered which of the two provides the best flavor. When served in a classic dish, such as lobster Thermidor, it is hard to tell the difference. Typically, the tail meat of most lobsters is sweet, succulent, dense, and highly valued. On harvesting, lobsters usually have their claws "banded", which makes them easier to handle and curbs their naturally aggressive and cannibalistic

behavior when captive. However, if banded for too long, the claw meat will start to atrophy.

SUSTAINABILITY Most American lobster from Nova Scotia and Newfoundland has to be a minimum size when landed. The size is measured along the carapace.

AVAILABILITY Whole: Live and cooked. **Frozen:** Cooked whole and frozen, extracted from the shell. Canned.

EAT Live: Freeze briefly or stun before boiling. **Cooked:** Boiled – 10 minutes per 1lb (450g); broiled, baked, both extracted from the shell and in bisque.

FLAVOR PAIRINGS Cream, butter, Parmesan, tarragon, parsley, chervil, paprika, white wine.

CLASSIC RECIPES Lobster Thermidor; lobster Newburg; lobster bisque; dressed lobster.

The large and heavy crusher claw is filled with dense, sweet meat that can be extracted whole to garnish a dish.

Once caught, strong rubber bands secure the claws so the lobster cannot attack.

Slipper lobster *Scyllaridae*

Colorfully named the shovel-nosed lobster, Spanish lobster, sand lobster, or locust lobster, slipper lobsters lack the meaty claws of "true" lobsters (much like the spiny lobster). Various species thrive on the sea floor in warm waters worldwide, mostly around Thailand, Singapore, and Australia. Close and commercially important cousins include the Moreton Bay bug (found in northern Australian waters), and the Balmain bug (found off the south coasts of Australia). Most slipper lobsters have a sweet, delicate, mellow taste and medium texture, firm to the bite.

AVAILABILITY Whole and tails.

EAT Cooked: Boil, steam, poach, deep-fry, grill.
FLAVOR PAIRINGS Butter, herbs such as tarragon, chives, and dill, garlic, citrus, lemongrass, soy sauce, chile.
CLASSIC RECIPES Seafood platter; grilled bug tails with garlic butter.

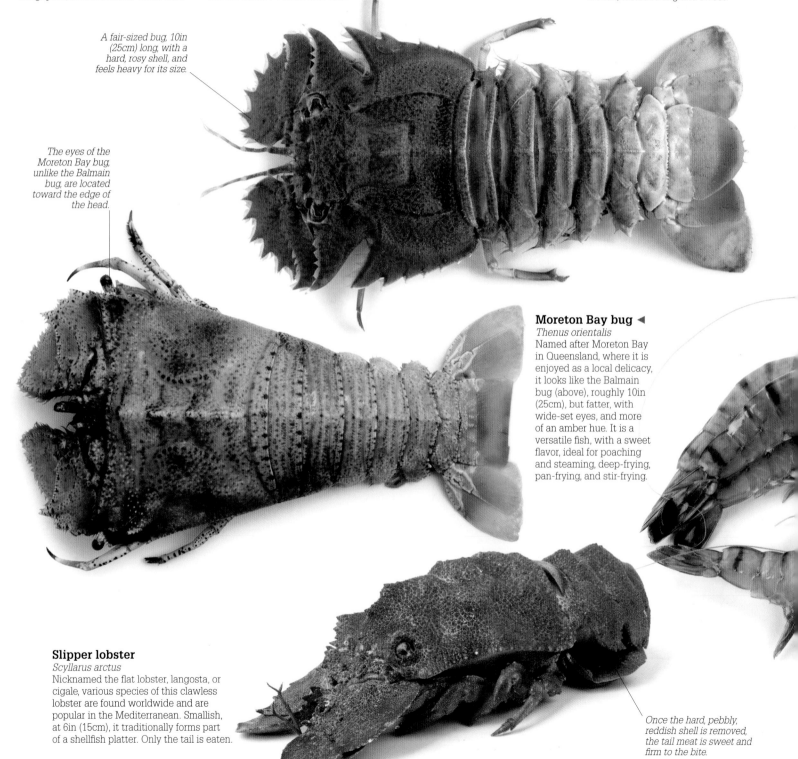

A fair-sized bug, 10in (25cm) long, with a hard, rosy shell, and feels heavy for its size.

The eyes of the Moreton Bay bug, unlike the Balmain bug, are located toward the edge of the head.

Balmain bug ▼
Ibacus peronii
Sometimes called a flapjack, or mud bug, this tasty Australian shellfish is especially popular in Sydney. Its meat, found only in the tail, tastes strong and sweet.

Moreton Bay bug ◄
Thenus orientalis
Named after Moreton Bay in Queensland, where it is enjoyed as a local delicacy, it looks like the Balmain bug (above), roughly 10in (25cm), but fatter, with wide-set eyes, and more of an amber hue. It is a versatile fish, with a sweet flavor, ideal for poaching and steaming, deep-frying, pan-frying, and stir-frying.

Slipper lobster
Scyllarus arctus
Nicknamed the flat lobster, langosta, or cigale, various species of this clawless lobster are found worldwide and are popular in the Mediterranean. Smallish, at 6in (15cm), it traditionally forms part of a shellfish platter. Only the tail is eaten.

Once the hard, pebbly, reddish shell is removed, the tail meat is sweet and firm to the bite.

Prawn and Shrimp

Prawns and shrimps thrive in all waters, cold and warm, fresh and marine. Widely popular, especially in Australia, the US, Europe, and Japan, prawns are extensively harvested and farmed. Varied use of the terms "prawn" and "shrimp" can be confusing. In the US, "shrimp" often means the same as "prawn." In the UK and Australia, "prawn" mostly refers to warm-water species, such as the giant black tiger prawn (*Penaeus monodon*), as well as some fair-sized cold-water species, such as the deep-water prawn (*Pandalus borealis*), while "shrimp" refers to

smaller species, such as the brown shrimp (*Crangon crangon*). The largest prawns are the warm-water, or tropical, variety, at least 14in (35cm), compared to cold-water shrimps, about 2in (5cm).

SUSTAINABILITY Tropical shrimp provide more than three-quarters of the world's supply. Found mainly in the Pacific and Indian oceans, they are harvested or farmed by Latin America, Australia, China, Vietnam, Sri Lanka, and Thailand. Tropical shrimp farms can cause damage to the environment. Mangrove swamps are flooded to make a site suitable

for farming. Toxic chemicals ward off disease and, after a few years, the farm becomes too polluted to sustain more farming. Some farms, however, have adopted responsible practices; check the label. The smaller, slower-growing, cold-water shrimp, found mainly in the Atlantic, Arctic, and Pacific oceans, are caught by the US, UK, Canada, Greenland, Denmark, and Iceland. Many fisheries have a minimum mesh size, as trawling for shrimp creates a huge bycatch.

AVAILABILITY Cold-water: Fresh and frozen; cooked as crevettes (poached). **Warm-water:** Cooked

and frozen; peeled and soaked.

EAT Cold-water: Serve defrosted as part of a salad; or serve as potted shrimps. Use the shells for stock and flavored butters.

Warm-water: Pan-fry, stir-fry, deep-fry, broil, grill, bake. For a sweet, roasted flavor, pan-fry in oil with vegetables. For a subtler flavor, simmer in water.

FLAVOR PAIRINGS Mayonnaise, capers, paprika, pepper, lemon juice.

CLASSIC RECIPES Cold-water: Shrimp cocktail; avocado, pear, and prawns. **Warm-water:** *Gambas pil pil* (garlic prawn); shrimp tempura.

Crevette rose
When poached, the white Central American shrimp (right) is often called a *crevette* (French for "shrimp"). It is wonderfully sweet and dense and makes an attractive rosy garnish to paella. Confusingly, crevette rose is also the name of a prawn from the Palaemonidae family.

Giant black tiger prawn ◄
Penaeus monodon
A meaty tropical prawn, which can reach 14in (35cm), it is harvested globally, and farmed extensively. When buying, check how responsibly the fish have been sourced and choose organically farmed. To grill, snip off the legs and antennae; then twist and pull out the tail section. The taste is mellow, honeyed, and succulent.

Pacific white shrimp
Litopenaeus vannamei
A popular shrimp species farmed in both Latin and South American countries, these white prawns are harvested, graded, and frozen for sale. Often large, up to 10in (25cm), they are meaty and sweet. The shells provide a tasty addition to shellfish stock.

Brown shrimp
Crangon crangon
Although measuring no more than 2in (5cm), this common shrimp is regarded as quite a delicacy, fetching a higher price than larger, warm-water species. Caught in the East Atlantic, it looks transparent when live, but turns amber-brown on cooking. Brown shrimps are traditionally served as potted shrimps. Although fiddly to peel, they are sweet, succulent, and absolutely delicious.

Deep-water prawn
Pandalus borealis
Valued for its sweet, mild taste, and succulent texture, it is also called the Greenland prawn in the UK, and the northern red shrimp or Alaskan pink shrimp in the US. A fair size for a cold-water prawn, at 2½in (6cm), it is always cooked on landing, and frozen for sale. The shells make a tasty stock, ideal for pilaf, risotto, and soup. They can also be processed together with butter, and sieved to make prawn butter.

Crab

Crabs come in all sizes and are a popular crustacean on many continents. The wide availability of crab (they are found in oceans worldwide) and the variety of species makes them a favorite in many countries. Crabs come from a selection of groups including the Cancridae, Grapsidae, Portunidae, Lithodoidae, and Majidae families. A crab has a carapace or cart as a main shell, legs, and in most cases claws, though the size of claws and legs varies from species to species. They periodically molt their shell as they grow—frequently in the first two years of life, and every 1–2 years thereafter. Crab provides two distinct meats: the white meat, found in the claws, legs, and main body, and the brown meat found in the carapace of the crab. As a general rule, the white is often the favored of the two and is more expensive. Brown meat from the carapace is well flavored. Some species are renowned for their white claw meat, specifically the Brown edible crab, Jonah, and Dungeness crab of the Cancridae group. Snow crabs and King crabs have valuable sweet succulent meat in their legs. Male crabs have larger claws and are therefore more valuable, hens are considered to have more intensely flavored brown meat and less white meat and are usually less expensive.

SUSTAINABILITY Many crabs are sustainably sourced, although depending on the species and the area of capture, it can be illegal to land crabs carrying eggs (berries). In some cases, it is illegal to land hen crabs. There is a minimum landing size in place globally for some species, measured width ways across the carapace. For the white meat, alternatives would be responsibly sourced prawns and scallops.

AVAILABILITY Cooked: Whole and claws. **Prepared:** Dressed/hand-picked; processed and pasteurized white and brown meat (usually frozen separately).

EAT Live: Boiling for 15 mins per 1lb 2oz (500g) is usual. **Cooked:** Toss into salads, rechauffé in pasta, rice dishes, and sauté. **Raw:** Sushi.

FLAVOR PAIRINGS Mayonnaise, chile, lemon, parsley, dill, potato, butter, Worcestershire sauce, anchovy paste.

CLASSIC RECIPES Thai crab cakes; chile crab; dressed crab (usually brown edible crab); potted crab (crab paste); pan-fried soft shell crab; Maryland crab cakes.

Blue crab
Callinectes sapidus
Native to the West Atlantic, this crab is seen in both Japanese and European waters. Known as "busters" or "peelers", blue crabs nearing a molting stage are held in tanks, so that once the carapace lifts away revealing the soft, delicate body underneath, they are harvested. The gills, mouth, and stomach sac are removed and the crab is frozen or sold fresh ready for the "soft shell crab" season. Alternatively, meat from these crabs is used for crab cakes, soups, and dips. The fresh season is usually late spring to early summer.

It is known as the "swimmer" crab because of the paddles it has in place of its back legs.

The blue crab can be identified by its beautiful blue claws and an olive brown carapace..

Once cooked, the shell becomes a vivid red. The best meat is found in the legs and claws.

Dungeness crab
Metacarcinus magister
A member of the Cancridae group, the Dungeness crab is found in the Pacific Ocean from Alaska to California, and is the most popular crab in the Pacific Northwest and western Canada. It can measure up to 10in (25cm). It's recognized for its delicate and sweet flavor, and is popular for a seafood platter, served simply with melted butter.

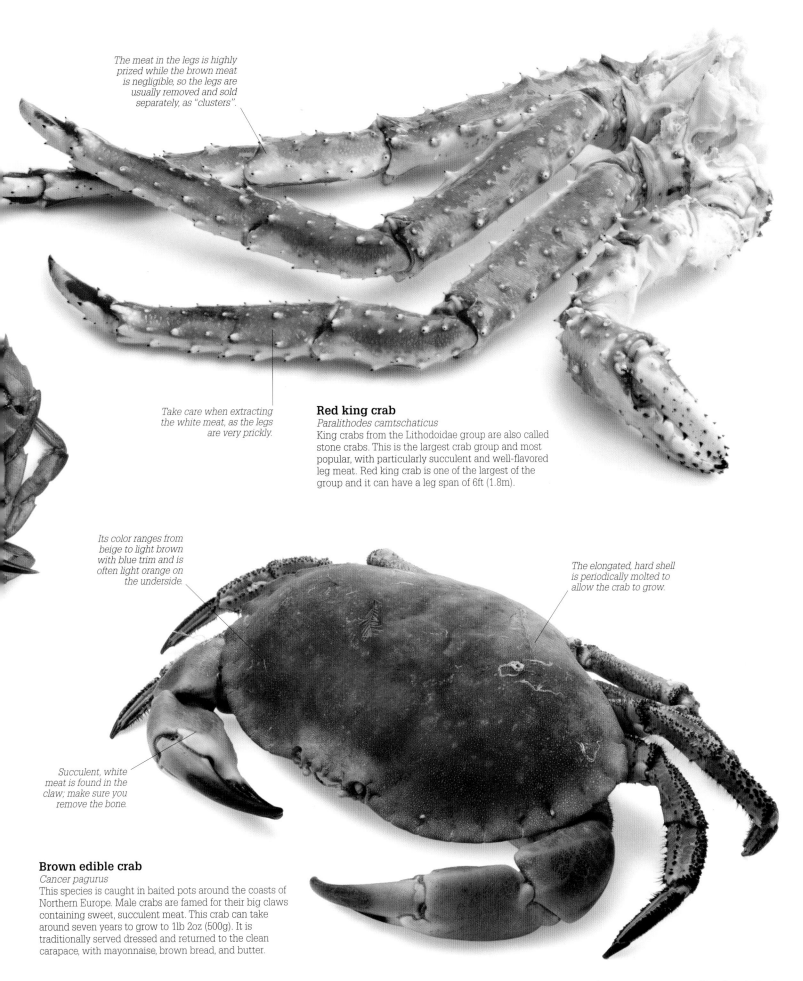

The meat in the legs is highly prized while the brown meat is negligible, so the legs are usually removed and sold separately, as "clusters".

Take care when extracting the white meat, as the legs are very prickly.

Red king crab
Paralithodes camtschaticus
King crabs from the Lithodoidae group are also called stone crabs. This is the largest crab group and most popular, with particularly succulent and well-flavored leg meat. Red king crab is one of the largest of the group and it can have a leg span of 6ft (1.8m).

Its color ranges from beige to light brown with blue trim and is often light orange on the underside.

The elongated, hard shell is periodically molted to allow the crab to grow.

Succulent, white meat is found in the claw; make sure you remove the bone.

Brown edible crab
Cancer pagurus
This species is caught in baited pots around the coasts of Northern Europe. Male crabs are famed for their big claws containing sweet, succulent meat. This crab can take around seven years to grow to 1lb 2oz (500g). It is traditionally served dressed and returned to the clean carapace, with mayonnaise, brown bread, and butter.

Squid *Cephalapod*

Although many species of squid have thrived for centuries in the world's oceans, it is only in recent years that this shellfish has become globally popular. Squid is now quite possibly the most widely consumed seafood, partly due to its availability. The common squid (*Loligo vulgaris*), popularly nicknamed "ink fish", is probably the best known. It ranges widely in size from a baby squid, measuring ¾in (2cm), to much larger specimens, some growing as long as 31–35in (80–90cm). The size of a squid is what determines the cooking method—whether fast or slow. The smaller the squid, the quicker the cooking; the larger the squid, the longer it will need in the pot. Squid is made up of a long tubular body (mantle), which, once prepared, is called a "tube". The body is flanked at one end by a pair of wing-like fins, which sometimes look like arrows, most famously on the arrow squid (*Nototodarus gouldi*). The live squid is covered in a reddish, purple or coffee-brown membrane, sometimes with intricate brown "veins" or markings, providing camouflage. The membrane is thin and easily pulled away, especially after the squid has been packed in ice and jostled around in its box. Attached to the head are 10 tentacles, two long and eight smaller ones. In the center of the tentacles is the hard beak (mouth-piece). The ink, after which the "ink-fish" is named, is contained in a small, silver ink sac in the tube. Running up the middle of the squid is an internal shell (or "pen"), which resembles plastic, and should be pulled away before cooking (see page 282). The flesh of a good-quality squid is white, turning pink as it decomposes.

AVAILABILITY Whole: Fresh, dried, smoked, and canned. Parts: Frozen tubes or rings; sometimes part of a mixed seafood cocktail.

EAT Cooked: Pan-fry, stir-fry, deep-fry, braise, or sauté. For rings or small pieces, broil or poach. Whole tubes, flattened out into a sheet and scored, these taste excellent when grilled. The tube can also be stuffed with a savory breadcrumb mix, couscous, quinoa, or rice. Choose a fair-sized squid, usually with a tube that is no more than 3–4in (7.5–10cm) long. Prepare it, and cut it into rectangles or rings; or leave whole, if grilling. **Raw:** In sushi.

FLAVOR PAIRINGS Chile, olive oil, breadcrumbs, lemon juice, garlic, scallions, mayonnaise.

CLASSIC RECIPES Fried calamari; squid cooked in ink; squid stuffed with rice; Sichuan-fried squid.

Common squid
Loligo vulgaris
The "ink fish" has gained a reputation for being tough and chewy, but is only ever so if it is overcooked. In a hot pan, the meat takes no time at all. At its best, it tastes tender and mellow, with a subtle, distinctive flavor.

The tough, wing-like fins are best either finely sliced or stir-fried, or reserved to flavor stock.

The long, fleshy mantle is often cut into rings. It's tasty and succulent if not overcooked.

The mottled skin is best peeled off and reserved for stock, as it toughens and shrinks around the flesh when cooked.

Eight arms are relatively short, while two are longer, and used to catch prey.

Octopus *Celphalapod*

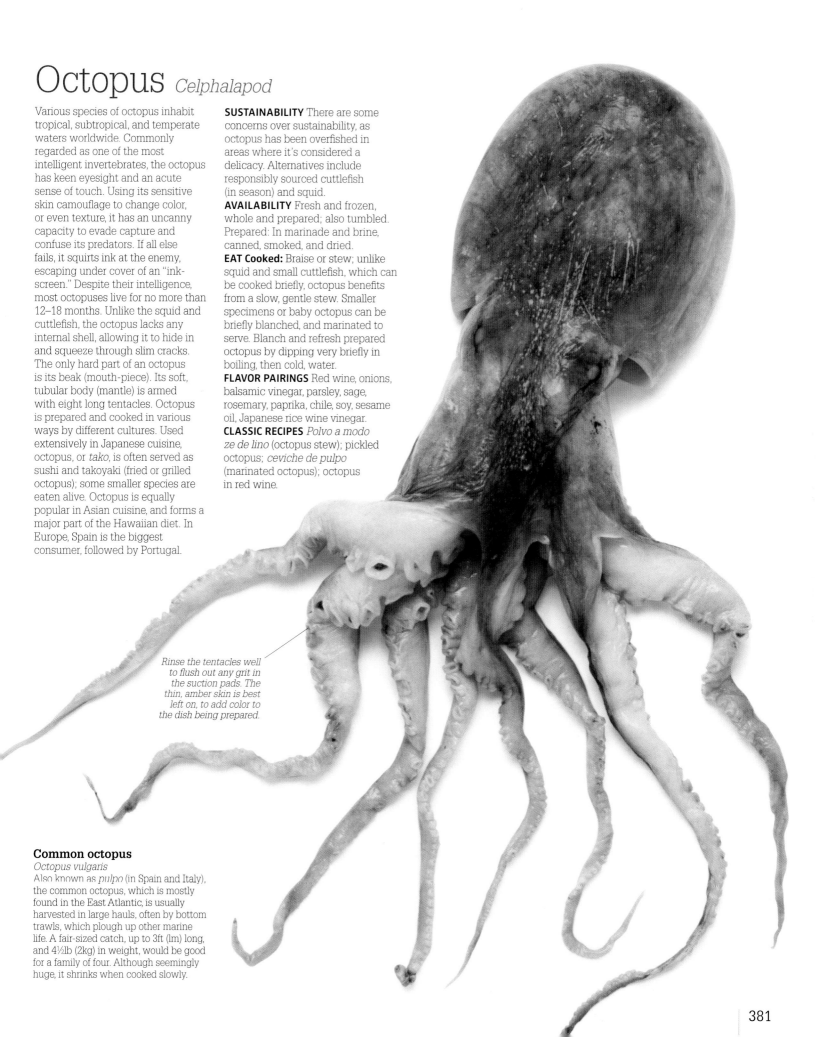

Various species of octopus inhabit tropical, subtropical, and temperate waters worldwide. Commonly regarded as one of the most intelligent invertebrates, the octopus has keen eyesight and an acute sense of touch. Using its sensitive skin camouflage to change color, or even texture, it has an uncanny capacity to evade capture and confuse its predators. If all else fails, it squirts ink at the enemy, escaping under cover of an "ink-screen." Despite their intelligence, most octopuses live for no more than 12–18 months. Unlike the squid and cuttlefish, the octopus lacks any internal shell, allowing it to hide in and squeeze through slim cracks. The only hard part of an octopus is its beak (mouth-piece). Its soft, tubular body (mantle) is armed with eight long tentacles. Octopus is prepared and cooked in various ways by different cultures. Used extensively in Japanese cuisine, octopus, or *tako*, is often served as sushi and takoyaki (fried or grilled octopus); some smaller species are eaten alive. Octopus is equally popular in Asian cuisine, and forms a major part of the Hawaiian diet. In Europe, Spain is the biggest consumer, followed by Portugal.

SUSTAINABILITY There are some concerns over sustainability, as octopus has been overfished in areas where it's considered a delicacy. Alternatives include responsibly sourced cuttlefish (in season) and squid.

AVAILABILITY Fresh and frozen, whole and prepared; also tumbled. Prepared: In marinade and brine, canned, smoked, and dried.

EAT Cooked: Braise or stew; unlike squid and small cuttlefish, which can be cooked briefly, octopus benefits from a slow, gentle stew. Smaller specimens or baby octopus can be briefly blanched, and marinated to serve. Blanch and refresh prepared octopus by dipping very briefly in boiling, then cold, water.

FLAVOR PAIRINGS Red wine, onions, balsamic vinegar, parsley, sage, rosemary, paprika, chile, soy, sesame oil, Japanese rice wine vinegar.

CLASSIC RECIPES *Polvo a modo ze de lino* (octopus stew); pickled octopus; *ceviche de pulpo* (marinated octopus); octopus in red wine.

Rinse the tentacles well to flush out any grit in the suction pads. The thin, amber skin is best left on, to add color to the dish being prepared.

Common octopus
Octopus vulgaris
Also known as *pulpo* (in Spain and Italy), the common octopus, which is mostly found in the East Atlantic, is usually harvested in large hauls, often by bottom trawls, which plough up other marine life. A fair-sized catch, up to 3ft (1m) long, and 4½lb (2kg) in weight, would be good for a family of four. Although seemingly huge, it shrinks when cooked slowly.

Cuttlefish *Cephalopod*

Popularly nicknamed "ink fish" for its ability to squirt ink at its enemies, the cuttlefish is often the tastiest but quite possibly the least appreciated member of the cephalopod group. Various species thrive in the depths of the world's oceans, except for North American waters. Cuttlefish are caught for their internal shell (cuttlebone) and the copious ink they produce to confuse their predators. The ink is harvested and pasteurized for commercial use, for dying pasta black, and for cooking: typically, risotto nero. Cuttlefish are mostly caught by trawl, and as bait for recreational fishing. With a wonderfully sweet, seafood taste, and firm, meaty texture, cuttlefish is enjoyed as a delicacy in many countries. If pan-fried for more than a minute, though, it will toughen and lose its translucency. The fish is particularly prized in the cuisines of China, Japan, Korea, Spain, and Italy.
AVAILABILITY Whole: Unprepared. **Frozen:** Ink and shell sold separately. **Preserved:** Dried.
EAT Cooked: Slice the body thinly and pan-fry, deep-fry, or bake. The legs and tentacles are best stewed slowly and extensively.

CLASSIC RECIPES Risotto nero; chile cuttlefish; soupies krasates (cuttlefish in wine); Tuscan cuttlefish salad.
FLAVOR PAIRINGS Red wine, garlic, red onions, balsamic vinegar, chile, lime.

Common cuttlefish
Sepia officinalis
Native to the East Atlantic and Mediterranean, it is one of the largest cuttlefish, at about 16in (40cm). The tough tentacles need to be tenderized in a slow stew or braised.

The frilly fins of the cuttlefish peel away with the flesh. They give shellfish stock a wonderful flavor.

Sea urchin *Echinoidae*

Prickly and uninviting, sea urchins thrive on the ocean floor. More than 500 species exist, most are edible. Sea urchins feature in Japanese, Italian, Spanish, and classic French cuisine. The edible part of the urchin is its roe, which needs to be carefully extracted. The entrance into a sea urchin is on its underside, through its mouth, which can be opened with a knife. First the viscera should be removed; then the creamy orange roe (attached to the top of the shell) can be scooped out with a spoon (see page 281). The resultant treat is small and relatively expensive, but offers an intense, creamy taste, much like seaweed. In Japan, the urchins, or uni, are eaten fresh with sushi, and fermented to form sea urchin paste.
SUSTAINABILITY In some cultures, especially Japan and the Mediterranean, sea urchins are popular as a delicacy, which has led to overfishing. There is no real alternative to sea urchin.

AVAILABILITY Whole and, in some countries, extracted from the shell.
EAT Usually raw, although they do add flavor to a creamy fish sauce.
FLAVOR PAIRINGS Lemon.
CLASSIC RECIPES *Linguine con ricci di mare*; sea urchin omelet.

Sea urchin roe
Pried out of its prickly shell, sea urchin roe is often enjoyed raw, but is equally delicious cooked. Add it to a cream, white wine, and fish stock for the perfect addition to pan-fried fish, such as turbot.

Sea urchin roe (or "tongues") have a umami (essence of loveliness in Japanese) that is delicately salty and rich.

Sea urchin
Echinus esculentus
Globular, pink, and spiky, the common sea urchin found in shallow waters off the British Isles can grow up to 6in (15cm) in size. Sea urchins are a challenge to prepare, but the seaweed flavor is strong and creamy—never pungent or fishy.

To avoid the spines, either split the urchin in half, or cut out the central beak and scoop out the middle with a teaspoon.

Peel away the outer membrane to reveal the tough, pure white body beneath.

These eight pairs of arms and two longer tentacles are used to capture prey and can be retracted completely into the body.

Goose barnacle
Lepadidae

The goose barnacle takes its name from its striking long, goose-like neck. Like other crustaceans, it lives attached to exposed rocks in many coastal waters, except in the Arctic. Barnacle meat comes from the creature's soft protruding body, covered in thick skin. Before cooking, the tough skin needs to be removed with the help of a nail; or it can be peeled away after cooking. The barnacle has a sweet seafood taste much like crab and crawfish. Cooked to perfection, it is succulent and tender; if overcooked, it is tough and rubbery. In Portugal and Spain, goose barnacle is prized as the iconic delicacy *percebes*.
AVAILABILITY Usually whole.
EAT Cooked: Steamed or poached; only 2–3 minutes in boiling salted water with a bay leaf and lemon.
FLAVOR PAIRINGS Lemon, butter, garlic.

Before cooking, remove the chalky (calcareous) plates and peel the skin away.

Goose barnacle
Lepas anatifera
A sought-after delicacy in several Mediterranean countries, goose barnacles are often enjoyed simply steamed over stock, then served straight from the shell. Measuring about 10in (25cm), two or three provide a good helping.

Sea cucumber
Stichopodidae

Although commonly found in the world's oceans, sea cucumbers are something of an acquired taste, with a rather salty, savory flavor and chewy, gelatinous texture. Reflecting their nickname "sea-slug", they shuffle slowly across the sea floor, scavenging for food. After being caught, the fish are gutted, boiled, salted, and dried, for long-term storage. To prepare, rehydrate the fish by soaking in water, and tenderize with extensive simmering. In China, the fish is a delicacy, slowly braised in rice wine and ginger. Sea cucumbers are also popular in the Philippines and parts of Europe, especially Barcelona.
SUSTAINABILITY Sea cucumbers have been overfished in the Mediterranean and other seas. Alternatives include whelks, which have a similar texture.
AVAILABILITY Whole, usually dried.
EAT Cooked: Soak and simmer, or braise.

FLAVOR PAIRINGS Southern European/Spanish flavors: Pil-pil chile, garlic, parsley.
CLASSIC RECIPES Braised sea cucumber with mushrooms; braised espardenyes.

Sea cucumber
Stichopus regalis
Enjoyed for centuries by fishermen, it is prized as a delicacy, eaten fresh in Japan, and dried in China. Typically slug-like in shape and size, it grows up to 8in (20cm).

Feather-like tentacles sweep up food from the sea floor.

Rows of tubular feet have tiny suction caps that help it move along the sea floor.

Some sea cucumbers discharge sticky threads from their base when they are attacked.

Hot-smoked fish

Hot-smoking is a technique of preservation in which fish or seafood is brined or salted for a short period, allowed to dry briefly, then smoked and cooked in a temperature-controlled kiln. An initial smoking takes place at a low temperature. The duration of this phase is dictated by the producer and the type of fish. Once the fish is impregnated with smoke, it is smoked for a second time at a higher temperature, which cooks the fish. Fish often treated in this way include mackerel, trout, and salmon, and shellfish include mussels and oysters. Hot-smoked fish has a lightly salted, densely smoked flavor, an opaque appearance, and a moist texture. Although products will keep for a number of days, hot-smoked fish generally have a shorter shelf life than cold-smoked fish.

BUY Choose fish that is moist, but not slimy, and has a strong, but pleasant aroma.

STORE Keep refrigerated, but not directly over ice. The salt added during the smoking process automatically gives the fish a slightly extended shelf life.

EAT Hot-smoked products can be eaten immediately or added to other dishes. Because they have already been cooked, care needs to be taken when reheating them or adding them to a hot dish. Serve them piping hot, but do not overheat, because it will toughen and change the texture.

FLAVOR PAIRINGS Horseradish, cream and sour cream, honey, soy sauce and sesame oil, dill, cilantro.

CLASSIC RECIPES Beef and smoked oyster pie; smoked mackerel pâté; smoked eel with beet and potato salad; smoked mackerel fishcakes.

Remove the sprat's head and peel away its skin to reveal a fillet with an excellent flavor.

Smoked sprats ▲
A popular treat and delicacy in Germany, Sweden, Poland, Estonia, Finland, and Russia, smoked sprats are also known by their Swedish name of brisling. They are smoked whole and, because of their soft bones, usually eaten whole—diehard fans may eat the head, too. The smoking process dries them somewhat and gives them a robust flavor.

Arbroath smokie
This is a speciality from Arbroath in Scotland. Gutted, small haddock, heads removed, are tied into pairs at the tail using locally sourced jute, dry-salted for an hour, and then densely smoked. Served as they are, or used in mousses and smoked haddock pâté, Arbroath smokies have an intense flavor.

The salting process makes the texture of the herring quite dry.

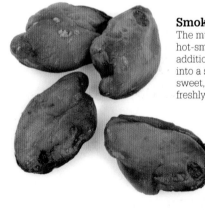

Smoked mussels
The mussels are cooked, brined, and hot-smoked. They are delicious as an addition to a seafood platter, or tossed into a salad. Smoked mussels are firm, sweet, and tasty. They are available freshly smoked or canned in oil.

Smoked oysters ▶
Firm and verging on tough, brined and cooked oysters are kiln-smoked for this speciality, which is popular in Asian cooking. Most are canned in oil; also available freshly smoked or vacuum-packed. The smoking process masks a lot of their natural taste. Use in beef and smoked oyster pie, or blend with cream cheese for a dip.

Smoked eel ▲
Firm and slightly rubbery, smoked eel is considered a delicacy, particularly in The Netherlands, so it is expensive. European and New Zealand eels are cleaned, dry-salted, and hot-smoked. The smoke cuts through the oily texture of the fish.

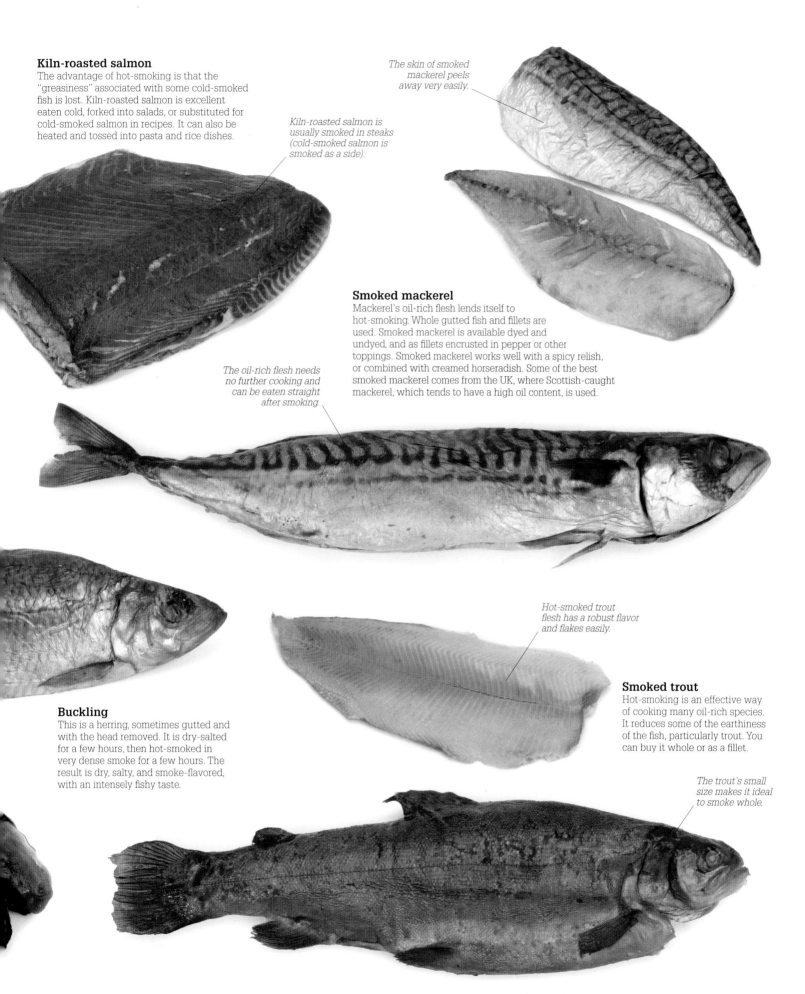

Kiln-roasted salmon

The advantage of hot-smoking is that the "greasiness" associated with some cold-smoked fish is lost. Kiln-roasted salmon is excellent eaten cold, forked into salads, or substituted for cold-smoked salmon in recipes. It can also be heated and tossed into pasta and rice dishes.

The skin of smoked mackerel peels away very easily.

Kiln-roasted salmon is usually smoked in steaks (cold-smoked salmon is smoked as a side).

Smoked mackerel

Mackerel's oil-rich flesh lends itself to hot-smoking. Whole gutted fish and fillets are used. Smoked mackerel is available dyed and undyed, and as fillets encrusted in pepper or other toppings. Smoked mackerel works well with a spicy relish, or combined with creamed horseradish. Some of the best smoked mackerel comes from the UK, where Scottish-caught mackerel, which tends to have a high oil content, is used.

The oil-rich flesh needs no further cooking and can be eaten straight after smoking.

Hot-smoked trout flesh has a robust flavor and flakes easily.

Smoked trout

Hot-smoking is an effective way of cooking many oil-rich species. It reduces some of the earthiness of the fish, particularly trout. You can buy it whole or as a fillet.

Buckling

This is a herring, sometimes gutted and with the head removed. It is dry-salted for a few hours, then hot-smoked in very dense smoke for a few hours. The result is dry, salty, and smoke-flavored, with an intensely fishy taste.

The trout's small size makes it ideal to smoke whole.

Cold-smoked fish

This method of smoking fish takes place over a period of days. The fish is brined, and a relatively heavy salt solution is used in order to extract as much moisture from the fish as possible. Temperature is crucial: the product should not reach more than 84°F (30°C), so as not to cook the flesh or encourage bacterial growth. The fish is smoked for between 1 and 5 days, the flavor becoming richer and more intense as time goes on. Some cold-smoked fish may then be cooked (such as smoked haddock, cod, and pollock). As cold-smoked fish is essentially raw, fish that is not going to be cooked is frozen at 0°F (-18°C) for around 24 hours to destroy parasites that may be present in the fish (this is a legal requirement in some countries). The flavor of smoked fish depends on how long a fish is left salted, and how long it is in the smokehouse. The taste of many fish—such as oily fish—is enhanced by smoking.

BUY Pick fish that looks dry, glossy, and smells smoked but not too strong.

STORE Smoked products have a slightly longer shelf life than fresh fish. They are never placed directly on ice, as with fresh fish, but must be chilled in the refrigerator.

EAT Smoked salmon and more artisanal products (such as smoked swordfish, grouper, and tuna) can simply be sliced and served with a squeeze of lemon juice and bread, or added to more complex dishes.

FLAVOR PAIRINGS Citrus, horseradish, delicate herbs including dill and flat-leaf parsley.

CLASSIC RECIPES Finnan haddock with poached egg; smoked salmon with capers; kedgeree; Cullen skink.

Atlantic smoked salmon

Both Scottish and Irish smoked salmon are considered a delicacy, but the price of wild salmon is prohibitively high, and most smoked Atlantic salmon is now farmed. It may be smoked over peat, applewood, or oak; whisky is also popular. Oak smoke can give an intense taste, peat smoke produces quite a sweet woodiness.

Traditionally, kipper is split down the back and smoked on the bone, but it is also available as a fillet.

Kipper

A kipper is a cold-smoked herring. It is split down the back and cleaned, brined, sometimes dyed, then smoked over sawdust fires. English herrings are often considered the best species of herring for smoking. Many kippers are particularly fine. Kippers can be broiled or jugged (boiling water poured over the fish and left to stand). They have a dense, intensely salty, sweet, and smoky taste—but it varies according to producer.

Finnan haddock

Named after the fishing village of Finnan, this smoked fish is popularly referred to as Finnan haddie, and was once the most popular type of smoked fish. To make it, the haddock is cleaned, the head is removed, then the fish is opened out flat (left on the bone), brined (sometimes with dye), and smoked—traditionally over peat. The taste is similar to that of smoked, undyed haddock. Finnan haddock with poached egg is a breakfast classic in the UK.

Bloater

A bloater is a smoked herring. Whole fish are dry-salted in barrels for several hours, then cold-smoked over smoldering wood to dry the fish, and give it a lightly smoked flavor.

The bloater's skin is easily pulled off to reveal the ready-to-eat flesh under the skin.

Dyed haddock fillets are excellent for kedgeree, as the color shows up well against the white rice.

Smoked haddock fillets

Dyed fillets (soaked in brine colored with tartrazine) and undyed fillets are available. A natural dye made with turmeric and annatto powder is now used by some producers. Dyed haddock can be slightly saltier than undyed, but this depends on the producer. Haddock is a sweet fish and smoking suits it well. Best poached in milk to draw out excess saltiness.

During the process, an exterior crust is formed called the pellicle. This is strongly smoked and dry. It is sometimes trimmed away and sold as smoked salmon trimmings, which are perfect for pâté.

Undyed haddock is a pale straw color. Avoid fish that has pink flesh and looks wet, as this is a sign of deterioration.

Smoked haddock is traditionally smoked with the skin on, unlike other white fish.

Smoked swordfish

For this product, swordfish loin is cold-smoked. It is served raw, thinly sliced, and has a delicate, subtle flavor. Swordfish is quite challenging to smoke, because it can take on a bitter aftertaste and be overpowered by the flavor of the wood used to smoke it.

Smoked halibut is best sliced thinly, as the fish has a slightly dry and firm-textured flesh.

Smoked halibut

Halibut has a delicate taste and the process of smoking it can overpower the natural flavor of the fish. Smoked halibut is available as a fillet or sliced. Serve the raw slices with a simple garnish of dill and a wedge of lemon.

Salted fish and Dried fish

The earliest form of preservation was to dry fish in the sun and wind. Other fish were preserved in brine or dry-salted. In the Mediterranean, eels, anchovies, sardines, herring, tuna, and roe were commonly salted. One of the earliest dried and salted fish, cod, was caught by boats that travelled long distances to fish it. The cod was cleaned, air-dried, and packed in brine or salt for the voyage home. The process of salting fish is influenced by the weather, the size and species of fish, and the quality of the salt used. The fish must be completely saturated with salt, or "struck through", to ensure that it will be safe to eat. There are two methods of salting—placing the fish directly in a brine or packing it in salt, which in turn creates its own brine as moisture is drawn from the fish. The amount of salt used differs from one fish and product to another. Fish may also be dried to remove moisture content but left unsalted. Stockfish is unsalted fish, usually cod, which is dried by the sun and wind on wooden racks, or in specially adapted drying houses. Other species of white fish, including ling, tusk, gray mullet, bonito, and saithe are dried, as are some shellfish, such as cuttlefish, squid, oysters, shrimp, and scallops. Some salted and dried fish are rehydrated, by soaking in several changes of water, to draw out as much of the salt as possible, and then cooked as a fresh fish (the flavor is more intense than that of a fresh fish and a gentle, lingering saltiness is evident). Some fish, such as Bombay duck and cuttlefish, are served dried.

CUTS Whole (gutted), split whole fish on the bone, shredded fish strips.

EAT Poach, pan-fry, or broil.

FLAVOR PAIRINGS Olive oil, garlic, orange, capers, onion, parsley, milk, coconut.

CLASSIC RECIPES Salt fish and achee; salt fishcakes; bacalao; brandade de morue (salt cod purée).

Salted anchovies

One of the most popular salted fish, anchovies are also brined. Intensely salty, they are often used to top pizzas or to garnish Mediterranean dishes such as salade Niçoise. They can be soaked briefly in milk before use to remove some of the saltiness; this softens and rounds the flavor.

Dried tuna loin is firm and dry, and best shaved or grated. It tastes very strong so only a little is needed to flavor a dish.

Maatjes herrings are usually eaten whole and unadorned, or simply with bread. They have a sweet, intense flavor.

Dried tuna loin

Mosciame del tonno is a delicacy in Italy and Spain (where it is also called mojama). Strips of tuna loin are salted and sun-dried, to make a firm slab that resembles a dried meat. It has a rich, meaty flavor and may be grated to add to pasta and salads.

Maatjes herring

Hailing from Amsterdam, maatjes herring is also known as virgin herring, as it is made from young fish that have not produced roe. The fish, caught around Norway and Denmark, are soused (soaked in a mild brine). They are only partly gutted, as the offal is key to the success of the curing process. A similar product from Germany is made using more intense brine.

Bombay duck

The small bummalo fish is native to Southeast Asia. It is eaten fresh in India, where it is usually fried to serve as a side dish. It may also be dried in strips and called Bombay duck. It has a strong, aromatic, fishy flavor.

Bombay duck is served in its dried state as an appetizer. It has a strong, hearty taste.

Dried shrimp

Unshelled shrimp, lightly salted and dried, are used extensively in China, Southeast Asia, and parts of Africa. They are usually added to a dish to give it a depth of flavor.

These have a distinctive smell that is strongly seafood-like and also sweet. Soak prior to use, or use dry as a seasoning.

These scallops have a strong flavor and very dry texture. Use dry or soak in water to rehydrate.

Dried scallops

Dried scallops are used extensively in the cuisine of the Far East. One popular recipe is as part of a spicy chile salsa. They add a dynamic seafood flavor and a certain sweetness to a dish when used whole or grated.

Salt pollock ▼

Alaskan pollock is abundant. Salted pollock is popular in the Far East and Caribbean. It requires a long soak before use; is excellent poached or used in fishcakes. It has a milder flavor than salt cod. Good with spices and mashed potato.

Salt pollock is usually sold as a fillet or in strips, often ready pinboned.

Salt mackerel is available both as whole gutted and salted fish, and as fillets.

Salt mackerel

This product is popular in the Far East, particularly in Korea. The fish must be soaked in cold water overnight before use. Poach for about 30 minutes and use for pâté or salad; it is also good pan-fried. After soaking, the fish still has a strong salty taste, and the flesh is a little fibrous.

Salt cod is sold as whole split fish, fillets, loins, and in strips. Strips are quickest to use.

Salt cod

Dried unsalted cod is called stockfish and used in several countries in soup and as an additional ingredient. Salt cod is prepared in Scandinavia, and is also a speciality in Portugal, which is exported globally. It requires 36–48 hours of soaking, in several changes of water, prior to use. A salty taste is present once cooked, and the flavor is strong and almost meaty, with little comparison to fresh cod.

Fish roe

Although the roe of both male and female fish is edible, it is the "hard" roe, or eggs, of the female fish that has gained extraordinary heights as a delicacy, and often fetches a premium price. The milt or "soft" roe is the soft male roe or sperm of some species, particularly herring, and it is also sometimes valued as a delicacy, especially in Europe. Several species of fish produce excellent "hard" and "soft" roe, whether for use as a garnish or stand-alone *hors-d'oeuvre*, and many countries favor specific varieties. In Japan, *kazunoko*, the salted eggs of herring, are most popular. In Southeast Asia, a particular favorite is crab roe, harvested from female mud crabs. In Europe, "*caviare*", originally the name for the eggs of sturgeon, has long been prized. Traditionally the three most celebrated sturgeon caviars—beluga, oscietra, and sevruga—were processed by the Russians and Iranians. Methods of preparation vary. With most "caviar"-type products, the female roe is harvested, rinsed to remove the egg membrane, lightly salted, drained of excess liquid, then packed. Many are also pasteurized to extend their shelf life by a few

months. Caviar substitutes treated in a similar way include the roe of Pacific salmon (or keta), Atlantic salmon, salmon trout, trout, lumpfish, capelin, carp (or icre), and flying fish (tobiko). There is even a seaweed caviar now available. Non-caviar roes are sold either fresh or preserved, whether salted and dried, or smoked. Most eggs are soft and translucent, with a salty taste and grainy texture.

SUSTAINABILITY The popularity of sturgeon roe has led to overexploitation, with many species now almost extinct. Sturgeon are now being farmed in France. Other alternatives include icre, herring roe, and keta.

AVAILABILITY Caviars: Fresh and pasteurized. Other roes: Fresh, salted, smoked.

EAT Usually raw, except for fresh cod and haddock roes, and herring milt, which is served cooked.

FLAVOR PAIRINGS Caviars: Melba toast, chopped egg white, chopped onion, parsley. Soft herring roes: Butter, capers, lemon. Smoked roe: Olive oil, garlic, lemon.

CLASSIC RECIPES Taramasalata; caviar with scrambled eggs; grated bottarga with truffle oil and linguine.

Sevruga caviar
After beluga and oscietra, sevruga ranks third in the line-up of popular sturgeon caviars. Of the three, sevruga eggs are the least expensive and most readily available, as the fish matures relatively early at 7 years old. Although small, the eggs are a rich metallic gray, with an intense flavor, often preferred to that of beluga or oscietra.

Salted herring roe
A popular alternative to caviar, lightly salted herring roe is marketed under various names. It is better than lumpfish roe, as it does not run color, making it ideal as a canapé topping.

Salted herring roe has a delicate fish taste with a slight lemony tang, and a hint of salt.

◀ Beluga caviar
Illegal in some countries, beluga is considered the grandest of caviars. The beluga sturgeon (*Huso huso*) is the biggest of the family and known to live for up to 20 years. The eggs are large, soft, and smoky gray in color. It is one of the most expensive caviars and traditionally served with a round-edge, mother-of-pearl spoon, to protect the eggs.

Bottarga di muggine
Huevas de mujol or *poutargue*
The amber-colored eggs of gray mullet, sometimes called the "poor man's caviar", are a Mediterranean delicacy. Traditionally, the eggs are washed, salted, pressed, and sun-dried, then dipped in beeswax to hold their flavor. To serve, the roe can be thinly sliced, or freshly grated and tossed into pasta (but not cooked).

Herring roe ▲▼
Marketed under a variety of names, female herring roe is now readily available and sold as a low-cost alternative to other caviars. It competes on the market with lumpfish roe, but is unlikely to be dyed, making it ideal as a garnish. Kazunoko, a salted variety, is a Japanese delicacy.

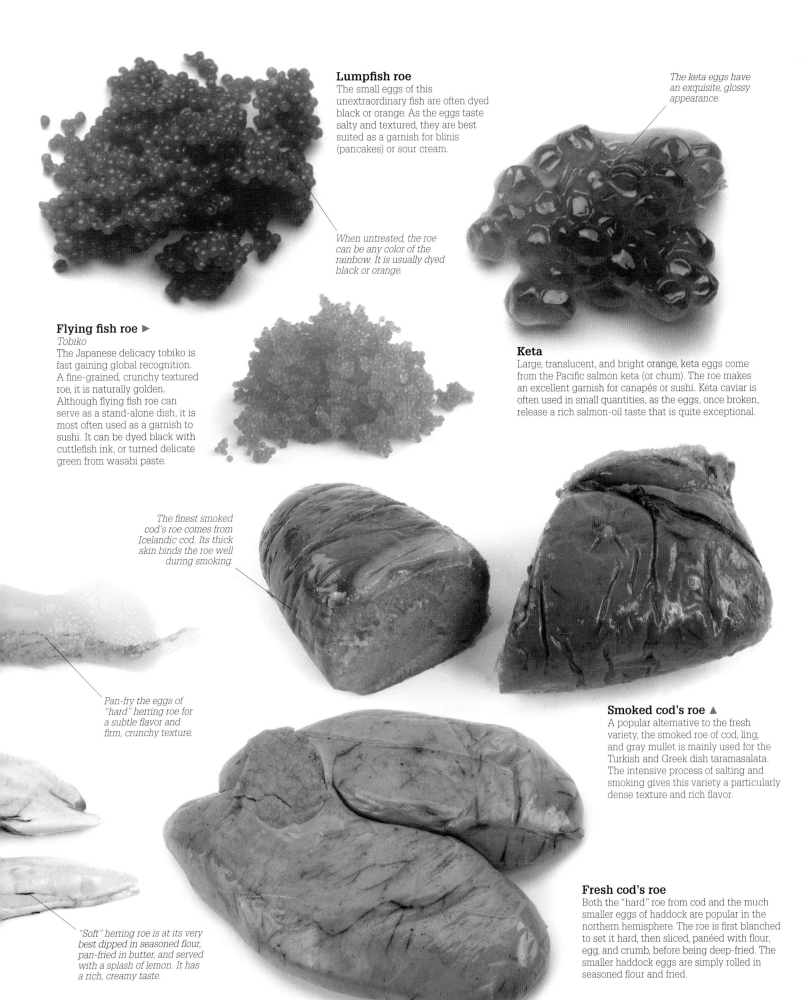

Lumpfish roe
The small eggs of this unextraordinary fish are often dyed black or orange. As the eggs taste salty and textured, they are best suited as a garnish for blinis (pancakes) or sour cream.

When untreated, the roe can be any color of the rainbow. It is usually dyed black or orange.

The keta eggs have an exquisite, glossy appearance.

Flying fish roe ▶
Tobiko
The Japanese delicacy tobiko is fast gaining global recognition. A fine-grained, crunchy textured roe, it is naturally golden. Although flying fish roe can serve as a stand-alone dish, it is most often used as a garnish to sushi. It can be dyed black with cuttlefish ink, or turned delicate green from wasabi paste.

Keta
Large, translucent, and bright orange, keta eggs come from the Pacific salmon keta (or chum). The roe makes an excellent garnish for canapés or sushi. Keta caviar is often used in small quantities, as the eggs, once broken, release a rich salmon-oil taste that is quite exceptional.

The finest smoked cod's roe comes from Icelandic cod. Its thick skin binds the roe well during smoking.

Pan-fry the eggs of "hard" herring roe for a subtle flavor and firm, crunchy texture.

Smoked cod's roe ▲
A popular alternative to the fresh variety, the smoked roe of cod, ling, and gray mullet is mainly used for the Turkish and Greek dish taramasalata. The intensive process of salting and smoking gives this variety a particularly dense texture and rich flavor.

"Soft" herring roe is at its very best dipped in seasoned flour, pan-fried in butter, and served with a splash of lemon. It has a rich, creamy taste.

Fresh cod's roe
Both the "hard" roe from cod and the much smaller eggs of haddock are popular in the northern hemisphere. The roe is first blanched to set it hard, then sliced, panéed with flour, egg, and crumb, before being deep-fried. The smaller haddock eggs are simply rolled in seasoned flour and fried.

Index

Page numbers in **bold** indicate information on the uses, availability, and sustainability of the fish, and their descriptions in the Fish Gallery.

Page numbers in *italics* indicate techniques and equipment used in choosing, preparing, and cooking the fish, including suggested Flavor Pairings.

The symbol (a) indicates an alternative, i.e. the use of a fish other than the one named in the recipe title.

Acknowledgments

About the Editor-in-chief

C.J. Jackson spent many holidays as a child in Scotland, catching and preparing fish. In the 1980s and 1990s, she worked in Australia, the Far East, the Middle East, North Africa, Switzerland, Spain, Italy, and France where she was exposed to seafood cookery in many of the world's great culinary traditions. In 1989, she enrolled as a student at the prestigious Leith's School of Food and Wine in London and went on to teach there, a post that gave her further opportunities to research into and write about seafood.

Today, C.J. is Director of the Billingsgate Seafood Training School, a non-profit organization situated above London's Billingsgate Market, the UK's largest inland fish market. Here she runs courses, teaching people how to select, prepare, and cook sustainable seafood. Working in this historical market, with its many wonderful personalities, the degree of expertise, and, of course, the range of fish, C.J.'s fish fascination is indulged every day.

C.J. is the author of *The Billingsgate Market Cookbook*, the co-author of *Leith's Fish Bible* and *The Illustrated Cook's Book of Ingredients*, and a contributor to the BBC's *Good Food Magazine*.

C.J. Jackson would like to thank the merchants at Billingsgate Market, but also my friends and colleagues, particularly Steve Clements from J. Bennett Exotics and Ron Peacham for their help in sourcing and identifying various exotic species; Mike Eglin from James Nash and Sons for his help in sourcing fish for photography; Chris Leftwich, Barry O'Toole, and Robert Embery of Fishmongers' Company and the fisheries inspectorate at Billingsgate Market; Paul Joy and Yasmin Ornsby from Hastings Fishermen's Protection Society for their help with the photography and an early morning trip to sea; Dr. Tom Pickerell for all his expertise not only about responsible sourcing, but also the shellfish industry; Mary-Clare Jerram, Sara Robin, and Andrew Roff at Dorling Kindersley for their focus and drive to complete this book and for Andrew's organizational skills; my team at the Billingsgate Seafood Training School for their patience; and especially, apologies to Colin and Joseph for all the "lost" weekends over the last 6 months—and while we were trying to move house!

Dorling Kindersley would like to thank everyone at Billingsgate Seafood Training School, including Ron Peacham and Adam Whittle; Yasmin Ornsby, Paul Joy, Ken Moss, Michael Adams, and Richard Adams at the Hastings Fishermen's Protection Society; Dr. Tom Pickerell from The Shellfish Association of Great Britain, for his advice on sustainability; Jocelyn Barker and Lowri Holness from The Alaska Seafood Marketing Institute; Stuart West, Ian O'Leary, and Myles New for photography; Luis Peral for art directing the photoshoot; Rob Merrett for prop styling; Katie Giovanni and Bridget Sargeson for food styling; Abigail Fawcett, Anna Burges-Lumsden, Jan Stevens, Katy Greenwood, Sal Henley, and Rachel Wood for recipe testing; Jenny Baskaya and Karen Van Ross for picture research; Roxanne Benson-Mackey and Charis Bhagianathan for their editorial assistance; Devika Dwarkadas, Divya PR, Heema Sabharwal, Katherine Raj, Kathryn Wilding, Danaya Bunnag, and Emma and Tom Forge for design assistance; Steve Crozier and Gary Kemp for retouching; Angela Baynham for proof-reading; and Sue Bosanko for the index.

Useful websites

Monterey Bay Aquarium Seafood Watch
www.montereybayaquarium.org/cr/seafoodwatch.aspx
Run by the Monterey Bay Aquarium, Seafood Watch is a website that advises consumers and businesses on the most sustainable seafood choices available. The site includes downloadable guides to the most sustainable fish and seafood choices by US region, as well as a national guide.

Fish Watch
www.nmfs.noaa.gov/fishwatch/
The National Marine Fisheries Service maintains this site, which lists sustainable fish and seafood choices as well as news and updates about US fisheries. It provides extensive information about selected species of fish and shellfish, including sustainability status, nutritional value, and life history and habitats.

The Marine Stewardship Council (MSC)
www.msc.org
An international organization that certifies sustainable fisheries. Check their website to find out which fisheries are certified in your area.

Seafood Choice Alliance
www.seafoodchoices.com
An international organization that works with the seafood industry toward a sustainable future.

SeaChoice
www.seachoice.org
A Canadian organization that partners with the Monterey Bay Aquarium Seafood Watch program to advise on sustainable fish and seafood choices for Canadian consumers and businesses.